Harold Gibbons

Harold Gibbons

*St. Louis Teamsters Leader
and Warrior Against Jim Crow*

GORDON BURNSIDE

McFarland & Company, Inc., Publishers
Jefferson, North Carolina

ISBN (print) 978-1-4766-7493-3 ∞
ISBN (ebook) 978-1-4766-3366-4

Library of Congress cataloguing data are available

British Library cataloguing data are available

© 2018 Gordon Burnside. All rights reserved

No part of this book may be reproduced or transmitted in any form or by any means, electronic or mechanical, including photocopying or recording, or by any information storage and retrieval system, without permission in writing from the publisher.

Front cover image of Gibbons and members of the union enjoying a night of baseball at Sportsman's Park, 1940s (Blanchard Studio, Bellevue, Illinois, 559.43, State Historical Society of Missouri, Photograph Collection)

Printed in the United States of America

*McFarland & Company, Inc., Publishers
Box 611, Jefferson, North Carolina 28640
www.mcfarlandpub.com*

In memory of my mother,
Mary Myers Burnside,
who taught me to love books

Table of Contents

A Note on Terminology   1

Introduction: A Word or Two About Gibbons   3

1. Young Gibbons   11
2. St. Louis' Warehousemen   21
3. Gibbons Gets His Way   28
4. Reds and Trots   37
5. Kavner, Saffo, Race Relations   47
6. Bernice Fisher and "Cab" Calloway   58
7. The Teamsters   69
8. Varieties of Political Experience   77
9. Mobsters Move In   91
10. Gibbons' Revenge   99
11. Gibbons a Racketeer?   110
12. Hoffa   119
13. Joe Costello and the Wildcat   129
14. "Vertical Improvement"   136
15. Gibbons Goes to Washington   148

Table of Contents

16. The Split	163
17. Hoffa Sets a Trap	170
18. Gibbons Relaxes	176
19. Calloway for Congress	191
20. "This Stupid War"	206
21. The Fall	225
22. Out to Grass	239
Chapter Notes	251
Bibliography	277
Index	283

A Note on Terminology

Teamsters Local 688, the main labor organization discussed in this book, is a *local union*. It is an affiliate of the International Brotherhood of Teamsters, or IBT, which is an *international union* as opposed to a merely national one. International unions are so-called because they have affiliated local unions in a foreign country. In nearly all cases, the foreign country is Canada.

The IBT refers to its top officers as the "general president," the "general secretary-treasurer," and members of the "general executive board" (which is constituted by the first two plus a dozen or so—the number varies—vice presidents). In this book, for simplicity's sake, those officers are called president, secretary-treasurer, and members of the executive board.

Books like this—concerning trade unions and other organizations, laws, regulations, official boards, etc. —tend to get crammed with acronyms and initialisms. I've tried to hold them to a minimum, but the following seemed unavoidable:

AFL—American Federation of Labor
AFSCME—American Federation of State, County and Municipal Employees
CIO—Congress of Industrial Organizations
CORE—Congress of Racial Equality
IBT—International Brotherhood of Teamsters
ILWU—International Longshore and Warehouse Union
LHI—Labor Health Institute (Local 688's medical clinic)
NLRB—National Labor Relations Board
RICO—Racketeer Influenced and Corrupt Organizations Act
RWDSU—Retail, Wholesale, and Department Store Union
SAC—special agent in charge (FBI)
UAW—United Auto Workers
UE—United Electrical Workers
UMW—United Mine Workers

Introduction: A Word or Two About Gibbons

> I came to St. Louis and discovered the most creative local union in the nation—Ernest Calloway[1]

In late 1946 or perhaps early '47, the St. Louis labor leader Harold Gibbons went to Chicago in search of a female organizer for his union. The majority of Gibbons' members were warehouse workers, and mostly men, but he was hoping to add people working in the next step up in the commercial-goods chain: sales clerks in the city's big department stores, most of whom were women.

In Chicago he found Bernice Fisher. A russet-haired, thirty-year-old white woman, Fisher, though not beautiful, was so lively that she trailed admirers, male and female, behind her. She was indeed a professional trade union organizer—but that was, as we say nowadays, merely her day job. Her chief interest in life lay in dissolving barriers between the white and black races. Fisher and a handful of friends at the University of Chicago had a few years earlier formed a group they called the Congress of Racial Equality, or CORE. With CORE as their organizational vehicle they set out to integrate restaurants, lunchrooms, bowling alleys, and other businesses that even in Northern cities routinely refused service to African Americans.

Fisher's group was little known outside Chicago except to scattered left-wingers like Harold Gibbons. Twenty years later CORE, along with two other direct-action groups—Martin Luther King Jr.'s Southern Christian Leadership Conference and the Student Nonviolent Coordinating Committee (SNCC)—would spearhead the movement that finally eradicated legal racial discrimination in America. (Casual discrimination, as everyone knows, remains.)

But that was in the '60s. Not 1947.

In St. Louis Bernice Fisher began signing up salesladies in Gibbons' union. Evenings she spent building a local chapter of CORE. For it she recruited a high school teacher, a one-legged war veteran, a sociologist, a historian of the world's religions, a future federal judge, various others, all of whom shared her sharp sense of revulsion when in the presence of racism. The new CORE group began tackling downtown eating places where discrimination reigned—which, St. Louis being then an essentially Southern city, was nearly all of them. CORE's philosophy was Christian-pacifist (Bernice Fisher was a Baptist). Its members dressed in their Sunday best and treated adversaries with respect. They would begin a campaign against, say, a restaurant that refused to serve blacks by first negotiating with the owner; then, if talks failed, leafletting passers-by on the sidewalk outside; and finally, if leaflets proved unavailing, sitting-in at the counter. Sometimes a campaign failed completely and CORE would move on temporarily to another business. All this required fortitude and time. Indeed, it took a full decade. But, scrupulous in its methods and trusting in its notion of justice, St. Louis CORE eventually got the job done. By the early 1960s, when the rest of America was just awakening to the movement for civil rights, CORE had defeated Jim Crow in downtown St. Louis.

Harold Gibbons meanwhile tried to keep mum about ties between his union and CORE because some of the merchants whose workers the union hoped to organize, especially owners of the department stores, weren't above suggesting to such workers that their so-called labor union was really a bunch of fanatic race-mixers.[2] Still, the connection was there for all who cared to see. CORE held meetings at the union's headquarters and used its equipment, especially the vital (in those days) mimeograph machine. Gibbons hired a number of CORE activists to serve on the union's staff and he himself sat for years on CORE's national board. (He quit when the integrationist organization went black nationalist in the late '60s.)

A word or two here about Gibbons. His dates are 1910–1982. He was a big, athletic man, handsome in a bust-of-a-Roman-senator way, especially after he began to lose his hair. His parents were Irish immigrants who had settled near Scranton, Pennsylvania, the father laboring as a coal miner. The family was large and poor. Gibbons' father died when Harold was a boy, after which the family moved to Chicago. There the son planned to make his fortune. "I was going to be an engineer and I was going to be a rich guy," he told a biographer.[3]

Instead, he fell in with a species of American we would today call liberal but which in the 1920s and early '30s often combined principles learned in the Progressive movement with membership in the Socialist Party. In Gibbons' case such people were often women, usually immigrants, frequently Jewish, and either industrial workers or trade union officials a couple of steps up from the assembly line. These wise women tutored Harold in the skills needed for a union career, particularly public speaking. Under their guidance he became a very effective stump orator as well as an imaginative and aggressive tactician.

In 1936–37 Gibbons was one of the hundreds of thousands of people caught up in the birth throes of the Congress of Industrial Organizations, a new labor federation. He rose with it. He became an official in a new teachers' union, then a leader of striking taxi drivers, then the regional director of a textile workers' group. In the spring of 1941 a still different CIO union sent him to St. Louis.

It was a fateful move for both Gibbons and the city. In St. Louis he rather quickly gathered together a dozen scattered warehouse workers' groups into what in time became one of the biggest, most powerful local unions in the nation. Gibbons dominated his union for thirty years.

However, this book is less about the union than how its boss used it to change his adopted city.

Harold Gibbons had learned from his Progressive-Socialist mentors how Robert M. La Follette, the greatest of American Progressives, had earlier in the century employed a social institution, the University of Wisconsin, to help his state's farmers and small businessmen in their struggles with adversaries, including big corporations.

Gibbons also had the aid of an institution, his union. We've mentioned his importation of Bernice Fisher of CORE to lead the desegregation downtown of St. Louis eating establishments. There is no other case like it in American history. Trade union leaders of the twentieth century, especially those of the old CIO, sometimes involved themselves in civil rights struggles. But they *assisted* others, usually African Americans who had begun the actions. Gibbons didn't merely assist. Not only did he light the match—he toted in the gunpowder and laid the fuse for the series of explosions that finally leveled Jim Crow throughout his city.

The creation of St. Louis CORE was Gibbons' glory. But there are other examples of gifts he gave, or at least tried to give, to the town—and to the nation as well.

Buses and trolleys. In late 1948 the private companies owning the city's bus and streetcar lines asked permission from the state's Public Service Commission to increase fares. Gibbons' union joined a veterans' group in sponsoring a petition drive against the fare hikes. It was winter and cold. Bundled up to their noses, the petitioners stood shivering at two booths, one at 8th and Washington, the other at Olive and Grand, collecting signatures from passers-by. (Bernice Fisher was a leader in this campaign too.) Some 20,000 signatures were sent on to the commission, which rejected the fare increases.[4] Union volunteers later participated in a campaign that resulted in the city's taking over the bus and streetcar companies. Bolshevism in public transit.

Community stewards. In 1951 or '52 (no one seems to have kept a record) Gibbons' union established what it called its "community stewards" program. A shop steward in a unionized workplace represents employees' interests versus those of the employer. Under Gibbons' program, members of his union began serving their home neighborhoods in a similar way. This they did by organizing a ward's residents to pressure their alderman or Democratic Party committeeman. A community steward could thus, for example, improve trash collection, erect stop signs at busy intersections, win playgrounds for the neighborhood's kids. The program made the union popular at the ward level—and, very soon, influential in the city's Democratic Party.

In 1949 Gibbons' organization, previously unattached, joined the International Brotherhood of Teamsters, becoming IBT Local 688. Both weal and woe followed. Mobsters who had in the early '50s seized control of several St. Louis Teamster locals cast their eyes on Local 688, but Gibbons, with the support of Jimmy Hoffa, a young vice president of the national union, found the means to fight them off. Hoffa in 1957 moved to Washington, D.C., as the IBT's president, and Gibbons went along to serve as his right-hand man. The community stewards program seems to have lapsed during these years. In November 1963 Gibbons broke with Hoffa over the assassination of John Kennedy and returned to St. Louis. He revived the community stewards program, though this time with an emphasis on the city's north side, which had become heavily African American.

Sewers. An unpleasant subject, but... In 1953 Joe Ames, a Local 688 staff member, learned that a civic group had failed in its attempt to collect enough petition signatures to call a referendum on a question that, if approved, would bring the many separate sewers in St. Louis and St. Louis County together in one big unified system. In St. Louis, as in most places, poor and laboring-class neighborhoods suffered the most from untreated— and often uncovered—sewage. Ames (who had come over from CORE) suggested to Gibbons that the union adopt the project. Gibbons gave his okay and also some money. "We didn't need much," Ames recalled.[5] Once again union volunteers went out seeking signatures. And got them. Voters approved the question in 1954, and the Metropolitan Sewer District began operations two years later.

Later, at Gibbons' urging, Local 688 members joined the petition drives that brought a community college system and a branch of the University of Missouri to St. Louis.

Vietnam. Gibbons was one of the handful of American union leaders who opposed the war. However, his opposition sometimes took forms different from theirs. Although Gibbons led marches, spoke at rallies, signed manifestos, etc., his more important antiwar work came about through his friendship with Henry Kissinger, President Richard Nixon's national security adviser. Gibbons and Kissinger had become friends when the latter was still a professor at Harvard. In the spring of 1972, with Kissinger ensconced in the White House, Gibbons traveled to North Vietnam as a member of a delegation of U.S. labor leaders, carrying with him a private message from Kissinger to the North Vietnamese urging them to resume suspended peace negotiations in Paris.

Later that summer he participated in the planning of a second, even more complicated journey to Hanoi, one involving not just Kissinger but also Jimmy Hoffa, who had recently been freed by the Nixon administration from a federal prison. This episode has long been obscure, largely because of the determined silence of the main players, both in the White House and in the Teamsters. But I think we've finally got it pretty straight here.

* * *

Gibbons died in November 1982. Given his role in St. Louis' history, his passing occasioned surprisingly little public notice. There were several reasons for this. He had made many enemies, who were no doubt simply happy just to see him go. The *Post-Dispatch*, the city's dominant newspaper, had always been cold to him. Then, too, Gibbons had nine years earlier been thrown out of his own union by a coalition of local dissidents and national Teamster bosses. A onetime Gibbons protégé said he had expected something like a day of municipal mourning for his teacher. "But it was so understated, a lack of acknowledgment of everything this guy had done. How could it be so little?"[6]

But nine years is half a generation. For most St. Louisans, Gibbons was by 1982 a fish that had quit pulling on the line.

I never met Gibbons. But in the spring following his death I wrote a long article about him that appeared in one of the city's tabloid papers. For the piece I interviewed a number of his associates, including the man who, after helping to drive Gibbons from office, took over his job as Local 688's leader. I put my notes away in a box when the article was published. Then years later, in 2005, I took them out again and began a new series of interviews with the idea of writing a book.

Gibbons is a difficult man to get into, psychologically. He left little by way of personal record. Although he was often described in the press as the "intellectual Teamster," and though he certainly loved books and was always quoting some writer he had just read, he didn't write much himself. Most of the formal speeches he gave and the articles he published, even many of the letters he sent, were composed by a ghost named John "Jake" McCarthy. Gibbons' collected papers include an unpublished diary he kept on a trip to North Vietnam during the war between that country and the United States, but otherwise much of the prose in the collection, though labeled as Gibbons', is probably McCarthy's.

What was he like? McCarthy, who worked closely with Gibbons for the better part of twenty years, said, "He was hard to get to know. He wasn't altogether convinced of his acceptance by others. In a sense, he was shy."[7] Gibbons' grown children all hooted at the idea of their booming, boisterous father's shyness. But McCarthy may have been on to something.

Take wit, for example. In interviewing his former associates, I often asked if Gibbons had a sense of humor. The interviewee's response was nearly always, first, a surprised look at the question itself, then a long obvious rummaging in memory, finally a confessed "Yes, maybe, I don't know." One person *did* know. Ron Gamache, the man who helped force Gibbons out of the union, complained to me that before Gibbons actually surrendered his office he stripped it of official papers. "There wasn't a scrap of paper left," Gamache said. The day we talked, Gamache was sitting behind what had been his predecessor's desk. He gestured toward its top drawer. In there, he said, left face-up, so as to confront the desk's new occupant, was a photo of Gibbons shaking hands with Richard Nixon. "He had kind of a weird sense of humor," Gamache said.[8] Gibbons was at the time on the Nixon White House's "enemies list."

So, having no direct line into Gibbons' mind or soul, I've had to rely on others to tell me what they saw him do. I owe particular thanks to Gibbons' daughter, Elizabeth Gibbons Vasquez, and his two sons, Patrick and Lawrence, each of whom has patiently endured long hours of conversation with me about the Gibbons family. Patrick and Larry Gibbons have also allowed me to examine their father's voluminous FBI file, which they obtained under the Freedom of Information Act.

The following people also took time to talk to me:

Marcus Albrecht, of Edwardsville, Illinois, a former Teamster and Gibbons protégé, currently an officer of the Illinois Education Association, who back in the 1980s helped create the Harold Gibbons archive at Southern Illinois University at Edwardsville;

the late Joseph Ames, of Silver Spring, Maryland, a onetime Local 688 staffer and original member of St. Louis' chapter of CORE, who went on to become a national vice president of the American Federation of State, County and Municipal Employees;

Ronald Borges, a former member of Local 688's executive board;

the late Ernest Calloway, Local 688's house intellectual and envoy to St. Louis' African American neighborhoods. When I saw him in February 1983, Calloway had been rendered speechless by a stroke. DeVerne, his wife, an impressive person in her own right—she had recently retired after a long career in Missouri's legislature—answered many of the questions I put to him;

William L. Clay, a retired Missouri congressman and an author whose dryly unsentimental book *Bill Clay: A Political Voice at the Grass Roots* is one of the best introductions I know to American politics. Of course it's especially good on St. Louis politics;

Sally Bixby Defty, a former reporter for the *St. Louis Post-Dispatch*;

the late Martin Duggan, a former editorial page editor of the *St. Louis Globe-Democrat*;

the late Thomas F. Eagleton, a retired U.S. senator from Missouri;

Michael Goebel, Local 688's former secretary-treasurer;

Gladys W. Gruenberg, a onetime Local 688 staff member who is today a retired business professor at St. Louis University;

the late Thomas J. Guilfoil, a St. Louis lawyer and financier ("half-assed banker" is the way he put it) and former treasurer of the Democratic Party of Missouri;

the late George Houser, of Newburgh, New York, a founder of CORE;

Gordon Hoener, a retired St. Louis stockbroker and nightclub entertainer;

Harland Horn, of Imperial, Missouri, a former secretary-treasurer of St. Louis' Teamsters Local 610;

Yuki Kato Keathley, of Pevely, Missouri, a onetime office manager of Local 688's Labor Health Institute and a personal secretary to both Harold Gibbons and Jimmy Hoffa;

Wanda Koss, a former secretary at St. Louis' Teamsters Joint Council 13;

the late Sheila Michaels, a onetime St. Louisan, CORE member, SNCC field secretary, and feminist leader. Of Gibbons she said, "Oh, I had such a crush on him as a teenager"[9];

the late John M. McGuire, a reporter for the *St. Louis Post-Dispatch*;

Shawn Murphy, a Scranton, Pennsylvania, historian who provided me with information concerning both anthracite mining in general and Archbald Patch, the Scranton-area coal camp where Gibbons was born and raised;

Keith Payne, a retired professional golfer and longtime friend of Gibbons;

Evelyn Rich, executive director of New York City's chapter of Americans for Democratic Action, who talked to me about CORE's Bernice Fisher;

Marvin Rich, Evelyn's husband, also of New York, a former Local 688 staffer and early member of St. Louis CORE;

James Robinson, of New York, another founder of national CORE;

Michael Ryan, a former education director for Local 688;

Levi Sanford, a former vice president of Local 688;

the late Ted Schafers, a retired reporter for the *Globe-Democrat*; the late Melburn F. Stein, a retired St. Louis police officer, who talked to me about St. Louis Police Department politics in the 1950s and '60s; and the late Jerry Tucker, of St. Louis, a former regional director of the United Auto Workers and onetime liaison between the UAW and Local 688.

For their generous assistance, I owe thanks as well to Stephen Kerber and Amanda Bahr-Evola, archivist and archives specialist, respectively, Lovejoy Library, Southern Illinois University at Edwardsville, where Harold Gibbons' papers are stored. Thanks also to the staff of the Western Missouri Manuscript Collection, Thomas Jefferson Library, University of Missouri at St. Louis, the site of Ernest Calloway's papers; to Nancy McIlvaney, associate director, Research Center—St. Louis, State Historical Society of Missouri, Jefferson Library, St. Louis; and to the staff of the John M. Olin Library, Washington University, St. Louis, whose holdings include Harry Vernon Ball's "Case History of a Labor Union: The United Distribution Workers."

I owe a particular debt to Ball, whom I never met. When he died in 2006, Ball was professor emeritus of sociology at the University of Hawaii. Sixty years earlier he had been one of the first—possibly *the* first—black person to be admitted to St. Louis' Washington University, an institution that, despite its abolitionist origins, was still whites-only until shortly after the Second World War. As a graduate student there, Ball came to know David Salmon, a political science instructor, and Joe Ames and Marvin Rich, two of Salmon's prize students, and also Bernice Fisher, then an organizer for Gibbons' Local 688. Among the latter four there occurred a fruitful cross-pollination. On one hand, they and a handful of other people formed St. Louis CORE. On the other hand, Salmon, Ames, and Rich followed Fisher onto the staff of Local 688, thereby further infusing the union, already flush with memories of the rebellious '30s, with the spirit that would distinguish the civil rights movement of the '60s. Harry Ball meanwhile interviewed Local 688 veterans for a master's thesis in sociology, "Case History of a Labor Union," a two-volume, six-hundred-page typescript whose bland title fails to suggest the riches it contains. When I started researching my own book, I was unaware that Ball's existed. Now that my book is finished, I can't imagine how I thought I was going to carry it off without having something like the earlier work to consult.

Also very helpful to me were Steven Brill's *The Teamsters* (Simon & Schuster, 1977), which concludes with a chapter on Harold Gibbons; David Salmon's privately printed memoir about his years as a Teamster; and a series of four articles about Gibbons that Sally Bixby Defty published in the *Post-Dispatch* in the spring of 1969.

1

Young Gibbons

According to Harold Gibbons, his long quarrel with Robert F. Kennedy began the moment they met.

It was Tuesday, September 2, 1958. Gibbons, a Teamsters Union vice president, was in Washington, D.C., to testify at Senate hearings on labor racketeering. Kennedy was the committee's chief counsel. Passing time before the session officially began, the two men, both descendants of Irish Catholic immigrants, chatted about their backgrounds. Kennedy inquired about the size of Gibbons' family. "I was the youngest of twenty-three children," Gibbons replied. Kennedy was clearly taken aback by this. Himself one of nine kids and soon to be the father of eleven more, the very competitive young lawyer assumed that Gibbons was exaggerating. He held fire for the moment, however, planning to ask again once Gibbons was formally sworn in—the idea being that the latter might, in repeating his answer, lay himself open to a charge of lying to Congress. Such anyway is how Gibbons later told the story. And it is a fact that, according to that day's hearings transcript, Kennedy very early asked his witness, "You were one of 23 children, is that right?"[1]

Strictly speaking, it was. Harold Joseph Gibbons was born April 10, 1910, to Patrick and Bridget Muldoon Gibbons. He was Bridget's thirteenth and last-born child. But Patrick had earlier been married to another woman, her name now unfortunately lost, who had borne him ten boys and girls. So, yes, Harold was indeed the youngest of twenty-three.

His parents were natives of Ireland, although Bridget, having been born on a packet bound from that place to England, grew up in the latter country. She came to the United States as a young woman, found work as a household maid, and in time married a considerably older man, the widower Patrick. Patrick was sixty-three when Harold came into the world. A child of County Mayo, Ireland, the elder Gibbons had emigrated to northeastern Pennsylvania's Lackawanna Valley, where he took up a career digging anthracite coal.

In 1910 the Gibbonses were living in Taylor, a village just south of Scranton. Taylor was a classic company town, named for a New York banker who was the controlling stockholder of the Delaware, Lackawanna & Western Railroad, the area's chief employer. Among other things, the railroad owned Taylor's two coal mines, the Pyne and the Archbald, the latter named for a judge who was one of the colliery's owners.² Patrick and his older sons worked in the Archbald mine. The family lived in a small company-owned frame house on Williams Street, directly opposite the colliery, in a section of the village known as Archbald Patch.

"Patch" was the word then normally applied by Americans of longer tenure to neighborhoods populated by Irish immigrants. The writer John O'Hara, born in 1905 in a Pennsylvania coal town forty miles south of Taylor, says in a story about a fictional patch that it "looks like a picture of Ireland, except that there are no thatched roofs."³ Archbald Patch was a little different, however. Although the section included Russians, Poles, Czechs, and other Eastern European immigrants, the majority of its residents seem to have been Welsh Methodists. "Archbald Patch was a Protestant community, and we were one of only two Irish Catholic residents," Harold Gibbons would later tell an interviewer. "That was when I first learned about discrimination. They let us know we were different."⁴

He liked to describe a Christmas Eve on which he and an older brother lay in the snow outside the Methodist church waiting to see Santa Claus hand out gifts to the Welsh Methodist children in the warm, brightly lit basement below.

"I'm pretty sure the story is apocryphal," said Gibbons' daughter, Elizabeth Gibbons Vasquez. "But it helps you to understand his worldview. It was like Ireland—Catholic and Protestant worlds and full of haves and have-nots. That's where, I think, Daddy's anti-institutional orientation started."⁵

The Gibbonses were certainly poor. Miners found it difficult to feed and clothe their children even in good times, and existence was especially hard during strikes, when there would be little or no income at all. "I guess my early boyhood days were the bleakest of my life," Gibbons later said. "But everyone else was eating potatoes for breakfast, lunch, and dinner, so I didn't realize it the time."⁶

Young Gibbons, early 1940s. The moustache soon disappeared. Photograph by R. H. Lanham, 559.4, State Historical Society of Missouri, Photography Collection.

1. *Young Gibbons*

Patrick Gibbons died when Harold was nine. "My father was a coal miner," Harold recalled on another occasion. "He had a little bit of prosperity when he ran a saloon and was a borough councilman, which was typical for the Irish. But most times, I remember, were pretty rough." Asked about boyhood heroes, he said, "I guess my uncles and my brothers were my heroes," pointedly excluding his father.[7] The narrator of John O'Hara's story accompanies a physician to a miner's hovel to treat a little girl ill with diphtheria. There the visitors find, beside the girl, her mother and the other children, but of the man of the house the only sign, hanging on a peg in a kitchen wall, is "a miner's cap with a safety lamp and a dozen buttons of the United Mine Workers of America."[8] Patrick Gibbons seems to have left about the same impression on his youngest son.

The Gibbons household was run by its women. Bridget was the dominating presence. She managed the twenty-three children as if they were an army company and she the first sergeant. "She'd come downstairs in the morning and one of her daughters would serve her breakfast," said Harold's eldest son, Patrick, named for the evanescent grandfather. "After breakfast she'd start assigning the chores."[9] Care of young Harold was assigned to his sisters, especially Annie, eight years his senior. The boys, until they married and left home, would dutifully bring their weekly pay to Bridget.

Gibbons family legend says there was a special relationship between Bridget and her youngest. Many miners' sons went to work as young as eight or nine, first in the colliery yard where, using their bare hands, they separated valuable chunks of coal from worthless slate; then, as they grew older, descending into the pit to dig at the coal face itself. Such was the fate of Harold's older brothers. But on the day Harold was born, Bridget looked up from her bed and announced, "This will be the last child I bear and he's not going to work in the mines."[10] And he did not. Protected by his mother, he was allowed to remain in school until he turned fourteen, which was late for a boy of his time and social class. The son's feelings for Bridget were equally strong. When she died, in 1940, Harold, then about to become a parent himself, suddenly developed an inflammation of the joints that doctors diagnosed as rheumatoid arthritis. The symptoms, which never recurred, were understood by family members to be an unconscious expression of grief at the loss of his mother.[11]

But that was of course much later. In the meantime most of old Patrick's twenty-three offspring grew to man- and womanhood and wandered away from home. The family remnant—Bridget, Harold, and sister Annie—moved into Scranton, where Harold dropped out of school to work in a diner. Thanks to the FBI, which for many years assiduously collected pieces of information about Gibbons, we know that the diner was called Yank and Bill's and sat on Providence Square in the city.[12] Harold spent five years there, first as a dishwasher and later as a short-order cook, putting in twelve-hour days seven days a week, for which he was paid ten dollars. This, as had his brothers with their colliery wages, he took home to Bridget.

Harold had by now become a big, strong, athletic young fellow. On one occasion he ran away to become a prizefighter—until his mother tracked him down and brought him home again. And he was beginning to attract women. The young fry cook had sleepy gray eyes, emphatic dark eyebrows, a long straight nose, and the sort of full-lipped mouth that novelists used to describe as "sensitive." His face would always be easy to pick out of a crowd. A friend from the 1930s and '40s remembered him as "exceptionally handsome."[13] A journalist who encountered Gibbons when he was nearly seventy said the labor leader was "still strikingly good-looking."[14]

* * *

In 1929 Bridget, Annie, and Harold moved to Chicago, where two of the older Gibbons brothers, leaving the miner's life behind, had become policemen. Harold went to work as a construction laborer and then as a shipping clerk in an electrical parts warehouse. He also took night classes at local high schools. In 1932, at the lowest point of the Great Depression, he lost the warehouse job. Unable to find other work, he began hanging around the YMCA, where, as a pupil enrolled in an adult education class, he happened to enter and win some sort of contest. The prize was a scholarship to the School for Workers in Madison, Wisconsin.

The School for Workers was (and remains today) a six-week summer session on the campus of the University of Wisconsin. It had been founded in 1925 to give young working women an introduction to "economics, sociology, speech, psychology and the like."[15] By the early '30s, however, the student body was composed largely of young men to whom it offered practical instruction in union organizing and collective bargaining. Harold, a ninth-grade dropout, had long entertained vague dreams of becoming a college graduate. "I was going to be an engineer and I was going to be a rich guy," he remembered. Instead, in August 1932, "I went up to the University of Wisconsin and there's a bunch of socialist kids there."[16]

Gibbons told different stories at different times about his political education. Sometimes he spoke as if he had ingested radicalism as a child, along with the potatoes eaten three times a day during coal strikes. "My dad was a union guy," he told a newspaper reporter, "and if you ever scabbed, it was never forgotten."[17] On other occasions, as in a 1976 interview by Steven Brill, a writer working on a book about the Teamsters Union, he hinted that the young fellow who arrived at the School for Workers in '32 had been a greenhorn with no politics at all. The "socialist kids" had made a special project of trying to convert him, Gibbons said. Evenings after class they would corner him in his dorm room and bombard him with economic and political theory. "The result was that a lot of the things that were part of my childhood growing up in the coal fields came back to me in a flood," he said. The "socialist kids" showed him a picture that he hadn't been able to put together for himself: "a society divided between those who own and those who work."

"I came away from there with the conviction that if I had any talent, any energies, any brains, I'm gonna devote it to the have-nots and not the haves," he told Brill. He had always known he had ability. "Like they used to say about John L. Lewis, he was in the dues manufacturing business, but if he was in the business of manufacturing sewing machines, he would have been a success there, too. And I suspect that I could have made a living in other ways, but I've never had a desire since those summers to do anything but be a trade-union man."[18]

Gibbons would return to the School for Workers every summer for years following that 1932 introduction, and even after ceasing to attend himself, would send lieutenants to soak in the school's atmosphere. But it was the original session that made him a socialist.

Socialism, be it noted, of a peculiarly Midwestern kind. The School for Workers was a product of the Progressive movement that dominated the Upper Midwest in the late nineteenth and early twentieth centuries. In 1894 a University of Wisconsin economist named Richard T. Ely, having decided he knew too little about trade unions, went off campus to join a union's picket line, an act that shocked some of his more cloistered colleagues.[19] Ely's walk became the germ of the Progressives' "Wisconsin idea," which was based on the conviction that a tax-supported institution such as a state university should benefit *all* of the state's citizens, including those who lacked the time or money to matriculate on its campus. The Progressives had a nearly religious faith in the ability of education to cure human ills, and they made a special effort to bring teachers into politics. In Wisconsin, for example, a university professor was drafted to write the state's workman's compensation law, which then became a model for the rest of the country. Other instructors went into the countryside to teach, say, crop rotation to farmers or accounting to merchants, thereby creating the nation's first extension programs.

The Wisconsin idea clearly made a strong impression on young Harold Gibbons. There's no evidence that he ever read much in Karl Marx or the other classical European socialist thinkers. But later, in St. Louis, he would create what might be called *extension* radicalism, employing the resources of a large local trade union in the same kind of community outreach that Wisconsin's Progressives had done with their state university.

When he returned home from the School for Workers in the fall of 1932, Gibbons formally enrolled in the Socialist Party. He also became acquainted with the person who would become his mentor in the Chicago labor movement.

Mostly forgotten now, Lillian Herstein was an important figure in her day. Born in 1886 to parents who were Lithuanian-Jewish immigrants, she grew up to be "an attractive little girl, with rosy cheeks and black hair" who made a name for herself as a fiery street-corner speaker during the big wave of industrial strikes that followed the close of World War I.[20] In the '20s she became the leader of Chicago's teachers' union. A protégé of John Fitzpatrick, the longtime president of the Chicago Federation of Labor, the city's AFL council, she would for many years reign as the lone woman member of the council's executive board. In 1932, with Fitzpatrick's backing, she ran (unsuccessfully) for Congress on a local third-party ticket but supported Norman Thomas, the Socialist candidate, for president.

Herstein was a Progressive, though of a slightly different cast than that found in Wisconsin. She sometimes taught at the School for Workers, but her deep pedagogical roots were in the Summer School for Women Workers at Bryn Mawr College near Philadelphia, which had been founded in 1921 by Progressive-minded women from the nation's upper classes.[21] Herstein's lifelong love was workers' education. She spent many summers at Bryn Mawr, where she specialized in the teaching of English and public speaking and was as progressive in her instructional methods as in her politics. About a class composed of young immigrant women, she recalled that "I had an interview with every girl. I'd get her talking, and I'd say, 'Now that's something you should write about'—their first day at Ellis Island, or the first accident on the job the girls witnessed." Herstein's pupils jumped at the chance to view themselves through the lens of language. "It was a great experience in their lives."[22]

Herstein was among those who lobbied Eleanor Roosevelt, a fellow Progressive supporter of the Bryn Mawr school, on behalf of federal aid to workers' education.[23] And in 1933, just months after Franklin Delano Roosevelt was inaugurated as president, one such a New Deal entity—the Emergency Education Program—was created, with several people from the Bryn Mawr school recruited to serve on its planning staff.[24] Herstein set up an EEP school on the campus of the University of Chicago.[25] She hired Gibbons as one of the school's instructors.

We don't know exactly how or where Gibbons and Herstein met. (Herstein was unclear about it herself. In a letter written to him years later, she reminisces about their days together at the University of Chicago. "Was that 1935?" she asks.)[26] We can be reasonably certain that it was somewhere on the local Socialist-Progressive-workers' ed circuit. Gibbons had divided his days in early '33 between laboring on a New Deal make-work construction project and reading in the Chicago public library, where he gave himself a crash course in history and economics. "Believe me, I read a lot of crap," he remembered. "But I also learned something from Stuart Chase [a liberal economist who had coined the phrase "a new deal"], Emma Goldman, and others."²⁷ On joining the EEP he underwent six weeks of teacher training, receiving for it $18 a week and three meals a day. That organization, a hastily thrown-together body intended to relieve a temporary crisis, had two aims: to furnish unemployed schoolteachers and other white-collar types with paychecks; and to employ them in instructing unemployed manual laborers in the skills they would need to function as potential leaders of trade unions, an institution the early New Deal saw as vital to industrial recovery. The six weeks' training was intended to teach the teachers how to speak the laborers' language. Gibbons, himself a manual laborer, already knew that language, so he naturally began to shine.

Gibbons was especially impressive at forensics, the art of public speaking. He may well have received coaching in this from Herstein, a noted local orator herself. In any case his ability on the stump, first cultivated in EEP teacher training, would long distinguish him among American labor leaders. "Gibbons was a brilliant guy, very articulate and interested in all political issues, domestic and foreign," recalled the late Senator Thomas F. Eagleton of Missouri, a sometime Gibbons ally of the 1960s and '70s. "It was a joy to hear him speak and to watch the audience which focused on him intensely. His vocabulary was first-rate. I do not think he had an extensive formal education, but he surely made up for that."²⁸

Gibbons not only stood out among the teachers in the EEP (which in 1935 was absorbed by the Works Progress Administration); he helped Herstein organize Chicago's EEP faculty as Local 346 of the American Federation of Teachers and was himself elected the new local's president.²⁹ At the AFT's national convention in 1936, a large, influential Chicago delegation nominated Herstein for the national union's presidency and Gibbons for one of its fifteen vice presidencies. Herstein was narrowly defeated, largely, she said, because of machination by the union's Communist faction.³⁰ But Gibbons was elected. Not bad for a man who, four years earlier, had had neither job nor trade.

His tenure as an AFT vice president was brief, however. The AFT was an AFL union. By March of 1937, Gibbons was moonlighting for the insurgent CIO. "In a stormy session in May 1937 [according to a later FBI report] the Chicago Federation of Labor voted to expel Local 346 of the American Federation of Teachers because of the activity of Gibbons, then its president, in organizing for the CIO."³¹ Herstein chose otherwise. Believing that Chicago teachers could not prosper outside the AFL, she voted to stay on with the older federation.³² She and her star pupil thus went their separate ways.

* * *

Gibbons' moonlighting in early '37 involved a strike by a group of taxicab drivers. The year had gotten off to an explosive start. In late December 1936 autoworkers in Flint, Michigan, had seized several General Motors plants and then held them for forty-four days in what they called a "sit-down strike," until the company finally gave in and recognized the autoworkers' new CIO union. Dramatic strikes, sit-downs and other types, immediately broke out in scores of cities and industries, most of them led by the CIO rather than the conservative old AFL. "It is difficult," a union veteran of those days has written, "to impart on ordinary paper the magic that surrounded the letters C-I-O in 1937."[33]

For three weeks in March, most of Chicago's cabbies went on strike against their employers. The episode began in a spasm of violence, with striking and nonstriking drivers fighting in the streets of the Loop, overturning each others' vehicles and setting them on fire. Gibbons had originally volunteered his services as the editor of the strikers' bulletin, but he became the de facto strike leader when the official CIO organizer was suddenly assigned elsewhere. Chicago's police intervened on the side of the owners. "Hundreds of guys were jailed and we moved the strike headquarters each night to avoid harassment," Gibbons remembered.[34] In an attempt to cripple the taxicab companies and at the same time dodge police clubbing, the strikers took to stealing parked cabs late at night and driving them off piers into Lake Michigan.[35] It was a tactic Gibbons would one day employ in another city.

The cab drivers won in the end, and Gibbons moved on to other struggles. According to the FBI, "he associated himself in a volunteer capacity with the CIO[,] and being a suave, young, militant speaker, he was accepted by Van A. Bittner, regional director of the CIO, and subsequently became one of his assistants in the Lake States area."[36] The CIO was dominated at the time by its two main founders, John L. Lewis, president of the coal miners' union, the United Mine Workers of America, and Sidney Hillman, president of the Amalgamated Clothing Workers of America. Van Bittner, a Lewis lieutenant, was soon replaced as head of the CIO's Midwest efforts by Frank Rosenblum, a Hillman man. Gibbons thus came under Rosenblum's purview. The two men would be friends and political allies for many years.

That summer Rosenblum sent Gibbons to South Bend, Indiana, to head up an organizing drive in a textile mill there. Most of the mill workers were women. They faced a variety of obstacles, the most formidable of which was a federal judge's injunction against putting mass picket lines around the mill, a stratagem the workers had used to keep out strikebreakers. Enforcing the injunction, local police escorted strikebreakers into the mill. Gibbons responded with an act of civil disobedience, directing the women to lie on their stomachs in front of police cars. The young organizer was jailed briefly on a charge of inciting to riot. Later all charges were dropped against him and other enjoined strikers when it was learned that the judge owned stock in the textile mill. The judge was in effect using the police force as security guards to protect his personal property, a not uncommon phenomenon then.

The strikers possessed no stock, of course, which established them in some people's minds (including, probably, the judge's) as no better than public nuisances. "We were outlaws," Gibbons told Steven Brill. "If you could have seen the way cops treated us in those days you'd understand a little more about why we became so cynical and disgusted about law and the establishment."[37]

"Class war" was no mere phrase to the hothead Gibbons. By late 1937 he was in Louisville, Kentucky, where Rosenblum had sent him to direct the organization of textile workers in five states of the Midwest and the Upper South. The salary was $35 a week, when money was available. ("We were on half pay most of the time," Gibbons recalled.)[38] Union organizing in the South, lower or upper, proved to be hard going. Again a majority of the mill workers were women—and so were most of the people hired by mill owners to act as strikebreakers. In one Louisville drive Gibbons repeated the tactic he had used in South Bend earlier. "Hundreds of women would lie down in the slush and mud to keep the scabs out," he said, "and there would be wild hair-pulling sessions among the women when the scabs would attempt to cross the line."[39] Years afterward, when the family had returned to Louisville for a visit, Gibbons reminisced one rainy evening with his son Patrick. "You know," he said, "this reminds me of a night when I and some guys were driving around this town with dynamite in the trunk, planning to blow some place up. But we couldn't find it because of the fog."[40]

Not surprisingly, some of Gibbons' CIO bosses were of two minds about him. "I was given all the dirty jobs because I was such a hell-raiser," he said. "Sidney Hillman fired me four times because I wasn't satisfied with [union] recognition, I wanted to fight for union-shop contracts. It took me years to realize Hillman was right."[41]

One spring evening he went downtown to Louisville's Tyler Hotel to preside at a meeting sponsored by a group called the American Friends of the Workers of Spain. The speakers were a married couple, Charles and Lois Orr. Lois, twenty-two at the time, had just returned from Spain, where she spent a year working for the Loyalist side in the civil war. Toward the end of that year she had been captured by Franco's insurgents and tossed into a prison camp from which she was eventually rescued by the American consul. After returning to the United States she had married Orr, an economics professor at Louisville University. They were now trying to raise money for republican Spain.[42]

Having spoken their piece and made their pitch, the Orrs invited Gibbons to come home with them for dinner. The home in this case turned out to be that of Lois' parents, William and Murah Culter. William Culter was a accountant who, at the urging of his wife, had taken a flyer on real estate and become moderately wealthy by turning a onetime gravel pit into a popular suburban development called Lakeside. It happened that, when the Orrs' car pulled into the Culters' Lakeside driveway, Lois' younger sister Ann was watching with a friend from the kitchen window. To the two young women, the stranger emerging from the car looked unhealthily gaunt. "Oh my God, would you look at what Lois just dragged in!" the friend exclaimed. "Well, he might not be so bad," Ann replied. Years later, she would tell her children she had gone out of her way that evening to be nice to Gibbons because her friend had said such a *mean* thing about him.[43]

Ann Maffette Culter was twenty. A small, strikingly pretty woman with black hair and olive skin, she was studying art history at the university. As compared to her sister Lois, whom her nephew Larry Gibbons describes as the "rough and tumble type," Ann was a Southern lady intellectual.[44] She played the piano and violin, painted and sculpted, was a voracious reader. But Ann had a rebel streak of her own: she was a leader of the local chapter of the Young Peoples' Socialist League, the youth auxiliary of the Socialist Party.

She was the belle of the campus radicals, he a handsome, dashing CIO organizer. It was 1938 and the world seemed to be sliding irresistibly toward social revolution. Ann's parents were opposed to any match between them. "These labor union things are never going to last," William Culter is said to have told his daughter. "How will he support you then?"[45] Ann didn't care. In early 1939 she and Gibbons ran off and got married.

There's a sequel to this story. Twenty years later, an FBI agent was sent down to Louisville to locate a copy of Harold and Ann's marriage license. Although no particular reason for the search can be seen in the available FBI records, it's likely that the agent's supervisors, working as they did in an atmosphere dominated by the puritanical J. Edgar Hoover, hoped to please their boss by demonstrating, through the absence of such a license, the Gibbonses' depravity. The agent reported seeking the license's origins at Louisville's city hall, at the county courthouse, and even in various courthouses across the Ohio River in Indiana, but he was finally forced to return empty-handed.[46] But no wonder he couldn't find the license in the places he investigated, said Patrick Gibbons.

"Father and Mother were married in Cincinnati."[47]

2

St. Louis' Warehousemen

In February 1937, as CIO fever swept the nation, the five hundred employees in the J. C. Penney Co.'s warehouse in St. Louis were among those infected.

Even a ripple in that city's warehouse business was bound to be consequential. Founded by French traders in 1764, St. Louis after the American Revolution became the new nation's inland entrepôt. Especially in the late nineteenth century, the city's many wholesale merchants "pushed aggressively into a rapidly expanding hinterland from the Mississippi to the New Mexico Territory and from Colorado to the Rio Grande.... Jobbers and retailers all along the tracks, in the small towns and in Little Rock, Wichita, Pueblo, Denver, Dallas, Houston, Fort Worth, Laredo, and San Antonio relied heavily upon St. Louis wholesalers for their supplies."[1] Those supplies, while awaiting shipment into the outback, occupied acre after acre of warehouses, many of them stacked along the Mississippi River levee, others filling the downtown area's southeast section, now the site of baseball's Busch Stadium. "St. Louis," said Ted Schafers, who in the late 1930s was beginning a long career as a reporter for the *St. Louis Globe-Democrat*, "was the warehouse capital of the United States."[2]

Penney's warehouse, in today's stadium district, was a big one. It occupied a thirteen-story brick building at the corner of Fourteenth and Spruce streets. Nowadays it's a hotel and condominium. The structure's outer face, designed by the trompe d'oeil muralist Richard Haas, has been painted to resemble a beaux arts apartment building complete with painted-on statuary, urns, and pilasters. Illinois commuters coming off the Poplar Street Bridge on their way to jobs in Missouri may glance up at Haas' whimsical work and smile, if in the mood for it. But there would have been few smiles around the place in the winter of '37.

"Warehouse workers were among the lowest paid, most insecure in the city," remembered Schafers. "Warehouses would hire them for Christmas and Easter and lay them off after the rush."[3] Top pay at Penney's was $23 for a six-day week. That was better than the $15 paid at the Brown Shoe Co. warehouse up at Seventeenth and Washington Streets, and certainly much better than the $8 paid at still other warehouses.[4] But it wasn't much if the warehouseman had a family to feed, house, and clothe. And because the seasonal nature of the job meant that there were always many more warehousemen than warehouse positions, those who were lucky enough to have positions took care not to offend supervisors who did the hiring—and grew quietly resentful as a result.[5]

Among Penney's employees was a former prizefighter who called himself Kid McCoy (no one seems to have known his real name). One February evening this McCoy happened to attend some sort of AFL meeting. Apparently inspired by what was said there, he began talking to coworkers about forming a union. Two dozen other Penney's employees accompanied the ex-boxer to a second labor meeting, this one run by an organizer for the CIO steelworkers. The organizer had little time to spare for warehousemen, but he gave McCoy and his friends a stack of blank CIO membership application cards and told them to go back to Penney's and sign up other workers there.[6]

Over the next six or seven weeks, Kid McCoy and his colleagues proceeded to collect signatures. Penney's managers, learning of this development, decided to stop it before it could bear fruit. One supervisor stationed himself in a car outside a tavern that the rebel warehousemen were known to frequent and wrote down the names of those he saw entering. The men he noted were Phil Reichardt, Max Voras, Bob Pentland—all of whom would indeed become longtime union leaders—plus McCoy and six others. Penney's promptly fired all ten.

But the rebels had been fortunate in their timing. Prior to the spring of '37, federal intervention in a labor dispute had nearly always favored the company involved rather than the union. But *NLRB v. Jones & Laughlin*, a U.S. Supreme Court decision handed down in April of that year, went the other way, permitting the National Labor Relations Board, until then a rather toothless New Deal agency, to punish a Pennsylvania steel company for doing just what Penney's had done in St. Louis: fire employees for trying to form a union. Penney's, moving to forestall a similar NLRB suit against itself, quickly hired back nine of the ten rebel warehousemen. Kid McCoy's job couldn't be salvaged because he'd also been accused of fighting in the workplace, a charge that placed him beyond the protection of the court's ruling. Like tens, probably hundreds of thousands of others before him, the ex-prizefighter vanished into the mists of trade-union history.

Penney's meanwhile did counterattack. In May it set up a company union. But Phil Reichardt, a thick-necked, heavy-shouldered South St. Louis dutchman who had taken McCoy's place as the rebels' main leader, responded to this tactic shrewdly. He and his friends turned out en masse for the company union's first meeting. Finding themselves in the majority, they took control of the organization—but only to let it wither away. Then they petitioned the NLRB to conduct a workplace election to determine which, the moribund company union or their own lively CIO group, would have the right to act as the warehousemen's bargaining agent. This election, held two months later,[7] the CIO group won by a margin of 124 votes.

New unions erupted in St. Louis that spring like bubbles in a stew. A headline on the front page of the April 2 *Post-Dispatch* told the story: "4000 Employees in 6 Industries and 107 Firms Involved—All but One in CIO." The most spectacular of these organizing drives was at Emerson Electric, a manufacturer of household appliances, where workers staged a General Motors–like sit-down strike that lasted a record fifty-three days. In the end other union leaders, fearing a public backlash against their own groups, talked the Emerson workers into leaving the plant and continuing the strike outdoors, in the usual manner. The Emerson strikers came marching out in a column, accompanied by a *Post-Dispatch* reporter. "The line of march was south in Twenty-first street to Locust," the reporter wrote, "east to Twentieth street, north to Washington and east to Eighteenth, past the company offices at 1824 Washington, where the marchers booed and shook their fists at the windows. Turning south in Eighteenth the strikers passed the Century Electric Co., at Eighteenth and Pine, where their union is conducting [another] strike. They booed the [nonstriking] Century workers who appeared at windows, and were greeted by strike pickets on the sidewalk."[8] These sentences form a kind of verbal snapshot of the way the CIO spread around the city.

No trade did more to sow the CIO seed than warehouse workers, and no group of warehousemen did more than Penney's. At some point that spring Phil Reichardt and Max Voras began carrying their lunch buckets over to the nearby Butler Brothers building, after Penney's the biggest dry goods warehouse in town, to spend the noon hour talking union with that firm's employees. Inspired, the latter formed a local union of their own. Like the managers at Penney's, those at Butler Brothers tried to head the rebels off by hastily throwing together a company union, but they capitulated when their workers threatened a strike. Butler Brothers recognized the CIO group in August and signed a contract with it two months later.

At Brown Shoe, a gangling freight checker named Bill Latal led the union drive. Born in 1894 in the city's Irish-Catholic Kerry Patch district, Latal was older than most of his coworkers. He had in the past been a foundry laborer, typesetter, bookie's runner, autoworker, and member of the old anarcho-syndicalist Industrial Workers of the World.[9] Latal organized a rally at which Reichardt, Voras, and other Penney's unionists addressed the Brown Shoe warehousemen. The latter were hesitant to join at first. (This may have been partly because when Brown's managers, true to form, started their own company union, they appointed a popular young man named Lou Berra as its president.) However, in a serious misstep, the company then suddenly announced a 10 percent pay cut for all employees. That decided the issue. When a subsequent NLRB election was held, Brown's warehouse workers voted unanimously for Latal's CIO group.

Similar victories were won by employees at Shapleigh Hardware, National Candy, American Wine, and three local coffee companies. Such was the campaigners' fervor that, as some of these names suggest, they were soon organizing food production workers as well as warehousemen, and women workers as well men. "And so it went," writes a sociologist who made as study of the St. Louis movement. "One warehouse or production plant after another organized itself, with the aid of the NLRB but with little or no help from the AF of L or the [national] CIO."[10]

With lots of local help, though. For, like so many people caught up in a popular movement's birth, St. Louis' warehousemen believed their cause transcended narrow personal interests—that it had political, even moral significance. By looking out for each other, they said, they could make the world fairer and more reasonable. If the crew at one warehouse went on strike, others hurried to join the picket. Warehousemen who were still drawing a paycheck docked themselves twenty-five cents a week to help those who had gone on strike and had none. "Mooching committees" solicited leftover bread, fruit, and vegetables from friendly grocers to feed strikers' families. Penney's Max Voras, a lanky, long-faced man, became an exemplary figure because he "spent much of his meager earnings on union activity and even paid the dues for a number of members."[11] Shared sacrifice lightened the warehousemen's hearts and made them carefree.

But they were also bitter people who felt no tenderness for their bosses. At one of the first firms organized, managers and union representatives gathered in the company's boardroom to negotiate a contract. The managers had earlier removed all ashtrays from the room, lest the employees begin feel too much at home there. Noticing this, the employees' spokesman dropped his lit cigarette on the floor and ground it in with his heel until the spot was thoroughly blackened. "Thereafter," writes an early historian of the St. Louis movement, "ash-trays were also provided for the union men when they met in the room. Great gusto is displayed by the men who witnessed this early scene when they talk about it today."[12]

Something should be said here about the author of these words, Harry Vernon Ball, Jr. A native of St. Louis, Ball was a child prodigy who, when he was only seventeen, became a graduate student in the sociology department at Washington University. He was also one of the first African Americans admitted to that university. (He may have been *the* first. Ball was so light-skinned that college officials may not have realized they were taking in a black man.) In 1948–49, while pursuing a master's degree in sociology, Ball, then twenty or twenty-one, spent a year examining the records of the warehouse union and interviewing its founders, which he then wrote up as his thesis. Later Ball went on to a distinguished academic career first in the Midwest and then at the University of Hawaii, where he finally escaped the racial toils of the mainland. But his book lives on in Washington University's archives. There it preserves warehouse veterans' memories of their struggles (the cigarette ground into the boardroom floor, for instance) and traces a decade's worth of the union's economic, social, and political twists and turns.[13]

By late 1937 some three thousand of the city's warehousemen had organized themselves into eleven local unions. These eleven, aware that they needed some sort of mechanism to coordinate their activities, formed what they called a Joint Advisory Council. Unfortunately, the JAC turned out to be faulty because the local unions, worried that they might lose their independence to it, provided it with neither a staff nor a treasury. The JAC functioned mainly as a pool from which volunteers could be called to proselytize among the employees of as-yet-unorganized companies.

It soon became obvious that this arrangement wouldn't do. In a hostile world, independence was a luxury that weak organizations couldn't afford. Humbled just months earlier, the warehouse owners began in the autumn of 1937 to regain their confidence. In November, Penney's suddenly laid off 135 workers, all of them union members. Managers at other companies started to ignore provisions in the union contracts they had earlier agreed to honor. These developments took the leaders of the eleven local unions by surprise and (writes Harry Ball) "demonstrated to them their vulnerability."[14]

In November 1938, seeking to reduce this vulnerability, the JAC sent four delegates to Pittsburgh for the CIO's first national convention. A photo shows three of them—George Seiler, Norman Twist, and Lou Berra (the one-time president of Brown Shoe's company union had left it for the CIO group)—out for a walk in that city. They might be dressed for church: each wears a white shirt, necktie, dark wool suit and vest, topcoat, and a hat with the brim pulled down over one eye. These were unostentatious radicals.[15]

The St. Louisans were shopping for a home in one of the new "internationals." In labor parlance, an international union (so called because it has at least some members in Canada) is in fact a national organization with which local unions affiliate. Such affiliation can provide a local union not only with help against recalcitrant employers but also protection from competing labor organizations. Unfortunately, there was no international for warehousemen alone. On the West Coast, the CIO longshoremen's union, the ILWU, which had won a great victory on the docks in 1934, surged inland like a big wave and signed up warehouse workers as well. In New York, both department store clerks and the workers in the warehouses owned by those stores went into another CIO union. (Meanwhile the conservative AFL Teamsters, affronted by the Communists who led the West Coast longshoremen, created their own warehouse division in an effort to keep the longshoremen at bay.)[16] Unhappy with the choices, the St. Louis delegates returned home unattached.

Then, weeks after their return, they learned that their locals had been more or less *assigned* to the New York–led international. This organization, which during its early years would bear several different names, eventually became known as the Retail, Wholesale and Department Store Employees Union—RWDSU for short.

RWDSU grew out of the secession, in early 1937, of ten New York locals from the old retail clerks' union of the AFL. Given a charter in the CIO, the new international gathered up sales and warehouse personnel in a variety of fields: dry goods, textiles, shoes, hardware, pharmaceuticals, and other commodities. Its president was Samuel Wolchok, a protégé of Sidney Hillman, president of the Amalgamated Clothing Workers and the CIO's most powerful personage after John L. Lewis.[17] Like his mentor Hillman, Wolchok was a Russian Jew who after emigrating to the United States became a New Yorker and a Socialist. Also like Hillman, Wolchok was a veteran of the sharp, sometimes homicidal fighting between Socialist and Communist needle-trade workers of the 1920s. He did not like Communists. Unfortunately for him, the early RWDSU's most vigorous affiliates were based in big New York department stores, such as Gimbel's and Bloomingdale's, and led by men and women who were either members of or close to the Communist Party. A historian who was an authority on department store unions (and a master of understatement) writes of Wolchok that "his strongly held political convictions rendered more difficult his later task of reconciling left and right wing factions within his union."[18]

In fact, there was something of a chronic standoff between Wolchok and his largely Socialist staff at RWDSU headquarters, on one hand, and the Communist leaders of RWDSU's New York locals, on the other, which had an inhibiting effect on the international as a functioning organization. A longtime local official (one admittedly close to the Communists) has described what he perceived to be the "Wolchok style" of union leadership: "The president is not a strong, powerful person. The locals are permitted to go their own way and not be interfered with by the international. That's the deal."[19]

RWDSU was plagued not only by ideological divisions but by differences involving job classification and geography as well. Although the majority of its members were New Yorkers, the international also "had substantial membership in St. Louis, Toledo and Detroit, [although] most of these members worked for wholesale houses, warehouses, or dairy companies rather than for retail stores."[20] RWDSU members who lived outside New York often complained that the international had little understanding of or interest in their problems.

This seems to have been especially true of St. Louis' warehousemen, who had had small enthusiasm for RWDSU in the first place. To them, membership in the international meant only a series of annoyances. Wolchok, they said, had increased local unions' per capita dues to the international, promising to rebate a percentage to umbrella groups such as the JAC, but the rebates never arrived. He had promised that RWDSU would create a special division for warehouse workers, but the division was never formed. It was the latter issue that most stuck in the St. Louisans' craw. If they couldn't have a warehouse international, they at least wanted an international with a warehouse division, such as the AFL Teamsters had instituted. The 1939 CIO convention insisted that RWDSU set up such a division, but Wolchok and his friends, apparently viewing such a group as a threat to themselves, did nothing about it.

At a conference in Cincinnati, Bill Latal and Phil Reichardt of the St. Louis group made a point of meeting openly with Harry Bridges, the Communist president of the West Coast longshoremen's union. But this was only a bluff. As Harry Ball tells it, the St. Louisans wanted "to create the impression that the warehouse unions would leave [RWDSU] if the orders of the convention were not followed by the leaders of the international." Unfortunately for the bluffers, a St. Louis warehouseman named Norman Twist, the leader of a faction opposed to Latal and Reichardt, "sneaked out of the meetings and telegrammed a pledge of loyalty to President Wolchok."[21]

Not that the New Yorkers didn't appreciate the St. Louisans' virtues. "The international did not know what to do about St. Louis," writes Ball. "There seemed to be a large number of shops organized, but also a total lack of unity and cooperation." Wolchok and his friends were particularly frustrated by the St. Louisans' refusal to behave as the more experienced New Yorkers thought they should. "However, the international officers were also aware of the militancy of the Warehouse Workers. They apparently believed that only a person equally militant could bring St. Louis workers into line with the desires of the top leaders."[22]

Leonard Levy, an RWDSU vice president, had a friend whose name was Harold Gibbons. This Gibbons was young, energetic, very militant—and at the moment unemployed. Hitherto the Louisville-based regional organizer of the CIO's new textile union, Gibbons had recently been "dismissed from the Textile Workers when he was discovered taking part in a Socialist Caucus at one of the conventions."[23] He was therefore available. Levy recommended his friend to Wolchok.

To Wolchok, Levy's candidate must have seemed just the person to tame those troublesome warehouse workers in the river city. So, in late May 1941, writes Ball, "the international sent Gibbons into St. Louis."[24]

3

Gibbons Gets His Way

Harold and Ann Gibbons, on arriving in St. Louis in the spring of 1941, rented a small house at 4826 Fountain Avenue, an older, pretty, working-class neighborhood, just east of North Kingshighway Boulevard. Fountain Avenue was then in the process of going African American. Ann, a Southerner, always spoke nostalgically of their years in the neighborhood. Its sensibly unhurried pace made her feel at home, she said.[1]

Not that they actually spent much time at home at first. Since their marriage, Ann had frequently traveled with her husband on organizing campaigns and she continued doing so in St. Louis. During these trips she made herself useful by commiserating with fretful wives, mimeographing leaflets, cooking big pots of hot soup for strikers. On at least one occasion she took a job in a textile mill so she could proselytize among its women workers. There were three Gibbonses now: Patrick Thomas Gibbons, named for the coal-miner grandfather from County Mayo, had been born the year before in Louisville. Harold and Ann carried him along on their campaigns in a laundry basket.[2]

But they did like St. Louis. Harold, when he came home from work in the evening, began dropping his loose change in a jar on the kitchen counter. They hoped to put together the down payment on a house of their own.

A stranger might have considered them unduly optimistic. Gibbons had received a cool reception from St. Louis' warehousemen. To them he was just another busybody sent by Sam Wolchok to harass them. And at first Gibbons' every word seemed to reinforce their expectations. Harry Ball writes that Gibbons' "efforts to defend President Wolchok and the other officers of the International, as he did for a period immediately after his arrival, only made the members more suspicious of him and his program."[3]

For Gibbons himself, St. Louis was a professional crossroads. His dilemma is well described by David Salmon, a political science instructor at Washington University who eventually left academia to join the staff of the warehouse union. "In the 1930s trade union leaders were, at heart, organizers," Salmon writes. "By the 1940s, they were obligated to become administrators and politicians or be cast aside or be coopted by those leaders who *had* made the change. Organizers operate best on instinct, and training comes almost exclusively from the school of hard knocks and gut reactions.... But when it comes to supervising employees, handling the organization's finances, carefully communicating in speech and writing, making long-term plans, and complying with the law, very few workers have the necessary background, personality or disposition to be this kind of leader."[4]

Gibbons was now thirty-one, but his bosses considered him something of an adolescent in occupational terms. "My reputation in the Textile Workers was as a hell-raiser and an agitator," he recalled. "They said I had too many strikes to be a good negotiator."[5] Gibbons might win recognition for a mill's workers, but the union hierarchy would then replace him with a more experienced and patient person to negotiate the actual contract. Him they sent to a new project elsewhere. "I never got to spend more than two or three weeks in the same place," he complained.[6]

To be successful in the trade-union world, an organizer had to light somewhere long enough to build a base of support around him. Gibbons realized that he would never be able to build such a base in the Textile Workers, which is why he agreed to go to St. Louis for RWDSU. In either union, though—the Textile Workers or RWDSU—the man he believed he must finally impress was Sidney Hillman, the real power behind both organizations. Gibbons said, "I took the [St. Louis] job to prove to Hillman that I could administer an outfit and accept responsibility, that I wasn't just another dime-a-dozen labor leader."[7]

He saw that, to win his RWDSU bosses' approval, he first had to pacify St. Louis' rebellious warehouse workers. But how was he to carry that off?

Another man might have tried a combination of muscle and manipulation. Gibbons knew that trick too. Levi Sanford, a onetime vice president of the warehousemen's union, said that when confronted by an angry crowd Gibbons would often pick out one especially unruly ringleader to serve as its representative and then, by silencing him first, silence the rest of the crowd with him. "He was a master of that," Sanford said.

> One of the things I learned from him was how to take control of a meeting of five or six hundred people. You'd go into a meeting, and some guy would get up yelling, and maybe he's drunk. And you'd just stare at him. You'd just look at him, dead in the eye, and never say a word. Pretty soon the rest of the audience would look around to see who you were staring at. And they'd figure out what was going on, and all of a sudden it gets real quiet—except for the drunk. He's still talking. You just look at him. Then you say to him, "If you don't have enough booze for all of us, shut the fuck up." And then you just move on because you've embarrassed the guy. Or you might say, "I've listened to you for the past two or three minutes and now I think you should let me carry on this meeting so these people can go home." And then the guys around him would get on him and shut the guy up. "Aw, man, shut up, we gotta get out of here!" This is what Gibbons taught me. And he would never raise his voice.[8]

Gibbons did not attempt this with St. Louis' warehousemen. He must have judged them too serious, and sober, for such a stunt. Instead, in August, he decided to separate two of the most respected—and also, probably, most recalcitrant—of the union's leaders from its members by putting them on a train bound for a six-week stay at his own alma mater, the School for Workers in Madison, Wisconsin. The two chosen were Sherman Wheeler, a warehouseman at Shapleigh Hardware, and Bill Latal of Brown Shoe.[9] But even this brought arguments. Gibbons had assumed that the Brown Shoe workers would be pleased by the selection of Latal, known affectionately to them as "Pappy," as their representative in Madison. But, no, they bridled at the suggestion. "They did not want 'any guy from the International' to think that he could tell them how to run their local," writes Harry Ball.[10] Gibbons lost his temper at this—which of course only stiffened the shoe warehousemen's resistance. They announced that *they* would hold an election among themselves to choose someone for Wisconsin. Then they elected "Pappy." The upshot was that Gibbons got the person he wanted, and the Brown Shoe workers got to show him they wouldn't be pushed around.

We don't know exactly what Latal and Wheeler heard during their weeks in Madison. No doubt they attended lectures on organizing, negotiating, creating welfare funds, and the like. But no matter which particular topics were taught, the underlying message would have been "industrial democracy," a Progressive, semi-socialist system of belief that, since capitalism had clearly failed (the Depression being proof of that), direction of a great industrial economy could no longer be safely left to private ownership alone. So who should share its direction now? Enlightened government (the New Deal) and industrial labor (especially the CIO). As the CIO's Sidney Hillman put it, "What labor is demanding all over the world today is not a few material things like more dollars and fewer hours of work, but the right to a voice in the conduct of industry."[11] To effectively exercise that voice, however, labor must first gather itself into strong trade unions. And those unions must not restrict themselves (as the AFL mostly did) to organizing, negotiating, etc., but must also become involved in the concerns—peace, war, prosperity—of the nation at large. Such a message—more or less the one Gibbons had heard from the young socialists on *his* first visit to the school back in '32—surely rang bells in the mind of Bill Latal, the former Wobbly. By the time Latal and Wheeler returned to St. Louis, they were much more open to Gibbons' notions. Indeed, Latal would for years thereafter be one of Gibbons' staunchest supporters. (About Wheeler, alas, we know little more than his name.)

As it happened, Gibbons' initial ideas were relatively modest. His chief proposal was that St. Louis' warehouse locals—the original eleven had now rearranged themselves as nine—restructure their umbrella group, the impotent Joint Advisory Council. Hitherto a loose association with (as its name implied) mainly advisory functions, the JAC as Gibbons saw it should be made a much more centralized organ capable of, first, defending member locals against counterattacks by employers and raids by competing unions, and, second, launching concentrated organizing drives of its own on the city's remaining nonunion warehouses.

He must have been persuasive, because the warehouse leaders did vote to restructure. The JAC was rechristened the St. Louis Joint Board of RWDSU. Whereas the JAC had operated on a largely ad hoc basic, the locals' representatives coming together at different times and places as need dictated, the new Joint Board was provided with a physical home: three offices and a meeting hall in a building at the corner of Seventeenth Street and Washington Avenue. More important, it was given a treasury, funded through a $1.50 per capita tax on each local's members. Libertarian critics of this scheme (including the union's historian, Harry Ball) were unhappy about this transfer of certain powers from the locals to the new central body, which they saw as a diminution of union democracy.[12] But theirs was a minority view. As another observer would note, "This revamping of the advisory council into a centrally controlled joint board was the first step toward the eventual merger of all St. Louis C.I.O. warehouse unions into a single, adequately funded local."[13]

Gibbons' second move reinforced the first. The workers at Rice-Stix Co., a big St. Louis dry-goods warehouse, were in 1941 being courted by two different CIO organizations, the Joint Board group and another affiliated with Harry Bridges' West Coast–like International Longshore and Warehouse Union. Each group had signed up an equal number of warehousemen, but Rice-Stix's owners were fearful of the ILWU because of its Communist reputation. Gibbons essentially "organized the bosses" (in trade-union parlance) rather than the workers, by fanning the owners' fears of communism. Rice-Stix recognized the Joint Board local outright, without bothering to ask its employees' opinion. This certainly was undemocratic—and dangerous red-baiting as well. But it was a coup for Gibbons: The Joint Board now represented 100 percent of the city's dry-goods warehouse workers. As Ball puts it, signing up Rice-Stix was "the single act most responsible for convincing the Warehouse Workers that Gibbons intended to organize and try to build a strong union rather than merely be a politician [angling] for the top offices of the International."[14]

Gibbons, writes David Salmon, had "gradually changed himself from a rabble-rouser into a manager, planner, leader and symbol of the [St. Louis] movement. In the process, Gibbons identified closely with the workers. He learned their names, ate with them, and knew their families as well as their hard work and job frustrations. He unified the membership around his leadership."[15]

* * *

Gibbons was in another way either shrewd or the beneficiary of very good luck: the persons he chose to be his top aides were also equipped to serve as ambassadors from the union to the ethnic neighborhoods in which they happened to live.

For example, Phil Reichardt of Penney's became the union's envoy to the large German-American community in South St. Louis. Bill Latal was a link to the Irish on the North Side. Ernest Conn, whose election Gibbons would soon engineer as the Joint Board's vice president, represented the city's African American community, then constituting about 13 percent of the population.[16] The city's Sicilians had carved a home for themselves out of formerly all-Irish blocks on the near North Side. Mainland Italians, on the other hand, were found atop The Hill, a long ridge running east and west above the city's railroad yards. The union's connection to both of these Latin groups was a man named Pete Saffo.

Saffo, when Gibbons met him, was a pasta maker for the Mound City Macaroni Co. He was on the payroll there in the spring of 1943 when volunteer organizers from the Joint Board suddenly appeared to proselytize among the firm's employees. Planting themselves just outside the main gate, the organizers handed leaflets to the workers as they passed to and from the job. This leafleting, though strenuous, went on for several weeks without much in the way of positive results. Most pasta workers were polite, but none was willing to stop long enough to discuss the leaflet's message. Saffo was thought to be particularly frustrating. Glancing at the proffered sheet, he would invariably hand it back with a quiet but audible laugh. It was only weeks later, after he had stepped forward to join the drive himself—and not just join but become instrumental in making it succeed—that Saffo explained what the joke was all about. The leaflets were in English, Saffo said, and he was one of Mound City's few pasta makers who could read anything but Italian.[17]

A small, frail man with large brown eyes, Saffo in photos resembles the typically haunted-looking existential hero of postwar French films. But he wasn't haunted at all. Cheerful and outgoing, Saffo had an extraordinary capacity for making new friends and smoothing away old hurts. The macaroni workers soon elected him their secretary, and not long after that he joined the staff of the Joint Board, where he rapidly became one of Gibbons' most trusted lieutenants. Saffo's good sense and warm heart endeared him not only to his boss but also to Ann Gibbons and the children, according to Elizabeth Vasquez.[18] Yuki Kato, Gibbons' longtime aide, probably spoke for most of the union's veterans when she said, "The person that was Gibbons' favorite was Pete Saffo. I think Gibbons always felt closest to Pete."

Kato herself, who, like Saffo, came to the union in 1943, represented no significant proportion of Missourians. Born and raised in Stockton, California, Kato was nineteen when she was interned shortly after Pearl Harbor and shipped with her mother and a sister to a "relocation camp" in the swamps of eastern Arkansas. The three women were held in the camp for the better part of two years. Finally released, they made their way north to St. Louis, where Kato enrolled in a secretarial course at Brown's Business School. She did well there but feared she would never find work because of the wartime hatred of things Japanese. However, the Joint Board staffers took her in. "Being socialists, they were inclined to help people," she said.

"It was a very close-knit group—of men, except for me. I was surprised they let me into their little circle." Kato began her career as a lowly filing clerk, but her intelligence, wit, and Saffo-like diplomatic skills ("I always knew who worked well with whom, and also who fought with whom") soon made her indispensable as an office manager. Like the other staffers, she was impressed by her new boss. "He was a great speaker, he could convince you

Members of St. Louis' warehouse union, 1941. Max Voras is fourth from left, front row. Phil Reichardt is at far right. Gibbons, far right, back row, had recently arrived from New York to direct the union. The warehousemen hadn't yet decided whether to keep him or ship him back. The other men in the photo are unidentified. Commercial Photo Co., St. Louis, 559.11, State Historical Society of Missouri, Photograph Collection.

of anything," she said. "But he was also very kind. People didn't always notice it, but he was a kind person. Whoever got in contact with him became very loyal to him."[19]

Pete Saffo, Lou Berra, Bill Latal, Phil Reichardt, Yuki Kato, Max Voras, and Ed Brown, who had come over with the Rice-Stix crew—these seven, plus one other person, who wouldn't arrive in town until shortly after the war, formed the heart of Gibbons' early operation.

Meanwhile the union continued to grow. Aided by volunteer organizers from established locals, the employees of three dozen other St. Louis firms—Mavrakos Candy and International Shoe among them—won union recognition from their employers. The process wasn't always smooth. In many cases an employer would come to terms only after his workers had walked out and closed down his business. But the victories steadily accumulated. By the end of the decade, according to a Joint Board researcher, the union had conducted organizing campaigns at forty-seven city businesses. Of those they lost five and won forty-two.[20]

In St. Louis as elsewhere in the early 1940s, trade-union organizing was made easier by the fact that labor was in short supply. Whereas during the Depression workers looking for jobs had far outnumbered the jobs available, now, with the drafting of millions of men into military service, there were more jobs than people to fill them. Labor shortages meant that a worker unhappy with his job could walk away from it confident that he would soon find another. Pay raises were another matter, though. Within days of the attack on Pearl Harbor, the leaders of both the CIO and the AFL issued a "no-strike pledge," promising to refrain from calling strikes until the war was over. In return, the government established a War Labor Board to adjudicate employer-employee disputes, including those over wages. Labor, business, and the public each had representatives on the board. (Gibbons served as an alternative labor rep on a regional WLB in Kansas City.) In theory all three groups would sacrifice equally, but as the war went on labor reps increasingly found themselves outvoted by the business and public reps. As a result, wages tended to stay flat while prices crept up.[21] By 1943 union members were growing restive over this discrepancy. Union leaders, squeezed between the no-strike pledge on one side and member discontent on the other, sought a nonwage means of relieving financial pressures on members. At the same time employers continued to seek a nonwage means of competing for workers. A solution, as both sides soon agreed, was employer-paid medical insurance. It was during these years that, to solve the manpower problem, U.S. companies began paying their employees' doctor and hospital bills.

In St. Louis, however, the warehousemen of the Joint Board went a step beyond creating a medical insurance program. They organized their own medical clinic—the Labor Health Institute, or LHI.

According to David Salmon, Gibbons got the idea from one Elmer Richman, a Hungarian-born physician who specialized in the treatment of allergies. Richman had for several years been promoting a small prepaid group health program in his adopted city. "Most of the members and affiliated medics were drawn from the liberal, socialistically oriented Saint Louis Jewish community," writes Salmon. Gibbons, on being introduced to Richman, was immediately enchanted by his notions. As a consequence the two programs, Richman's little prepaid group and Gibbons' ambitions for the LHI, "were joined."[22]

Earlier the Joint Board had moved its headquarters south several blocks, from Washington Avenue to a five-story yellow brick structure, a former warehouse (appropriately enough), at 1127 Pine Street. The clinic was to be situated on the building's fourth floor. Doris Preisler, a registered nurse and local Socialist activist, designed its layout. Lou Berra, the former Brown Shoe warehouseman, was appointed the clinic's business manager. Richman became the medical director, heading up an inaugural staff of six physicians and dentists. The LHI opened its doors to patients on November 15, 1945.[23]

The clinic was financed entirely by employers. The first of these was the Ravarino and Freschi Spaghetti Co. (a competitor of Mound City Macaroni, Pete Saffo's former employer), which had in May of the previous year signed a contract agreeing to contribute 3.5 percent of its annual payroll to a Joint Board-run fund for the medical care of the company's employees. Thereafter, nearly all contracts negotiated by the union contained similar clauses. These agreements entitled warehouse union members to prepaid basic doctor and dentist office visits, hospitalization, specialist care, lab studies, outpatient surgery, psychological counseling, and other services, including a pharmacy where prescriptions could be filled at cost. In 1947 most employers raised their LHI contributions from 3.5 percent to 5 percent of payroll, providing coverage for a warehouseman's family members as well.[24]

One big hurdle remained. The union had since its beginning enjoyed warm relations with St. Louis University's Firmen-Desloge Hospital, a Jesuit institution. In the summer of 1943, for example, in an era when the arrival of hot weather brought with it widespread fears of polio, the union donated a badly needed iron lung to the hospital. A union spokesman said Firmen-Desloge had been singled out in this way because of its traditional willingness to treat all people, poor warehousemen included, regardless of their ability to pay. Unfortunately, creation of the LHI, which the hospital's directors saw as a competing institution, chilled the relationship. Indeed, in April 1947 Firmen-Desloge suddenly announced that it would no longer welcome to its medical staff doctors who were also on the staff of the LHI. The city's other Catholic hospitals followed suit. Gibbons feared that Washington University's Barnes Hospital, a secular institution, would do the same, in which case LHI-affiliated physicians would be forced to choose between continuing to work at the clinic and losing their privileges at a teaching hospital. Such a contest, Gibbons knew, the LHI was bound to lose.

He wasted no time responding. On the very evening of the Jesuits' announcement, the union, in Harry Ball's words, "took immediate steps to procure a hospital of their own." Gibbons and his friends inspected a vacant eight-story apartment building on Lindell Boulevard in the city's fashionable West End, just across the street from the Chase Hotel. Determining that the structure could be converted for use as a union-operated hospital, they "paid a sum running into the thousands of dollars and procured an 'earnest money contract'" on it.[25] As it happened, the union did not in the end buy the building. Firmen-Desloge's directors, evidently deciding they would rather compete with a clinic than a whole new hospital, soon reversed course and dropped their ban on LHI affiliation. The union halted the purchase of the building and got its earnest money back.

With that, the situation was more or less as before the Jesuits' decision. But the brief episode had given St. Louis a glimpse of Gibbons steel.

4

Reds and Trots

The Labor Health Institute, once it had been dreamed up by Gibbons and Dr. Richman, received its formal approval from delegates to the warehouse union's first "all-city shop conference." This occurred at the DeSoto Hotel in March 1944. The conference, which would become an annual (or on occasion biennial) event, was like a political convention. Two hundred delegates, representing some six thousand union members, attended the 1944 event. A photo shows them seated in the hotel's banquet hall, the men in suits and ties, the women wearing hats. A banner overhead reads, "Every Member an Organizer."[1]

Gibbons gave the keynote speech. He talked about the Roosevelt administration and how, its attention having shifted from depression to war, was now in some ways less friendly to labor. "We must become interested in politics," he told the delegates. "Every time we turn around we run up against some government agency. Because the bosses are in control of those agencies, they see to it that they get out of the agencies what they want. It is our job to wrest control of the agencies of government so that we instead of the employers will enjoy the benefits we rightly deserve as producers of all the wealth of the world."[2]

The War Labor Board was one of the "boss-controlled" federal agencies Gibbons had in mind. In tune with many other CIO leaders, he charged that although employers had promised, in exchange for labor's no-strike pledge, to maintain contracts negotiated before the war's start, many had in fact not done so. "The bosses have been chiseling on that agreement after Pearl Harbor, behind the no-strike pledge," Gibbons claimed. He said he hoped to see the whole WLB swept away—and the no-strike pledge with it. Conference delegates agreed. Before leaving the hotel, they voted unanimously to repudiate the pledge.[3]

In this the warehousemen were following the lead of John L. Lewis' United Mine Workers, who the year before had not only dropped the no-strike pledge but, war or no war, also shut down the nation's bituminous coal mines in a series of strikes that brought the miners a healthy wage increase. Lewis had been painted as a traitor to the war effort by the respectable press—and by some union papers as well. Gibbons persuaded the Joint Board to send Roosevelt a telegram defending the miners' actions. The wire "caused a slight furor" at the May 12, 1943, meeting of St. Louis' Industrial Union Council, the coordinating body for the city's CIO organizations. Indeed, to show its displeasure with the warehousemen's move, the council passed a special resolution affirming its support of the no-strike pledge "without qualification."[4]

"I think I know the origin of this resolution," Gibbons told the council that evening. "It represents a certain school of thought."[5]

He meant the Communists. Communist trade union policy in St. Louis was directed by a man named Bill Sentner. The son of a Russian-Jewish tailor, Sentner had grown up in the city. He happened to be working at Emerson Electric on that day in March 1937 when employees seized the plant and began their two-month-long sit-down strike. Leadership in the new CIO unions frequently devolved upon energetic people partial to one or another left-wing philosophy—socialism, communism, Trotskyism, syndicalism. At Emerson Electric it devolved upon Sentner, a Communist. He and a small group of friends formed the plant's workers into a local of the United Electrical Workers Union (UE), an international whose own top leaders were Communists. Because St. Louis was home to a number of electrical parts companies, UE soon became strong there. By the mid–1940s, in fact, UE locals made up the city's largest single labor bloc and as a result dominated the Industrial Union Council. Naturally the council tended to follow the Communist Party line.[6]

Not that that line was especially alarming. Although the Communists enjoyed a reputation as uncompromising revolutionaries, their revolutionism had in fact dwindled during the late '30s. In June 1941, with the German army's invasion of Russia, it disappeared altogether. Politics for the Reds had suddenly become reduced to a single end: defeating the Germans—an end requiring the unhampered production of armaments by Russia's allies, especially the capitalist United States. Just yesterday fierce critics of peaceful relations between labor and management, the Communists now became strong advocates of it. In St. Louis, for example, Bill Sentner transformed himself into the very model of a moderate labor leader. *Time* magazine would report in 1945 that Emerson Electric had been losing money until a new chief executive "sat down with Bill Sentner, boss of the C.I.O.'s United Electrical Workers and one of the country's few Communists who frankly calls himself a Communist. Together they worked out a successful labor-management plan, adopted a profit-sharing program.... In two years [Emerson] was in the black."[7]

4. Reds and Trots 39

But as the Communists moved to the right, other trade unionists went leftward. Furthest to the left were those who, in the late 1920s, had been expelled from the Communist Party because of their allegiance to the ideas of the deposed Soviet leader Leon Trotsky. Although not numerous, the American Trotskyists were for a time influential in the labor movement.[8] Within their ranks could be found shrewd union leaders, including the strategists behind a spectacularly successful Teamsters strike in Minneapolis in 1934. The Trotskyists' position on World War II was the mirror image of the Communists'. Whereas the Reds believed that all other questions should be set aside until the war was won, the Trots argued that both sides, the Allies as well as the Axis, were capitalist powers and, because they were, workers had no concrete interest in which turned out to be the victor. Having no such interest, the Trots said, workers' trade unions should drop the no-strike pledge and all other self-imposed limits and return instead to the *real* war, against the capitalist ruling class.

Without necessarily accepting Trotskyist logic, many CIO leaders agreed with some of its corollaries, especially that concerning the no-strike pledge. Among these was Gibbons. We don't know how or when he became acquainted with the Trots. It could have been as early as the Minneapolis strike of 1934, or as late as 1936–37, when, Trotsky himself having ordered them to do so, the American Trots briefly enrolled in the old Socialist Party, where Gibbons was then still a member.[9] (The Socialist soon expelled the Trots as mischief makers.) In any case he was by the early '40s attending occasional Trotskyist meetings in St. Louis, according to FBI memoranda, and had come under bureau surveillance as a suspected Trot.[10]

Gibbons' politics must have been all right with Latal, Reichardt, and the other warehouse leaders. In July 1943 the Joint Board went so far as to call for the "immediate formation of an Independent Party of Labor and Working Farmers" for the following year's presidential election, a resolution whose endorsement Gibbons also sought at the next meeting of the Industrial Union Council.[11] Since the Communists were then pushing a fourth term for Roosevelt, the warehousemen's proposal may have been intended as a provocation. When the council refused even to consider the third-party idea, the Joint Board voted to disaffiliate from it. As Harry Ball notes, Lou Berra, the warehouse union' s spokesman, "denounced the manner in which deals had allegedly been made to give the Communists positions on the [council's] executive board out of proportion to their membership in the local CIO. He argued that such a policy could not have helped but lead to discrimination against the Warehouse Workers, who he claimed had gained the unending hate of the Communists for [their] complete freedom from 'Red' elements."[12]

Berra's words sound today like typical Cold War rant, but in 1943–44 the Cold War was still several years in the future. Russia and America then stood shoulder to shoulder as military allies. Within the CIO, however, a kind of Cold War prelude was already unfolding. Among its member unions the no-strike pledge had become the cause of growing unhappiness. That unhappiness exploded during the one and only legal U.S. strike of the World War II era, the Montgomery Ward walkout of 1944–45.

This episode began in late 1943 when the mail-order giant suddenly canceled its contract with the warehousemen laboring in its Chicago hub. Those workers, all RWDSU members, went on strike in April 1944. During the course of that year the walkout spread to Ward installations in Baltimore, Detroit, Denver, and Fort Worth. Because Ward had, by canceling the RWDSU contract, defied a War Labor Board order, the strike was in effect sanctioned by the federal government. (When Ward's president, an old-fashioned conservative, refused to give in, the government briefly seized his company. A once-famous news photo showed soldiers in full combat gear removing the president's chair from his office—with him sitting in it.) Since the government and most other unions, CIO and AFL alike, were on RWDSU's side, the strike should have been successful. But it failed. And that failure was largely due to the Communists.

Shut down in Chicago and elsewhere, Ward simply shifted its warehousing functions to a branch in St. Paul, Minnesota. There the employees were members not of RWDSU but of Harry Bridges' International Longshore and Warehouse Union. Bridges happened to be a particularly enthusiastic supporter of the no-strike pledge. When RWDSU asked ILWU members in St. Paul to respect their picket lines, they agreed at first to cooperate. Bridges, however, ordered them to continue handling Ward merchandise. His decision was backed by other Communist-led unions, including Bill Sentner's UE. But what really irked the strikers was the fact that among Bridges' allies were some sections of RWDSU itself, including the always militant Red warehouse and department store locals of New York.[13]

Gibbons found himself in the middle of this fight. Indeed, he had been a member of the two-man delegation sent to St. Paul to appeal to the ILWU local there. The other man, leader of a Chicago grocery clerks' union, was named Sidney Lens.

We should say a word about Sid Lens here. Short, bald, voluble, emotional, he was born in 1912 to Russian-Jewish immigrants. His mother, enthralled by news of the Bolshevik Revolution, instilled in her son a passion for socialism. Young Sid received his baptism of fire when, working as a fourteen-year-old busboy at a summer hotel in the Adirondacks, he talked his young colleagues into striking for more pay. "It was an exhilarating experience but not a fruitful one," he later wrote. "The county sheriff unceremoniously shook me out of bed, took me for a thirty-mile ride into a wooded area, slapped me around a bit, and left me miles from nowhere with my suitcase for company. I should have felt pained and angry, and I did to an extent, but I also felt exalted—I had joined a great fraternity."[14] Lens and Gibbons became good friends during the St. Paul trip. In later years, when Lens began writing books about the labor movement, he included in them stories about the St. Louisan that would be of great value to a biographer.

The mission to St. Paul didn't go so well, though. "Gibbons and I spent hours taking to a woman who was the top official of the [ILWU] in the Twin Cities," Lens recalled. "She was taken with Gibbons personally, a tall and exceptionally handsome man, but his charm availed little against communist politics. She insisted that her members would pack [Ward's] Chicago orders because 'we have to win the war.'"[15] In vain did Gibbons and Lens protest that they also wanted to win the war but saw no need to wreck a union in the process.

The strike sputtered throughout '44 and '45, but finally exhausted the Chicago warehouse local that had started it in the first place. That local died shortly after the war's end. International RWDSU, which now found itself effectively shut out of the nation's second largest city, emerged from the affair badly damaged. Within the CIO many trade unionists, already impatient with the Communists because of the no-strike pledge, had grown furious over what they saw as the Reds' betrayal of the Ward workers. Gibbons may have been especially bitter. He seems to have taken that bitterness out on the Reds back home.

By 1945 a group of anticommunist insurgents had won control of the United Electrical Workers local at Emerson Electric, the site of the 1937 sit-down strike and Bill Sentner's old bailiwick. Sentner and his friends found themselves under siege in both St. Louis UE and the city's CIO Industrial Union Council. According to Sentner's biographer, Gibbons conspired with Jesuit priests at St. Louis University to frighten Catholic electrical workers away from their Communist union leaders.[16] In 1946 the warehousemen, who had quit the Industrial Union Council three years before, returned to join the new Emerson group in urging "local unions to ferret out proponents of Communism and Fascism within their ranks." Since there were few if any fascists in the local CIO, Sentner and his allies were clearly the resolution's real targets. Nevertheless it was approved. A Sentner lieutenant charged that the resolution was motivated by spite rather than genuine political differences. Gibbons, this man maintained, "deeply resented" the fact that the electrical workers had for years outmaneuvered the warehousemen in St. Louis labor politics.[17] There may have been some truth in his argument, for Gibbons was not a man without vanity. But by 1946 similar resolutions were being passed by CIO organizations groups all around the country. Largely this was due to growing animosity between the United States and the Soviet Union, the beginnings of the true Cold War. Still, the Communists had undercut themselves in the unions through what was seen as their rigidity on the no-strike pledge and their misbehavior during the Montgomery Ward affair.

In late 1946 Sentner's chief aide was defeated in his bid for the presidency of the city's Industrial Union Council, signifying that his union's long slide was well under way. Two years later international UE took itself out of the CIO, thereby avoiding expulsion with nine other Communist-led unions. As happened in other cities, St. Louis' UE locals were soon absorbed by anti-communist labor organizations. Meanwhile Bill Sentner was hauled into court and convicted of plotting to overthrow the U.S. government. He never actually went to jail but instead remained free on a series of appeals while earning a living as a maintenance electrician at a St. Louis hospital. Sentner finally left the Communist Party following Nikita Khrushchev's 1956 speech denouncing Stalinism. He died not long afterward of a heart attack at the age of fifty-one.

* * *

All the more ironic, then, given the vengeful way Gibbons pursued local Communists, is a memorandum of July 1948, from J. Edgar Hoover to the FBI's special agent in charge (SAC) in St. Louis. The memo, which bears the heading "Detention of Communists in the Event of Sudden Difficulties with the Soviet Union," concerns what the bureau referred to as its "key figure list." Should war break out between America and Russia, such memos said, the "key figures" named on that list were to be arrested and put in camps apparently like that in which Yuki Kato found herself at the start of World War II. Hoover's memo focuses on "key figures" in St. Louis. At its bottom are four blank squares, evidently photographs that have been deleted since Hoover's time. Two of the squares have names under them. An expected name—"William Sentner"—turns up beneath one square. The other is labeled "Harold Joseph Gibbons."[18]

Communists in St. Louis considered Gibbons and his friends a "bunch of Trotskyites."[19] So did the FBI. But why should the bureau lump together as possible domestic threats two left-wing groups that famously hated each other? And whereas the Reds had for a while in the '40s numbered in the tens of thousands, the Trots probably never possessed as many as a thousand members. Why then worry about them at all?

The answer, in short, was a man named Farrell Dobbs. A thin, good-looking fellow with Republican inclinations—he had voted for Herbert Hoover in 1932—Dobbs was stunned by the social havoc wrought by the Great Depression. He was loading coal trucks in Minneapolis when he met—and was greatly impressed by—three tough Irish-American brothers named Dunne. One evening he happened to encounter one of the three at the bar in a coal-yard saloon. As Dobbs later recalled the event, "I took a place next to him, and after engaging him in a little small talk, I came right to the point.

4. Reds and Trots

"'Are you a communist?' I asked.

"'What the hell's it to you?' he shot back.

"'I heard that you are,' I told him. 'If it's so, I guess that's what I want to be.'"[20]

The Dunnes were Teamsters and Trotskyists, and Dobbs joined both groups as well. With the brothers he helped lead the great Minneapolis strike of 1934. But the real flowering of his talents came later. Before Dobbs, most Teamsters were truck drivers who made short-run deliveries within a single city or town. Dobbs took them out on the nation's highways. He and the Dunnes began in Minneapolis, where they required all drivers coming into the city's freight terminals to join the Teamsters Union. Having accomplished that, they radiated outward signing up drivers (and warehousemen) and negotiating contracts for them, first in Minnesota and then throughout the Midwest. By 1938 Dobbs and his friends had expanded their system into a kind of trade-union empire, an eight-state Teamsters organization—they called it the Central States Drivers' Council—that stretched from Michigan into the Dakotas and represented a quarter of a million drivers. Other IBT organizers traveled to Minneapolis to study Dobbs' methods. Among these was a young Detroit man named Jimmy Hoffa.

"I learned a great deal in those days," Hoffa later wrote, "but I would have been a dunce not to have done so. I was studying at the knee of a master who understood all of the intricacies of organizational work, fathomed the responses and reactions of employers, and comprehended the many problems of his union at home base. Instinctively, Farrell Dobbs always thought ahead and planned accordingly."[21]

Dobbs made enemies as well, of course. In an international union as severely decentralized as the Teamsters, many local leaders were displeased by empire-building. Especially displeased was Dan Tobin, the IBT's longtime president, who felt threatened by Dobbs' rise. And Tobin's friend President Roosevelt, then trying to ready Americans for World War II, evidently stirred uneasily at the thought of allowing a radical, antiwar party to maintain a strategic grip on trucking in the nation's vast heart. Beginning in May 1941, there was a two-pronged attack on the Minneapolis Trots. First Tobin sent to the city carloads of his toughest street fighters, including Hoffa, in a physical attempt to break up the truckers' union. Then, that invasion having failed, the Roosevelt administration indicted eighteen Trotskyist union leaders on charges of plotting to overthrow the government. ("I suffered torn loyalties when Dobbs and the Dunnes were arrested," Hoffa wrote.)[22] The eighteen were quickly convicted and, after appeals failed, went to prison in early 1942.

Gibbons in St. Louis was having troubles of his own. The city then possessed *two* warehouse unions. There was Gibbons' CIO bunch, but also an AFL group, Teamsters Local 688, led by a smiling, moon-faced man named

Larry Camie. Since its inception in 1941 Camie's union had been making periodic raids on Gibbons' membership. Gibbons was looking for ways to retaliate. In November 1946 he spotted what seemed a fine opportunity when a third group, Teamsters Local 600, broke into open rebellion. These were short-haul freight drivers who had become dissatisfied with both their employers and their own elected officers. In fact Local 600 was just then in trusteeship, being run not by its officers but by a representative sent in by the IBT.

Local 600's insurgency had flared when its member drivers at a big trucking firm, the Daniel Hamm Drayage Co., at Second and Tyler Streets, walked off the job to protest what they saw as dictatorial behavior by a foreman. Siding with the employer, the IBT trustee declared the action an illegal strike. But this only stoked the rebels' anger. Within weeks the wildcat had spread to five other firms and involved hundreds of drivers. Striking and strike-breaking Teamsters began fighting each other at freight terminal gates. Local 688's Larry Camie was himself involved in at least one of these fights, on the strikebreakers' side.[23] What had begun as a minor set of grievances was described by the IBT trustee as "a struggle for control, in which the insurgent group has challenged the regular officers of the union. Insurgents have threatened to form an independent union."[24]

An independent union? As Gibbons must have seen it, fate had placed before him two groups of people who, if combined, might prosper together. On one hand were the renegade but leaderless Teamsters of Local 600, and on the other the Minneapolis Trotskyists, not long out of prison, veteran union leaders who now had no union to lead. He decided to aim for a match.

The FBI caught wind of the affair by eavesdropping on a January 1, 1947, phone conversation between Farrell Dobbs and the eldest of the Dunne brothers, Vincent Raymond, known to friends as Ray. Dobbs was speaking from the group's new headquarters in New York, Dunne from an outpost in St. Paul. The former told the latter to proceed to St. Louis and "immediately get in touch with Harold J. Gibbons." Gibbons, Dobbs said, had promised to pay for Dunne's travel and room and board. Another man, whom the FBI listeners believed to be James Cannon, the founder of the Trotskyist movement in the United States, urged Dunne to travel under an alias lest he be discovered and "bring the hornets down on him." Dunne agreed, saying he would call himself "Ray Rodney."[25]

Dunne left for St. Louis. After a day or two Dobbs followed him there. Meanwhile in that city tensions continued to mount. On January 9 Dunne wrote an unnamed comrade to say, "This has been a hectic period of three days and nights. The situation is almost an unbelievable one. Gibbons and his 6000 warehouse workers has [sic] a frank and pointed warning from [name deleted by the FBI] of the Teamsters. [Deleted] tells him that he has been ordered to start the fight to take over Gibbons' union. [Deleted] gave Gibbons a few days or even a few weeks to think it over.... He offered Gibbons a top place in the new set-up, $8,000 a year with expenses and a Cadillac, etc. He said he wanted it 'peaceful,' but would take it the other way if necessary."

Reading FBI documents is complicated by the bureau's practice, before releasing them under the Freedom of Information Act, of deleting some names mentioned in them. The Teamster leader who threatened Gibbons was probably Larry Camie, but we can't be certain about that. In any case, Dunne says that Gibbons had asked for time to think the proposition over. Meanwhile both Gibbons and Dunne were busily proselytizing among the wildcat drivers. "I must follow it very closely," Dunne writes, "and have organized meetings of the truck drivers' leaders and with Gibbons and part of his staff for at least one meeting per day for the next period."

Dunne notes that the impatient Dobbs had actually managed to reach St. Louis before him. "I arrived late Tuesday—Farrell will probably stay a week or two with me.... Our impression is that we may win Gibbons and his second in command [probably Lou Berra] for the party. It is also possible that we may win two or three of the leading truck drivers. Gibbons is still quite a bit the Social Democrat [a mild, nonrevolutionary socialist in Trot parlance], but he *is* thinking politically [Dunne's italics]."[26]

As it happened, Dunne and Dobbs had arrived too late to contribute much to the strike. On the same day Dunne wrote his letter, the IBT announced that it had expelled six wildcatters and put another twenty-five on five years' probation.[27] Many of the wildcatters had already lost their jobs to nonunion drivers, and they now wandered away in search of new work. A remnant would carry on with the strike until June, when the NLRB held an election to determine whether IBT loyalists or the insurgent group should represent Local 600's drivers. That election the loyalists won. The wildcat was officially over.

The Trotskyists themselves were finished in St. Louis—and as far as that goes, in serious trade union work anywhere in the United States. They did have one more shot at recruiting Gibbons. This occurred on November 4, 1948. Again a record of the meeting comes from the FBI, which seems to have planted a microphone somewhere in the Trots' Minneapolis office.

Gibbons, who apparently was in the city on other business, had dropped by for a visit. Ray Dunne was the senior man on hand. Harry Truman had just confounded popular expectations by defeating Thomas Dewey in the election for the presidency, and that event, and its implications for politics in the United States, provided the main topic of conversation. Gibbons and Dunne talk about the prospects for a socialist revolution. Dunne claims to be optimistic. Gibbons says he doesn't "think the revolution will come about without another war." The palaver, which began in the late afternoon and continues till midnight, grows increasingly testy. The St. Louisan accuses the Trots of being "neurotic." Another Trot tells Gibbons, "You are completely off base—now cut that stuff out!" According to the FBI's transcript, "Hal [Gibbons] says he can't think politically and knows this from being in the SP [Socialist Party]. He says he is too tied up in his work to join a party of this type and he would just as soon live a 'normal life' like other people."[28]

With that declaration, Gibbons appears to have broken his connections with the Trotskyists. If he and Dunne or Dobbs ever met again, the FBI has no record of it. Ironically, it was six months *after* this final, quarrelsome visit to Minneapolis that the bureau put him on the list of people to be rounded up "in the Event of Sudden Difficulties with the Soviet Union." In time, however, the bureau did decide that the St. Louisan wasn't a public threat, at least not in the sense originally suspected. A 1953 memo reported that Gibbons hadn't attended a local Trot meeting in six years. "In view of his inactivity," wrote St. Louis' SAC, "it is felt that he should no longer be scheduled for apprehension as a dangerous subversive and it is therefore requested that he be removed from the Security Index List and his Security Index Card be cancelled."[29]

Even so, the FBI would watch him for the remainder of his days.

5

Kavner, Saffo, Race Relations

Civil war broke out in RWDSU following the failed Montgomery Ward strike. Many members were angry at the international's own Communist-led locals. The tone was set by a January 1945 editorial in a newspaper published by a RWDSU district in northern New Jersey. The paper demanded punishment for the leaders of New York City's Local 65, who were, the editors claimed, "prepared to unhesitatingly sacrifice the trade unions of America in order to carry out the program of Earl Browder and the Communist Party."[1]

Local 65 was a warehouse and retail workers' union, the biggest in New York. In many ways—in its political activism, its welfare programs, and the enthusiastic participation of its members—Local 65 was quite similar to Gibbons' group in St. Louis. Because they were so much alike, Gibbons and the leaders of the New York union would eventually reconcile. They would in the 1960s be allies against the Vietnam War, for example. And Gibbons would even send promising Local 688 staff members to the New York union for training, as he had earlier sent them to Wisconsin's School for Workers.

But not in 1945. Just days after the New Jersey paper's editorial appeared, St. Louis' own Joint Board passed a resolution calling on RWDSU to remove Local 65's leader "and have the International take over the local until the Communists could be cleaned out of positions of dominance." "Our International has put up with this fifth columnist too long," Gibbons told his members. "When every section of the CIO, from President [Philip] Murray on down was supporting the Ward strikers, this tool of Moscow was attacking the strikers in the press and in effect scabbing on his own International."[2]

Sam Wolchok, RWDSU's president, would have very likely loved to strip Local 65 and its sister unions of their Communist leaders, but he was powerless to do it. So, hoping to play it safe, he took *no* action. And because he didn't, complaints went upstairs to the CIO instead. Murray, the federation's president, appointed a New Jersey RWDSU official to investigate the matter. This man accused Wolchok and his friends of diverting financial aid intended for the Montgomery Ward campaign to other uses. A sizable RWDSU caucus—it took the name Decent, Democratic Trade Unionism, or DDT for short—announced that it would challenge Wolchok and the other officers at the international's November 1946 convention. One of the most vocal DDT founders was Harold Gibbons.

At that convention, critics of what they saw as the do-nothing Wolchok administration succeeded in electing two of their own to the international's executive board. Unfortunately—such is the political life—those two soon went over to the Wolchok side. By this time, the pro- and anti-Wolchok forces so disliked each other that they had all but forgotten Montgomery Ward and the Communists. Staffers at RWDSU's headquarters in New York began to speak of Gibbons himself as a particularly annoying foe.

That autumn a thirty-four-year-old New Yorker named Dick Kavner happened to wander into RWDSU's offices. Rumpled, overweight, already losing his hair, Kavner resembled one of the lesser villains in a Humphrey Bogart movie. A former RWDSU organizer, he had just been discharged from wartime service in the Air Force and was looking for civilian work. Not everyone at the international was happy to see him. In some quarters he was considered quarrelsome and overly aggressive. Still, he was welcomed by Wolchok and his friends, who announced that they had just the job for him. They sent him west to St. Louis to become Gibbons' assistant.

Actually, as Harry Ball tells the story, Kavner was hired to serve as *Wolchok's* secret agent in Gibbons' local union. "Kavner's assignment was to make reports of everything Gibbons did, including reports on his correspondence and phone calls." Over the long term, Ball writes, Kavner was to "make friends for the International and take over the Joint Board."[3]

"So Kavner came to St. Louis to dethrone Gibbons," said Levi Sanford, a former warehouse union vice president. "But when he got here, he and Gibbons had a long conversation about the situation. Gibbons said to him, 'The hell with those guys. Why don't you come in with me and be my ramrod? You and I can make this thing go!'"[4] Kavner agreed and became, in effect, a double agent.

For months he pretended to do the RWDSU leader's bidding, but actually served as *Gibbons'* spy inside the Wolchok administration. Then, in the fall of 1947, the DDT caucus was defeated on an important vote at the annual convention, and this turn of affairs apparently emboldened Wolchok and his friends. Within days "the St. Louis Joint Board began to feel the effects," Harry Ball writes. Several of Gibbons' staff members (including its lone female organizer/business agent, Bernice Fisher, about whom we'll hear more later) were fired outright by RWDSU. And "organizer Kavner was ordered to report back to the offices of the International in New York."[5]

Wolchok had begun to suspect his spy. When Kavner arrived, in late November, the international's president insisted that he sign a loyalty oath.

5. Kavner, Saffo, Race Relations 49

Kavner, realizing that the game was up, refused the oath, abandoned the masquerade, confessed his allegiance to the St. Louis organization, and resigned his RWDSU job. He also forwarded to Phil Murray a report detailing various Wolchok administration sins, including its plotting against Gibbons. According to Levi Sanford, Kavner walked out of the international's offices and never returned. "He was an outlaw to New York after that."[6]

It was Gibbons' turn then. On December 3 the St. Louisan received a letter from Wolchok saying that he was dismissed as the leader of the city's warehousemen. But could Wolchock make the firing stick?

No, he could not. From the start RWDSU had been plagued by the inability of St. Louis' workers to feel at home in the international. But they *had* now grown comfortable with Gibbons. Arnold Rose, a sociologist who studied the union in the late '40s accurately described the situation: "Wolchok had sent Gibbons to St. Louis to control the Joint Board for him, but Gibbons came to express the attitudes of the local leaders better than they were able to themselves. Gibbons provided sophistication, technique, and increased direction to a union that already had democracy and militancy."[7] Firing Gibbons made no sense to the warehousemen, so they lined up behind him and fired Wolchok and the international instead.

On January 13, 1948, a special gathering of two hundred shop stewards voted unanimously to disaffiliate from RWDSU and turn the Joint Board into an independent union. Three nights later, four thousand of the rank and file gathered at Kiel Auditorium to ratify the stewards' decision. The Joint Board was renamed the United Distribution Workers. Bill Latal continued to serve as the union's unpaid president, Gibbons as its salaried director.[8]

Not that the warehousemen intended to remain independent, vulnerable to union-busting efforts by powerful employers and membership raids by other unions, such as the Teamster group they had fought off the year before. The new, six-thousand-member United Distribution Workers was a big local, but not big enough to wander in a world of wolves. So it was that participants at the Kiel Auditorium rally also resolved that "our officers be authorized to secure affiliation with another national labor organization."[9]

* * *

Dick Kavner was the ingredient that, once added to the mix, gave the warehouse union its distinctive quality. Kavner, as Levi Sanford notes, became Gibbons' "hard drive." Some found him sinister. Gladys Gruenberg, a retired St. Louis University professor who in the late 1940s worked for the union teaching grievance procedures to shop stewards, remembers Kavner as a "strong-arm kind of guy, a muscle man."[10] Ron Borges, a young warehouse union official of the 1970s, said that Kavner, his mentor at the time, once ordered him to leave a testimonial dinner the two were attending in New

York. "The next day he explained that some mobsters had come into the room. Not wannabes, the real thing. 'If you're going to be involved in this local, you can't know those guys,'" Borges said Kavner told him. But *Kavner knew them*.[11]

Kavner actually had several skills, the most important of which may have been literary: he wrote the agreements the union negotiated with employers. He never failed to include the details that more hurried writers sometimes overlooked. "Those contracts were *this* thick," said Gibbons' son Larry, gesturing with thumb and forefinger.[12] Noting that the warehouse union was known for abiding faithfully by the terms of its contracts, a management lawyer once said, "There's no reason for Gibbons not to observe the agreement. They're written on his terms of heads-I-win, tails-you-lose."[13] That was Kavner's doing.

But he could be a "muscle man" too, as he demonstrated during a strike on St. Louis' near North Side in the summer of 1948.

The J. H. Grady Manufacturing Co. made baseballs and softballs. Its workers, almost all women, spent their days sewing covers on the balls. A majority had signed cards giving the warehouse union permission to represent them in bargaining with their employer, but Grady refused to recognize the union. The women struck, throwing a picket line around the plant. Grady's supervisors, all men, made a point of elbowing their way roughly through the line, meaning to intimidate the pickets. Kavner, whom Gibbons had assigned to run the campaign, hauled off and slugged one of these men—whereupon he was arrested and taken around the corner to the Carr Street police station. Bailed out, he returned the next day to find that Grady had hired a photographer to take pictures of the pickets, a tactic the women found even more threatening than jabs from the supervisors' elbows, because it made them feel exposed. Kavner and Pete Saffo jumped the photographer and broke his camera. Kavner was arrested again, and this time *he* got slapped around on the trip to Carr Street. He was jailed several more times before the Grady strike ended—ended, despite his efforts, in defeat for Grady's workers.[14] If nothing else, though, Kavner won the respect of his colleagues.

Not that they necessarily *liked* him. The late Joe Ames, who worked with Kavner in the early 1950s, recalled him as "tough, abrasive, and highly principled."[15] To Marvin Rich, another warehouse staffer of those days, Kavner was "very able, talkative, hard-driving—and also a pain in the ass at times."[16]

"Kavner was a *bastard*," said Levi Sanford with an explosive laugh. "He was a Jewish fella. Nobody liked him. I *know*. I was a black guy and nobody—" Here Sanford brought himself up short, deciding not to follow the thought out.

"Well, you shouldn't say nobody likes you, especially on the staff of a union," Sanford went on. "But Kavner and I had a lot in common. Kavner kicked butt. He'd fire you, he'd cuss you out in front of everybody, he wouldn't give a care what was going on. He was a hell of a guy. *I* liked him."[17]

We've already mentioned Pete Saffo, who was in contrast to Kavner almost universally popular in the union. The son of a large, Italian-speaking family, Saffo was a conservative man in many ways. "Pete was a nice Italian kid who grew up on The Hill," said Patrick Gibbons. "He wasn't an ideologue like my father and Kavner."[18] In 1945, when Harold Gibbons happened to be out of town, Saffo drove Ann to the hospital to give birth to their daughter Elizabeth. Shocked to discover that Ann wore no wedding ring, Saffo worried that the nurses would think her unmarried. Two years later he again served as Ann's chauffeur when Larry was born, but this time came prepared for the occasion. Before they entered the hospital, Saffo produced a gold band and slipped it on Ann's finger. "She wore it for the rest of her life," Elizabeth Vasquez said.[19]

If Kavner served as Gibbons' truncheon, Saffo was his emollient. "I've never met anybody as good with people as Pete was," said Larry Gibbons. "He had wonderful people skills."[20] "Pete knew more about Democratic Party politics than any other person in St. Louis, including the professional politicians who were supposed to know about them," said Joe Ames, who among his other accomplishments served a term as a Democratic member of Missouri's legislature.[21]

"Pete was a real sweet guy," recalled Ron Borges. "He dressed very well. Every day he smoked one cigarette and drank one martini—no more, because of his health. He knew a lot of people, including mobsters. Dick Kavner knew mobsters too, but he *talked* about knowing them, and Pete didn't. Where Saffo was quiet, Kavner was loud, boisterous, flamboyant. Where Saffo had one drink, Kavner would have many. Kavner sometimes rubbed people the wrong way. Saffo almost never did."[22]

As Levi Sanford saw it, Saffo's most important contribution to the union was the ease with which he dealt with "certain elements." "Elements" is a word one hears around union people: it signifies the criminal and semi-criminal types often found nibbling at a city's smaller, more vulnerable business and labor organizations. "Pete knew everybody in St. Louis—*every*body," Sanford said. "Kavner was Gibbons' hard drive, but Pete was his stand-up guy to the elements in the community. Although he weighed about only eighty-five or ninety pounds, Pete could keep everything on a peaceful level."[23]

Saffo and Kavner became Gibbons' top lieutenants. In his memoirs, the academic-turned-union-official David Salmon refers to the three men as the warehouse union's "Triumvirate." "Pete described their close relationship and how they handled disagreements," Salmon writes. "They had a rule that if any two disagreed on an item, their vote would prevail." Kavner once complained that Gibbons would try to manipulate the vote by taking either him or Saffo aside and offering a favor in return for voting the way he wanted. Salmon, however, maintains that such occasions were rare. "Actually, Gibbons usually went along when he was outvoted by the other two."[24]

For a time the triumvirate was a quadrumvirate. Lou Berra, the former Brown Shoe worker whom Gibbons picked to run the Labor Health Institute, was in the late '40s frequently perceived as his chief's most trusted associate. Gibbons' Chicago friend Sid Lens, for one, considered the easygoing Berra to be either second or third in the warehouse union's chain of command.[25] But in the early '50s, as we'll see, Berra made a misstep from which he couldn't recover and got shunted into a sinecure instead.

* * *

When they left RWDSU the warehousemen had urged their leaders to find them a new home in another international union. But which might that be? Harry Bridges' ILWU in the CIO and the AFL Teamsters both possessed large warehouse departments. (Although Bridges' union, being Communist-led, was definitely out.) And there were yet other internationals that, albeit lacking formal warehouse sections, might be willing to adopt a "miscellaneous" local—one that, like the St. Louisans', encompassed a variety of trades. But by 1948 the St. Louisans comprised coffee and candy production workers, pasta makers, retail sales clerks, office secretaries, even taxicab drivers as well as warehousemen. Some critics thought that was carrying miscellany a bit far.

Another obstacle involved union democracy. All trade unions, AFL and CIO alike, claimed to be democratic. But power in unions, as in all human institutions, inevitably gravitates toward the top. Most U.S. unions, even those that seemed practically bolshevik in the '30s, had since developed administrative styles that differed little from those seen in government agencies or private corporations. Dave Beck, an international Teamsters executive, was only more frank than other labor leaders when he once told a journalist, "I'm paid $25,000 a year to run this outfit. Unions are a big business. Why should truck drivers and bottle washers be allowed to make big decisions affecting union policy?"[26]

But for Gibbons unions were, as he frequently said, "a movement, not a business." His notion was shared by the organization's other socialists, a group that included among others Dick Kavner, Bernice Fisher, the old Wobbly Bill Latal, Carl Leathwood, an Oklahoma labor journalist who came to town to edit the union's bimonthly tabloid newspaper, *Midwest Labor World*, and Elmer Richman, the Labor Health Institute's medical director.

Gibbons and the others believed in what a later generation would call participatory democracy—self-government by, precisely, "truck drivers and bottle washers." In April 1948 the warehouse union held its annual all-city shop conference. (Victor Reuther of the United Auto Workers, another socialist, gave the keynote address.) In their most significant piece of business, the delegates created a Shop Stewards' Council, which they designated as the union's ruling body. This council was to be constituted by some 300 shop stewards, each of whom would be elected by 25 of his or her shop-floor coworkers, to represent their particular concerns. Meeting once a month, usually in the Kiel Opera House on Market Street, the Stewards' Council was to establish policy for the union on a wide range of issues, among them enforcement of contracts with employers, organizing strategy and tactics, political action, alliances with other organizations, and staff salaries, including Gibbons' own. (In 1948 Gibbons and other staff members each drew $90 per week, plus $5 a day for expenses. By 1951 most staff salaries had climbed to $125.)[27]

Bill Latal, president of the local, chaired the sessions of the Stewards' Council. Gibbons, heading an administrative staff of business agents, was a kind of prime minister. To help prepare the stewards for their role as intermediaries between the shop floor and the council, the union in January 1948 launched a yearlong series of special classes. (Gibbons maintained all his life a near-religious belief in the meliorative powers of education.) Victor Reuther returned to town to lead one session. Margaret Dagen, a young high school teacher from the suburbs, taught others. A series of classes called "Leadership Problems in the Shop" was team-taught by Dagen, Gibbons, Kavner, Berra, and Leathwood.[28]

Sid Lens, Gibbons' comrade from the Montgomery Ward strike, in 1949 published a book in which he hailed the St. Louis union, and especially its Stewards' Council, as a model for the entire U.S. labor movement. The warehousemen, he wrote, have "organized a system of group meetings which is more important for the future of American labor than all of the pronouncements of the big brass put together.... If its present policies continue, it will weather the storms of the future far better than other groups. Such methods of involving the rank and file are essential if labor is to move beyond its present status."[29]

But the Stewards' Council system turned out to have certain limits. Although council sessions were intended to deal primarily with issues bubbling up from shop floors, shop-floor meetings (of work crews and their stewards) soon became haphazard, easily postponed or canceled for one reason or another: illness, the lack of a meeting place, the intervention of other union business.[30] Crew members themselves often skipped meetings, despite having voted to fine themselves $3 for each absence. "In the last analysis," writes David Salmon, "aside from the wages and working conditions in their own shops, most members were not very interested in the programs of the local. Not even the fines that were levied for non-attendance of shop and community meetings could change that intransigence."[31] Oscar Wilde is supposed to have said that "the trouble with socialism is that it would take too many evenings." Many among the warehouse rank and file would have agreed. Although shop-floor meetings never ceased altogether, they became both irregular and less intimate, bringing together workers and stewards in ever larger masses rather than in separate small groups. In those masses, stewards rather than workers tended to do the talking. Repetition of slogans tended to replace frank discussion. It wasn't the village-hall democracy Gibbons had had in mind.

Another limitation on union democracy was Gibbons himself. He soon discovered that there were questions on which he did not *want* majority opinion to prevail. One, for example, involved the maintenance of discipline among stewards. Harry Ball describes a session of 1949's all-city shop conference in which Gibbons introduced a resolution that would permit the Stewards' Council to remove a steward whom it judged to be violating union policy. Dick Kavner rose to speak against the proposal. He argued "that the very basis of democracy in the Union seemed to be that the stewards were *elected by their crews* and were supposed to represent the views of the crews to the Council [Ball's italics]." Gibbons defended his resolution "on the grounds of Union solidarity and administrative efficiency, and as a measure needed to prevent any possible raids on the union." The delegates eventually approved Gibbons' idea by a large margin—even though, as Ball noted, the applause following his speech "did not nearly match that which Kavner had received."[32]

"This was a controlled democracy," writes David Salmon, who was in a position to know. Still, there's no denying that Gibbons enjoyed wide popular support among his union's members. Partly this was because he and his staff consistently negotiated higher wages and better benefits for them. But there was more to it than that. The charismatic, ceaselessly energetic union boss made membership itself an exciting thing. According to Salmon, even warehousemen uninterested in the boss' political and social views "were united in pride of their union and, indeed, formed a cultural alliance."[33] Gibbons' brain seemed to teem with interesting projects, for which, from an organization possessing thousands of members, he never failed to recruit hundreds of eager volunteers. Hundreds doesn't sound like much. But they would begin to tell.

* * *

Another area in which Gibbons did not welcome majority rule was race relations.

The warehouse union acquired its taxicab drivers' unit in 1945 following a particularly violent strike that originated at Deluxe Taxi, an African American firm. According to Harry Ball, the violence was largely the work of St.

Louis' mostly white police department, which, he says, traditionally exercised little restraint in clubbing black strikers. But the strikers themselves made contributions to the mayhem, Ball writes. They formed what they called "education committees" that cruised the city's streets beating up nonstriking drivers.[34]

Launched that spring by sixty Deluxe drivers, the strike eventually spread to other taxi companies, and by late summer half of the city's five hundred black cabbies had walked off the job. Gibbons' organization provided financial aid to the strikers. Then, in November, after Deluxe and the other firms had finally agreed to recognize them as a trade union, the drivers became Local 22 of what was then still the old St. Louis Joint Board of RWDSU. "They did not logically belong to this union," notes the sociologist Arnold Rose, "but no other union wanted them, largely because they were Negroes."[35]

St. Louis was then known as a "border" city. Marvin Rich, a warehouse union staffer in the late '40s and early '50s, laughed bitterly when he recalled the phrase. "Yes," he said, "it was a Southern city with a Northern exposure or a Northern city with a Southern exposure, take your pick."[36] Border cities were believed (mostly by whites) to be less harsh in their racial practices than those further south. In St. Louis, for example, there was no segregated seating on buses and streetcars. But Jim Crow was as much the rule in schools and housing, in restaurants, hotels, theaters, bowling alleys, and other forms of public accommodation, as in any town in Mississippi or Alabama.

Trade unions in the city weren't significantly better. AFL unions were traditionally whites-only. CIO organizations, except for a few like Gibbons' warehousemen and Bill Sentner's electrical workers, did little more than pay lip service to the idea of racial equality. Although preaching integration on one hand, they neither encouraged black participation in union activities nor did much to protect black rights on the job. "In several respects," noted one observer, "the unions in St. Louis are less equalitarian than are some unions in the deep South."[37]

As individuals, white warehousemen were no less racist than other unionists—and not particularly embarrassed to admit it either. In 1949 Gibbons hired a research team led by the sociologist Arnold Rose, then teaching at Washington University, to survey his members' attitudes. (The union split the project's costs with the American Jewish Committee.) Rose had a few years earlier been a coauthor of Gunnar Myrdal's *An American Dilemma*, a book instrumental in focusing white liberals' attention on the snares of racism. Rose's work on St. Louis warehousemen was eventually published as *Union Solidarity: The Internal Cohesion of a Labor Union*.[38] (Harry Ball conducted some of the surveys involved in the project.) Race wasn't the book's only topic, but its racial implications were certainly the most disturbing. For example, readers learned from Rose's work that 84 percent of white St. Louis warehouse union members believed that African Americans should not be permitted even to live on the same block as white people. A still higher proportion, 88 percent, said black people shouldn't be allowed to live in the same building as whites. Sixty-nine percent went so far as to say they personally disliked working beside blacks.[39]

Such as it was, the good news in Rose's report was that three-quarters of the warehousemen polled *did* favor equal treatment for blacks and whites in *union-related* matters—strikes, meetings, grievance filings, and so forth— and that only a very small number (5 percent) were critical of the union's own efforts to reduce discriminatory barriers in general.[40] Gibbons hoped to build on these sentiments, slowly eliminating racist thinking in white members by increasing their sense of union solidarity.

Since his arrival in St. Louis in 1941, the union boss had made a point of discouraging racial discrimination in the union's social activities. In 1943, for example, the warehousemen canceled a planned excursion on the Mississippi because the boat's captain refused to carry African American passengers. For business meetings and conferences Gibbons and his staff contracted only with those few downtown hotels that did not practice overt discrimination. In 1948 the union formed what it called a Democratic Rights Committee, chaired by Ernest Conn, a black Rice-Stix shop steward, to take positive steps toward uprooting prejudice. Conn's group sponsored an annual Christmas party, the summer picnic, and various softball games, all interracial. Gibbons received dire warnings about those parties, his son Patrick recalled. "'Harold, you can't do that. People will get drunk and kill each other,' they said. But there was never any racial trouble at those events, although one time a jealous woman did get mad and cut up her boyfriend."[41] The Democratic Rights Committee also published a handbook informing members about their rights on the job.

Inevitably the workplace, not social gatherings, became the chief theater in Gibbons' antiracism campaign. The Democratic Rights Committee very soon discovered, for example, "that the democratic rights of members most frequently infringed within the shops were the rights of Negro members to the use of the same eating facilities as those used by other members and the right to [job] upgrading based upon seniority."[42] Under the committee's direction, the union refused to sign contracts with firms that favored one race or another—and refused to let its members seek such favors as well. On at least two occasions in the early '40s Gibbons faced down wildcat strikes by white warehousemen protesting the assignment of more desirable "white" jobs to black workers. The wildcats were settled quickly, writes Harry Ball, "by the union's standing firm and threatening to expel any member who did not follow the no-discrimination policy."[43]

Gibbons never entirely extinguished racist tendencies in his union. When, in years to come, groups of insurgents would periodically rise against him, they were invariably white and some at least were motivated by resentment of his egalitarian racial policies. But until almost the end he triumphed over these malcontents by persuading a majority of members to see things his way. "[Gibbons] controlled the ship," recalled Marvin Rich, an original member of the Democratic Rights Committee. "He pretty well got what he wanted. He got what he wanted because members trusted him."[44]

6

Bernice Fisher and "Cab" Calloway

In the late 1940s Gibbons launched his first major extension program, an application of the Wisconsin Idea, to his adopted city. It wasn't an abstract notion with Gibbons, but rather grew out of his concern for the warehouse union's members—"citizen-members," he called them. As he saw it, "any local, state or national problem affecting the social and civic well-being of our citizen-members is the concern of our union." Such problems, he said, "range from adequate health protection to adequate transportation facilities and garbage collection."[1] For a union whose African American membership was considerable,[2] St. Louis' "social and civic" problems certainly included Jim Crow. But African American warehousemen couldn't be freed from the toils of institutionalized racism without doing the same for *all* of the city's black residents.

A huge assignment. How and where to begin?

In late 1946 or early '47, Gibbons persuaded a thirty-year-old, Chicago-based RWDSU organizer named Bernice Fisher to come to St. Louis to work for his union. Fisher's experience was with retail sales clerks, and since Gibbons was then trying to organize department store salespeople in his city, hiring her made sense on that score alone. But Ernest Calloway, an old Chicago friend (about whom we'll hear more later), informed him of her other assets. Although many people like to think of themselves as revolutionaries, Fisher was the rare real thing.

Born in Punxsutawney, Pennsylvania, in 1916, and raised by a single mother in Rochester, New York, Fisher possessed a strong religious bent—Baptist in her case—that seems to have manifested itself in childhood. As a young woman she became a divinity student at first the University of Rochester and later at the University of Chicago. But no denomination could contain her. When she died, of a stroke, at age forty-nine, the program printed for her funeral bore a quote from Reinhold Niebuhr: "Religion is God looking over your shoulder."[3]

James Farmer remembered meeting Fisher in Chicago in 1941. She was "wiry and impulsive," he writes in his memoirs. "Her clothes were sometimes ill-matched, her reddish-blond hair often in disarray, and her hose frequently had crooked seams and runs, which she failed to notice. Bernice was completing her master's thesis in religious education. I think there was nothing on earth that she did not feel strongly about. An avid reader of such modern theologians as Kierkegaard, Buber, and Niebuhr, she always knew precisely how many angels could dance on the point of every needle."[4]

Farmer, Fisher, and four or five others, some white, some black, were also then studying Gandhi's notion of satyagraha, nonviolent direct action. From time to time they were advised by a young pacifist named Bayard Rustin, later one of Martin Luther King Jr.'s chief lieutenants. The little group decided to try applying satyagraha to whites-only businesses around the University of Chicago campus. Dressed in their Sunday best, speaking quietly and respectfully, they first attempted to reason with the owner of a Jim Crow lunchroom or bowling alley, seeking to persuade him to change his policies on moral grounds. If reason failed, the group's members were prepared to "sit in"—that is, take seats at the business' counter and politely refuse to leave until the owner finally agreed to serve African American customers along with whites. (Actually, "sitting in" was a later term. The group's original members, being CIO sympathizers as well as Gandhian Christians, used the phrase "sitting down.") Having had some success in Chicago (though apparently without having to actually sit-in), the group branched out in 1942, forming a loose network of like-minded people in several other cities. This network they called the Congress of Racial Equality, or CORE.

Farmer, a charismatic black man, became CORE's longtime national chairman, Fisher, a white woman, its first national secretary. "She was a dynamo," recalled the late George Houser, another of the group's founders. Farmer made the speeches and held the press conferences, but, said Houser, "Bernice did most of the actual work—drafted the leaflets, ran them off on the mimeograph machine, etcetera. She *followed through* on things."[5] James Robinson, another member of the original Chicago group, remembers Fisher as "extremely lively—her eyes seemed to *bounce* at times. She could be sarcastic and often spoke ironically. CORE was serious business, but we had a lot of fun." Fisher never married but instead lived most of her life with her mother, who dutifully moved from town to town with her adventurous offspring. According to Robinson, a Chicago CORE member named Smith was in love with Fisher, but she didn't return the interest. "They would have made a good match because Smith was a quiet man who would have let her take charge," Robinson said. "Bernice was going to wear the pants in any relationship."[6]

Arriving in St. Louis sometime in the winter of 1946–47, Fisher was soon introduced to a small group of liberals who shared her hatred of racism.

Mostly whites with a sprinkling of African Americans, mostly middle-class, mostly associated in one way or another with Washington University, these people gathered periodically at the Delmar Boulevard apartment of Margaret and Irving Dagen to talk about social and political problems. They called themselves Humanity, Inc.[7]

Some we've already met. Maggie Dagen was a high school teacher who sometimes led shop-steward classes for Gibbons' warehouse union. David Salmon, a Utah Mormon with a doctorate from Stanford, had only recently come to St. Louis to teach political science at the university. Harry Ball, Marvin Rich, a precocious teenaged freshman, and Joe Ames, a veteran of the recent war in Europe, were college students. Irv Dagen, Maggie's husband, a businessman who was then enrolled in the university's law school, Charles Oldham, another law student, his wife Marian, a schoolteacher, and Billie Ames, at the time Joe's wife, were also members of the group.

Two were worldlier than the others. Ames, then twenty-two, had lost a leg during fighting in Germany. He and Marvin Rich met over a game of pool in the university's student activities center. "Even missing one leg, he was a pretty good pool player," said Rich.[8] A large, confident young man with a crooked grin, Ames had been raised by a Democratic family in a rural Missouri town populated by unionized railroad workers. "I fell in love with jazz, especially Duke Ellington and Louis Armstrong, and played clarinet myself in a jazz band," he recalled in an interview. "All these factors, plus common sense, probably inclined me to be liberal concerning race."[9] Rich, slight and bespectacled, the son of a poor baker, had entered Washington University at the age of sixteen. There he became active in Hillel, the Jewish students' organization, and also helped form a campus chapter of Americans for Democratic Action, a liberal organization. Off campus, he somehow became involved in everyday ward politics in the city's north-central African American Ville neighborhood. Salmon, Rich's classroom professor, was much impressed one day when the youngster took him to meet a more nuts-and-bolts political science instructor, Jordan Chambers, the powerful Democratic boss of the city's mostly black Nineteenth Ward.[10]

Bernice Fisher, not long after her arrival in town, was invited to the Dagens' home for a Humanity, Inc., meeting. The topic was Jim Crow. Maggie Dagen, who chaired the session, began by describing a recent visit to a department store. There she had encountered one of the store's African American maids eating a sandwich in the restroom. When Dagen asked why, the maid said, "Because I'm not permitted to eat at the lunch counter." Dagen having finished her tale, Fisher talked about CORE and its work in Chicago. The difference between discussing and doing became suddenly, blazingly clear to all her listeners. About that evening Dagen would later write, "Bernice Fisher galvanized the group into action."[11]

6. Bernice Fisher and "Cab" Calloway 61

Not long after that evening the members of Humanity, Inc., changed the group's name to St. Louis CORE. Fisher became their coach.

In those days downtown St. Louis treated its black people meanly. On one hand it took their money and on the other it humiliated them in both large and small ways. Downtown barred black customers not only from its eating places but, except in cases like that of the aforementioned maid, from its restrooms too. As Gibbons once put it, "You couldn't find anywhere outside the black community for a woman to eat or go to the john when she was shopping."[12] Downtown's tone was set by three big department stores. Fisher and the other CORE members suspected that if they could persuade one of those stores to desegregate, the other two—and also the district's many smaller businesses: restaurants, diners, cafeterias, drugstore soda fountains—would desegregate as well. For its test case, CORE began with Stix, Baer & Fuller, the second largest and most prestigious of the department stores.

Stix sat at the corner of Sixth Street and Washington Avenue, in the heart of the business district. The store's principal owners, the Baer family, were well-known Jewish humanitarians and philanthropists, and Fisher and her friends hoped they would be more open than other big merchants to the dismantling of racial barriers.

St. Louis CORE in its campaign at Stix followed the steps developed earlier by its Chicago precursor. Beginning in July 1948, one set of polite, well-dressed CORE members tried negotiating with Stix executives while another set handed out leaflets to passers-by on the sidewalk outside the store. These initial talks lasted off and on for almost a year, but produced no agreement. Therefore, on Saturdays in the spring of '49, carefully selected teams of racially integrated CORE members began sitting-in in the store's main lunchroom. Periodically the sit-ins would cease for a fresh round of negotiations. This phase of the campaign went on for several months, but again was unavailing: satyagraha had encountered a more sullen form of passive resistance. In November 1949, nearly a year and a half after the campaign's start, CORE concluded that Stix was for the time being anyway unbudgeable. The group's members voted to reverse their strategy and tackle smaller downtown businesses instead of big stores like Stix.

The decision proved to be wise. In 1951, after a yearlong CORE siege, the downtown Woolworth's finally agreed to serve African American customers at its lunch counter. By early 1953, according to a history of national CORE, "two [St. Louis] Sears Roebuck outlets, the Greyhound terminal, and all but one of the downtown dimestores completely integrated their eating facilities."[13]

Each step of this process had its own particular characters, scenery, denouement. Joe Ames, for example, recalled being assaulted by a young follower of Gerald L. K. Smith, a once-notorious anti–Semite and racist whose organization, the Christian Nationalist Party, was then based in St. Louis. Ames, it may be recalled, was particularly vulnerable because he had lost a leg during the war. He said, "We were sitting-in at the Forum Cafeteria on North Seventh Street. I was outside handing out leaflets. I had become friendly with the cop on duty, a man who was counting days until retirement. One day the cop went down the street to get a Coke at a drugstore. The moment he was gone, a car carrying Gerald L. K. Smith people pulled up at the curb. A big kid got out and jumped me and snatched away my leaflets. The cop came running back. Seeing him, the kid jumped back in the car, and the car started to pull away—but couldn't. Because all of a sudden it found itself blocked in by a black-and-white patrol car."[14]

In the 1960s civil rights demonstrators down South would frequently be beaten by local vigilantes *before* being jailed by the police. St. Louis, a decade earlier, was different. There the conservative city fathers moved swiftly to smother controversy before it could hurt business. During CORE's sit-ins, the police acted not so much to protect demonstrators from vigilantes as to maintain the peace by keeping the two sides separate. Meanwhile the press ignored all signs of conflict. "I remember happening upon a sit-in at a downtown St. Louis lunch counter in about 1950, shortly after I joined the *Post-Dispatch* as a reporter," writes Richard Dudman, later the paper's star war correspondent in Vietnam. "As I recall, an editor told me the newspaper knew all about it and there was no need for a story." And, indeed, the paper printed nothing about the sit-ins. Years afterward Dudman asked two retired editors why the *Post* had suppressed such a dramatic story. The editors maintained "that the policy was appropriate, considering racial tension at the time, earlier interracial violence and the influence of such racists as Gerald L. K. Smith in the community." The editors went so far as to argue that the blackout *helped* CORE's long campaign by keeping it peaceful. Dudman, however, suspected that the silence of the city's liberal journal very likely *protracted* the campaign unnecessarily by encouraging downtown's merchants to hold out against it. And in any case, notes Dudman, "one result of the news blackout is that history books do not yet mention an innovative, peaceful and successful St. Louis venture in breaking down racial segregation."[15]

Dudman's reminiscences, published in the *Post-Dispatch* as "St. Louis' Silent Racial Revolution," appeared long after the events it described. Whether despite or because of the news blackout, CORE's campaign was eventually successful. The Greyhound bus station and the dime stores had caved in by '53. In March 1954 Stix began serving black people in its first-floor dining room, and Famous-Barr, the biggest of the three big department stores, served them in its basement dining room. (Scruggs Vandervoort Barney, the smallest of the three, had capitulated earlier.) And in 1958 Stix integrated its last, most upscale room. By then ten years had passed since CORE began its work, and the campaign wouldn't be truly complete until the city's board of aldermen, after several earlier failures to do so, passed a public accommodations ordinance in 1961.[16] As Dudman said, CORE's efforts over the decade 1948–58 had constituted a revolution in the city's racial practices. But it was a revolution with the tempo of an underwater ballet.

All the more ironic, then, were Gibbons' recollections. "We used the union as a social force," he said in a 1977 interview. "Our [union] led the whole goddam fight. We picketed the theaters. We went down and sat in restaurants.... We raised hell. We busted the city wide open."[17]

Not only did this "busting open" take years to accomplish, and not only was the "hell raising" considerably quieter and more polite than the phrase suggests, but Gibbons appears to have participated in little of the busting and hell-raising himself. Not that he hadn't a good reason for his abstention. In 1949, at the same time CORE was conducting sit-ins at Stix's eating facilities, Gibbons' union was trying to organize that store's sales force. Bernice Fisher, for one, was involved in both projects. Stix's managers fought back by claiming, plausibly enough, that the two besieging forces were in fact one and the same organization, probably thereby trying to stir both racist and anti-union sentiments among their white employees. Gibbons, seeking to deny the allegation, in '49 issued a press release officially severing the union from CORE.[18]

But of course Stix was right. St. Louis CORE and the warehouse union were, if not the same thing, tightly bound up with each other. Fisher wasn't alone in being deeply involved in both organizations. CORE's Maggie Dagen taught classes for union members. Marvin Rich joined the union staff in 1950 after graduating from Washington University. Joe Ames went to work for the union part-time while he was still a college student, and then in 1951 became a full-time staff member and one of Gibbons' political advisors. David Salmon gave up his Washington University professorship to enlist with Gibbons in 1953. Leon Higginbotham was briefly both a CORE member and a union staffer before going on to law school (and eventually to a seat on the U.S. Court of Appeals). Alice Peurala, later the feminist leader of a Chicago steelworkers' local, was one of a number of white rank-and-file warehousemen who participated in CORE's efforts.[19] Black members, especially drivers from the union's taxicab unit, played an especially important role in the sit-ins. The warehouse union also provided CORE with financial support, a place to hold meetings, and the use of office equipment, including the instrument without which such a group was in those days helpless: a mimeograph machine. "On Fridays," said Rich, "I would use that machine to crank out some 1,500 to 2,000 leaflets, which we would then hand out on Saturdays at the weekly demonstration outside Stix, Baer & Fuller."[20]

Gibbons himself was "sort of a father figure" to CORE activists, Joe Ames said.[21] He was father to St. Louis' early civil rights movement as well.

* * *

Bernice Fisher's stay in St. Louis was to be a brief one, about two years. Even so, she left a lasting impression. She so ably coached her successors in St. Louis CORE that, as we'll see, the organization's legacy can still be felt in the city today.

She helped change the city in other ways too. In late 1948, for example, the private firms operating St. Louis' bus and streetcar lines sought permission from the state to raise their fares. Fisher and other warehouse leaders formed a committee to fight this proposal. They set up two street booths—one downtown at Eighth and Washington, the other at Grand and Olive in the West End—and from these points collected signatures on a petition to oppose the increases. Twenty thousand names were quickly gathered and taken to the capital in Jefferson City, whereupon the relevant state commission rejected the fare-hike requests. Others involved in the protest committee were Robert Pentland, a Penney's warehouseman who with union help had just been elected to the state senate, and the local officers of a war veterans' group. According to Harry Ball, though, it was the energetic Fisher who most deserved credit for the committee's success.[22] Then, three years later, another petition drive launched by the union resulted in the municipal takeover—socialization—of the bus and streetcar companies themselves.[23] Although Fisher wasn't around for this epilogue, her spirit could be sensed in it.

Teamster politics helped drive her away. In January 1949 the warehousemen became an IBT local, a development that will be described in the next chapter. That March, only weeks after the union had affiliated with the Teamsters, several AFL internationals—among them the IBT and a retail clerks' group with which the former had often been at odds—came together as a nationwide coalition aimed at organizing the employees of a variety of retail businesses, including department stores. Gibbons, who had for some years been trying to organize St. Louis' department stores, welcomed the coalition. But no sooner had the coalition's formation been announced than Dave Beck, the IBT's executive vice president, pulled his international back out and ordered its member locals to sever all relations with the retail clerks.

Gibbons and his friends were baffled by the directive. Nevertheless they obeyed Beck's orders. They locked the retail clerks out of the coalition's local office and even sent members to picket grocery stores that had contracts with the clerks.

Fisher was appalled. "Bernice Fisher refused to participate in a drive to organize already-organized establishments [the grocery stores]," writes Harry Ball. "She considered it to be 'raiding.'"[24]

The previous year's city-wide shop conference had authorized the hiring of an education director for the union. Fisher now applied for that job, hoping it would excuse her from the attack on the retail clerks. Gibbons refused to give it to her, primarily, Ball says, because he knew the anti-clerk campaign was unpopular throughout the warehouse union. Gibbons feared that if he were to give Fisher the alternative work she sought, others would demand it as well, thereby starting a slide that might result in the complete unraveling of union discipline. He told Fisher she must either participate in the action or resign from the union. Following principle as always, she took the latter course.

Fisher moved to New York. There she worked as an organizer for several unions, including the American Federation of State, County and Municipal Employees, where, in the 1960s, she would briefly be reunited with Joe Ames. In the same years she frequently visited the Riches, Marvin and his wife Evelyn, and served as godparent to their son, Gordon. She seems not to have formed long-term relationships except for that with her mother. Movement gossip, abetted by Farmer's memoirs, said she had an unrequited passion for James Farmer. "My sense is that she never had affairs," said Evelyn Rich. "She was a very serious person. She was too busy to have affairs."[25]

Fisher joined a mostly black Baptist church in Brooklyn and became the head of its social action committee. Her specialty was Jim Crow housing. Speaking of her committee work, she wrote in 1962 to a St. Louis friend: "I'm a professional race relationist—an appellation I once abhorred. Actually I love my job. I get the chance to take complaints and then go into the field and begin enforcement of the law against discrimination in housing. I've learned to make a comparatively weak law work. (Some nasty landlords have protested my belligerancy [sic]!) ... Say hello to Hal and the boys. Give my love to the Dagens—in case you're speaking at the moment. Of course, give my best to The Senator."[26]

Four years later she was dead from the stroke.[27] The Hal mentioned in her letter was Gibbons. The Dagens were of course Maggie and Irv. The "in case you're speaking" probably referred to the differences, sometimes ideological, sometimes personal, often both at once, that tend to erupt among intense political types. The letter's recipient was Ernest Calloway and "The Senator" was his wife DeVerne, who had recently been elected to Missouri's legislature.

Ernest Calloway had come to St. Louis in early 1950, more or less to take Fisher's place as a sparkplug in both the warehouse union and its extracurricular anti-racism programs. "Ernest Calloway was a philosopher," said Mike Ryan, a onetime Gibbons lieutenant who is today a retired political consultant. "He was the idea guy. He planted ideas with Gibbons and then created ways to implement them."[28]

A stocky, copper-skinned man, Calloway was forty when he hooked up with Gibbons. His father had been a coal miner and a lay preacher. The family lived in an eastern Kentucky mining community that was dominated by volatile white mountaineers. "I grew up hating white people," Calloway once said in an interview. "A friend of mine was lynched in 1933. They tied him to the back of an automobile, dragged him up the mountain, poured gasoline on him and set him on fire. Later I went up to see the remains. It took me many years to forget the smell. Later I found hatred a waste of time. What you have to work with are institutions, laws, customs. I have spent fifty years working hatred out of my system."[29]

Escaping Kentucky and the miner's life, young Ernest went on the road as a hobo. One evening, as he wandered in the mountains of Baja California, he spied a beautiful naked woman approaching through the mist. In her presence, he later wrote, he found himself "enveloped by an unusual sense of comfort and peace." Suddenly the woman changed into a great bald vulture. Calloway backed away in horror, at the same time thinking he perceived something familiar in the creature. "The face was the mirror of evil and I saw my own drab, rudderless, non-caring existence within [it]."[30] A life devoted to selfish pleasures would ruin him, he concluded. The vulture woman vanished. Calloway headed back to the United States and a life in the labor movement.

In 1934 he won a scholarship to A. J. Muste's Brookwood Labor College in suburban New York, a leftish training ground for many CIO leaders-to-be. (Visiting faculty included Norman Thomas, Upton Sinclair, John Dewey, and Reinhold Niebuhr.) The middle '30s he spent organizing unemployed councils in Virginia. In 1938 Calloway traveled to Pittsburgh seeking a job with the CIO steelworkers but was, he believed, blackballed by the Communists because he belonged to a rival socialist faction. In Chicago later that year, he became a founder of a union for redcaps, the black men who toted passengers' luggage in railroad terminals.

Drafted in 1940, Calloway refused to report for duty, not because he was a pacifist but because the armed forces, in their practice of racial segregation, treated African Americans unfairly. "Being a Negro," he was expected to "suffer the indignities of second-class citizenship and at the same time assume first-class responsibility to the state," he told his draft board.[31] Therefore he declined to serve. For its part, the government declined to prosecute, presumably for fear of risking embarrassing publicity. In the late '40s Calloway took ship for England, where he attended Oxford University on a scholarship provided by the British trade union movement. He was introduced at a party to Lady Nancy Astor, a Virginia-born aristocrat who told him that black people should allow benevolent whites to direct their lives for them. "It was at this point that our conversation became slightly heated," Calloway recalled.[32]

6. Bernice Fisher and "Cab" Calloway 67

The year before he went to England he had married the former DeVerne Lee, a tiny bundle of energy who was herself an activist. The daughter of a Memphis railroad laborer, Lee had worked her way through college before going off to India to serve in the Red Cross during World War II. In Bombay she led a protest against the segregation of white and black U.S. servicemen in the Red Cross' swimming pool. At different times in the 1960s both Calloways would run for public office: she won, he lost. Mike Ryan said that Ernest Calloway was too cerebral for retail politics. "DeVerne was much more direct, the real politician in the family," according to Ryan. "She knew how to work a crowd, make connections. They should have run *her*" for the office her husband sought, Ryan said.[33]

In 1949 Ernest was making plans to return to Oxford on a Fulbright scholarship when he happened one day to encounter Harold Gibbons in a cocktail lounge. They had earlier met during the Chicago taxicab strike of 1937. Now, over drinks, Gibbons invited Calloway to spend three or four months in St. Louis setting up a research office for the warehousemen's organization. "I came to St. Louis and discovered the most creative local union in the nation," Calloway recalled long afterward. "I finally decided to give up returning to Oxford and cast my lot with Gibbons instead."[34]

Calloway was accordingly on hand in December 1951 when Gibbons and his friends, having launched one campaign against Jim Crow in city lunchrooms, took on the Jim Crow education system as well. Under the aegis of its Democratic Rights Committee, the warehouse union submitted to the city's school board a fourteen-page paper entitled "Planning for an Integrated School System in St. Louis."[35] According to Marvin Rich, he, with Irv Dagen and Charles Oldham, CORE's two law students, did the actual writing of the document. Calloway served as their inspiration and advisor.[36]

Missouri's constitution, like those of some other Southern and border states, forbade the teaching of white and African American children in the same classrooms: segregation was the law as well as the custom. But the authors of "Planning," who began the paper by tracing the history of U.S. Supreme Court decisions on school segregation, noted a progressive weakening of the court's defense of the practice, and predicted that, if it were to be true to its own logic, the court would soon have no choice but to find that these state laws violated the constitution of the United States. St. Louis, the authors argued, should be prepared to act on that inevitable ruling. They suggested eight steps the school board could take to prepare for desegregation, one of which was the immediate assignment of some black teachers to white schools and some white teachers to black ones, a possibility unanticipated— and therefore not expressly forbidden—by the state.

Calm practicality was the note struck throughout the document. Gibbons wrote the introduction (or at least had his byline applied to it). Only too aware that many of his own union members were themselves school segregationists, he tried to step carefully. "We wish to emphasize ... that we are not presenting this plan for the purpose of advocating the end of segregation," he wrote. "We are assuming that segregation will be ended within the next few years. In formulating this plan, we have only sought to determine how best to prepare for the change."[37] This was disingenuous. Gibbons and his friends knew that merely by raising the subject in the first place they were bringing both the change and peaceful public acceptance of it that much closer.

Of course they were right. St. Louis' school board formally rejected the paper's arguments in 1952, but just two years later, in May 1954, the U.S. Supreme Court did at last declare school segregation unconstitutional. St. Louis' schools then desegregated with hardly a murmur of protest.

In 1955 Calloway was elected president of the city's NAACP chapter. That group, composed mostly of clergymen and other middle-class professionals, had until then focused on legal strategies, filing lawsuits against various Jim Crow practices. Calloway introduced it to direct action. Under his leadership the NAACP's primary target became jobs, with the group petitioning local branches of large companies such as Coca-Cola and Lever Brothers to hire black people. Calloway's NAACP adopted something like the CORE double-whammy: negotiations first, then, if talking produced no results, picket lines and threats of consumer boycotts. At the same time, of course, Calloway himself—whom Gibbons had dubbed "Cab," after the popular band leader of that era—remained an employee of the warehousemen's union. Assigned to a department run by David Salmon, he conducted research, taught classes, and wrote manuals for shop stewards.

Everyone understood, however, that his chief energies were to be reserved for work on behalf of the city's African American population. Salmon raised the point one day while conferring with Gibbons about budgetary matters. Why, he asked, must his department be responsible for Calloway's salary? "Gibbons told me that Cab was his, and my, contribution to the Saint Louis community."[38]

7

The Teamsters

In 1948, after they came home one evening to find their Fountain Avenue home burglarized, the Gibbons family moved to Kirkwood, a middle-class suburb on St. Louis' southwestern edge. Ann Gibbons, who had enjoyed life on Fountain Avenue, always regretted leaving it. "Mother really felt very isolated in Kirkwood," said her daughter Elizabeth Vasquez. "Nobody was an artist there, nobody went barefoot, nobody was interested in labor unions." Ann considered Kirkwood provincial. Vasquez recalls a morning when she refused to go to school because the headline in that morning's newspaper was "Gibbons Indicted" and she feared that her friends would make sneering remarks about it. Ann tried to reassure her daughter. "No one here reads the paper," she said.[1]

With the new home came a shift in the domestic mood. Union friends had felt free to drop by the Gibbonses' more or less at will, especially on weekends. "In the late '40s and early '50s couples gathered at our house on Friday nights to drink and talk and debate issues," said Patrick Gibbons. "It might go on until two in the morning, and it could get loud. Harold was always the loudest."[2] Ann, who had small children to raise—in 1948 Patrick was eight, Elizabeth three, Larry only a year old—began to balk at these get-togethers. She found her husband's poker games particularly trying. "Mother stopped him from having poker games at the house because the players drank too much and cussed too much, and she didn't want that in her home," said Vasquez. "She wasn't precious. She just thought the games got too wild."[3]

Ann was a reserved woman who was drawn to books and music. Gibbons was, most of the time, a noisy extrovert. Their energies were mismatched. Ann, possessing the normal person's stamina, would be exhausted after a day's cooking, housekeeping, and child care. But Gibbons wasn't a normal person: he could go for several days on no more than brief catnaps. This gave him a great advantage at work, in negotiating contracts, for example. In extended contract talks, the employer's chief negotiator would often tire at some point and have to be replaced by another person. Precisely because he was fresh, the new man was unlikely to have all the prior session's twists and turns lodged in his memory. But Gibbons, who, with his tremendous endurance, could remain steadily at the table without taking a break, would have lost track of nothing. "Because he remembered and they didn't, Father could sometimes slip a previously discarded point *back* into the bargaining," Vasquez said. "And this time the company might agree to it."[4]

Once a long night of talks was concluded and a contract agreed to, Gibbons would want to celebrate. "But the art museum and the symphony wouldn't be open at two in the morning," said Patrick Gibbons with just a touch of irony. "So he'd go to the saloons."[5] Then after the bars finally closed he might, rather than wake Ann and the kids, sleep it off in his office or check into a hotel.

Gibbons was all thumbs as a homebody. His children, in their seventies now, often speak of him as if he had been not their father but rather a somewhat distant uncle. "I've told you Harold wasn't good with children," said Patrick. "He didn't know what to do with them. He came to visit my wife and me once and I introduced him to my nine-year-old stepson. Harold just sat there looking at the boy. Finally he said, 'So, you want to play some gin rummy?'"[6]

By the early '50s Gibbons was away from home a good deal of the time. His absence increased Ann's sense of isolation. She hadn't learned to drive a car, which only made the problem worse. "Ann did not have an automobile at her command and was constantly asking for rides from other people," writes David Salmon, his "constantly" implying that as time passed these benefactors became increasingly less eager to help out.[7] Larry Gibbons said, "Slowly but surely Mother got stuck at home with us kids."[8]

Harold Gibbons' own life had plenty of stress in it, but then he seems to have enjoyed stress as long as it was accompanied by novelty. Gibbons hated being bored. When his days seemed repetitious he tended to fall into what David Salmon refers to as Gibbons' "periods of ennui." On such occasions the union boss might simply disappear for a time. "So far as I could determine, Gibbons' outages [an interesting word] were not drunken sprees but rather a compulsive need to get away from boredom and the pressure of routine," writes Salmon. "The need was evident even in the early days when, as Bill Latal reminisced, the militants collected money among themselves to get him out of town; in those days it was on the Greyhound bus."[9]

Gibbons' life was now touched by moral ambiguity as well as stress, because he had taken his warehousemen into the Teamsters Union.

The process was complex. After leaving RWDSU in January 1948, Gibbons spent most of the following year seeking a new international for his now independent CIO union. One possibility was the United Auto Workers. Jerry Tucker, a St. Louis-based protégé of the late Victor Reuther, said that

Gibbons discussed such a move with Victor's brother, the UAW's president Walter Reuther. These talks came to nothing, Tucker said, because although Gibbons felt closer to the Reuthers than to anyone else in the labor movement, he insisted on a larger role in their organization than they could provide. "Harold wanted to be in line to be made the director of an eight-state UAW region, part of the union's hierarchy," Tucker recalled. But if Reuther had given Gibbons that post he would have angered UAW leaders who were senior to the St. Louisan in terms of experience and years of union service. "And who also were *autoworkers*, not warehousemen," added Tucker. "As the story goes, Walter couldn't make it happen for Harold, so Harold took the option of going with the Teamsters."[10]

A second possible new home for the warehousemen was the Amalgamated Clothing Workers. According to Harry Ball, the price of admission to that international was the dismemberment of Gibbons' organization. The St. Louis union was *too* miscellaneous for the ACW, which was willing to take on the retail clerks but wanted neither the warehouse workers themselves nor "the cabs, the small pickle houses, or many other parts of the local."[11] Gibbons' members had already let him know that they would refuse to be broken up and dispersed among other unions, so he quickly refused the ACW's bid.

The most surprising of Gibbons' explorations that year were those conducted with eight rebellious RWDSU locals in New York City. These eight were the Communist-led warehouse and department store groups he had so bitterly denounced for betraying the Montgomery Ward strike just a few years before (see Chapter 4).

This is a difficult story to pin down, mainly because few of its actors ever committed their recollections to paper. With the coming of the Cold War in 1946–48, some leaders of Communist unions, now uneasy with the guidance they received from the Communist Party, began thinking about making other arrangements. A sign of this was an article that appeared in the *New York Times* in September 1948. According to the reporter, several Communist-led RWDSU locals in New York were talking to non–Communist locals about forming a new international. Sam Wolchok, RWDSU's president, had informed the reporter that "the leader of the movement to form an independent department store international was Harold Gibbons, a former extreme right-winger who fought Mr. Wolchok last year on the grounds that he was not 'tough enough' on the Communists…. Now, Mr. Wolchok added, Mr. Gibbons is trying to team up with New York's leftist locals in an effort to set up a competing group that would also include elements from Detroit, Toledo and elsewhere."[12]

Gibbons' friend Sid Lens has partly confirmed Wolchok's story. Lens' own Chicago grocery clerks' local had left RWDSU in 1946 to join an AFL international. Two years later, he writes, he and Gibbons entered negotiations to bring as many as ten breakaway New York RWDSU locals into, not a new international, but a "special department" of Lens' AFL international.[13] The fact that most of these locals were Communist-led posed no problem for Lens, a former Trotskyist who saw Communists as badly educated comrades rather than villains. Gibbons, much disgusted by the New York locals' behavior during the Montgomery Ward strike, seems to have blamed that behavior not so much on the local unions themselves as on the party chieftains who ordered it. He appears to have viewed Lens' plan as an opportunity to detach the New Yorkers, whose ideas on the role of trade unions in domestic affairs were similar to his own, from a party, the Communists, whose international affairs served the interest of a foreign nation.

Lens' plan fell through, largely because the leaders of his AFL international couldn't guarantee that the envisioned "special department" would not be raided by other AFL unions. And, Lens writes, "in any case, Jimmy Hoffa, then a teamster vice president but already recognized as the power behind the scenes, entered the auction at this stage, and he had more to sell than I did."[14]

Lens seems to be telescoping the events of different years here. According to Gibbons himself, he wasn't introduced to Hoffa until 1952 or '53.[15] The Teamster officer who, in Lens' words, "entered the auction" in 1948 was Dave Beck, executive vice president of the IBT and, although the septuagenarian Dan Tobin still occupied the president's chair, the union's de facto boss.

The only first-person account of the "auction" we possess comes from the seller, Larry Camie. Camie, it may be recalled, was the leader of Teamsters Local 688, St. Louis' *AFL* warehouse union.[16] Local 688 was about a third the size of Gibbons' CIO group. Its members worked mostly in lumberyards and in building-supply and grocery warehouses. In 1946–47 raids by Camie's people on the CIO local had led Gibbons to retaliate by importing the Trotskyists mentioned in Chapter 4. After that episode, relations between the two groups evidently improved—to the point where, by early 1949, Camie and Gibbons were discussing a possible merger.

Camie gave his version of the story when he appeared before the McClellan Committee nearly a decade after the fact. "On or about January 17, 1949," Camie began, he traveled to Chicago for a meeting of the Teamsters Union's warehouse division. While strolling one day in the hotel lobby he happened to encounter Dave Beck, who suggested that they go upstairs for a private talk. Camie went to the room indicated—and found not Beck but Gibbons waiting for him. Then, Camie said, "Mr. Dave Beck came into the room and said that Mr. Gibbons was applying to the International Teamsters for a charter for his warehouse union.... Mr. Beck said, 'I want to consult with you as we have one charter now for a warehouse union [in St. Louis], and what do you think about it?' I said to Mr. Beck I thought two charters would be confusing for the same type of work which would be overlapping and more confusion, and the proper thing to do was take Mr. Gibbons' union and merge it with 688 and have one union. Mr. Beck said, 'Well, why don't you fellows think it over?'"

At this point in Camie's testimony, the committee's chief counsel, Robert Kennedy, interrupted to ask, "You went back and worked out the details with Mr. Gibbons?"

"That is correct," said Camie.

"And the unions were merged?"

"The two unions were merged," Camie agreed.[17]

On January 25, just eight days after the Chicago meeting, the shop stewards of Gibbons' union gathered in the ballroom of St. Louis' Jefferson Hotel to take up the proposed merger. Some stewards must have been doubtful about the deal at first, because the vote on it came only after an extended debate. According to Calloway, "several hours of discussion followed, [but] as discussion went on, the wisdom of the proposal became more apparent. The vote was taken, with only seven out of more than 300 stewards present in opposition."[18]

No doubt a big chunk of the discussion Calloway mentions involved money. Camie received $36,000 in the deal, $12,000 for each of the three years remaining in his term as the old Local 688's president. Another $42,000 was split among the six members of the old local's executive board. On the rare occasions that Gibbons mentioned these sums, he said his union had given the six men "severance pay." Larry Gibbons said simply, "Father paid them to go away."[19]

After the Senate hearings of a decade later, Robert Kennedy expressed shock at the arrangement. "Here a labor union became nothing more than a commodity to be bought and paid for on the open market," he wrote in a book about his investigations of the Teamsters.[20] He meant that the members of Camie's group had been given no say in the matter. Whereas Gibbons had sought and received approval of the merger from his shop stewards, Camie had sought it only from his suborned executive board. Camie claimed to see nothing wrong in this. Like Dave Beck he was essentially a businessman: he had founded Local 688 in the first place—why shouldn't he be paid for giving it up? Besides, he argued, his members were better off under the new regime. The old Local 688 had neither a pension plan nor other benefits, but Gibbons' group possessed both, including free medical care from the Labor Health Institute. Camie told the Senate committee, "I felt, in the merger of Mr. Gibbons' union and the union that I represented, that the members would benefit by a merger, and we merged the unions."[21]

The newly combined organizations took the name the Camie group had used since its founding: Local 688 of the International Brotherhood of Teamsters, Chauffeurs, Warehousemen & Helpers of America. It had about eight thousand members.

The transaction caused a stir in the world of labor. As the *New York Times* reported, "the 'merger' caught other CIO leaders off guard. There was talk that the teamsters had served notice on Mr. Gibbons to turn over the local or face raids." The newspaper itself adopted this version of the event, as can be seen in the headline slapped on the story: "AFL Teamsters Raid CIO Local in St. Louis, Add 6,000 Members."[22]

So was Gibbons the architect or the victim of the Camie deal? In a sense he and his St. Louis warehousemen *had* been captured by an alien entity. (Gibbons would later tell his son Larry that tears ran down his cheeks as he wrote the letter in which he formally resigned from the CIO.)[23] Many of the CIO's founders had been socialists of one brand or another, and even in the 1950s most CIO leaders still talked as if they were part of a great reform movement. The Teamsters, on the other hand, were one of the most conservative of the old AFL craft unions: words like "social" and "movement" made IBT veterans squirm. Also, CIO organizations were relatively free of labor racketeering. Partly this was due to their social-mindedness, partly to the fact that their memberships, typically employed in mass-production industries—autos, coal, steel, etc.—worked under contracts that were negotiated across entire industries and under much public scrutiny, which made them difficult to fiddle with. Whereas companies with Teamster contracts were by comparison smaller, more insular, and much more private, a situation that sometimes allowed both company executives and union leaders to carve out creative little rackets for themselves, usually at the expense of union members. Some leaders of Teamster locals were notorious for their crookedness.

Gibbons was certainly aware of the problem. Larry Gibbons remembered asking his father about connections between Teamsters and mobsters. "He said that probably somewhere close to a third of the locals were gangster-influenced."[24]

But if Gibbons saw his union as having been hijacked by villains, he gave no sign of it. In fact he argued, in a statement released two days after the merger, that the IBT was the best possible home for his warehousemen. Unlike RWDSU, he said, the Teamsters were serious about organizing. (Beck had just launched a $20 million drive to sign up new members, including warehouse workers.) The IBT had promised not to interfere with either the St. Louis union's enlightened racial practices or its political radicalism. Best of all, the Teamsters were willing to let the new Local 688 remain thoroughly miscellaneous. As Gibbons put it, "in our union we have organized workers in a number of fields and our membership has been solid in the determination that our group which has worked together for years shall not be split along more rigid jurisdictional lines. Only the Teamsters were willing to give such assurances."[25]

Gibbons had another, very practical reason for joining the IBT. His Chicago friend Sid Lens, faced with a similar choice a few years earlier, had taken his own local into not the Teamsters but the Business Service Employees, an AFL international closely allied with the Chicago Teamsters. Indeed the existence of that close alliance had been for Lens the deciding factor. His reasoning had to do with transportation history. In postwar America, freight increasingly was hauled over the road in trucks rather than by railroad, as it had in the past. And because truck drivers could shut down a company by preventing it from receiving or shipping freight, they had become the most sensitively placed workforce in the nation. Lens had learned this the hard way. On an occasion when he was still with RWDSU, Teamster drivers had refused to honor a picket line around a department store he was trying to organize, and his organizing efforts failed as a result.[26] After that, Lens always tried to stay on the Teamsters' good side. "From a strategic point of view," he wrote in 1949, "they are today even stronger than Reuther's auto workers or [Philip] Murray's steelworkers."[27]

Gibbons in 1949 badly needed to improve *his* union's strategic position vis à vis recalcitrant employers. As Harry Ball describes it, "one of the primary reasons for the Union's desperate need to affiliate with an international was the severe defeat it was suffering at the time in its drive to unionize the … J. H. Grady Manufacturing Co."[28] Grady was the baseball- and softball-making firm that had provided Dick Kavner with such a baptism of fire (see Chapter 6). That thirteen-month campaign had cost the warehouse union $125,000 (more than $1 million in today's dollars).[29] Even worse, Grady had practically from the strike's start begun hiring replacement workers ("scabs," in union parlance), and when the strike finally failed those strikers who had held out—the toughest, most spirited of them, that is—found they had no jobs to go back to. Union morale suffered.

The Grady Co. had had more than stubbornness going for it. Early in the walkout, a circuit court judge issued an injunction sharply restricting the picketing the strikers could do. The federal Taft-Hartley Act, passed by Congress just two years before, in 1946, tied strikers' hands as well. Back during Roosevelt's New Deal, the federal government had been friendlier to labor: For example, St. Louis' warehousemen had won a strike against a local hardware company by picketing not only the company itself but also a bank that happened to have the hardware company's president on its board. This had embarrassed the bank's other board members and they pressured the hardware man to give in and settle the strike.[30] But the Taft-Hartley law outlawed such maneuvers (called "secondary boycotts"), which precluded their use against Grady. "Every time we turn around we run up against some government agency," Gibbons had grumbled in the early '40s. Now, in the late '40s, the complaint seemed even more apropos than before.

Government wasn't the union's big problem, however. The big problem was the local's own inability, despite having begun the strike with the backing of a large majority of Grady's workers, to prevent it from manufacturing and—especially—*shipping* finished softballs and baseballs. If he hadn't known it before, Gibbons learned from the Grady strike the same lesson Sid Lens had learned in Chicago: truck drivers held the power. St. Louis' warehousemen should become a *Teamster* organization because they could then, in league with Teamster drivers, control the shipping of both a manufacturers' raw materials and its finished products. In such a situation a firm like the Grady Co. would be forced to negotiate.

* * *

Gibbons had one other reason for hooking up with the Teamsters. He was, after all, a man of strong personal ambition. "I was going to be an engineer and I was going to be a rich guy," he once said, describing himself at twenty. "Daddy was driven by a need to achieve and be recognized," said Elizabeth Vasquez. The engineer dream dissipated, but Gibbons had intended from the start of his career as a trade unionist to rise as high in the labor movement as talent and fortune would take him.

His closest RWDSU friend was a tough little Russian-Jewish immigrant named Larry Steinberg, the boss of a big warehouse local in Toledo, Ohio. Gibbons named his second son after Steinberg. Although Larry Camie didn't mention it, Larry Steinberg sat in with Gibbons on the negotiations that brought the St. Louis warehousemen into the Teamsters.[31] And soon after the St. Louis merger was announced, Steinberg pulled his own local out of RWDSU and brought it into the IBT alongside Gibbons'.

RWDSU warehouse leaders in Detroit and New York (not, however, including the Communists) did the same thing, thereby forming a former RWDSU warehouse caucus in the Teamsters. Gibbons was from the start the caucus' leader. Of course the IBT was a conservative AFL union dominated by truck drivers, while the warehousemen were johnny-come-lately leftwingers from the CIO. But it was at least conceivable that the leftish warehouse Teamsters might in time come to dominate an organization hitherto run by right-wing truck-driving Teamsters, and, if so, Gibbons might then rise to the organization's very top.

It surely didn't seem a *likely* prospect. Still, who knew what opportunities tomorrow might bring?

8

Varieties of Political Experience

Gibbons' career as a social revolutionary in the CIO had about it a certain abstract moral ease that began to fray when he joined the Teamsters. During the 1950s he also got involved in St. Louis city politics. His aims there followed naturally from his concern for the union's "citizen-members." "We have," he liked to say, "broader concerns than the eight hours we spend in labor. Our wives, our children, our homes, indeed our leisure hours mean that we have a stake in the community and the neighborhood in which we live."[1] "Community" and "neighborhood" are pleasant, wholesome words. However, in order to effectively defend *specific* St. Louis communities and neighborhoods, Gibbons became an active leader of his adopted city's Democratic Party. That complicated his ethical choices as well.

St. Louis was then sixty-one square miles of factories, stores, government offices, domiciles, etc., plus 850,000 human beings—all shoved up against the Mississippi River. For reasons we need not go into here, the city had decades earlier separated itself politically from St. Louis County, which surrounded it on all but the river side.[2] The county itself remained largely rural and agricultural. "Even Clayton, the county seat, had the leisurely ambiance of a small Missouri town," writes Maggie Dagen in her memoirs.[3] And since Clayton began (as it does yet today) at Skinker Avenue, demarcating the west end of Forest Park, the great green common laid out for the 1904 St. Louis World's Fair, St. Louis the city was a tightly closed-in place.

This closed-in-ness determined the nature of the city's politics. St. Louis couldn't grow past Skinker on the west, because of the historical event mentioned above, and couldn't expand eastward because of the Mississippi. By the 1940s the Democrats pretty much ran the municipal government (the Republicans having dwindled into minority status during the Depression) but they had split into two wings. One wing was especially focused on the closed-in problem. Fearing competition from cities that were free to expand geographically (and rapidly doing so), this wing's adherents hoped to rejuvenate their dark, Dickensian warren by clearing out its worst tracts and replacing them with airy green spaces full of new light industry. Robert H. Salisbury, a political scientist then at Washington University, dubbed this wing of the Democratic Party the "Forces of Progress." The opposing wing was a motley lot of ward healers, owners of slum properties, small shopkeepers, and trade unionists rooted in precisely the older neighborhoods that the Forces of Progress were eager to clear out. This faction Salisbury called the "Politicians."[4]

The two factions, it should be noted, were tendencies, not organizations, not actual political parties. Their shapes were constantly shifting—a person who sympathized with the Forces of Progress on one question might well switch over to the Politicians on the next, then back again on a third. Even so, the two labels provide a useful way to look at the municipal politics of those days.

Raymond Tucker was the uncontested leader of the Forces of Progress. A stocky man in wire-rimmed glasses who would soon become St. Louis' mayor, Tucker had begun as a professor of engineering at Washington University. He made his political reputation by securing the passage of an ordinance that rid the city of its perpetual haze of coal smoke. To his mind industrial smoke and traditional ward politics were both symptoms of urban decay. "A successful air pollution program cannot be achieved through partisan politics of favoritism to either individuals or large corporations," he once told an audience. "If you pursue a program that affects everybody but your friends you will find you have many friends and an awful lot of smoke."[5] Tucker's own friends included the city's business elite (represented by a group called Civic Progress); its major newspapers, especially the liberal *Post-Dispatch*; and most of its educated middle class.

The leaders of the Politicians faction were much less prepossessing. Other things being equal, Gibbons might have thrown in his lot with the Forces of Progress on at least some issues. But since he was boss of a trade union many of whose members lived in neighborhoods the reformers wanted to raze, he nearly always sided with the Politicians group.

In 1948, for example, the Forces of Progress asked voters to approve a bond issue that would pay for the demolition of many blocks of tenement housing in a district known as Mill Creek Valley. Mill Creek neighborhoods, which ran roughly from Fourteenth Street west to Grand Boulevard, were inhabited almost entirely by black people, many of them poor newcomers from the South. The warehouse union came out strongly against the bond issue. Dick Kavner, addressing a session of the union's Stewards' Council, noted that the proposal concerned demolition alone—it said nothing about constructing replacement dwellings. Ernest Conn, the African American chairman of the union's Democratic Rights Committee, argued that given St. Louis' endemic neighborhood segregation, tearing down the Mill Creek slums would leave their residents homeless. "The homes for the displaced people, most of whom are Negroes, just don't exist," he said.[6]

The phrase "displaced people" had come to the United States from Europe, where the recent war had turned millions of people into homeless refugees. "Let's Don't Create a D.P. Problem in St. Louis," cried an advertisement that the warehouse union placed in all three daily newspapers.[7] The bond issue's opponents, who included the city's NAACP chapter, campaigned more energetically than did its supporters, and as a result the proposal was defeated by a wide margin.[8] So Mill Creek's tenements, unlovely as they were, remained for a time.

But this was the era of "urban renewal." In St. Louis as well as in many other postwar U.S. cities, reformers had economic logic on their side. Concerning Mill Creek Valley and a mostly poor white district called Kosciusko, two historians write:

> From city officials' perspective, urban renewal and inner-core industrial redevelopment were not simply an exercise in public good but an imperative move for fiscal solvency. As planning research indicated, slums such as [Mill Creek Valley] and Kosciusko used more than 40 percent of the city's fire, police, road, health, and sanitation services while returning only 6 percent to the city in property tax revenues. This was clearly an insoluble situation. The war on the slums, then, was more a war waged by reformers and downtown corporate interests against small-time slumlords than on working-class blacks and whites. It amounted to a bitter land struggle between Civic Progress business leaders and petty landlords, in which the exercise of eminent domain and the funneling of resources by the municipal government clearly favored the interests of Civic Progress. Nevertheless, working-class blacks and whites were the collateral damage of the renewal war, as they bore the brunt of the headache ball and bulldozer.[9]

In a 1955 referendum, St. Louis voters, reversing their decision of seven years earlier, approved bond issues totaling $110 million, which (augmented by another $1 million in federal money) was used to clear land for a number of projects, including three express highways: one through Mill Creek Valley, another through Kosciusko, and still another through the middle of the Italian community on The Hill. Twenty thousand black Mill Creek residents would lose their homes to these projects, as would several thousand more white people from The Hill and Kosciusko. "In addition, hundreds of small business, religious, and community institutions were displaced or obliterated, along with their dense social networks."[10] Destruction of Mill Creek homes was to be alleviated to some extent by the construction of acres of public housing on the city's near North Side. (Displaced Hill and Kosciusko residents, mostly white and therefore unhindered by the color of their skin, simply melted into other white neighborhoods.) Having little choice, many Mill Creek Valley residents abandoned their homes for these new housing complexes, which in the future would become the source of a whole new set of urban problems.[11]

Urban renewal's opponents could do no more than delay the inevitable. After the victorious bond vote Ray Tucker, now St. Louis' mayor, refused to enforce the city's rat-control ordinance in Mill Creek and Kosciusko on the grounds that since the two districts were soon to be demolished under the urban renewal program, money spent on their upkeep would be wasted. "Public indignation rose at reports of children being attacked [by rats]," noted one observer. "Community stewards" for the doomed districts sought help in this matter from their colleagues in Local 688. "Finally, the union went to court for a writ of mandamus ordering enforcement of the law."[12]

But in the end, the buildings in the two districts had to come down. The razing of Mill Creek Valley and Kosciusko was a disaster for its inhabitants and a political defeat for Gibbons and his associates, including the other members of the Politicians faction. We don't know exactly how Gibbons reacted to this defeat, but must assume that it only strengthened his resolve to defend surviving neighborhoods, especially those that were home to Local 688 members. The experience surely confirmed in his eyes the value of the "community stewards" program mentioned above.

"Community stewards" was another Gibbons invention. The program, which seems to have begun in late 1951 or early '52, was patterned on the shop-steward system practiced by most trade unions. A community steward, who was chosen by the Local 688 members residing in a given ward, operated there more or less the same way a shop steward does in the workplace. He or she conducted public meetings to which neighbors could bring "community grievances" concerning, for example, "the slow removal of fallen trees or garbage, the need for playgrounds, [and] the location of bus stops."[13] These grievances the steward then took up with the relevant alderman or Democratic Party committeeman. Gibbons described the process this way: "If, let's say, we needed a playground in the neighborhood, we'd have our steward get all our members in that neighborhood together and start raising hell. We'd call a meeting, and you know when you're talking about a playground it isn't just for Teamster members. So our guys would get every goddamn neighbor to go to the meeting, too. In the 24th Ward [the large Italian colony known as The Hill], which was our best ward, we'd have 1,500 or 2,000 people, when the ward committeeman might get 150 to his meetings. He'd die. And you know he'd listen to us."[14]

According to a graduate student who spent the summer of 1959 studying Gibbons' union, Local 688 appointed one community steward for every twenty-five of its members living in a given ward. That year there were 225 stewards, which, if union membership had been spread evenly around the city, would have meant eight stewards for each of its twenty-eight wards. In fact, writes the student, "There are very few Teamsters living in Wards 6, 23, and 28, but otherwise members of the local are fairly equally distributed in other wards."[15] The 225 community stewards weren't equally zealous, the grad student noted. When they came together to compare notes in monthly meetings at the union hall, no more than a hundred would ordinarily be present. And only "about 50 stewards form the 'hard core' of the assembly."[16]

Still, in politics fifty "hard core" ward workers can be a mighty army, especially if properly armed. Money arms. Local 688's members had earlier voted to assess themselves 25 cents a month to build a special fund for political purposes. "I don't recall much conflict between community stewards and Democratic Party regulars," said Mike Ryan, a later Local 688 staff member. "We had money. We worked *with* party people. They figured out real fast that we could have spent that money in other ways."[17] Add to that thought the sociologist Arnold Rose's finding that a higher percentage of warehouse union members (and their families) typically came out to vote on election day than did the general run of St. Louisans.[18] So there were several reasons why party regulars would have welcomed close cooperation with the union. As early as 1956 a *St. Louis Globe-Democrat* reporter was writing that "these community stewards had supplanted practically the local party committeeman as the people most capable of 'getting things done in the neighborhood.'"[19]

The reporter probably exaggerated a bit. It's unlikely that many community stewards took on Democratic committeeman jobs themselves. But in a ward where Local 688 had a large number of members—and especially where, as in the aforementioned Ward 24, Pete Saffo's base, it had influential members—the party committeeman was almost certain to soon start seeing things the union's way. Some party regulars were annoyed by what they felt to be the union's aggressiveness. "They're trying to take over," complained Jack Dwyer, committeeman for Ward 4. "I don't have anything against labor, but they wouldn't let me tell them who should be president of the Teamsters. I don't see why they should tell me how I should run my ward."[20] The independence of Dwyer, who was also St. Louis' city treasurer, chairman of the city's Democratic central committee, and a chief leader of the Forces of Progress faction, was probably never really in much danger. But the fact that even he could feel threatened shows how high Local 688 energies then ran.

* * *

Gibbons had two partners in the Politicians faction.

Lawrence "Larry" Callanan was the business manager of AFL Steamfitters Local 562. The Fitters, as they were known, were plumbers who installed heating and cooling systems in large construction projects such as office buildings, hospitals and schools. Relatively few in number (about a thousand), they wielded an unusual amount of power because of their strategic position in St. Louis' construction industry. Local 562 was an "Irish" union, meaning that its roots lay deep and thick in the old immigrant Irish neighborhoods of the city's near North Side. It had, for example, a long association with the Hogan gang, a Democratic Party grouplet that in years past had also sometimes engaged in bootlegging and bank robbery. Even in Callanan's time, writes one historian, "the connotation of something unlawful, corrupt, or even violent clung to the Fitters, a sentiment that set them outside the normal ebb and flow of machine politics, St. Louis style."[21] Callanan, a boisterous, black-haired, combative man, had himself served a prison term for armed robbery. His brother Tom, a onetime undertaker who had been elected the city's sheriff, was Larry's more or less respectable public face in politics.[22] Like Local 688, Local 562 maintained a special political fund, but it was much larger than the warehousemen's and was used primarily to maintain political friends in office, those friends then being expected to do what they could to facilitate the building projects that kept Steamfitters employed. So tempting was the size of the fund that Larry Callanan frequently had to fight off efforts by other Fitters to replace him and get their own hands on it. As might be expected, he and his union were often in newspaper headlines.

The third leader of the Politicians faction was Morris Shenker. A Jewish immigrant from Ukraine, Shenker had at age fifteen come alone to St. Louis, where he proceeded to attend night classes in high school, then college, then law school, all the while supporting himself by running a small grocery store during the day. As a young lawyer he earned a reputation as a defender of the underdog, frequently representing clients, many of them black, who couldn't pay for his services. They were lucky to have him. An otherwise hostile journalist would note that, during Shenker's first twenty years of practice, the lawyer "compiled an amazing record as a defense attorney, winning acquittals for roughly four out of five of his clients. Of the convictions that he appealed and that reached the Missouri Supreme Court, only two were sustained."[23]

Shenker was a tall, stooped man with the mouth of a disappointed catfish. Fame, or at least notoriety, came to him in 1950–51 when he represented some professional gamblers in a Senate investigation that became a sensation when broadcast on nationwide television. In St. Louis, where in early '51 the investigating committee, chaired by a U.S. senator named Estes Kefauver, conducted two days' worth of sessions, the *New York Times* reported that "housework, movies and many business houses suffered as local talent testified before the crime investigators. Bars and taverns were crowded. Watchers blocked sidewalks in front of demonstrator [TV] sets in store windows."[24] Shenker's law practice prospered as a result, but his growing celebrity eventually drew him into circles that proved to be ethically dubious. Tom Eagleton once said of his friend, "As a criminal lawyer he obviously knew criminals"— implying that Shenker had come to know some of them a bit too well. Nevertheless, the lawyer was an important figure in St. Louis' Democratic Party. He was smart, a skilled fund-raiser, and loyal, three qualities highly prized in the political world. "In politics, there are workers and 'claims agents,'" explained Eagleton. "Workers actually work in supporting a candidate. 'Claims agents' claim to work but don't actually do it. I can't recall Morris ever refusing to do something I asked him to do. If he said, 'I will help you,' he meant it."[25]

Gibbons, Callanan, and Shenker were not necessarily friends. Shenker defended Gibbons in at least one criminal case in the early '50s, but aside from that we know almost nothing about the relationship between them. And according to Joe Ames, the one-legged war veteran who had become one of the Teamster boss' political experts, "Gibbons had very little to do with the Callanans outside Democratic Party politics."[26]

Still, the trio had no difficulty coming together to fight the Forces of Progress. At stake in the struggle was not just the physical preservation of older St. Louis neighborhoods but also the historical, constitutional, and political webs in which those neighborhoods were embedded. Take, for example, the city's ward system. Each of the city's twenty-eight wards was represented by an alderman elected by the ward's residents. Since many wards had originated as immigrant enclaves, their aldermen tended to identify with one ethnic group or another: Germans in the south; Irish in the north; African Americans in Mill Creek Valley and in Jordan Chambers' near northwest; Italians on The Hill; and Lebanese (but called "Syrians" in St. Louis because Lebanon, at the time of emigration, was a still a province of Syria) and Slavs along the river on the near southeast. Each ward was a little satrapy run by the alderman or, more often, the (usually) Democratic committeeman who had engineered the alderman's election in the first place. The alderman or committeeman maintained himself by doling out patronage jobs or other favors.[27] A person's view of such favors was often colored by how high or low he or she was in the social scheme of things. Tom Guilfoil, a former slum kid who grew up to become became a powerful St. Louis lawyer and Democratic Party leader, once compared the typical party committeeman to a "chancellor of equity." The committeeman, Guilfoil said, "knew where to put in the fix, although it wasn't really a fix. You took someone ground up by the system, and you went down to city hall and got your people out of trouble."[28]

Some fixes *were* real, of course. Guilfoil, orphaned as a small child, was raised by a grandmother and aunt who lived in Lafayette Square, in the riverfront Ward 7, which was governed by Syrians with help from Serbs and Croats. In those days, said Guilfoil, many small neighborhood stores had a "book shop," a curtained alcove in which one could place bets on horse races and lottery numbers. These book shops were as ubiquitous—and as popular—as the corner tavern, and although illegal, far from secret. (Guilfoil's grandmother and aunt ran a little store in the rooming house they owned. "When I was fifteen I could pick the winners of the 'baby' [two-year-old horse] races," he said.)[29] The bookies were allowed to operate unmolested by the police (and by local government officials, including judges) in return for considerations that would certainly include voting the right way on election day.

Such practices disgusted members of the Forces of Progress faction. (Most St. Louis ward bosses were associated with the Politicians group.) That distaste can be felt yet today in a series of drawings by the *Post-Dispatch*'s great editorial cartoonist Daniel Fitzpatrick. These pictures, which Fitzpatrick began publishing periodically in 1931, dealt with especially egregious cases of political corruption in the city. Most showed the same basic scene: a dark, gulch-like urban passageway whose criminal denizens have just the moment before fled into sewers and doorways, thereby avoiding exposure to light. "Rat Alley" was the name Fitzpatrick gave this passageway. His first "Rat Alley" cartoon concerned a state legislator who had been discovered laundering the swag from a bank robbery. Many later pictures had to do with the politics-gambling nexus in the city's wards, especially the riverfront wards (like young Tom Guilfoil's), which Fitzpatrick seemed particularly to dislike.[30] The artist, who plainly admired Ray Tucker, had many admirers himself (including, as we'll see, Harold Gibbons). And because Fitzpatrick's work served as the *Post-Dispatch*'s public face for many of that paper's readers, especially those who wouldn't take the time to read actual editorials, the "Rat Alley" series was wonderful propaganda for the Forces of Progress group.

An early, though indirect, clash between the two factions came in March 1951, during a special election held to replace a recently deceased St. Louis congressman. The late lawmaker had been a Democrat; his district normally went Democratic and, other things being equal, it probably would have gone Democratic on this occasion as well. However, for the Republican candidate the nearly contemporaneous TV broadcast of the Kefauver hearings came as an early Christmas gift. Arguing that the Democrat in the race had been "hand-picked" by Morris Shenker, suddenly infamous as a gamblers' lawyer, the Republican barnstormed around town alerting voters to the menace of what he called "Shenkerism." Almost immediately this theme was taken up by the newspapers. The *Post-Dispatch*, usually Democratic, joined the normally Republican *Globe-Democrat* in endorsing the GOP candidate. The election was a crucial event, declared a *Post* editorial, because it would "[help] decide how tight the Shenker-Callanan control is going to be in St. Louis."[31]

The Democrat lost. As did, a month later, the Democratic candidate for president for St. Louis' Board of Aldermen. In this case the party hopeful was much more Gibbons' protégé than Shenker's. (A *Globe* columnist wrote that the Democrat's campaign "was mostly run from the office of Local 688 at 1127 Pine St.")[32] But he was also a member of Shenker's law firm, a bit of information that the Republicans publicized widely. Again the Kefauver hearings had an effect. On election day the Republican turnout was especially heavy in the city's West End. "A part of this [the heavy GOP turnout] can be attributed to the simple fact that ... these are Republican wards, historically," noted a postmortem written by Local 688's political experts. "Undoubtedly, however, the anti–Shenker campaign played a large part in it. Too many television sets in these wards."[33]

A year later, in the primary election of 1952, the Forces of Progress faction borrowed the "Shenkerism" tag from the GOP and applied it liberally to their opponents in the Politicians wing of their own party. They did vary the language somewhat. Since the latter faction's Sheriff Tom Callanan was himself seeking reelection at this time, the Forces of Progress campaigned against the "Shenker-Callanan machine." Tom Callanan was defeated, as were most of the other candidates endorsed by the Politicians, including a number of their ward committeemen. "A Great Day at the Polls," exclaimed the headline over the *Post-Dispatch*'s day-after lead editorial.[34] The Politicians had now lost three elections in a row. Some machine.

A showdown between the factions came in the mayoral primary of 1953. Just as the Kefauver hearings had worked against the Politicians' chances in the previous three elections, so did two acts of violence occurring in February of that year. Early in the month a bomb blew the front porch off Tom Callanan's house; two weeks later a second bomb destroyed Larry Callanan's union office. Although neither crime was ever solved, police suspected renegade Steamfitters in both cases. After Tom's defeat in the sheriff election, his brother had put him on the Fitters' payroll earning $150 a week as the organization's welfare and education director—a move that, the police said, was unpopular with some members. In any case the bombings, happening as they did so close to the primary election, were likely to negatively color the thinking of at least some voters.

The primary was held in March. Ray Tucker, running for public office for the first time, was the candidate of the Forces of Progress. The person backed by the Politicians group was Mark Eagleton, a successful corporate lawyer of Irish-Catholic background (and the father of the future senator) who, relatively new to partisan politics, had been a Republican only a few years earlier. "He'd been on the U.S. legal staff at Nuremberg and was now counsel for the Anheuser-Busch brewery and the baseball Cardinals," recalled Joe Ames. "A brilliant man."[35]

And an unsophisticated one as well, according to Tom Guilfoil. "Mark had been a Republican most of his life," said Guilfoil. "I don't know that he ever understood the dynamics of the Democratic Party. He was a magnificent speaker but he had a tendency to go down into the river wards and say, 'I can promise you an honest administration because I'm rich—I don't need money.' Well, this was not long after the Depression."[36] To voters in those wards, Eagleton's message sounded smug and condescending, Guilfoil said.

But the election was close, Eagleton losing to Tucker by only 1,600 votes out of the nearly 100,000 cast. Joe Ames blamed the defeat on Gibbons. The amputee war veteran had gone to work full-time for Local 688 after graduating from Washington University in 1951. By '53, although he was still handling some contract negotiations, his real focus was politics, serving as a middle man between Gibbons and Democratic ward leaders. Gibbons, Ames said, was "one of the best combinations of principle and ability I've ever run into. But his political judgment wasn't always good." Ames said he spoke to Gibbons just before the '53 mayoral primary, suggesting that the union put extra people and money into Ward 8, another riverfront ward run by a Syrian-Slav group but one that had on this occasion lined up with the Forces of Progress. "I knew we couldn't win the ward but I thought we could cut Tucker's margin enough there to allow Eagleton to win the city," Ames said. Gibbons, believing Eagleton already had the election sewed up, refused to make the extra effort, according to Ames. But Gibbons was wrong. "Tucker took the 8th with enough votes to win the city."[37]

That hurt. With Tucker's victory, Gibbons and the other members of the Politicians group lost all serious access to the mayor's office for at least a dozen years, because Tucker would be reelected twice, in 1957 and again in 1961. Gibbons' miscalculation (if Ames is correct and that's what it was) would prove costly for his side in several ways.

In the police department, for example. As a result of city-state disputes during the Civil War, official control of St. Louis' police force was wielded not by the city itself but by Missouri's governor.[38] But the governor usually allowed himself to be guided in these matters by his political allies back in the city. Under the previous municipal administration, police policy had generally been set by a state senator named Edward J. "Jelly Roll" Hogan. Hogan was the leader of the remnant of an Irish-American gang that, at different times over the years, had mixed Democratic Party politics with various illicit endeavors. Throughout the first half of the century the Hogan gang had struggled for control of the city's North Side wards with another, very similar group, this one headed by a family called Egan. In 1953 the leader of the remnant of *that* gang was a certain Mike Kinney, who, like Jelly Roll Hogan, had a long-held seat in the state senate. With the victory of Ray Tucker and the Forces of Progress, Hogan, an ally of the Callanans, was suddenly on the outs vis à vis City Hall and the police department. Mike Kinney was now in.[39]

8. Varieties of Political Experience 87

"Police Shake-Up Makes Chapman Detective Chief," announced the *Post-Dispatch* within seventy-two hours of Tucker's victory. This purge ("Nine officers were demoted, including lieutenant colonels, majors, captains, and lieutenants") was led by James Chapman, the department's brand-new chief of detectives. The new chief, whom a photo accompanying the story shows to be a dapper, smiling, confident-looking man, came to the job with a history. "Chapman was reported to have had a dispute last year with Lawrence Callanan, boss of the Steamfitters Union and brother of former Sheriff Thomas F. Callanan," the *Post-Dispatch* article said. "Lawrence Callanan was said to have threatened to send Chapman 'to the sticks,' a quiet district with few opportunities for recognition."[40] The electoral triumph scored by the Forces of Progress had spared Chapman his trip to the sticks. And who in particular was responsible for Chapman's good luck? "Chapman was in with the group with Mike Kinney," recalled Melburn Stein, a once well-known St. Louis police officer of the 1950s. "Mike Kinney was the one that promoted him right on up. He rode the political ride right on up."[41]

As we'll see, relations weren't all that smooth to begin with between Gibbons and the police department. With Chapman in a position of power, they would grow worse.

But it wasn't always the Forces of Progress that came out on top in these contests. Tucker and his allies did succeed in rebuilding large chunks of downtown St. Louis (Busch Stadium replaced the old warehouse district, for example, and the desolate old waterfront became the site of Eero Saarinen's gleaming Gateway Arch.) But the reformers could go only so far. In 1950 and again in 1957 they strongly supported referendums on rewriting the city's charter, or constitution. Both measures were intended by their sponsors to simplify St. Louis' government by reducing the number of its elected officers. The '57 referendum, for instance, asked voters to cut nearly in half (from twenty-eight to fifteen) the number of city wards—and thus also the number of aldermen representing them on the Board of Aldermen. The change would have removed from public office a fairly large number of the mayor's enemies and significantly increased his own power.

Both proposals were defeated by the Politicians faction. And, especially in 1957, Local 688 led the way. Robert H. Salisbury writes that "the Teamsters were particularly active, using the charter campaign as a means for strengthening their program for local political participation on an issue in which their interests coincide with other major groups in the city population."[42] Two Gibbons aides acted as captains in this effort. Sidney Zagri, a brilliant but restless lawyer had been in the dress manufacturing business in Chicago when Gibbons persuaded him to come to St. Louis to direct the union's community stewards program. Hitherto a rather loose network, the stewards were turned by Zagri into something approaching a political machine. The other captain was Ernest "Cab" Calloway, Gibbons' ambassador to the black community. Calloway had not long before gotten himself elected president of the city's NAACP chapter. According to David Salmon, "possibly the NAACP was the deciding factor in [the referendum] and Cab played an important role."[43]

This was an impressive demonstration of political muscle. Observing it, many people would have agreed with the anonymous St. Louis politician who earlier told a *Globe-Democrat* reporter, "Give me Gibbons and Local 688, and you can have the rest of the Democratic organization—Jack Dwyer [the party's city chairman], Tony Sestric [the party committeeman for Ward 8], the whole lot. Gibbons is the man to watch."[44]

* * *

But we're getting ahead of ourselves here. Gibbons wasn't as politically powerful in the early '50s as he would be later in the decade. Nor was he, though a leader of the Politicians faction, nearly as well known as Morris Shenker and Larry Callanan. In fact, it had been only recently that he and his union had received much attention from the city's newspapers. The first extended piece about the local seems to have been Harry B. Wilson's "Between the Lines" column in the *Globe-Democrat* of October 23, 1951.

According to Wilson, Local 688 had the week before thrown up informational picket lines at the doors of three St. Louis breweries (Falstaff, Hyde Park, and Griesedieck Brothers), an action which, because truck drivers from other Teamster unions refused to cross those lines, effectively shut the breweries down. In noting the action Wilson's column showed how far Local 688 had come since its defeat by the J. H. Grady Co. three years earlier. As may be recalled, the union had lost the Grady strike because it couldn't prevent that firm, a baseball and softball manufacturer, from making and shipping balls. That setback had helped persuade Gibbons to take his people into the Teamsters; the brewery action was evidence that IBT affiliation had strengthened the local. According to Wilson's piece, the informational picket had occurred because Local 688 wanted to sign up the breweries' clerical workers. "The pickets went out for what one union leader called 'an advertising campaign,'" writes Wilson. "The union was advertising several things. One, of course, was the fact that the brewery office workers had never joined the union."

But there was more to the advertising than that, the columnist continued.

> By suddenly closing three breweries, Local 688 gave the office workers a demonstration of strength. It flexed its muscles in public, trying on a small scale for much of the same sort of psychological reaction nations hope to get when they put on huge parades of their military might. What the union wanted was to show the office work-

ers that they don't have to worry about company retaliation if they join the union. At the same time, Local 688 was pushing the breweries around to show them that they had better not try to push Local 688 around.... The strategy was uncommon, and so is Local 688. As unions go, it is a newcomer. This year saw its tenth anniversary. But in some respects, Local 688 is the most potent local union in this part of the United States.[45]

We might note here Wilson's suggestion that joining Local 688 wasn't necessarily the idea of the brewery workers themselves, that the decision whether ultimately to join was not so much theirs as their employers'. If Wilson's view was correct, the union had moved closer to adopting the traditional AFL-Teamster tactic of "organizing the bosses" rather than directly proselytizing workers, a method more characteristic of the CIO.

In March 1952, six months after the Wilson column in the *Globe-Democrat*, the *Post-Dispatch* published a Sunday feature article about Gibbons. This also appears to have been the first of its kind. The writer, Peter Wyden, begins his piece (headlined "Labor Boss") by reprising Gibbons' life to date: his coal-camp youth, adventures in the CIO, marriage to Ann, arrival in St. Louis, and his fruitful shepherding of the warehouse union there. At forty-one, Wyden writes, Gibbons was "6 feet 1½ inches tall, weighs 194 pounds, and what little hair is left above his towering forehead is turning gray. Though he never finished high school, his sensitive face, dark blue suits and his voice—well modulated unless aroused—give him the air of an easy-going college administrator."

A photo shows the Gibbons family at home in front of the fireplace: Ann smiling into the camera, five-year-old Larry at her knee, twelve-year-old Patrick and seven-year-old Elizabeth on the floor playing with some kittens—while an unsmiling Gibbons, sitting off to the right in a dark suit and tie, looks more like a visitor than a family member. Which in a way he was. "In an average week," writes Wyden, "the local may have 24 picket lines going in three separate strikes and Gibbons may pop up at any one of them at 4 a.m. to see whether anybody is in trouble.... Often he gets through much too late to travel to his sparsely furnished frame house at 466 Julian, Kirkwood, and sleeps a few hours in a downtown hotel. His wife never expects him for dinner except Sundays and his neighbors don't know him because he is never home."

As for Gibbons' union, Wyden writes, it "consists largely of workers in industries once thought impossible to organize," but now its ten thousand members make it the biggest in Missouri. "In the last decade many members have more than quadrupled their wages. They have also acquired a catalog of benefits, including virtually unlimited hospitalization and medical care, without charge, for members, their spouses and children; drugs and eye glasses at cost; free dental care except for bridgework and dentures which are supplied at cost; free home nursing service; employer-paid pensions; free employment service; and free legal advice."

Gibbons throughout the interview played down his own role in Local 688's affairs. "Gibbons says he has little personal power over such decisions [endorsing political candidates] or the use of the union's $800,000 assets. Right now, for instance, he is negotiating for a $5-a-week raise for himself and his staff (they are all paid as much as Gibbons and nobody has had a raise in five years)." According to the union boss, recommendations on political endorsements were handled by one union committee and those on pay raises by another. Wyden seems to have found the comment unduly modest. "Today Gibbons can pull strings in local politics and the national labor movement," he writes.[46]

The union had clearly come a great distance since 1937, when a few hundred warehouse workers had dug in their heels and challenged their employers. Its members, once ill-paid seasonal workers, were now as economically secure as many of their white-collar neighbors, maybe more so given the medical care they received from the Labor Health Institute. Along with its political clout in St. Louis' wards, the local had elected one of its own, Bob Pentland, to the state senate and even picked up some influence in Congress. ("United States Senator Thomas C. Hennings Jr. thought enough of the votes of Local 688 to start his campaign with a speech before some of its members," noted Wilson of the *Globe*.)[47] What's more, as Gibbons pointed out to the *Post*'s reporter, the local, once a rickety affair that had to carefully watch its nickels and dimes, was now rather prosperous.

Prosperous enough to attract envy. Indeed, as we're about to see, Gibbons had excellent reasons for looking as grave as he does in the photo accompanying Wyden's article. It's never smart to talk about how rich and successful you've become. Gibbons should have kept especially quiet concerning that $800,000.

By March 1952 envy was stalking him.

9

Mobsters Move In

"By the 1940s," writes an authority on crime in the twentieth-century United States, "the local power structure in many cities was a quadripartite alliance of organized crime, elements of organized labor, elements of the business community and the Democratic Party political machine, including district attorneys and top police brass."[1]

St. Louis was never a mob town like Chicago, Cleveland, or even Kansas City. But it did have mobs. As in most cities of the time, the St. Louis mobs' main business was illegal gambling. Although relatively harmless in itself, illegal gambling tended to spawn worse practices—the corruption of officials, loansharking, the easy use of violence to collect on bad debts—that spawned still others. One was labor racketeering.

Three ethnicities dominated organized crime in St. Louis in the 1940s and '50s: Sicilian-Americans, Lebanese-Americans (in St. Louis called "Syrians"), and people of more or less Irish-American descent. The Sicilian gang was sometimes said to be subservient to the old Al Capone organization in Chicago. The Syrians were rumored to be intertwined with the Democratic Party organizations that usually controlled St. Louis' riverfront wards. Because the Sicilian and Syrian mobs mainly exploited people in their own ethnic neighborhoods—people too fearful or too proud to complain about them— little information about those gangs was available to titillate the city's newspaper readers. But the Irish-American mob made up for that lack.

The boss of the Irish-American mob was Frank "Buster" Wortman. His base of operations was actually across the river in East St. Louis, Illinois. Wortman had risen to power in the late 1940s after snipers picked off, one after another, over a period of several years, the bosses of the mob of which he himself had previously been a mere member. These nemesis-like shootings made a deep impression on a whole generation of people on both sides of the river. For a time in the 1950s Wortman lived in an otherwise quite ordinary ranch-type house in Collinsville, Illinois—but one surrounded by a moat. Wortman's adventures, so unlike those of the quieter Sicilians and

Syrians, made him possibly the best-known person in the region after Stan Musial.

"Wortman was a gambling man, primarily," recalled a *Post-Dispatch* reporter who covered him in those years. "He dabbled in other fields, such as labor racketeering, trucking, juke boxes, pinball machines, racehorses, real estate developments, restaurants, nightclubs and loan companies. But income from those ventures was a trickle compared with the big money that comes from gambling with the wraps off."[2]

Still, trickles help. Some of the Wortman gang's racketeering involved St. Louis Teamsters. Mobsters took over the management of three Teamster truck-drivers' locals simply by marching in and announcing that, unless they were hired as "bodyguards," they would murder the locals' officers. They did the same thing at Joint Council 13, the coordinating body for area Teamster groups. Once ensconced in these organizations, the "bodyguards" worked out sweetheart contracts with employers, adapting the original union contracts so that both employers and mobsters made money—at the expense of the actual union members. Then, in either late 1951 or very early '52, evidently thinking that these conquests had come off quite smoothly, the mobsters looked around for another Teamster group to invade.

"One day," Harold Gibbons later recalled, "one of my guys was grabbed in a bar by one of those hoodlums and told that either we put some of their people on the payroll or he was going to kill me." Though not entirely innocent of violence themselves, Local 688's leaders apparently hadn't before this encounter run into out-and-out mobsters. "Well, we didn't know a goddamn thing about hoodlums," Gibbons said. "But Dick [Kavner] knew Jimmy [Hoffa]. So we went over to Detroit and talked to Hoffa."

We've already encountered Jimmy Hoffa, the rising young vice president of the IBT. He told his visitors that they had two choices, Gibbons recalled. One, they could do what the gangsters said and "just put somebody on the payroll. They won't bother you. No one's going to get killed. [But] at the end of six months you'll be taking orders from this guy you put on the payroll. And he'll be running the local." Or, two, "get yourself a pistol and the first son of a bitch who walks in the door you shoot him in the head."[3]

Hoffa seems never to have tried this himself. Detroit was a rougher town than St. Louis. Confronted by a whole bestiary of mobs, Hoffa learned early in his career to barter with them, even to use them for his own purposes, meanwhile keeping the Teamster local of which he was president free of their control. On at least one occasion he went so far as to deliver a sister IBT local of jukebox workers into the hands of people he knew to be Mob members.[4] But Hoffa was in fact wrong about there being only two ways to deal with gangster problems. For example, Sid Lens, Gibbons' old RWDSU comrade, managed to throw out the mobsters who had invaded his grocery clerks' local

9. Mobsters Move In

in Chicago. He did this by befriending a *Chicago Tribune* reporter who then wrote a series of articles that, casting a bright public light on the invaders, persuaded them to go away and leave his local alone.[5]

As we'll see, Gibbons eventually attempted an amalgam of the Hoffa and Lens methods. After talking to Hoffa, he and Kavner returned to St. Louis and acquired some guns. Joe Ames said, "We kept pistols around the union's Pine Street office that year. I remember somebody hid a sawed-off shotgun in a golf club bag."[6]

In January 1952, having received a new threat, this time over the phone, Gibbons went to the police department seeking permits that would allow him and staff members to carry those guns legally. The police put him off, he said. In March, after new phone threats, he went back to ask for police protection. He was told only that the cop on the beat would keep an eye on the union hall. Looking for something a bit more concrete, Gibbons appealed to one of the city's five police commissioners. Again nothing happened. Some years later a St. Louis police captain explained it all to a Senate investigating committee.

> Well, in January 1952 [the captain said], Mr. Gibbons made an application to the police department to carry a revolver. Now that application was in the form of a private watchman's license. Nobody in St. Louis is given a permit to carry a revolver other than law enforcement officers like myself or licensed beat watchmen or licensed watchmen for particular premises where they are employed. When Mr. Gibbons went to our personnel office to fill out this application he was told he would have to get his employer to fill it out, stating what his job was with the company and the necessity for carrying the revolver. Mr. Gibbons did not come back to process the application. So on our records it shows it as an application that was denied.[7]

In other words, the only pistol permit available to Gibbons was that for a watchman, but Gibbons couldn't fill out the application himself because the filling-out had to be done by his employer. And Gibbons had no employer. Besides, he never came back to "process" the application. That took care of the permit problem so far as the police department was concerned.

Writing about this episode, a historian of the Teamsters Union who has no particular liking for Gibbons notes that, despite his pleas for help, St. Louis' police "made no special assignments and posted no guards. By this time Gibbons had every reason to feel vulnerable. On March 14, 1952, the same month he reported getting threatening calls, an official of the Laborers Union was murdered as part of someone's effort to take over that local. A few months later, in August, a second official in the same local was killed. The police never arrested anyone for either killing."[8]

To be fair, St. Louis' cops had reason to dislike Gibbons. For one thing, his union was thought to be sometimes overly physical in strike situations. During the aforementioned Senate hearings, the testifying police captain was asked whether other Teamster locals in the city were as vexatious to his department as Gibbons'. "No," he said, "we find this type of violence, this type of organizing, picket-line disturbances, and whatnot, is common practically only to Local 688 or to unions that are dominated by Harold Gibbons."[9]

Realizing that they were on their own against the mobsters, Gibbons and his staff refused to disarm. "I did not want [the guns] to be a deep, dark secret, however," Gibbons said later. "I called in the editor of the *Post-Dispatch* and Fitzpatrick, the cartoonist, and we had lunch."[10]

Irving Dilliard was not the *Post*'s editor but rather the editor of its editorial page. (Joseph Pulitzer II, the paper's publisher and chief editor, may have been unavailable or simply not interested in the controversy.) Dilliard was a prominent defender of constitutional rights, especially the rights of free speech and a free press. Like Gibbons, he and Daniel Fitzpatrick were men strongly influenced by Progressive thinking (probably directly in the case of the cartoonist, a Wisconsin native). But whereas Gibbons' Progressivism stressed bringing the poor and powerless into self-help organizations, Fitzpatrick's and Dilliard's brand was more individualistic and favored the independent business person and the professional. Fitzpatrick's cartoons especially show a suspiciousness of trade unions and a clear antipathy toward what he saw as thoughtless, self-centered union leaders such as John L. Lewis of the coal miners. As might be expected, the two newspapermen were supporters of Ray Tucker and the Forces of Progress.

In his conversation with Dilliard and Fitzpatrick, Gibbons presumably described the threats to himself and Local 688, his difficulty in getting protection from the police, and his conclusion that in the absence of such protection the union had no choice but to defend itself with pistols. According to Gibbons, the police commissioner with whom he earlier conferred had said "he could not condone this thing [the guns]. I told him I did not expect him to, but I wanted him to be aware of what was taking place."[11] Dilliard and Fitzpatrick very likely said something similar: they couldn't condone the firearms either. And Gibbons probably repeated what he'd said to the commissioner, that he mainly wanted the police and press to be *aware* of the situation. He may also have asked the newsmen to publish an article about the gangster threat (as Sid Lens had persuaded the *Tribune* to do in Chicago), if only thereby to reduce the chances of gunplay in the city's streets. We can be fairly sure that, even if he did not request such an article, he hoped that Dilliard and Fitzpatrick, being news people to whom he was offering a news story, would produce one on their own.

But no such article appeared. Silence came from the *Post-Dispatch*, as it had earlier come from the police department. The message seemed plain. Neither institution would help protect Local 688 from the invading gangsters;

nor, should the union insist on defending itself, would either the police or the journalists affirm its right to do so.

Two years later, after a federal grand jury had indicted Gibbons and his friends for taking vigilante action during the mobster crisis, no one from either the newspaper or the police department came forward to suggest extenuating circumstances. And five years after that, when the episode was rehashed yet again before a Senate committee, both the newsmen and the cops denied being told about the weapons. The police commissioner sent the committee an affidavit saying, "I do not recall Mr. Harold Gibbons' ever contacting me or notifying me that his associates would be carrying guns to protect themselves." In an affidavit of his own, the *Post-Dispatch* editor Irving Dilliard said that "to the very best of my recollection, no reference to carrying guns was ever made by Mr. Gibbons for me to hear on any occasion."[12] However, it seems unlikely that Gibbons would have concocted stories that the prominent persons named in them could deny so easily. Moreover, as his lawyer reminded the committee, those persons did not actually deny being told by Gibbons about the guns. They said only that they couldn't *recall* him doing so.

The issue was of course moot by the time of the Senate hearings. But it was all too pressing in 1952, when a shooting war with the mob seemed inescapable. "Gibbons sent his wife and kids out of town," said Jake McCarthy, a public relations man then with the Catholic archdiocese. "I remember Ted Schafers of the *Globe-Democrat* telling me that Gibbons wouldn't live out the year."[13]

* * *

"That's when I first met Mr. Hoffa," said Yuki Kato of the 1952–53 mobster crisis. "He came to St. Louis. He sent some other guys, too."[14]

Hoffa told several different stories about his visit to the city. Some of these stories contradicted others, but their common theme was that he had saved Gibbons from the gangsters and that he did it by threatening them with gangster connections of his own. According to one set of interviewers, "Hoffa [said he] sent a henchman to guard Gibbons and flew down to negotiate with the head of the East St. Louis underworld. He hammered out one of his usual non-crusading agreements—'You leave us alone, and we'll leave you alone. If you get into trouble with the police, we'll help you out, and if we get in trouble you help us out, but stay away from our organization.' It took a week of bargaining, during which Hoffa, for safety, kept within fighting distance of his armed opponents. The Detroit underworld passed the word along that Hoffa was dependable, and Gibbons never had any more trouble."[15]

Like many of Hoffa's other underworld stories, this one can neither be disproved nor verified. But there's no dispute about the henchman he assigned to protect Gibbons. That was Barney Baker, a professional thug.

Baker's real name was Bernard Max Becker. He grew up on New York's waterfront, where as a young man in the 1930s, standing six-four but then weighing a mere 175 pounds, he became a prizefighter.[16] According to Joe Ames, young Baker sailed across the Atlantic to Germany to work as a sparring partner for Max Schmeling, a boxer who briefly took the world heavyweight title away from Joe Louis. Said Ames, who was told the story by Baker, the American got lucky one day and knocked the German down. "Schmeling maintained that he had slipped," Ames said. "Sitting on the canvas, he took off one of his shoes, peered into it, and started yelling at his trainers, '*Vere ist der resin? Vere ist der resin?*' Later Barney got knocked down too. He pulled off his shoe and, mimicking Schmeling, yelled, '*Vere ist der resin?*' He was a funny man."[17]

And a scary one as well, when paid to be. Back in New York, having blossomed into his normal weight of more than three hundred pounds, Baker became a dealer in physical intimidation. His specialty was "belly-bumping," which is pushing people around without actually laying hands on them and making oneself open to an assault charge. "When I put my belly against another guy's belly, that guy is going to move," he once told Ted Schafers of the *Globe-Democrat*.[18] Baker usually worked for trade unions, though not always. "He spent most of his life on the edge of the Mob," Ames said.[19]

By early 1952 Baker, who was white, had somehow become the leader of a mostly African American Teamsters warehouse local in Washington, D.C. He was also co-chairman of a labor committee supporting the nomination of Averell Harriman, a wealthy New Deal figure, for president of the United States. Gibbons, who had endorsed Harriman (probably because the latter possessed what were then considered advanced views on civil rights), sent Ames and Ernest Calloway to work for him in the District of Columbia's presidential primary. (Harriman won the primary but was later defeated by Adlai Stevenson for the Democratic nomination.) It was during this campaign, Ames said, that he came to know and like Barney Baker. Gibbons himself met Baker that year at a Washington banquet put on by the liberal Americans for Democratic Action.

Not long after this, Baker was deposed from his union post amid accusations of financial impropriety. In November 1952 Hoffa sent him to St. Louis as a bodyguard for Gibbons. After the first mobster threats, Ann Gibbons had taken the three children and fled to her parents in Louisville; but they soon returned, and in July the family moved to a new home in Kirkwood. The house, at 308 Altus Place, had two stories, the first gray stone, the second frame, and a few smallish windows, with a stoop for a front porch. It looked like a fortress.[20] Barney Baker, who joined the family as an armed guest, soon made himself popular there. "He was a sweetheart," said Elizabeth Vasquez, who was seven at the time. "I can remember him sitting in our kitchen and me sitting on his lap," said Larry Gibbons, then five. Their mother was under the impression that Baker was mentally retarded. Vasquez said, "Even as a child I knew he wasn't very bright." Ann once discovered Larry playing with a .45-caliber pistol that Baker had left lying around the house. Despite this, Vasquez said, "Mother liked him."[21]

Joe Ames described Baker as "childlike." Even so, he added, "Barney Baker was the man I'd want with me if I was ever in a fracas. Not just because he was big. He was scary. He looked tough—and he *was* tough."[22]

While Baker guarded the Gibbons family, the militants of Local 688 prepared to repel the mobsters. Levi Sanford, twenty-three that year, was working as a clerk-typist at the Brown Shoe Co. warehouse on the corner of Seventeenth and Washington. An African American born in Mississippi and raised on St. Louis' North Side, Sanford had, after a year at a black college, been forced to drop out and go to work to support his family. Gibbons, Sanford said, was much admired by Brown Shoe workers (especially, for some reason, he said, by those of German or Bohemian descent, of which Brown Shoe then had many). "They believed in Gibbons," said Sanford. "They said, 'Well hell, we're not going to let anything happen to this guy, because he's our leader. He's a stand-up guy and we're with him a hundred percent.'"

About the mobsters, Sanford said, "They wanted to get rid of Gibbons. They wanted him dead bad."

Several times during the winter and spring of 1953, said Sanford, union staffers came by Brown Shoe and Local 688's other shops to announce, "We've got problems tonight. Come down to the hall. Everybody's going to have to have a gun."[23] As many as seventy men would show up at the Pine Street office on those evenings carrying hunting rifles and shotguns. Fortunately, each of these calls turned out to be a false alarm. It's possible, Sanford suggests, that word that union members were arming themselves spread around the city and was itself sufficient to forestall an attack from the Wortman gang.

In February 1953 the mobsters seized control of a fourth Teamsters local by forcing the president to resign and electing one of their own in his place. But now they had pushed their luck too far. Dave Beck, the IBT's president, invalidated the election results and placed the local in receivership, probably at the behest of Jimmy Hoffa—who in turn was probably responding to a new call for help from Gibbons. On Thursday, March 5, a Beck emissary named Thomas Flynn turned up in town to announce that "an investigation aimed at checking a threatened gang invasion of several teamsters' locals has been undertaken by the AFL International Brotherhood of Teamsters," although, when reporters tried to question him further, Flynn "refused to discuss details or to outline his program of action."[24]

The next day Gibbons led a raid on the offices of Teamsters Joint Council 13 at 4141 Forest Park. The raid did *not* make it into the newspapers. Neither

Flynn nor Barney Baker nor Jimmy Hoffa, whom the papers reported being in town that day, participated.

A man who *was* present that morning, the one-legged war veteran Joe Ames, remembered that the raiding party set out from the union hall in a convoy several cars long. Each car was equipped with some sort of "phone" that could receive calls but not transmit them. Gibbons had told the raiders to bring guns, Ames said, "but my recollection is that there were no more than three or four pistols, including one that was so rusty that it could not possibly be fired."

The raiders parked in various spots around the block in which the council building was located. Gibbons and George Seiler, a founding member of the warehouse local, proceeded to go inside. The plan, Ames said, was for those two to confront the council officers and "lay the papers on them"—that is, announce that the joint council was in trusteeship and that the now-ex-officers must get out. If either they or their "bodyguards" refused to cooperate, Seiler was to go immediately to a pay phone and tell the men waiting in the cars outside to come charging in. Ames remembered beginning to worry about the soundness of the plan when, just before they entered the council building, Gibbons turned to Seiler and said, "George, I hope you've brought some dimes."[25] Ames recalled, "I was in a car driven by Phil Reichardt [another founder of the local] and he and I had a dispute when we found that we could not receive anything on the 'phone' because we were in an area where the building blocked transmission; he refused to move because Gibbons had told us to stay in the assigned location. We finally settled it by my taking one of the 'phones' and going down to the nearest corner, where I could use it to signal him to come if we got the message. We didn't get one."[26]

Fortunately for all involved, the raiders met no resistance. Buster Wortman was not on the premises, Ames said. As far as that went, Ames was personally unconvinced that Wortman had been involved in hijacking the Teamster groups in the first place. The hijackers, he said, might have been an "offshoot" of the Wortman mob, led by a certain William "Bozo" Remphry. (The *Post-Dispatch*, in a story about the IBT's placing the joint council in trusteeship, mentioned Remphry's name along with those of Buster Wortman and a certain Rolla "Blackie" Dean. So Ames may have been correct.)[27] It's hard enough to take a man named Bozo seriously. But Bozo Remphry wasn't in the council office that day either. No one of any particular notoriety was there. Those who were present, said Ames, lay down their pencils or playing cards, or whatever they happened to have in their hands at the time, and filed meekly out of the council building, leaving it in the possession of Gibbons and his raiders.

And with that bit of opéra bouffe, the mobster crisis suddenly came to a close.

10

Gibbons' Revenge

Harold Gibbons, in a kind of summing up near the end of his career, remarked to an interviewer, "I just don't have anything called fear as far as my personal safety [is concerned]."[1]

It might have been true. But probably wasn't.

Most people, especially men, don't care to recall moments when they've been frightened. Instead they perform a kind of unconscious mental alchemy, changing what originally was fear into annoyance, anger, or even rage. Gibbons' actions following the mobster crisis of 1952–53 suggest that such an alchemy occurred in him. First came the fright, then the rage.

On Thursday, March 18, 1953, twelve days after he and his friends raided the headquarters of Joint Council 13 (see Chapter 9) and won it back from the Wortman gang, Gibbons brought together his union's Stewards' Council for a big meeting at the Kiel Opera House. Afterwards he made sure the meeting's gist was provided to the local press.

Thus, according to the next day's *Post-Dispatch*,

> drastic measures to rid the AFL Teamsters Union of gangsters who have infiltrated several St. Louis locals were voted last night by about 400 shop stewards of Local 688, AFL Warehouse and Distribution Workers, a Teamster affiliate.... [A union spokesman] explained that gangsters, using threats of force to silence union officers, have interposed themselves in negotiations between teamsters' locals and employers several times in the past two years. After intimidating the unions' representatives, they solicited fees from employers to obtain union agreement to contracts scaling down original demands.... The gangsters made no effort to obtain membership cards in the union, the *Post-Dispatch* was told, but merely acted as unofficial agents. Some were carried on payrolls, presumably as "bodyguards."[2]

The Wortman mob was running a "sweetheart contract" scam, one of the oldest of labor rackets. After seizing control of the three Teamster truck-drivers' locals, the gangsters worked out new terms with the employers involved. Under these new terms, the employers got cut-rate labor in return

99

for payoffs to the mob. Mobsters and employers became "sweethearts." The victims of the scam were the three locals' members.

With Gibbons, as with most trade unionists, it was an article of faith that racketeers couldn't take over a union without the cooperation, often the encouragement, of the employer. If an employer were to refuse to rewrite the contract in a way benefiting him and the racketeer, the racketeering would turn out to be profitless. If all employers refused their cooperation, most labor racketeering would simply disappear. But employers rarely did refuse, in Gibbons' experience. The temptation was too great. To fight racketeering, it was therefore necessary to take on the employers as well as the mobsters. It seemed clear to Gibbons that some employers of St. Louis Teamsters had been in cahoots with the Wortman gang. He may have suspected that employers were even involved in the plan to kill him.

The big "drastic measure" that Gibbons proposed, at the Stewards' Council meeting, was that the warehousemen of Local 688 help warehouse owners resist the kind of temptations to which some trucking company owners had succumbed. Toward that end, Local 688 should announce that if any warehouse company under contract to the local were to begin dealing with a person "other than an accredited union officer," the local would immediately strike *all* St. Louis warehouses. A single sweetheart deal would therefore automatically result in a warehouse general strike. The Stewards' Council approved Gibbons' proposal.

Gibbons, who seems to have been ferociously angry once it became clear that he and his family were safe, was preparing for industrial war.

He had the support of the international. At the end of March the IBT, which had already placed Joint Council 13 and the three truck drivers' locals in trusteeship, added a taxicab drivers' group, Local 405. (Local 405 was made up of white drivers; black drivers remained for the time being in Local 688.) Thomas Flynn, a union vice president who had come to town as the representative of IBT President Dave Beck, told reporters that the move was the "latest step in reorganization of the Teamsters' union here, which includes investigation of a threatened gang invasion of several locals."[3]

In fact, the real, hands-on "reorganization"—of Local 405 anyway—was undertaken not by Flynn but by the man whom the IBT would soon appoint the taxi local's trustee, the huge belly-bumper, Barney Baker.

In early April, Baker was pulled over by a police patrol for running a stop sign and found to be carrying a loaded .38 Smith & Wesson revolver in his overcoat pocket. The traffic stop wasn't fortuitous—the cops seem to have been lying in wait for him. The arresting officer, no rookie, was a lieutenant in the department's Intelligence and Hoodlum Squad. As this man later told a Senate committee, "[Baker's name] came to my attention in 1953, when he came in as a Teamster boss for Local 405. He was supposed to be the strong-arm man, and the rumor had come back to us that he was going around beating cab drivers and forcing them into the union."[4]

Whatever the truth of the rumor, the police took Baker for a mobster himself (a not so unreasonable assumption, of course). They intended to see him prosecuted on the weapons charge. But, as sometimes happens, what looked like a simple criminal case had a political side to it. Ray Tucker, of the Forces of Progress faction of the Democratic Party, had two days before Baker's arrest crushed his Republican opponent in the general mayoral election, thereby gaining the mayor's office and with it the upper hand in the city's police department (see Chapter 8). As noted, the dapper James Chapman, himself an adherent of the Forces of Progress faction, was appointed by Tucker the department's new chief of detectives. Larry Callanan, of the Politicians faction, had the year before threatened to have Chapman banished "to the sticks." Now the tables turned. Elections do have consequences. Chapman, formerly a police captain but now a lieutenant colonel, said, "he believed the concealed weapons case against Baker was one of the strongest he had ever known."[5] It wasn't strong enough for the city's prosecutor, though. That man, a friend of Gibbons and Morris Shenker of the opposing Politicians faction, was highly critical of the traffic stop. Through a spokesman he said, "Baker's arrest on a traffic charge was merely a pretext for watching him." In fact, the prosecutor's office announced that the cops' search of Baker and his car had been illegal. Charges against the belly-bumper were dropped.[6]

The Wortman gang meanwhile remained very quiet. Levi Sanford suggested that Pete Saffo, Gibbons' diplomat extraordinaire, had worked out some sort of private understanding among the three main local mobs, the Sicilians, the "Syrians," and Wortman's bunch. "Pete had a lot of influence in St. Louis," Sanford recalled with a deep laugh. "A *lot* of influence. Pete took care of the heavies."[7]

On the other hand Tom Guilfoil, the lawyer and Democratic Party pro, said he doubted that Gibbon's had been in serious danger from Wortman's gang, whatever Gibbons himself thought. "He had lots of protection," Guilfoil said of Gibbons, hinting that this protection was furnished by the Sicilians and Syrians. "Wortman's activities were always strange and difficult to understand. The principal names on *this* side of the river were not part of [Wortman's] activities."[8]

On April 20, Dave Beck's man Flynn announced the trusteeship of two more Teamster organizations, one of them Local 682, whose members were drivers of ready-mix cement trucks. Trusteeship is similar to receivership in bankruptcy. Appointed by the international's president, a trustee wields virtual dictatorial power over the local union or joint council placed in his care. Local 682's trusteeship seems to have been the result not of infiltration by gangsters but because of suspected malfeasance on the part of the local's own president. In mid–May that official was one of nine area labor leaders indicted by a federal grand jury on charges of extorting money from contractors. (Larry Callanan of the Steamfitters was another of the indictees. After vanishing for several days Callanan, escorted by his lawyer Morris Shenker, walked into a police station and surrendered.)[9]

The cement-truck drivers happened at the time to be deadlocked in negotiations with their employers—thirty-five sand, gravel, and cement dealers—over a new contract concerning wages and benefits. The drivers were then earning from $1.70 to $2.12 an hour, most of them in the lower range. They wanted an additional 25 cents an hour and other benefits. The dealers were standing fast at 7½ cents.[10]

These talks would have interested no one but the dealers and drivers had not St. Louis been at the start of what promised to be a busy building season. Money fairly sloshed around the city that year, partly because of federal spending fertilized by the Korean War. Scheduled summer projects included a new administration building at Lambert Field (the municipal airport), the expressway (now U.S. 40/Interstate 64) through Mill Creek Valley, schools, hospitals, suburban subdivisions, and public housing complexes. (A photo on page 3A of the April 10 *Post-Dispatch* shows city officials gazing up at the steel skeleton of the new Wendell Oliver Pruitt Homes on Carr Street, "a 1736 unit project for Negro tenants," many of them refugees from Mill Creek. Pruitt Homes would eventually become part of the larger—and soon-to-be notorious—Pruitt-Igoe housing complex.) An estimated $100 million was to be spent on these endeavors—a bit less than $1 billion in today's money.

All would require cement.

But the cement drivers, caught in the coils of trusteeship, were now without the services of their elected leaders. Gibbons was appointed to head a committee acting for the drivers.[11] Thus it was that the boss of Local 688, so fired up by the Wortman gang's threats that he was ready to take his warehousemen into a general strike against warehouse owners, found himself representing an altogether different Teamster group, the cement-truck drivers, in contract talks with the dealers of ready-mix cement. The prospects for an easy agreement clearly weren't promising. And, should those talks fail, a strike was set to start on Tuesday, May 19.

They did fail. "Drivers' Strike Forcing Rapid Halt in Building in City, County," exclaimed the *Post-Dispatch*'s front-page headline for Wednesday, May 20. "All Major Construction Expected to Stop by Friday," said one subhead. "Virtually All Housing Jobs Reported Shut Down," said another. And it wasn't only the city's 550 cement-truck drivers who had refused to report for work that morning. Because the allied building trades chose to respect the drivers' pickets, some 20,000 other construction workers—carpenters, electricians, iron workers, sheet-metal workers, bricklayers, laborers—were laying down their tools as well.

10. Gibbons' Revenge

The strike would last eighty-six days.

To outward appearances it was an undramatic event, surprisingly so considering its size, length, and impact on the city. Newspapers for the spring and summer of 1953 report none of the picket-line skirmishing so common in such walkouts. As far as can be told, not a single striker spent as much as an hour in jail. In an important sense the strikers were mere onlookers. The real struggle went on offstage, between Gibbons and Ray Tucker.

This wasn't clear at first, because Flynn continued to be presented to the press as the strikers' spokesman. In fact, Flynn was soon badly hurt in an auto accident and was out of action for months.[12]

Insofar as he had ever really been the Teamsters' top man in the ready-mix strike (which is doubtful), he now left that role to Gibbons.

Tucker had also kept his head down at the beginning. He must have found a construction workers' strike especially trying. He had taken office just weeks before, his head full of plans for municipal improvement. In mid–June he demonstrated his political and financial muscle by adding to Civic Progress, his semiofficial advisory council, ten new members, including three big bankers and the CEOs of Anheuser-Busch, Southwestern Bell, Monsanto Chemical, the May Co. department stores (owner of downtown's Famous Barr store), and International Shoe.[13] Thus reinforced, Tucker at last grew impatient with the pace of strike negotiations. On the last day of June he issued what was basically an order that the two parties come down to City Hall and settle their differences. He was, the mayor said, especially unhappy about the interruption of work on the new crosstown expressway and the airport administration building. "In its earlier stages I felt that a solution would be easier if the city did not interfere," Tucker said. "Now, however, the situation has become critical; the public good must take precedence over any special interest."[14]

"Mayor Tucker is dead right," said the *Post-Dispatch* in an editorial. "The construction industry is virtually at a standstill at a time when building should be close to its peak.... The parties need to be brought together and that is Mayor Tucker's purpose."[15] The Forces of Progress had spoken.

"Gibbons and Tucker never got along very well," Joe Ames said.[16]

Gibbons probably considered the mayor a hypocrite. Throughout the cement strike Tucker positioned himself as a neutral referee looking down on both the drivers and cement dealers, whom he termed "special interests." But Gibbons had a different view. Aware that the dealers' chief negotiator, a lawyer named Michael Aubuchon, had also been the manager of Tucker's campaign in that spring's primary and general mayoral elections, Gibbons no doubt suspected the mayor of secret sympathy for Aubuchon's ready-mix clients.

As might have been forecast, the Tucker-sponsored driver-dealer talks held at City Hall were no more productive than the earlier ones had been. So the strike dragged on.

By late July St. Louis was enduring record heat, which further frayed people's nerves.[17] Leaders of the other construction unions were beginning to grumble about the ready-mix drivers. Word began to go around town that Gibbons, and thus the strike, had spun out of control. St. Louis' public prosecutor, the same Politicians-faction sympathizer who had earlier shielded Barney Baker from the gun-toting charge, now empaneled a circuit court grand jury whose ostensible task was to probe the strike's causes but was in fact probably intended to nudge it toward a settlement. More ominously, in U.S. district court another grand jury began weighing possible indictments of labor racketeers in the St. Louis region. An editorial in the *Post-Dispatch*, appearing under the headline "Work for Grand Jury," praised the seating of the circuit court panel, while, alongside the editorial, a Daniel Fitzpatrick cartoon showed, skulking in a weed patch, two men labeled "St. Louis Labor Racketeers." One skulker is saying to the other, "Looks like they're all after us now."[18] St. Louisans might be forgiven if, seeing that particular newspaper page, they confused the work of the circuit court grand jury and that of the federal court.

Meanwhile, a Mrs. Mava Miller, the wife of a sheet-metal worker who, like many others in the construction trades, was spending his days at home because of the strike, organized a group of distraught spouses to call for an end to the walkout. She herself believed in trade unions and even occasional strikes, she said, but the cement drivers were being selfish. Mrs. Miller and her group threatened to picket the Teamster pickets at the cement, sand, and gravel sites.[19]

Tucker, seeking deliverance from this mess, had called on both sides in the strike to submit their dispute to binding arbitration. One evening he took thirteen minutes on KSD-TV, then the city's sole TV station, to present to the public his argument for arbitration.[20] Endorsed by both the *Post-Dispatch* and the *Globe-Democrat* as well as by the circuit court's grand jury, the idea was wildly popular. The cement dealers agreed to it. In an ad they ran in both papers they all but begged their opponent to do the same

HAROLD J. GIBBONS
ARBITRATE ...
The community demands it!
Mayor Tucker recommends it!
The grand jury recommends it! ...
Now it's up to you!
What is your answer, Mr. Gibbons?[21]

Gibbons toyed publicly with the arbitration idea for some time, first hinting that he might be open to it, then slowly backing away. For example, he borrowed a tactic that Walter Reuther of the UAW had famously tried against the big auto companies: Gibbons announced that the cement drivers would go along with binding arbitration, but only if the dealers would open their financial records to the arbitrator, thereby substantiating or failing to substantiate their argument that they couldn't afford the raises the union wanted. "Arbitration carries with it a responsibility on both parties to make available all facts necessary to arrive at a just and equitable decision by the arbitrators," Gibbons said. "To arbitrate without all the facts is to engage in a pointless and unfair procedure."[22] As the auto makers had refused Reuther's demand, the dealers' Michael Aubuchon refused Gibbons', stating that under a free-enterprise system companies had the right to keep their finances secret.[23] Gibbons, who had no doubt counted on that response, then withdrew his offer, the maneuver having allowed him to escape arbitration once again and, at the same time, perhaps gain credit with the public for appearing more reasonable than the dealers.

Finally, on Friday, August 7, with the strike eighty-one days old and the construction season at least half over, Gibbons called the cement drivers out to the Joint Council 13 hall on Forest Park Parkway to vote on the arbitration question. Of this event the Teamsters made a little show. They invited reporters from both newspapers, the foreman of the circuit court's grand jury, and Mrs. Miller, the leader of the unhappy construction workers' wives, to come sit in the hall's bleachers and witness the voting. Once the drivers had marked their ballots, they filed past the bleachers, one by one, dropping them in a box at the feet of Mrs. Miller and the grand jury foreman. Dick Kavner announced the results: 242 drivers had voted against arbitration, while only 34 voted for it.

"This rules out forever any possibility of arbitration," declared Kavner. "It is now up to the employers to assume their responsibility to the community and begin negotiating a settlement."[24]

A large collective groan can be imagined escaping City Hall. Cow-like, the strike lumbered on.

A *Post-Dispatch* editorial of Monday, August 10, suggested that the paper had just about run out of patience with one of the parties in the dispute and might soon say so openly: "Unless the strike ends now, St. Louis will begin to believe what it does not like to believe—that *somebody* does not want it to end" [emphasis in the original].[25] Few readers can have thought the paper meant Aubuchon and the dealers.

But later that same day, the walkout's eighty-fourth, a possible savior arrived in town. This was Jimmy Hoffa.

Hoffa was then largely unknown outside his own city, Detroit. He had a dozen years earlier helped drive the Trotskyists, including his former teacher Farrell Dobbs, out of trade unionism. After that, using tactics he had learned from Dobbs, he built strong IBT networks, first in Detroit, then in Michigan, then throughout the states of the Midwest, from the Dakotas to Ohio. At the

IBT convention of 1952 Hoffa had made a bargain with Dave Beck: he would support Beck for the presidency of the international if, in return, Beck gave him a free hand in his own part of the country. Among those who had been unlucky enough to get in his way, Hoffa was considered brutal and unforgiving. But in St. Louis in August '53 he was all smiles.

On Tuesday the 11th the two sides came together in the mayor's office. Michael Auchubon again represented the cement dealers. Hoffa and Beck's man Tom Flynn, finally recovered from his road accident, sat in for the drivers. Gibbons was absent, which in itself must have lightened the atmosphere. Hoffa did the rest. "We got them laughing," he told reporters afterward, "and when you get them laughing things smooth out."[26]

Still amiable, the two negotiating teams adjourned to more comfortable private rooms upstairs at the Missouri Athletic Club on Washington Avenue. There they spent the next nine hours hammering out the terms of a new contract, emerging at 2 a.m. Wednesday, August 12, to announce that the strike was finally over.

After breakfast and a shave, the former antagonists trooped down to City Hall to have their picture taken with Mayor Tucker. According to the *Globe-Democrat*, Gibbons, who had been waiting at a hotel for word to join the caravan to City Hall, was deliberately left cooling his heels by Hoffa and thus missed an opportunity to appear in the celebratory photo. Both the *Globe* and the *Post-Dispatch* credited the IBT, and Hoffa and Flynn in particular, with ending the crisis. Both papers blamed Gibbons for its prolongation, though without naming him specifically. As the *Globe-Democrat* said, St. Louis' Teamsters had been so unreasonable that even their own international came to perceive it. "What other conclusion is to be drawn when a protracted, seemingly insoluble strike is settled almost immediately by the simple expedient of national officers of the union coming in to by-pass the local officers and negotiators?"[27]

To Hoffa, in other words, went the credit for the city's sudden sense of relief.

Less remarked upon was the new contract itself. It gave the cement drivers an employer-financed medical and life insurance plan, paid sick leave, more vacation days, a mechanism for filing grievances, and what was essentially a rental fee for those union members who drove their own ready-mix trucks. As for wages, all drivers were to receive an immediate 15-cent-an-hour wage increase, retroactive to May 1, plus another 7 cents an hour to follow on May 1, 1954, for a total of 22 cents. The drivers had sought an extra quarter an hour (the dealers countering with 7½ cents). They fell 3 cents an hour short of their target.

Hoffa, speaking later in the day to strikers gathered in the joint council hall, told them, "In my opinion, this settlement represents total victory."[28] He

10. Gibbons' Revenge

was right: the settlement won by St. Louis' cement-truck drivers in the summer of 1953 was about as total as labor victories ever get.

But Hoffa, coming away from that late-night session at the Missouri Athletic Club, must have known that the new contract wasn't really his doing. He had only given the cement dealers someone to whom they could surrender without losing face. It was Gibbons who, in his fury, drove them to the point of surrender.

Hoffa had been shocked, he told Gibbons, by the cement dealers' refusal to allow the St. Louisan to add his own signature to the others' on the document. "There are some men in Detroit who dislike me," he said, "but those fellows back there actually hate you."[29]

Which was only fair, because Gibbons appears to have been extremely angry at them.

* * *

Long and bitter though it was, the cement drivers' strike was surprisingly peaceful in physical terms. But a brief taxicab drivers' walkout, occurring just months after the cement settlement, did get explosive.

Gibbons often said he dreaded taxi strikes because they were so difficult to control. That's because strikers can achieve little by picketing the taxi company's office; instead they must somehow interfere with the company's actual operations, which are performed out in the city streets, by scores of drivers in scores of moving automobiles. Striking cabbies pursue strikebreaking cabbies in cabs of their own, and the result is chaos: scattered confrontations resembling old-fashioned cavalry skirmishes—except that in this case the horses are made of glass and steel. Naturally people get hurt.

On the first day of December 1953, 116 employees of St. Louis' Yellow Cab Co., all owner-operators of the cabs they drove, went on strike in an attempt to force the company to recognize Local 405, a Teamster organization, as their bargaining agent. (Yellow Cabs' non-owner drivers were already union members.) Although Barney Baker had earlier been appointed Local 405's trustee, he was now outranked by Gibbons, who in July had become the trustee for the entire joint council. The belly-bumper was again just a soldier. Gibbons acted as general. Dick Kavner, Gibbons' "hard drive," served as commander in the field.

Questions about the '53 walkout (and another taxi strike, to be described later) gave Gibbons a good deal of trouble when he appeared before the McClellan Committee in 1958. To avoid possible perjury charges, he claimed to have "no recollection" of encouraging specific acts of violence against strikebreakers. He admitted that such acts had occurred in other instances but argued that union members were only defending themselves from thugs hired by cab company owners. Speaking generally, he said he opposed the use of violent tactics in strikes because they were usually "counterproductive," dissipating public sympathy for the strikers themselves.

There was certainly plenty of violence in the '53 strike. According to newspaper reports, a nonstriking Yellow Cab driver was treated for a head injury after three men in another car forced his cab to the curb and one of them then pulled him from his vehicle and punched him in the face. Several other Yellow Cab drivers filed complaints alleging similar assaults. Police arrested seven Teamsters in these incidents, one of whom was Kavner.[30]

But the most spectacular incident in the strike came to light only five years after the strike ended. In 1958 a former Gibbons loyalist told the McClellan Committee that he had, at Gibbons' and Kavner's behests, stolen a Yellow Cab and driven it off the embankment into the Mississippi River. According to this person, whose name was Oldron A. Mitchell, the plotters had arranged for a woman sympathizer to telephone the dispatcher and request a cab to fetch her from the Missouri Athletic Club. When the cab arrived and the woman was settled in its back seat, she pretended to suddenly recall that she had inadvertently left some item behind in the club. She asked the cabbie to go into the club and get it for her. Then, once the driver had left his machine, Mitchell came out of the shadows where he had been waiting, jumped behind the wheel, and drove away with both the cab and the "passenger."

"The young lady that was in the cab I let out in front of the bus terminal," Mitchell informed the McClellan Committee.

What happened after that? he was asked.

"As soon as she got out and I saw her safely across the street, I took the cab and run it in the river."

How did you do that? a senator asked.

"I went down over Broadway to Delmar, back from Delmar to Lucas, downhill at Lucas Avenue and built up momentum as much as I could in the car, and jumped out of the car at the last street before you hit the levee. The car went in the river."[31]

The cab remained there undiscovered and unsuspected until Mitchell, by then a member of a cabbies' group *opposed* to Gibbons, told his story to the McClellan panel. On hearing his tale, the authorities sent divers down to search the river's bottom. They found the hijacked Yellow Cab, all right—and also a station wagon with a male corpse sitting behind its steering wheel. The dead man, police eventually decided, was a suicide who had no connection to the taxi strike.

To return to 1953: on Saturday, December 5, a squad of policemen marched into the main ballroom of the Hotel Jefferson, at the corner of Twelfth and Locust, which that evening happened to be the scene of the Jefferson-Jackson Day Dinner, the local Democratic Party's annual fundraising event. Several hundred party bigwigs watched as the cops arrested

10. Gibbons' Revenge

Gibbons and took him away to jail. U.S. Senator Paul Douglas, an Illinois Democrat and the dinner's featured speaker, stood shaking his head in dismay, according to Tom Guilfoil, who was also in attendance that evening. Some, at least, of the participating cops no doubt enjoyed the assignment, said Guilfoil. "There was one faction of the police force, the same people who were for Tucker, who were anti–Gibbons," he recalled.[32]

Taken to police headquarters, the Teamster boss was charged with "suspicion of assault and malicious destruction of property" during the cab strike. Chief of Detectives James Chapman, Mayor Tucker's favorite policeman, announced the arrest to the press. Then early Sunday morning Morris Shenker posted a $500 bond, restoring Gibbons to freedom.[33]

Although Gibbons was certainly guilty of at least conspiring to commit (if not actually committing) the crimes alleged against him, the charges were soon dropped for lack of evidence. On the other hand, something that is not evidence, though it can carry near-evidentiary weight—a person's notoriety—was born that year. Earlier we suggested that Gibbons wasn't well-known among St. Louis' public before 1953. But the two strikes, the cement drivers' and the cabbies', seemed to take care of that.

Thirty years later, not long after Gibbons' death, a writer went around town asking people what they recalled about him. Memories were fuzzy, dates and details treacherous. But one mental picture appeared indelible: the cab in the river. Some St. Louisans could still see that.

11

Gibbons a Racketeer?

"There was great antipathy toward Harold among business people in St. Louis," said the lawyer Tom Guilfoil. To them, "he was virtually a Communist. He was worse than a Communist: he was a *pure* communist—he was a Trotskyite."[1]

Few St. Louis businessmen would have known a Trotskyist from a Rosicrucian, but many resented Harold Gibbons because in winning sharp wage and benefit increases for warehousemen, cement truck drivers, and other Teamsters, he interfered with their operations and ate into their profits.

In 1953 several business groups banded together to hire a private detective named Fred Bender to gather evidence of crimes suspected to have been committed by the union boss. Bender, when interviewed some years later, declined to identify these groups but he succinctly spelled out why they wanted to rid the city of Gibbons. "Gibbons looked like he'd take over the whole community," the detective said. "Gibbons was a brilliant planner on any kind of strike work. He won one strike after another, no one would work in any plant he was striking. There was a lot of smoke in those grand jury investigations, but nothing ever stuck."[2]

Gibbons became the target of a *series* of grand juries, the majority of them, Bender was saying, encouraged—perhaps instigated is not too strong a word—by business people. The first and most extensive of these investigations was federal. Empaneled in late July 1953, during the cement drivers' strike, this panel went nowhere at first because the local U.S. attorney had little enthusiasm for the project. Then, in December, after the U.S. Justice Department was accused of dragging its feet on the case, Attorney General Herbert Brownell sent one of the department's own to St. Louis to take over. This was Assistant Attorney General Max Goldschein, a career federal prosecutor who earlier had been attached to Senator Estes Kefauver's committee in its crusade against gamblers (see Chapter 8).

Goldschein was known as a courtroom terrier. The unenthusiastic local U.S. attorney tried to refuse his help. "Washington offered to send Goldschein when needed," he said, "but I didn't think there was enough evidence of labor racketeering to place a man of Goldschein's caliber in charge of a jury."[3] But the local man was overruled and Goldschein came to town.

Brownell and Goldschein, incidentally, were members of President Dwight Eisenhower's administration, which, inaugurated just eleven months before, had brought the Republican Party to power in Washington for the first time in twenty years. Gibbons had not previously worked within a GOP context. Throughout his earlier career as a labor leader, Democrats had dominated the federal government and also Missouri's state and big-city governments. Now that situation had changed. However, as we'll see, Gibbons would find Republican politics no whit less complicated than the Democrats'.

In any case, Goldschein not only came to St. Louis but by February 1954 he had Gibbons back in a jail cell, this time for refusing to surrender to the federal grand jury subpoenaed financial records of Local 688 and the Labor Health Institute.

"It was terrible," Gibbons recalled years afterward. He was put in a cell with three other men, two of whom took turns buggering the third. "It was the worst experience I ever had in my life."[4]

Gibbons saw the subpoena, which demanded *all* union and LHI records between 1949 and 1954, as a fishing expedition rather than an honest effort to get at particular transgressions. He refused to submit to it. At this point, however, according to David Salmon, IBT President Dave Beck entered the fray. Beck, Salmon says, "induced" Gibbons to fire the man who was then Local 688's lawyer (not Morris Shenker, who had briefly represented Gibbons after his December 1953 arrest) and replace him with a former Republican governor of Kansas named Payne Ratner. Ratner, with Beck behind him, threatened to have Local 688 put in trusteeship unless Gibbons agreed to turn the books over to him.[5] The books were duly surrendered, and Gibbons and Lou Berra, who had been incarcerated with him, were released from jail.

Goldschein's focus then shifted to Berra. The latter was approached by a plainclothes cop who announced that Goldschein and Chief of Detectives James Chapman wished a private conversation with him. Goldschein, according to the plainclothesman, was seeking information about suspected financial shenanigans at the Labor Health Institute, where Berra was the business manager. In a deposition given a few weeks after this, Berra said, "He [the plainclothesman] told me that Mr. Goldschein would not embarrass me before the grand jury in trying to implicate me with any questions.... I told [the cop] that I saw no reason at this time to meet with Goldschein and Chapman because they probably wouldn't believe me anyway. Even if I told them the truth."[6]

Photos show Berra to have been a slight man with an apprehensive smile. Yuki Kato remembers him as "a nice guy, but not very forceful."[7] To David Salmon he was an "upbeat, pleasant fellow [who] always had a joke."[8] Originally a warehouse checker at Brown Shoe, Berra had become Gibbons' chief lieutenant soon after the latter's arrival in town in the early 1940s. The two made an effective team. Gibbons, hotly eloquent before a crowd, could appear withdrawn in intimate, one-on-one conversation; Berra would then step in with small talk and badinage to keep things rolling. By 1953, however, Berra increasingly found himself supplanted by Dick Kavner and (especially) Pete Saffo. But he remained a member of Local 688's inner circle.

In April 1954, after he had refused to meet with Goldschein and Chapman, Berra was subpoenaed to testify before the grand jury. Under questioning, he happened to mention nine pistols and shoulder holsters that the union had purchased the previous year. These were new guns, acquired after the successful recapture of the joint council building in March 1953. Fearing retaliation for that act by the Wortman gang, Local 688 staffers had wanted weapons more trustworthy than the old (and, in at least one case, rusty) pistols they had carried on that raid.[9]

Not only did Berra mention the guns in his grand jury testimony—he also revealed that it was Saffo who acquired them. Then, apparently realizing that he had exposed the union to questions it might not want answered, he closed his mouth and would say no more about anything.

But of course he'd already gone too far. Goldschein naturally wanted to hear more about those pistols. He subpoenaed Saffo. The latter, called to the witness stand the very next day, refused to answer any of the twenty questions put to him. The judge found him in contempt of court and sent *him* to jail to think things over. It did no good for Local 688's lawyer to argue that the guns had been acquired in the first place because "St. Louis authorities did nothing to protect the [union's] organizers" from mobsters.[10] Saffo sat in his cell for forty-seven days until, in early June, an appellate court ruled that he need not answer eighteen of the twenty questions lest they violate his Fifth Amendment rights. As for the two questions that the appellate court did allow, Saffo was able to answer those in a way that incriminated neither himself nor others. He was then excused to go home.

Meanwhile, between February and May, federal agents examined the five years' worth of subpoenaed Teamsters books, looking for possible illegalities. They combed through not only the records of Local 688 and the LHI but also those of four other locals (including the taxi drivers' and the cement-truck drivers') for which Gibbons had been appointed trustee by the IBT. Finally, as a result of all this labor, on May 20 Gibbons and a Local 688 staffer named Ed Brown were indicted for filing with the U.S. Department of Labor a false report concerning political contributions. That was it. The government could dig up no other serious problem. Nor did this one stick. The indictments of Gibbons and Brown were soon dismissed because the action involved was found to be not a crime but only a bookkeeping error.

11. Gibbons a Racketeer?

From left, front row, Pete Saffo, Lou Berra, Gibbons, Ernest Conn, 1950. The other men in the photo are unidentified. Photographer unknown, 55.38, State Historical Society of Missouri, Photograph Collection.

The grand jury also handed down some indictments that were unrelated to the books' audit. Dick Kavner and seven cab drivers from Local 405 were charged with interfering with interstate commerce because they had roughed up a nonstriking driver during the previous December's taxi walkout. However, these indictments were also dismissed, in this case because although Kavner and the strikers were clearly guilty of assault—they had shoved the cabbie around and broken his eyeglasses—that assault was judged to have had nothing to do with interstate commerce and therefore wasn't a federal crime.

Lou Berra was indicted for obstructing justice and income tax evasion. This charge also was unconnected to the government's audit. Chief of Detectives Chapman had turned up a painting contractor who claimed that he'd paid Berra, the LHI's business manager, a series of kickbacks in return for assignments to paint various union properties, including the union's headquarters building at 1127 Pine. The contractor said Berra had encouraged him to destroy the canceled checks involved: hence the obstruction of justice charge. And Berra had filed no tax return on the checks he received: hence the tax evasion charge. On his side, Berra argued that the checks were loans rather than kickbacks. He also pointed out that the contractor, facing tax charges of his own, had agreed to testify against the Teamster in hopes of lenient treatment from the government. But in the end Berra was convicted and sentenced to two years in the penitentiary. Yuki Kato took over his post at the LHI.

It seems pretty clear now, from reading Goldschein's description of the canceled checks, which sound like payoffs of some sort, not loans, that Berra had indeed defrauded his own union.[11] Even so, after his release from prison in 1956 he was allowed to return to Local 688 in a series of sinecures that he quietly filled for what remained of his working career. Union staffers couldn't help being fond of the man. "They were disappointed that Berra had made this slip," writes David Salmon, one of the staffers, "but their loyalty to him continued."[12]

Probably there was more to it than simple affection, real as that was. For years afterward rumors about Berra floated around the world of St. Louis labor. Jerry Tucker, a onetime regional leader of the United Auto Workers, referred to those rumors when he said, "People used to talk about how Lou had taken a fall for Harold, for the union. And that it wasn't all Lou's doing."[13]

Berra's "fall" involved those nine pistols. When, in the early spring of '54, Goldschein and Chapman made their initial approach to him, they had already elicited from the painting contractor the admission that he and Berra had conspired to swindle Local 688. Goldschein hoped to use this confession to force Berra to testify in turn against Gibbons concerning the guns and other sensitive matters. But after mentioning the guns on his initial grand jury appearance, Berra dug in his heels and refused to proceed, thereby blocking one of Goldschein's avenues to information that might incriminate the union. Pete Saffo blocked another by sitting out those forty-seven days in a city jail cell.

Because no other such avenue revealed itself, the inquiry into the pistols' origins went nowhere in the end. But certain interesting questions remain. Why, for example, did Berra, a founder of the warehousemen's union and a party therefore to all of its secrets and sensitivities, call the guns to the attention of the grand jury in the first place? Had he calculated that Goldschein might be satisfied with mere mention of the guns and, as a result, cut him some slack on the paint scam? Why did he name Saffo as the man who acquired the guns? Was it jealousy? Did he think that he could thereby rid himself of a rival for his old position as Gibbons' chief sidekick?

Why, for that matter, were Gibbons and his friends so reluctant to talk about it? Again we can only hazard guesses. Pete Saffo admitted that he'd used union money to purchase the shoulder holsters (he entered them in the books as "office supplies"), but never let on where he got the pistols that went in them. One possibility was Joe Costello. Costello, about whom we'll say

11. Gibbons a Racketeer?

more later (see Chapter 13) owned a taxicab company, though the police always suspected him of using it as a front for what they believed was his main business, the buying and selling of stolen goods, including firearms. Not a Sicilian himself, Costello operated under the protection of the city's Sicilian mob. Costello, the cab company owner, and Gibbons, the trustee for the cab drivers' union, did business together. When in town, Barney Baker tended to shuttle between the union hall and Costello's office.[14] Saffo knew everyone, especially in St. Louis' Italian and Sicilian communities. So it's conceivable that Saffo got the pistols for Gibbons by way of Costello. But, if so, and given Costello's reputation, Gibbons wouldn't have wanted that bit of news appearing in the public press.

Not that such information would have made any difference to his detractors. They believed they already knew what Gibbons was. "Racketeer" was the word Goldschein had tossed around since his arrival in St. Louis, and "rackets" and "racketeering" invariably appeared in *Post-Dispatch* and *Globe-Democrat* articles describing the targets of Goldschein's grand jury. And, in fact, different St. Louis-area grand juries did indict a number of labor leaders on racketeering charges that year. Among the latter was Larry Callanan, boss of the Steamfitters Union and a leader with Gibbons of the Politicians faction in city politics; Callanan was eventually convicted of shaking down a pipeline contractor and sentenced to a dozen years in prison.[15] But Goldschein's grand jury produced no racketeering indictment of Gibbons or any other Local 688 member except the hapless Lou Berra.

Goldschein could have saved himself time and trouble if he had begun his investigation by speaking to Captain Thomas Moran, commander of the police department's Bomb and Arson Squad. Moran probably would have told him what, some years later, he told Robert Kennedy of the McClellan Committee. Asked his opinion of Gibbons' organization, Moran said he'd experienced a lot of problems with it. Too often, he complained, the union had resorted to physical intimidation in its organizing campaigns and strikes. But, Moran went on, "I would say that at no time during all the trouble we had with 688 to our knowledge was there any attempt at extortion."[16] It was a tough but honest union.

A similar conclusion was eventually reached by Daniel Bell, the labor columnist for *Fortune* magazine. Bell, a sociologist who would later become well-known as the author of *The End of Ideology* and other books, published in the May 1954 issue of *Fortune* a column about trade union corruption in St. Louis. Bell had been reading the *Post-Dispatch*, which by then routinely lumped Gibbons in with local labor leaders suspected of racketeering—and Bell did the same. Gibbons, after reading his column, wrote to the journalist threatening to sue him for slander. Bell then took another look at the matter. He discovered that he had in fact confused several federal grand juries, including one across the Mississippi in East St. Louis, Illinois, which had investigated certain construction union bosses there. Bell also noted that a major complaint of Goldschein's grand jury about Local 688 had nothing to do with criminal behavior. The union, the grand jury claimed, was driving businesses out of St. Louis. "Evidence was received that firms employing over 1000 men and women had in recent months decided to leave the area," the jury had said in an interim report. "The reason most frequently given was the inability to accede to the demands of Local No. 688, and still remain competitive."[17]

This was an odd accusation for such a body to make, Bell decided. After thinking it over, he wrote an extensive correction for the July issue of *Fortune*.

> In recent years [Bell said] St. Louis has become the capital of labor rackets in the construction industry. Following a *Post-Dispatch* expose, a Federal grand jury in July, 1953, indicted fifteen A. F. of L. construction union leaders for extortion. In a follow-up this May, two other grand juries indicted eighteen more persons....
>
> Behind the charges against [Gibbons'] Teamsters, as distinct from the racketeering accusations against the East St. Louis construction union leaders, is the fear of many St. Louis business leaders that the Teamsters' aggressive bargaining tactics are driving industry out of the area. A number of firms such as J. C. Penney, Warner-Hudnut, and Walgreen have shut down warehousing operations. But in most cases the chief reason was the condition of the warehouses or a change in merchandising methods.
>
> The simultaneous indictments of the two grand juries, however, had actually clouded the issues. Many rumors about Gibbons had floated around St. Louis. But the grand jury's indictment carried no charge of financial malfeasance against Gibbons. In fact the charge against Gibbons was purely a technical one.[18]

Unfortunately, few people in St. Louis were likely to catch a correction in a business magazine like *Fortune*. In his own city Gibbons would wear a faint but undeserved reputation for crookedness for the rest of his days.

* * *

In the summer of 1953, as the grand jury Max Goldschein would eventually lead was being empaneled in St. Louis, another investigation of Teamsters was under way in the halls of Congress. Republicans, who had been the minority party for a generation, were now eager to use their new majority-status perquisites, including committee chairmanships, to correct what they believed to be distortions wrought in the nation's life during the Roosevelt and Truman years. Many in the GOP believed that the greatly increased power of trade unions was one of those distortions. The IBT had become the nation's fastest-growing union. Certain Republicans in the House of Representatives, convinced that Jimmy Hoffa was a labor racketeer, launched a probe of Teamster locals in Detroit and Kansas City thought to be under his influence.

Their investigation, however, was shut down very soon after it began— shut down by other Republicans.

11. Gibbons a Racketeer?

It happened like this: one day in November, Representative Wint Smith, a Republican of Kansas and the chairman of the House Subcommittee on Labor, which was holding hearings in Hoffa's own Detroit bailiwick, was called away from the hearing room to take a telephone call. When Smith returned to the room he declared that the hearings were "suspended." A reporter asked him why. Gesturing toward the ceiling, Smith said, "The pressure comes from way up there, and I just can't be any more specific than that." Another committee member, Representative Clare Hoffman, Republican of Michigan, added that "powerful men in Washington have passed the word down to 'go easy, or get out.'"[19]

That mysterious phone call to Smith interred all talk of an investigation. Nothing more would be heard about Republicans getting tough on the IBT.

There were two reasons for this. First, Dave Beck, the new president of the IBT was himself a Republican. It wasn't unheard of for a trade-union leader to belong to the Grand Old Party—John L. Lewis himself was an adherent—but it was unusual, and party leaders didn't want to lose the few they had. What's more, the dynamic young Jimmy Hoffa, who clearly intended to one day replace Beck as IBT president, had, after spending some years as a lukewarm Democrat, recently become an increasingly important factor in Republican politics in Michigan. Now those two old right-wingers Smith and Hoffman intended to disturb Hoffa by poking around in his back yard? Cooler heads in the party thought that didn't make good sense.

The second reason was even more immediate and practical. In 1953 Republicans held a one-vote majority in the U.S. Senate. To maintain that majority, they needed to successfully defend every seat up for reelection in 1954, including, as it happened, a seat in Michigan. That state's GOP was expecting to get Hoffa's endorsement for its Senate candidate. No one in either the state or the national party wanted to risk forgoing his involvement in that campaign.

Hoffa understood that he had this claim on the party. On learning that Congressmen Smith and Hoffman had him targeted for investigation, he naturally looked around for Republican help. For $200 a day he hired the services of Payne Ratner, the same man Dave Beck would foist upon Gibbons during the grand jury investigation of 1954.[20] Ratner had been the Republican governor of Kansas in the early '40s, when Wint Smith, not yet a congressman, was serving as chief of Kansas' highway patrol. So they had a prior acquaintance. Ratner later freely admitted that he'd approached Smith on Hoffa's behalf during the Detroit hearings, though only, he said, to seek a brief postponement and to complain that Hoffman was being rude to his client. Smith, Ratner said, had promised to make the hearings more "dignified, fair and courteous."[21] But of course he eventually did more than that.

However, Ratner lacked the clout needed to kill the investigation himself.

Instead, the former governor seems to have served as a middleman between Hoffa and Republicans much more influential than Wint Smith. Who were these Republicans? Smith never said. But earlier that year the Washington correspondent of the *Post-Dispatch* had talked to Clare Hoffman, and afterward he wrote, in a passive sentence intended to shield whoever had informed him, presumably Hoffman himself, that "it was learned that three cabinet officials—Agriculture Secretary Ezra Benson, Budget Director Joseph M. Dodge and Attorney General Herbert Brownell Jr.—had been consulted on the committee's activities and had asked that the committee turn over whatever it finds to the proper administration officials for correction rather than exposing the matters in public hearings."[22]

In this context "the proper administration official," the official responsible for making "corrections," would almost certainly have been the attorney general, and this particular attorney general also happened to be President Eisenhower's chief political advisor in domestic affairs. So if one had to bet on the identity of the person who telephoned Wint Smith "from way up there" that day in November 1953, one would have to choose Herbert Brownell. If this is so, then with that phone call Brownell made himself Jimmy Hoffa's protector.

A year later, Michigan's Teamsters did endorse the Republican candidate for reelection to the U.S. Senate. In supporting him, writes Hoffa's most recent biographer, "Hoffa forged a permanent alliance with the Republican Party that proved highly profitable for him personally and for the Teamsters."[23]

Hoffa thus escaped a jam by placing himself in the care of one of America's two great political parties. But he bet on the wrong horse. The one-legged Joe Ames once said that Gibbons wasn't talented when it came to political handicapping. Hoffa was that way too.

In the elections of November 1954 Michigan's Teamster-backed Republican senator was defeated by his opponent, one result of which was to give the Democrats a slim but effective two-vote majority in the U.S. Senate. When, three years later, that body decided to investigate labor racketeering, it chose John McClellan, an Arkansas Democrat, to chair the investigating committee, and McClellan picked Robert Kennedy as the committee's chief counsel. John Kennedy became a committee member. Later Hoffa maintained, and with some justice, that the Kennedy brothers then rose to power on his back.

12

Hoffa

Despite his claims, it's never been clear that, aside from loaning him the belly-bumping Barney Baker, Jimmy Hoffa actually did much to protect Harold Gibbons from Buster Wortman's mob. But he said he did, and Gibbons believed him. Gibbons believed that Hoffa saved his life. And Hoffa did successfully conclude the cement-truck drivers' strike, which, without his aid, and given the enmity that had so hotly flared between Gibbons and the cement dealers, might have gone on until all parties were permanently embittered. On both those counts Gibbons no doubt felt grateful to the Detroit Teamster. That gratitude would become one ingredient in their long partnership.

Hoffa was forty in 1953. An early biographer described him as follows: "thick legs, thick wrists, broad heavy shoulders, large feet.... His eyes are small, bright, gray-green, hard. He has big, hard, callused hands and stubby fingers."[1]

Then again, he was only five feet five. When he and Gibbons stood together they looked like the old comic-strip characters Mutt and Jeff.

Hoffa, like Gibbons and many other labor leaders of their generation (Ernest "Cab" Calloway among them), was the son of a coal miner. Hoffa Senior escaped the pits to become a coal broker, but didn't prosper at it and died when Jimmy was only seven. Jimmy mostly grew up in Detroit. While in his early teens he dropped out of school to work in a Kroger's warehouse. At seventeen he organized a successful strike there by persuading his fellow laborers to refuse to unload an unrefrigerated carload of strawberries until the company, fearing the strawberries would spoil, agreed to restrain a bullying foreman.

It must have thrilled him to learn that a group of normally passive men will follow a kid, even a runty kid, into action, if the kid seems to know what he's doing. *Stepping up* became his habit. Years later, Local 688's Levi Sanford watched a middle-aged Hoffa move through a St. Louis shop introducing himself to its workers. He had, Sanford recalls, an easygoing, no-bullshit-between-you-and-me way of marching up to a perfect stranger and saying, for example, "Goddammit, your glasses don't fit right, why don't you go get them fixed!"[2] Hoffa had learned that constant, unceasing forward motion—aggressiveness, some might call it—wipes out all sorts of disadvantages. Energy and chutzpah count for more than physical size.

By the time he was twenty-three, Hoffa had become an organizer for Detroit's joint council of Teamsters. He worked with truck drivers, whose company he would always prefer to practitioners of other IBT trades, including warehousemen. Compared to St. Louis, Detroit in the 1930s was a frontier town. Among poor and laboring people it was a place where the gambler Moe Dalitz, who then owned a chain of laundries, and the mafioso Angelo Meli, who controlled the jukeboxes, were respected figures. Such men, noted the journalist Murray Kempton, were not industrial giants. "But they were outsized by comparison with the average entrepreneur in Hoffa's path, who was, more often than not, a truck driver whose scrabblings had earned him three or four trucks of his own. This was a society that, being too narrow to offer room to truly large-scale proprietors, quite naturally invested the gangster with a status disproportionate to his real position in the economy; and he was the biggest businessman with whom Hoffa had to deal."[3]

Hoffa, having little choice about it, therefore learned to treat with businessmen who were also gangsters. In 1937 the Teamster joint council won a surprisingly peaceful citywide truck strike—largely, Hoffa's associates said, because he had earlier formed friendships among certain Italian-American families, especially Angelo Meli's, one of whose usual services was renting out thugs to employers who used them to beat up strikers. "It wasn't that Jimmy had made any alliances with those guys during the 1937 strike, because he didn't," recalled one Teamster. "It was a matter of knowing who was going to hurt you and then asking them to back off."[4]

Hoffa's own methods weren't so different from the gangsters'. Thaddeus Russell, his most recent and friendliest biographer, writes that Local 299, Hoffa's longtime Detroit base of operations, grew *because* its leaders used violence as a tool. Local 299 specialized in "organizing" employers rather than workers. "The local's business agents first approached the owner of a firm," Russell writes, "and told him that if he did not enroll his employees with the union, his trucks would be bombed. Next, if the employer refused to capitulate, they bombed his trucks. In the mid-1930s the local gained a reputation as the most violent, lawless union in an unusually lawless, violent city."[5]

Hoffa was not in his own view a cynical man. Rather, he saw himself as the boy in the fable who blurts out that the emperor is naked—except that, for him, not just the emperor but nearly *everyone* was naked, and the only person clear-eyed and forthright enough to point that out was Hoffa himself. He had the rigid wisdom of a disappointed adolescent—and the brittleness that goes with it. He was once invited by an MIT professor to have dinner with the latter and ten of his brightest graduate students. Hoffa agreed, but announced that he would stay only as long as the students asked him *intelligent* questions. He began the evening with a brief talk, after which, the professor writes, "my carefully selected audience blasted him with questions for almost three hours. He responded agilely. Finally, after a perceptive, emotional monologue on the history of labor legislation, the 'tough' Jimmy Hoffa burst from the room in tears."[6]

Of the conflicts involving Hoffa's local, the most violent were those with competing unions. In 1941 a CIO truck drivers' organization tried to sink roots in Detroit. "They wanted to take the Teamsters over," said a veteran of that affair. "We had a real out-and-out battle with those fellows ... and it was one of those old-fashioned fights with sticks. And it even got to the pistol business."[7] Not long afterward, RWDSU, whose St. Louis affiliate was just then coming under Harold Gibbons' care, launched an organizing campaign among Detroit's retail clerks. This alarmed the leaders of the Teamsters' joint council, who, as Hoffa put it, feared they might "wake up some morning and find out that the clerks, being CIO[,] would be in a position to refuse delivery from an A.F. of L. driver."[8] To counter RWDSU, the Teamsters first set up a local of the AFL's own retail clerks' affiliate. Then, employing methods they had used against the Minneapolis Trotskyists and the more recent CIO drivers' union, Hoffa's people patrolled Detroit's streets beating up RWDSU organizers. "In an act of desperation," writes Thaddeus Russell, "twenty Teamsters ambushed and stomped [RWDSU's] regional director Tucker Smith and put him in the hospital with a concussion."[9] (Smith, restored to health, would be Norman Thomas' running mate on the Socialist ticket in the presidential election of 1948.) According to a pair of Hoffa biographers, Ralph and Estelle James, "Hoffa himself gave more than one vicious beating to rival leaders. He even led an attack on [RWDSU's] Detroit headquarters."[10]

The Teamsters acted with "desperation" in this episode because their opponents had put up such fierce resistance. In fact, Detroit's RWDSU local managed to hold on to a majority of the city's retail clerks until the RWDSU international split apart in 1948. After the split, a number of the Detroit RWDSU local's leaders went over the IBT, along with St. Louis' Gibbons, Toledo's Larry Steinberg, and other rebels. Still later, when Hoffa finally gained the IBT presidency in the late 1950s, he hired several former RWDSU leaders as aides. Having struggled with them so mightily in Detroit, he knew just how tough they could be.

Meanwhile, although he met occasional checks at home, Hoffa was increasingly successful in the larger world. By 1942 he had negotiated a statewide contract granting big wage increases and other benefits to Michigan's Teamster truck drivers. By 1953, through the creation of a network he called the Central Conference of Teamsters, he was hammering out such agreements on a regional basis in the Midwest and upper South. Thaddeus Russell argues that Hoffa's popularity among IBT drivers, though shocking to outsiders, had a simple explanation: those contracts lifted thousands of hitherto poor laboring people into the American middle class.[11]

Hoffa's dominance of the big Central Conference automatically made him a power in the international. Dave Beck, upon being elected IBT president in 1952, was easily persuaded to turn over his more mundane duties to a new vice president, Hoffa, so that he, Beck, could fill a loftier and more glamorous role. Hoffa was perfectly happy to let Beck distance himself from the union membership. About Beck he would say: "Don't forget he'd go and talk to the medical profession, Chamber of Commerce, Kiwanis, the President of the United States—he'd got to the top rung, he was no longer meeting with business agents, and truck drivers and people who are down to earth, who can take the heat. It's like eating in the best restaurants, then one day your car breaks down and you've got to walk into a hot-dog joint—you're a little hesitant about walking into that joint. That's what happened to Dave."[12]

Meanwhile, having been handed those more mundane tasks, Hoffa immediately began using them to build his own network of followers. According to another Hoffa biographer, the unwitting "Beck made speeches on foreign affairs; Hoffa undercut him by handling wages and working conditions.... When a problem arose anywhere in the country, Beck sent Hoffa in to straighten it out. And in each place Hoffa took over for himself. Minneapolis, Philadelphia, Cleveland, and St. Louis fell to Hoffa, and he laid siege to New York."[13]

St. Louis was a particularly important conquest. There, having already won Gibbons' gratitude in the Buster Wortman affair and the cement-drivers' strike, Hoffa began to ply him with gifts. He had during the cement-drivers' strike appointed Gibbons trustee for Joint Council 13 (in which Gibbons installed Pete Saffo as secretary-treasurer of one of the city's two big freight-drivers' locals). Even better, Hoffa placed in Gibbons' care his own special baby, the Central Conference of Teamsters, whose headquarters was transferred from Chicago to Local 688's headquarters at 1127 Pine Street in St. Louis. (Supervision of that office, whose primary function was the researching, collating, and writing of contracts for member unions throughout the conference's twenty-two states, Gibbons assigned to the former college teacher David Salmon.)

These jobs weren't just patronage. They were important to Hoffa, and he needed them done well. In those days Teamster officials, including those of the Detroit man's own Local 299, tended to be distinguished primarily by their muscle. They were, as a character in a Saul Bellow short story puts it, "goons, mostly, apart from Harold Gibbons, who was highly urbane and in conversation, at least with me, bookish in his interests."[14] Hoffa recognized Gibbons as a man who, in Gibbons' own satirical phrase, "knew how to open an envelope" (that is, without destroying its contents in the process). He saw that Gibbons was also good at recruiting other envelope-openers: people like Pete Saffo, Joe Ames, Bernice Fisher, Ernest Calloway, David Salmon, Marvin Rich, even the hard-case Dick Kavner with his gift for writing airtight contracts. When Hoffa assigned a task to Gibbons and his crew, he knew it would be carried out intelligently.

Which certainly included the task closest to Hoffa's heart. Though it was never announced publicly, Gibbons was appointed chief strategist and manager of Hoffa's drive to be elected IBT president at the international's convention in 1957. "Harold orchestrated the whole campaign," said John J. "Jake" McCarthy, a public relations man Gibbons had hired to assist him. "I know that because we ran the whole thing out of St. Louis."[15]

* * *

Gibbons and Hoffa spent a lot of time together in the early '50s, becoming not just allies but friends as well. They were in some ways very different kinds of men. Gibbons liked to read, especially social critics such as John Kenneth Galbraith and Simone de Beauvoir. Hoffa, when he read, preferred trucking statistics. Gibbons was a socialist, Hoffa a Republican who had little interest in politics except as it affected the Teamsters. And although both men put in long hours at work, the Detroit man, a teetotaler and nonsmoker, usually went home to his family afterward, whereas the St. Louisan was more likely to head toward his city's nightclubs and saloons.

Both were dedicated trade unionists, but they operated out of different labor philosophies. Gibbons always remained a CIO man at heart. The CIO, born during Roosevelt's New Deal and nurtured by it, liked to see itself as a force for broad social reform. The AFL, on the other hand, focused on improving its own members' economic interests. No other AFL chief ever put this difference between the two federations better than Hoffa, who once said, "That political or social stuff—ah-h. It's not important. I don't think the drivers expect me to be holding social gatherings for them or to go on the air and tell what's wrong with Germany or Italy. Running a union is just like running a business. We're in the business of selling labor. We're going to get the best price we can."[16]

In other ways, of course, Gibbons and Hoffa were alike. Both, coming of age in the early years of the Depression, went almost without hesitation into the trade union movement. Because respectable society, including its legislators and magistrates, then tended to favor employers over employees, neither Hoffa nor Gibbons had much respect for the law and its enforcers. Hoffa liked to brag that during one strike he had been arrested sixteen times in a single day. As for the St. Louisan, a journalist once noted that "there is something of the revolutionary's hatred for the police in Gibbons."[17] Both men spent numerous brief stays in jail (brief, that is, until Hoffa's federal incarceration of 1967–71), often on what they themselves considered trumped-up charges. As a result, they tended not to look too closely into the ethics of other men with police records—a practice that would get them both into trouble.

The insecurity of the Depression years had scratched deep grooves in their personalities. Although the quarter century from 1950 to 1975—the period of their own personal successes—would be an era of great general prosperity, they disbelieved in its permanence. According to Ralph and Estelle James, even the conservative Hoffa saw American capitalism as too inherently unstable to survive for long. Another big crash was inevitable. Once again, the overproduction of goods would lead to an economic smash-up and, like that of the '30s, throw millions of people out of work. The Jameses, whom Hoffa allowed to spend months closely following his day-to-day activities, write:

> The final result, which Hoffa discusses frequently in private conversation, is the radicalization of the American labor force, and the flowering of left-wing political movements. Despite his emotional attraction to a vigorous free enterprise economy, his numerous private financial deals, his advocacy of business experience for union leaders, and his support for many Republican candidates, Hoffa believes (just as he was taught by [Farrell] Dobbs in the 1930s) that capitalism is doomed. He is in the incongruous position of one who likes the present system, but does not believe it can work.... We have several times heard Hoffa predict a return to the violence in the streets that he witnessed during the Great Depression. Should this happen, he is prepared to lead the hungry masses forth.[18]

Gibbons became a socialist as a result of the Great Depression of the '30s. Hoffa, the rugged individualist, expected to be *forced* to adopt socialist politics by a depression still to come.

In the meantime, the two men often traveled different routes to reach the same conclusion. For instance, Gibbons hated racism. Hoffa, who seems to have had no particular feelings about it one way or another, was nevertheless aware that employers often used it to pit white laborers against black ones, thereby making their coming together as members of a trade union particularly difficult. Gibbons sharpened Hoffa's awareness of this common practice. "By all accounts," writes Steven Brill, "it was Gibbons ... who got Hoffa to reverse his earlier track record in Detroit of tolerating Teamster discrimination against blacks and to push courageously and successfully for integrated Teamster locals, even in the most virulently racist areas of the

South and Midwest."[19] The St. Louisan taught his Detroit friend well. Ernest Calloway, Gibbons' African American lieutenant, recalled watching Hoffa on one occasion dress down the assembled members of a whites-only local in Baton Rouge, Louisiana. According to Calloway, Hoffa told them, "You can segregate your schools if you want to but you can't segregate the Teamsters."[20]

On a more personal level, the two men shared an enthusiasm for physical exercise. Hoffa, when visiting the Gibbons home in Kirkwood, liked to get down on the floor of the living room and challenge his host to a pushup contest. He was especially impressed by Harold's ability to do many pushups while Ann Gibbons reclined, like Cleopatra on her barge, along her husband's spine.[21]

Gibbons and Hoffa found they could relax together. Patrick Gibbons, Harold's elder son, recalls as a boy riding along one wintry evening as his father and Hoffa traveled to a labor banquet somewhere over in southern Illinois. Drowsy in the back seat, he half-listened as they reminisced about close calls they had survived, labor eccentrics they had known. For young Patrick, the murmur of their voices seems to have merged with the warm air issuing from the car's heater. As he tells it, he might have been listening to a comfortably married old couple. Today Patrick says, "I never saw them as anything but cordial with each other."[22]

At some point, there arose a vague understanding that the two men would one day *share* the Teamsters Union's leadership. That is, Hoffa would with Gibbons' help win the international presidency in '57 and, after serving a term (or possibly two, or even more; this part seems to have been especially cloudy), would help elect Gibbons in his stead. The arrangement was apparently similar to that rumored to have been made in the early 1990s by two British Labour Party politicians, Tony Blair and Gordon Brown. They were said to have agreed that, if Blair became prime minister, he would later resign the post in favor of Brown. Something like that did happen eventually, but not before the friendship had soured beyond repair.

There would be strains in the Gibbons-Hoffa friendship as well.

* * *

One early strain involved the Missouri-Kansas Conference of Teamsters, a body that coordinated IBT activities in the two states. The presidency of the conference was another of Hoffa's gifts to Gibbons. The St. Louisan had earlier been named trustee for several Kansas City, Missouri, locals. Those trustee jobs had irritated Roy Williams, the burly Ozarks farm boy who had become the strongman among that city's Teamsters. Gibbons now began his tenure as conference president by replacing officers in the Kansas City locals under his jurisdiction. "St. Louis has tried to take over the Kan City Jt. Council," Williams complained to a friend. "Told Jimmy Hoffa over my dead body."

Williams' words, spoken during a March 1954 conference session in Kansas City, were overheard by Dick Kavner, who jotted them down in a notebook. Kavner's notes provide a glimpse into what might be called Teamster politics at the precinct level. Unsurprisingly, the Missouri-Kansas Conference soon split into two factions, with Gibbons, Kavner, and Pete Saffo, the St. Louis representatives on one side, and Williams and his Kansas City associates on the other.

Kavner's notes show a good deal of unpleasant bickering occurring in these meetings. Simple jealousy was obviously a factor. Williams, who groused that Teamster locals in his city were required to clear proposed strikes with Hoffa, whereas those in St. Louis were not, seems to have felt like a less-favored sibling. Hoffa may have intended him to feel that way. Another thing that Kavner's notes reveal is Hoffa's practice of playing people against each other, thereby keeping all involved guessing about his own intentions. An example is Kavner's summary of the February 1954 meeting in Miami. On one hand, the participants agreed that "Roy would now cooperate and work with Gibbons and Kavner." However, "Kavner's suggestion that a Mo-Kan [gathering] would be called to explain the agreement was vetoed by Hoffa." In other words, Hoffa gave Gibbons authority over Williams but then refused to make that authority public. Later, in the March meeting, Hoffa asked Gibbons and Williams to shake hands. Gibbons refused, arguing that a handshake would do nothing to settle the serious differences between them. According to Kavner's notes, Hoffa berated Gibbons for this refusal, saying "that he talked with less sense than a 21-year-old."[23]

Gibbons and Williams were both Hoffa protégés. But Williams was also in a sense a protégé of Kansas City's North Side mob—and, since that group was a tributary of Chicago's old Capone organization, known around that city as "The Outfit," a protégé of the Outfit as well. (For more on the relationship between the Chicago and Kansas City mobs, at least as it concerned rake-offs from Las Vegas gambling, see Nicholas Pileggi's *Casino*, Simon & Schuster, 1995.)

Although long suspected, these latter ties wouldn't be clear until forty years later when Williams, by then president of the IBT, was convicted of trying to bribe a U.S. senator. Williams then admitted to having for decades taken orders from the boss of the Kansas City mob. He claimed to have had no choice about it because the mobsters had threatened his life and those of his wife and children. "They were going to kill the others first and then me."[24]

He was, however, compensated for his troubles. In 1955, a year after Gibbons and Williams had these early run-ins, Hoffa set up the Central States Pension Fund, into which employers of the region's Teamsters paid $2 per employee per week, or around $1 million a month. With steady increases in both the number of workers covered and the rate paid, the fund would over time become enormous—a big bank. The Outfit and its allies used the bank to build or buy casinos in Las Vegas. Hoffa used it to pursue his overarching ambition, becoming president of the IBT. Just as, to cultivate a powerful state senator, say, a regular bank might loan him money on especially easy terms, the Central States Pension Fund began making friendly loans to people in a position to help Hoffa attain *his* goal. Not all of these people were Teamsters. Some were Midwestern mobsters who controlled not just Teamster locals but also entire joint councils. (Hoffa was never able to establish similarly fruitful relations with either Teamster leaders or gangsters on the East and West coasts.) "Hoffa wasn't a hoodlum," said Jake McCarthy. "But he understood politics. He knew he had to get along with Chicago and Cleveland [another mob center] to become president."[25]

So it was that when Hoffa formed the Central States Pension Fund he placed Roy Williams in a seat on its board of directors. Williams' role there was to cast the mob's vote regarding applications for loans from the fund— particularly loans involving Las Vegas casinos in which the Chicago and Cleveland organizations had significant interests. For performing this service, the satellite Kansas City mob paid him $1,500 a month.[26]

Assuming he knew about it, Gibbons wouldn't have found the arrangement especially shocking. According to two of his children, he estimated that about a third of the nation's Teamster locals were mob-influenced.[27] Such influence was a fact of life to him, like humid summers in the lower Mississippi River Valley. To Gibbons, the important point was that two-thirds of Teamster locals were *free* of mob control. Jake McCarthy, some years later, tried to explain the mob-IBT connection in a column he wrote for the *Post-Dispatch*. Mobsters in the union, he said, "were pretty much left alone to do their own thing as long, as they didn't mess up a national or bargaining agreement." Meanwhile, good guys like Gibbons focused on helping members improve their lives. "Well, how could they exist side by side?" McCarthy asked rhetorically. "Easy. The reformers worked where they had the power to work. After that, nobody got in anybody else's way. It was an intensely political thing—like the way Congress works. Like the board of directors of a few companies. Like your average city fathers in your average mob-dominated metropolis. There is the answer to getting it straight, you see?"[28]

Mob penetration of American big-city government was common in the late nineteenth and the first half of the twentieth centuries. In some immigrant neighborhoods, people we would today call mobsters bossed political party factions. (See, for example, Chapter 8, which discusses the frequently violent feud between the Egan and Hogan gangs in Democratic Party politics on St. Louis' North Side.) In Chicago the Outfit long ruled the populous First Ward (which includes the Loop), choosing its alderman, municipal judges, even its police captain. According to his biographers, Chicago's Mayor

Richard J. Daley, feeling that he had no choice, "treated the syndicate as just one more [Democratic] machine constituency."[29] Similar situations obtained in most Northern cities with large European immigrant populations. (Chicago's First Ward was heavily Italian.) Though they sometimes murdered each other, mob bosses had little to fear from civil authorities. The federal government was no threat to them because it traditionally left criminal justice to local government. Local government was no threat because it usually included some of the mob bosses' friends.

This situation eventually changed, of course. The children of immigrants moved to the suburbs and the old political machines, which depended on immigrant votes, began to fall apart. Starting in the 1960s, the federal government moved, cautiously at first, then with increasing vigor, into the enforcement of civil rights laws in the South (long the main bulwark of "states' rights": the notion that the federal government should stay out of local or regional matters, such as race relations) and, in the North, into the prosecution of various Italian-American mobs that government prosecutors had come to see as one great Mob, which they called the Mafia or Cosa Nostra. By century's end both legal Jim Crow and the older ethnic mobs had all but been erased from American life.

But that was far from the case in the 1950s. No one knew it better than Harold Gibbons. Despairing of police protection, either local or federal, Gibbons believed that he had little choice but to try to handle preying mobsters through cunning and careful diplomacy. It's likely that one of the things that attracted him to Jimmy Hoffa was the latter's possession of precisely those qualities. If Jake McCarthy is correct, Gibbons agreed with Hoffa that the latter had to have the support of the Chicago and Cleveland mobs to become president of the union. Ergo, bargaining with mobsters was going to be part of the plan.

Still, the whole thing must have rankled. Gibbons didn't want to shake hands with men like Roy Williams, even if Teamster politics seemed to require it. Then, too, although he and Hoffa were friends, they certainly weren't going to be equals. Hoffa was the boss. Gibbons could plainly see that friendship was much less important to the Detroit man than other things, definitely including the presidency of the Teamsters Union. There lay the limit to cordiality.

13

Joe Costello and the Wildcat

Mobster, gangster, hoodlum: which of those slippery terms best fit Gibbons' friend Joe Costello? The papers sometimes referred to him as a "police character," meaning that he was often arrested but spent relatively little time in jail. A *Post-Dispatch* photo from the 1950s shows him, slim, sandy-haired, neatly dressed in a suit and snap-brimmed hat, leaving police headquarters after yet another interrogation. He looks like a rough-edged Bing Crosby.

Costello was in his forties then. Of Irish extraction, he had grown up in a formerly Irish North St. Louis neighborhood that later turned Sicilian. A close childhood friend was John J. Vitale, who would become a boss of the city's Sicilian mob. Vitale was Costello's protector. According to an FBI informant, "In fact, Costello would be nothing were it not for the backing he receives from John Vitale.... Costello is intensely disliked by numerous St. Louis hoodlums, but they will not bother him because they are afraid of retaliation by Vitale."[1]

Costello was the owner of the Ace Cab Co., whose office and lot were at 1835 Washington Boulevard. The police suspected him of using the company as a front for the fencing of stolen goods, especially firearms and jewels. But fate, one night in October 1953, made him something more than a small-time crook. An Ace cabbie came in to tell his boss that he'd just dropped a drunken man and woman at a seedy motel out on U.S. Route 66. The pair were carrying a bag full of money, said the cabbie, who suspected they were embezzlers. Costello passed this information on to a crooked police lieutenant he knew, and the cop immediately drove to the motel and arrested the couple, delivering them and the money to a police station. Or rather, he took the couple and *half* the money, some $300,000, to the station. Another $300,000 simply vanished and was never accounted for.

The missing money became a St. Louis legend. The FBI believed the crooked lieutenant passed it to Costello, who then forwarded it to Chicago, where it was laundered by the Outfit. Ted Schafers, the *Globe-Democrat* reporter, who knew Costello and covered the story for his paper, disagreed.

He said Costello didn't even know there *was* another $300,000. Schafers believed the drunken couple buried the money in the ground somewhere just hours before they were caught.[2]

In any case, the drunken couple weren't embezzlers. They had kidnapped and murdered a six-year-old Kansas City boy named Bobby Greenlease. The $600,000, it turned out, was a ransom paid to the kidnappers by the boy's wealthy father.

In those relatively innocent days, the Greenlease case was a shocker. Apparently one of the persons most shocked was Joe Costello. In October 1954, almost exactly a year after little Bobby's murder, he was taken to a hospital with a bullet wound in his chest. Costello said he'd shot himself accidentally while cleaning a pistol. A friend of Costello's, the belly-bumping thug Barney Baker, told his wife that Costello, remorseful over his unwitting involvement in the Greenlease case, had meant to commit suicide.[3]

Although he survived the shooting, however it came about, Costello soon afterward began a lengthy and eventually fatal deterioration. He turned out to have an alcoholic illness as implacable as Bobby Greenlease's killers. After increasingly numerous arrests, other suicide attempts, a prison term on an illegal gun possession conviction, and a bar fight in which he shot and killed another man, he died from his disease in 1962.

Before then, however, he participated in a curious episode with Harold Gibbons.

No one knows exactly how Gibbons and Costello became connected. Both were restless night owls, so chances are that they had occasional drinks together in the city's saloons, especially those along De Baliviere Avenue, a strip of nightclubs between Delmar and Forest Park, which was Costello's special playground. (Costello was a co-owner of the strip's Tic Toc Club—indeed, it was his partner there whom he killed, shortly before his own death, on the sidewalk outside the club's front door.) And of course Gibbons and Costello knew each other through labor negotiations. Costello's employees were members of Teamsters Local 405, and Gibbons was the local's trustee. Employers and union bosses are normally adversaries, but for one thing, at least, the night life, these adversaries seem to have shared a common affection.

It may be recalled that St. Louis in those days had *two* Teamster organizations for cab drivers. Local 405 was for white cabbies. African American drivers, whom Gibbons had helped organize in 1945, remained a unit of the warehousemen's union, Local 688.

In August 1956, at Gibbons' direction, Local 688's Phil Reichardt, recently named acting secretary-treasurer of Local 405, signed an agreement with the city's four largest taxicab companies to add black drivers to their hitherto all-white workforces. But when the black drivers showed up for work on the morning of Saturday the 18th, the white drivers parked their vehicles and went home.

That evening some seven hundred white cabbies met in the ballroom of the Kings Way Hotel to discuss the issue. As the *Post-Dispatch* reported: "St. Louis taxicab drivers, on strike since yesterday against the trustee of their union, Harold J. Gibbons, president of Teamsters Joint Council No. 13, voted last night to withdraw from the Teamsters and form an independent union.... Speakers at last night's meeting emphasized that the crux of the dispute was Gibbons' denial of local autonomy to the taxicab drivers. The strike was touched off by the hiring of Negro drivers by companies which had been using only white drivers."[4]

The white drivers' strike was a "wildcat," one called by workers without their union's approval—and sometimes against the union itself. This strike was the latter sort. The white cabbies were striking for the same reason that some Southern communities of those years closed their public schools and sent white pupils to white "private academies," thereby attempting to sidestep the Supreme Court's *Brown v. Board of Education* decision of two years earlier. The intention was the same in both cases: avoiding racial integration.

Gibbons was away in New York that weekend. Phil Reichardt ordered the cabbies back to work, but they refused. This put him in a serious fix. Local 405 was bound by contract to furnish drivers for the city's taxicabs. If the local couldn't do that—if it couldn't control its own members—it would be of no use to the cab companies. As a trade union, it would be finished.

Reichardt was helpless. But Joe Costello stepped into the breach. Some drivers from Costello's company had walked out with the others on Saturday, but then showed up for work Monday morning. The *Post-Dispatch*, in those days an evening paper, reported that "Ace Cab Co.'s drivers refused to go along [with formation of a new union] and were operating as usual today."[5] Because Costello's cabs were running, the city had *some* white taxi service. Local 405 remained semi-functional. The strike was incomplete.

A spokesman for the strikers emerged on Monday. This was thirty-three-year-old Donald Cortor, who, as it happened, was relatively new to the taxi business. Unlike the vast majority of his colleagues, Cortor possessed a college education, having earned a degree in commerce and finance from St. Louis University. He liked driving a cab, he told reporters, "because it is a good, friendly life and there are lots of people to talk to."[6]

Cortor, an articulate young man, was aware that the race issue was tricky. He had no racial prejudice himself, he said, maintaining that the white drivers' chief concerns were, first, their finances and, second, their right to self-determination. Longstanding tradition in St. Louis dictated that white drivers transport white passengers and black drivers carry black ones. If, under a new policy, black drivers were allowed to carry white passengers as well as black ones, white drivers would lose money. "We will accept Negro drivers when we can do it without hurting our pocketbooks," said Cortor. "The breakdown of segregation is coming, but we resent his [Gibbons'] policy being forced on us now."[7]

The wildcat was bitter from the start. Cortor, announcing that the strikers had formed a new, independent union, the Taxi Drivers Welfare Association, complained to reporters that he was receiving threatening phone calls. He wasn't alone. Gibbons' daughter, Elizabeth Vasquez, eleven at the time, remembered being sworn at by an angry anonymous caller. (Her father, when he returned from New York, told her, "You shouldn't worry about a man who threatens a little girl, because he'll never have the courage to follow through on his threat.") Murah Culter, Ann Gibbons' mother, who happened to be visiting when the strike began, took a similar phone call. She immediately gathered up the three children and swept them off to Louisville. "We were gone the same day!" Vasquez said.[8]

Barney Baker reappeared in town on the evening of Tuesday the 21st. The next morning, he drove with a lawyer down to police headquarters to ask if there were a warrant out for his arrest. According to a news story, Chief of Detectives James Chapman, who since 1953 had accumulated a fat file of the belly-bumper's many run-ins with the law, replied that "he had no reason to arrest him, but would do so if Baker is seen in company with any hoodlum."[9]

That night Costello intervened in the strike again. A wildcatting driver complained to police that he had been forced off the road by two carloads of men, one of whom, an Ace Cab Co. driver, then struck him in the face with a baseball bat. (Fortunately, the injury wasn't serious.) Descending immediately afterward upon the Ace lot, police arrested four suspects: the Ace cabbie, two well-known local thugs—and Barney Baker. The four soon went free because neither the wounded driver nor a friend who had been riding with him could identify them as their assailants. ("If I did," said the friend, "it wouldn't be safe to walk the streets at night.")[10] Before letting him go, Chief Chapman told Baker it would be unwise to remain in St. Louis much longer. The belly-bumper took the advice to heart. An article in Friday's newspaper noted that he "went to Lambert-St. Louis Field this afternoon and was believed to be planning to head back East, cutting off a look-in on the current taxicab strike."[11]

Gibbons meanwhile returned from New York. He spent the rest of the week huddled with groups of strikers, peeling off two or three here, a dozen there, persuading them to give up the wildcat and return to work. He must have been grateful to Costello, Baker, and the others for the holding actions they had performed in his absence. Gibbons was no pacifist when it came to dealing with people he saw as enemies of his union, including rebellious members. On the other hand, the baseball-bat episode had been, as he saw it, all-too thoroughly covered by the press, the reporters having received help from Chief Chapman, who showed them the fat dossier he'd accumulated on Barney Baker. Assistance from Costello and Baker clearly wasn't the best kind of public relations for Teamsters. In a transparent attempt to muddle the issue, Gibbons announced on Thursday that he was putting fifty cars on the city's streets to protect *nonstriking cabbies.*

His words brought a quick, sardonic retort from the editors of the *Post-Dispatch*: "Not only did Mr. Gibbons accept the sudden assignment here of a one-time muscle man on the New York waterfront [that is, Baker]; he also ordered 50 automobiles to patrol the streets as 'protection' of drivers who have declined to go on strike.... The single victim of violence in this dispute has been a man who is striking, not one of Mr. Gibbons' boys. On that evidence, at least, those who need protection are the strikers, not the Teamsters. In any event, the police department is the proper agency for enforcing the law. If Mr. Gibbons' crowd needs protection the police are the people to see."[12]

That line about seeking police protection surely made Gibbons smile. But even if it had been available, neither side really needed such protection now. Once back in town, Gibbons had been busy offstage. First, he persuaded the owners of the idled cab companies to meet with their drivers and urge them to give up the wildcat. (One of these owners, the Laclede Cab Co.'s Alfonso J. Cervantes, a rising young member of the Politicians faction of the city's Democratic Party and a sometime Gibbons ally, would be elected mayor in 1965.) Second, he recruited Teamsters from other locals to drive taxis as strikebreakers. The possibility of losing their jobs for good may have intimidated the strikers even more than goons swinging baseball bats. Hearing this news, the rebel ranks began to crumble. By Wednesday morning, August 29, eleven days after the wildcat's start, large numbers of strikers were ripping up their picket signs and trudging back to work.

Within twenty-four hours it was all over. Don Cortor, the wildcat's leader, announced that the Taxi Drivers Welfare Association, the strikers' alternative union, would be disbanded. He advised drivers to return to Teamsters Local 405.

On the same day Pete Saffo, who had meanwhile become secretary-treasurer (and thus boss) of Joint Council 13, declared that strike leaders would go on trial before the council on charges of "conduct detrimental to the union." If found guilty, they faced possible expulsion from the union. "We cannot let them get away with a wildcat walkout," Saffo told reporters.[13]

Cortor said he doubted he would ever drive another St. Louis cab.

* * *

Nor did he. Two years later, in September 1958, during hearings in Washington, D.C., Cortor told the McClellan Committee that he had undergone trials at several different levels of the Teamsters Union, beginning with that conducted by Joint Council 13, which found him guilty, and concluding in 1957 with one run by the international itself, in which his last appeal was denied and he was formally expelled.

Cortor was called to testify about the St. Louis cab wildcat because the committee's chief counsel, Robert Kennedy, had taken a strong dislike to Jimmy Hoffa, whom he saw as a crook, and because Gibbons, who had by then become Hoffa's right-hand man, simply had to be a crook himself, at least as Kennedy saw it. Cortor was called to provide evidence against Gibbons.

Gibbons did not come out of these hearings well. For one thing Kennedy, in taking Cortor through an account of the wildcat, did so in a manner that allowed him to play down the racial angle. Cortor said the white drivers refused to integrate their union local for reasons that, although perhaps not entirely virtuous, were economic rather than racist (to safeguard their monopoly of white taxicab passengers), and also to protest what they saw as Gibbons' tyranny. "Were you objecting to having colored drivers?" Kennedy asked. "No," said Cortor. "I have never in my life raised my voice on integration, either in the cab industry or anything else."[14]

Kennedy subpoenaed Joe Costello and asked him a series of questions that were as thoroughly unfriendly as those asked of Cortor were friendly. Costello took the Fifth Amendment on every one. Kennedy probably preferred it that way. His questions were pointed enough in themselves to convincingly paint Costello as a member of St. Louis' criminal underworld.

And Costello's name came up frequently of course when, eight days later, Gibbons appeared before the committee himself. Soon after the session began, Kennedy asked him whether he had during the taxi strike "condoned the hiring of these gangsters and hoodlums to patrol the streets of St. Louis."

Gibbons, assuming (or pretending to assume) that Kennedy was referring to the Teamsters assigned to cruise the streets protecting cabbies loyal to the union, hotly denied they were hoodlums. "Look at the list," he told Kennedy. "There are four pages of them. You can check them. I question whether you will find any of them with a police record. They are all rank and filers, right off the trucks, garages, and warehouses."[15]

But Kennedy wasn't interested in rank and filers. He had a list of his own, one very likely provided by Chief of Detectives Chapman. Kennedy's list was of thirteen hard cases whom *Costello* had sent into the streets at the strike's start. Heading it were the names of Louis Shoulders, Jr., (son of the crooked police lieutenant in the Greenlease case) and William "Shotgun" Sanders, both of whom were suspected murderers.[16] The other eleven names were almost as notorious.

Worse was to come. It turned out that Costello had *billed* Gibbons for the thugs' time. (The amount was $2,900, or roughly $223 per thug.) And that Gibbons had paid it. And that Kennedy had learned about both the billing and the payment. Gibbons was clearly embarrassed by the association with his gangster benefactor. "It was only after the thing was going that Joe Costello asked me to reimburse him for the money," he told the committee. "I even talked to my attorneys, [asking] do they have a legal claim on our union."[17]

We don't know what the lawyers said concerning Costello's legal claim, but his moral claim, even with the suspected murderers thrown in, might have given them something to ponder. Gibbons had been the protector of African American taxi drivers since the end of World War II, when, because no other union would accept them as members, he brought them into the warehouse workers' organization. And now he had forced the integration of Local 405. Aside from the cabbies themselves, few white people noticed. But African Americans did. When, some years later, Gibbons came under fire for other reasons, the publisher of the *St. Louis Argus*, a black weekly, reminded his readers that, whatever his other sins, the union leader "practiced what he preached.... For what the Teamsters did in the hiring of Negro cab drivers on regular lines, alone, Gibbons is due a note of confidence."[18]

Without Costello's help, however, Gibbons might not have pulled it off.

Why did Costello do it? Surely not for the $2,900, or even for the twelve-day monopoly his Ace Cab Co. enjoyed while the other taxi firms were paralyzed by the strike. Like other outlaws, he may have been one of those socially conservative people who are offended by irregular phenomena like wildcatting. Or he may have simply taken a dislike to Don Cortor. So far as is known, Costello never discussed his motives for helping break the taxi wildcat. He may not have been clear about them himself. Although not yet fifty, he had only six years more to live. His alcoholic disintegration was increasingly apparent to everyone around him. "He was buying Scotch by the case," an acquaintance remembered. "He called me one time to play golf with him and Vitale. That was okay, but it was three in the morning when he called.

"You could see the decline in the man."[19]

Costello's actions in the wildcat remain a mystery. We must content ourselves with the thought that the unjust sometimes become agents of justice. And that, when the story of desegregation in St. Louis is finally written, Joe Costello should get at least a paragraph of his own.

14

"Vertical Improvement"

Jake McCarthy went to work for Gibbons in 1954, a year after the Wortman episode. He was then twenty-eight. After wartime service in the Navy, McCarthy had spent a year in Greenwich Village trying to write a novel. When the novel refused to jell, he returned to his hometown to edit the Catholic archdiocese's tabloid newspaper, the *St. Louis Register*. "One day in early 1954," he recalled, "I was having lunch in this bar and ran into Jack Walsh, the archbishop's public relations man. He told me Harold Gibbons was looking for someone to do PR."[1]

Gibbons was. The Teamster leader hoped to at least soften the effect of the charges that Max Goldschein's federal grand jury was expected to level against him and Local 688. "In those days the United Auto Workers was the only union that understood public relations," said McCarthy. Gibbons, who admitted that he knew nothing about PR, had nonetheless seen how successfully it had been employed by corporations to augment their power in the postwar world, and he concluded that trade unions had no choice but to use it too.

Young McCarthy, a six-four giant of a man, had the brief nose and long upper lip that once immediately marked a person as Irish. He knew little more about PR than Gibbons did. His maiden effort for Local 688 was an expensive full-page ad extolling the union's civic-mindedness. The ad appeared in the city's newspapers in early March 1954.[2] Unfortunately the ad's layout was so crowded—it featured, along with a half-dozen photos of warehousemen and -women performing good deeds, explanatory lines of text set in type so small as to be nearly illegible—that it may have repelled more readers than it attracted. In any case, the ad's message couldn't begin to compete with the big, clear headlines that the grand jury would dish up concerning labor racketeering—and do so on the front pages of those same papers, day after day, throughout that spring.

Whatever mild good will McCarthy's ad did inspire must have seemed uneconomical to his new employer, because it wasn't used again.

McCarthy's next big promotion, in April 1955, was an evening of boxing. Sponsored by Joint Council 13, the event, held at the city's Kiel Opera House on Market Street, was to raise money for the National Polio Foundation. Pete Saffo and Barney Baker (of all people) served as "co-chairmen." Two pairs of welterweights were the headliners. But the star attraction turned out to be Ruby Goldstein, a man who, in an era when prizefights were broadcast in prime time on network television two evenings a week, was the nation's best-known ring referee. A New Yorker who happened to be visiting St. Louis that week, Goldstein agreed to work one of the preliminary bouts in return for the $18.60 he needed to buy the striped shirt and black shoes required for the job. Goldstein's prelim, an eight-round match, included a local heavyweight named Sonny Liston. The future champion hadn't hitherto shown much promise. ("He is big and powerful but has lacked fire in the ring," noted the *Post-Dispatch*'s boxing writer.)[3] On this night, though, he demolished his opponent. Goldstein and Liston made the Teamster fights the talk of the town.

The union's charity evenings became an annual event. When boxing's popularity began to wane in the early 1960s, the prizefighters gave way to singers and comics. Jimmy Durante headlined the '63 affair, which, along with a briefer boxing card, featured George Jessel, George Raft, and a young rock-and-roller named Bobby Rydell.

One charity receiving money from these events was Dismas House, an abandoned North Side school that the criminal-defense lawyer Morris Shenker and a Jesuit priest named Charles Dismas Clark had turned into a halfway house for ex-convicts. Perhaps the most famous of the Teamster shows, a 1965 extravaganza featuring Frank Sinatra, Dean Martin, and Sammy Davis, Jr., then known in the fan-magazine press as the "Rat Pack," dedicated its gate to this project.

But we're getting ahead of ourselves here. Jake McCarthy in the mid–'50s became Gibbons' ghostwriter as well as his impresario. Eloquent though the Teamster boss could be on a speaker's platform, he fell dumb when confronted by a typewriter. "He was very well-read, but couldn't write a lick," McCarthy recalled.[4]

McCarthy filled a serious need. By the middle 1950s Gibbons had become something of a public figure on the national level (though a villain to many St. Louisans). He was an early member of Americans for Democratic Action, then well known as an organization of socialist and near-socialist intellectuals of the 1930s who had reconstituted themselves in the postwar world as anti–Communist liberals—as indeed the left wing of the Democratic Party. (Its members included Eleanor Roosevelt, the historian Arthur Schlesinger, Jr., and the economist John Kenneth Galbraith.) ADAers and their friends admired such Gibbons innovations as the Labor Health Institute;

they began inviting him to give talks at their meetings and write articles for their magazines. Hence the need for a ghostwriter. For years McCarthy turned out speeches, lectures, articles, even letters over Gibbons' signature. Before long, Gibbons was routinely described in the press as the "egghead Teamster." As Elizabeth Vasquez has said, "The ideas were always Father's but the speeches and articles probably came from Jake."[5]

Gibbons and McCarthy became friends. They were two bright men who shared a particular political outlook: socialism as refracted through an Irish-American Catholic background. (McCarthy's father sold real estate, but his grandfather, with whom he preferred to identify himself, had been a streetcar conductor—indisputably a proletarian.)[6] And they both liked to drink. Pete Saffo and Dick Kavner went home to their families at the workday's end. But Gibbons, as his son Larry has said, "was out until the bars closed almost every night. Everybody in the St. Louis nightlife knew Father, and he knew them."[7] McCarthy, who could be combative in print but in the flesh possessed a rare generous willingness to consider the opinions of others, also enjoyed the saloon world. He must have been restful company for his employer.

Gibbons on his nightly rounds was unencumbered by the mores of Kirkwood. When Larry Gibbons became a college student he would sometimes be allowed to accompany his father. "We'd start around eight with a couple drinks, then we'd go to dinner," he recalled. "We'd have a big dinner, with wine, and sherry afterward. Then, around ten or eleven, we'd go drinking seriously." Moving from club to club, father and son would trade drinks with gamblers, entertainers, politicians, and other insomniacs. Finally, at four or five o'clock in the morning, they would arrive for breakfast at the Chase Hotel. "After that, Father might look at his watch and say, 'What the hell, it's too late to go to bed now—let's just head for the golf course.' And we'd go out and play golf till dark."

"It was tough trying to hang out with Father because he could drink as much as two normal men and never get drunk," said Larry. "The number of men who became alcoholic working for him is legend, and I think Jake McCarthy may have been one of those."[8]

* * *

Liquor aside, Larry's story suggests that Gibbons—with his mornings on the golf course, breakfasts at the Chase, etc.—had begun living beyond his means. In 1957 he was making $15,000 a year as secretary-treasurer of Local 688, about three times the national average and considerably more than the $120 (salary plus expenses) per week he had pulled down as chief of St. Louis' warehouse union in the old RWDSU a decade earlier.[9]

Still, circumstances had changed in that decade, and Gibbons helped force the changes. In what seems to have been the first article about him in a national magazine, the author noted the St. Louisan's efforts against racism and then went on to add: "Although interested in unions as a twenty-four-hour-a-day social force, Gibbons knows that union leaders do not live by social work alone. Progress has been achieved through acquiring power and using it. As head of 40,000 Teamsters in the $400,000,000-a-year wholesaling business here, he can put pressure on the life-lines of many businesses. His union's decision to respect—or not to respect—picket lines of other unions can make or break strikes. When he strikes, he strikes for the jugular."[10]

The forty thousand Teamsters mentioned were those belonging to the sixteen local unions represented by Joint Council 13 (including the ten thousand members of Local 688, the council's largest). As the council's president Gibbons must have sometimes harked back to the J. H. Grady strike of 1948, which his warehouse union had lost because it couldn't persuade truck drivers to cease delivering the horsehide and cork that Grady needed to manufacture baseballs. Now he was the leader of both the city's warehousemen *and* its truck drivers—a figure of consequence in St. Louis' economy.

He was a consequential figure also in its politics. According to a *Globe-Democrat* article of 1956, "Politicians fear Gibbons because he is on the way to becoming the most powerful among them. As to his political potential, one shrewd observer said, "Give me Gibbons and Local 688, and you can have the rest of the Democratic organization—Jack Dwyer [then the party chairman], Tony Sestric [an influential alderman], the whole lot. Gibbons is the man to watch."[11]

Gibbons had become an important man.

"He was a *conceited* man," the former congressman William L. Clay, a sometime ally, sometime rival, said several years ago.[12] Elizabeth Vasquez, Gibbons' daughter, thinking of her father's boyhood back in Archbald Patch, put it a little differently. She said, "Daddy was driven by a need to succeed and be recognized, and not be a poor, ragamuffin coal camp kid."[13]

The coal-camp ragamuffin blossomed in the late '50s. He became known as not only the most intellectual but also the best-dressed labor leader in America. The chic look did not come painlessly. "Father was very self-conscious," Larry Gibbons said. "He once went to a negotiating session wearing a sport coat he had just bought for afternoons at the racetrack—a brown and white check. It was so flashy and cool-looking, he thought. But then he looked around the table and saw that everyone else had on either black or dark blue. From that day on he never bought anything but a charcoal gray or navy blue suit."[14]

The new clothes were expensive. Elizabeth Vasquez remembers a friend of her mother's once asking, "How is it that your husband is so fabulously dressed? You don't dress like that." "The family," replied Ann Gibbons, "can only afford one peacock."[15]

Ann may not have known it, but the family wasn't paying for even that one peacock. Of course neither were Local 688's members nor the employers with which the local negotiated contracts. Jimmy Hoffa saw nothing wrong with running sideline businesses, some of which worked against his own members' best interests.[16] Gibbons didn't do things like that, and as a result he would eventually die, if not quite poor, then in modest circumstances compared to some other trade-union leaders. Asked on one occasion about his stock portfolio, he replied, "I never wanted a portfolio, never had a portfolio, never intend to have a portfolio."[17] And he meant it. What Gibbons did have, though, especially as he came into increasingly important offices in the IBT, was expense accounts. He always argued that the fine clothes, gourmet dinners, nights in fancy hotels, etc., were necessary because they put him on an equal footing with the executives and politicians he dealt with, and that, moreover, he must "expense" the luxuries involved because he couldn't afford them on his own. But even his defenders agreed that Gibbons went far beyond reason in this case. By the early 1970s, when he was near the top of the IBT hierarchy, he was claiming more in reimbursement for expenses than all of his brother hierarchs combined.[18]

Ann Gibbons feared that her husband was hastening after false gods. "Mother didn't like the jet-set sort of executive lifestyle that Daddy took on when he started to rise," said Elizabeth Vasquez. "She didn't see any need for vertical improvement."[19]

Pricey wining and dining weren't the only problems. "Gibbons had a way with women," said Ted Schafers, the *Globe-Democrat* reporter. "He was a big, good-looking guy who stayed in good shape."[20] He attracted pretty women and they responded. As far back as 1950, a former RWDSU colleague had told the FBI that "Gibbons has the reputation of being 'crazy about women' and of being of poor moral character in this regard."[21] Gibbons' affairs were no secret among his friends. Sid Lens, his old RWDSU pal, recalled that "once at a party at our apartment Gibbons literally had to sneak out a back door to escape a woman who was begging him to take her away from her husband."[22] When Elizabeth Vasquez was fourteen or so, someone told her that her father had been seen in the company of a Hollywood actress named Linda Darnell. Gibbons took his daughter aside and tried to explain the situation. "'You might hear about my having dates with women,'" she remembered him saying. "'If you do, I want you to know it means nothing to me. I love your mother. It's just that sometimes I have to go to social functions, but your mother doesn't like them, so I ask other women to go with me instead.'"[23]

Elizabeth Vasquez, musing on her parents' relationship, told the writer Steven Brill, "As close as they were, sexual fidelity, at least on his part, was not part of the marriage contract. There's no use kidding about that."[24]

14. "Vertical Improvement" 141

Ann and Harold Gibbons (second and third from left) at a union party, 1953. Photograph by Edward H. Goldberger, 559.56, State Historical Society of Missouri, Photography Collection.

Vasquez maintained that her father's adulteries had no particularly deleterious effect on her mother. In 1957, however, Ann Gibbons underwent a lengthy hospital stay for depression. ("Frankly," writes David Salmon, who had befriended Ann and, as a result, became increasingly disenchanted with Gibbons, "I felt that he needed the treatment more than she.")[25] "She was never really the same after that," said Vasquez. "She lost her confidence about dealing with the outside world."[26]

The outside world wasn't being kind to her. The FBI, which had quit watching Gibbons in the late '40s, when he turned out not to be a communist after all, took him up again in the late '50s when he became known as an associate of Jimmy Hoffa's. Agents went through five years of Gibbons' income tax returns. They interviewed his auto dealer, his banker, his real estate agent (learning, for example, that Gibbons was making $86.96 monthly mortgage payments on the Kirkwood house he had bought in 1952.) J. Edgar Hoover, the FBI's chief, sent men to grill people living near the family's new home on Altus Place. Be careful, he warned them. "It may be noted that Mrs. Gibbons has reportedly been subject to 'breakdowns' in the past," Hoover wrote in a memo, "and it would be most embarrassing to the Bureau if neighborhood gossip were to arise as a result of your contacts which might be seized upon by Gibbons and others allied with him as an excuse for criticizing the Bureau's operations."[27]

In later years Ann rarely left home except to go to the grocery store or the hairdresser's. She had not been enthusiastic about moving to Kirkwood in the first place. Now if she went outdoors she risked encountering neighbors who might have been discussing her and her husband with FBI agents. "Her world became completely relegated to books," Vasquez said. "She really sort of retrenched."[28]

The critic Irving Howe, writing about the adulteries of the early American socialist Eugene Victor Debs, suggested that "perhaps anyone who leads opposition minority movements must bear so much pressure that it causes internal cracks of character or aggravates those already present."[29] Although she may have had fissures of her own, Ann Gibbons was clearly a casualty of her husband's "internal cracks of character."

* * *

Gibbons continued in the late '50s to expand his union's benefits package. Local 688 bought three hundred acres of rolling land outside the small town of Pevely, Missouri, thirty miles south of St. Louis. On that property in 1958 the local opened a summer camp that provided its members with low-cost sleeping quarters, a cafeteria, a swimming pool, a lake for fishing and boating, and a nine-hole golf course. Gibbons, tying it to the Labor Health Institute's medical insurance program, talked employers into financing the camp's operation. "Many of our members were from the slums," he said. "I saw the health-and-recreation camp as the only way to get their kids some fresh air and a decent place to play."[30]

But the grandest expression of what David Salmon has called his boss' "edifice complex" took shape several years after the Pevely camp was established.[31] Gibbons had in 1955 moved his union's headquarters from its downtown Pine Street location several miles west to a six-story office building on South Kingshighway Boulevard. This structure—called the "Magic Chef Building" after its former tenant, a stove manufacturer—cost Local 688 a million dollars. But the Magic Chef Building was itself but a way station. In 1960, at Gibbons' instigation, Joint Council 13 formed something called the Council Plaza Redevelopment Corporation, which body, after buying a large parcel of land at the west end of the now-desolate Mill Creek Valley—the decaying neighborhoods from which the city, in its drive for "urban renewal," had evicted thousands of poor black people (see Chapter 8)—proceeded to launch an urban renewal project of its own.

14. "Vertical Improvement"   143

Teamsters Council Plaza, as the project was called, would cost considerably more than the Magic Chef's million, but because its financing was so complex, its lenders so numerous, and the lawsuits it eventually inspired so densely thicket-like, we can't even now say how much more it was.

Council Plaza was a village—a bit of socialist Scandinavia (at least as Gibbons and his friends imagined it) set down at the junction of South Grand and Forest Park. The Plaza boasted an office building for Local 688 and the other Teamster locals, another building for the Labor Health Institute, a pharmacy, restaurant, beauty salon, barber shop, bakery, dry cleaners, underground parking garage, even a gas station. Its permanent residents—as opposed to those who merely held day jobs there—were the six hundred elderly inhabitants of a pair of apartment towers, the Plaza's showpiece. Gibbons regarded most retiree complexes as "high-rise deep freezes." But Plaza residents enjoyed shopping expeditions, evenings at the theater, tickets to baseball and hockey games. "It's not just brick and stone," said Gibbons. "We've created a way of living. These old people are really vibrant—they're busy as bees. They've got floor delegates and trash committees and transportation committees and painting classes and they run their own show."[32] "Most services are manned on a volunteer basis by the residents," explained a Local 688 report. "No resident serves less than two hours a week in volunteer services."[33] In other words, the Plaza's old folks couldn't have lived deep-frozen lives even if they had wanted to.

These were Local 688's mellow years. A retired truck driver who joined the local during this period said,

> Man, I used to love to go down to Council Plaza. It even *looked* pretty. The sun would hit those towers and they' d just shine.
> There was the LHI—it paid all your medical expenses. The pharmacy. The restaurant. I used to go to shop stewards' meetings in the restaurant. 688 was big on meetings. There was a three- dollar fine if you missed a meeting. They wouldn't push hard to collect the fine, but if somewhere down the road you decided you wanted to file a grievance against your company, somebody would say, "Well, I see you've been missing a few meetings." They'd file your grievance but wouldn't work it too hard, if you know what I mean. But I didn't mind the meetings. I liked getting together with the guys. The beer was free. And it gave you a chance to get out of the house.[34]

But Gibbons' socialist village had problems from its start. Although Gibbons had hoped to bring all the offices of Joint Council 13's member unions into the headquarters building (hence the name Council Plaza), most of the big locals insisted on remaining where they were, scattered around the metropolitan area. Among the refuseniks were the cement truck drivers, the over-the-road freight drivers, the local freight drivers, the beer truck drivers, and the dairy products drivers. They pleaded poverty, citing the Plaza's high rents. But in fact, writes David Salmon, "the leaders of these locals were most reluctant to come under Gibbons' tutelage."[35]

Nor was the Plaza the only place where Gibbons ran into resistance.

"Nobody loves a rich uncle," he liked to say.[36] The more successful and powerful Gibbons became, the more enemies he made—including some among St. Louis' Teamsters. This was especially true of Teamster truck drivers, who traditionally looked down on their warehouseman brothers, and of many of the drivers' leaders, who believed that one of them, not the warehouseman Harold Gibbons, should be running Joint Council 13.

In 1957 the council was released from the trusteeship in which Dave Beck, prompted by Jimmy Hoffa, had placed it during the invasion by the Buster Wortman gang four years before. Gibbons, who had been serving as the trustee, scheduled a date in early January '58 for the election of a slate of council officers. The voting was to be done by the half-dozen or so officers of each of the council's thirteen member locals. Gibbons announced his candidacy for the post of council president, expecting to win easily. He was in for a shock.

His opponent was Eugene Walla, president of Local 682, the cement drivers whom Gibbons had led to victory in the bitter construction strike of 1953. A popular, colorful figure—he wore cowboy hats and drove a Cadillac whose hood ornament was a pair of actual Texas long horns—Walla quickly pulled together an anti–Gibbons coalition of surprising strength. Gibbons estimated that he would beat Walla by at least thirty votes. And just to be safe, the night before the election he wined and dined several dozen prospective voters at one of the city's most expensive restaurants. "I had the thing signed, sealed, and delivered," he told the McClellan Committee a few months afterward. Wrong.

"I lost," he confessed. "I didn't collect on those votes. These are people who ate the food and didn't deliver."[37]

Actually, Gibbons didn't lose. He did defeat Walla in the end, but only barely, with the help of votes furnished by a Florida-based carnival workers' union that the prescient Jimmy Hoffa had gerrymandered into the St. Louis joint council just before the polling began. The carnival workers cast six votes. Six was the margin Gibbons won by.[38]

* * *

Dramatic though some of these local struggles were, they probably got less of Gibbons' time than did Hoffa's own campaign for the IBT presidency. The Detroit man was then relatively unknown outside his own Central Conference, which was good in a way because it gave Gibbons and Jake McCarthy, his PR specialist, a blank slate to write on. McCarthy devoted some time in 1955 to composing a brief biography of Hoffa that was distributed throughout the international as a pamphlet. Gibbons, probably helped by academic friends from Americans for Democratic Action, arranged for the high school dropout Hoffa to deliver a lecture at Harvard on the economics of trucking.[39] In April 1956 Gibbons and McCarthy organized a hundred-dollar-a-plate dinner in Detroit at which Hoffa was the guest of honor. The diners were some of that city's political and business elite. They presented Hoffa with a check for $265,000, which he then turned over to a representative of the state of Israel, who announced that the money would be used to build an orphanage in that country.

"Harold Gibbons, suave St. Louis Teamsters boss, and the public relations men were trying to create a new image of Hoffa," writes an unfriendly but not inaccurate Hoffa biographer. "The picture of a brawling associate of the underworld would not do for what they had in mind. The new Hoffa was presented as a humanitarian, a broad-minded student of world transportation problems, a man of deep insight into international politics."[40] Hoffa himself was amused by the effort. "For once I'm going to be a Boy Scout," he said.[41]

The Israel connection was probably Gibbons' idea. (Hoffa, as he himself never hesitated to point out, had no interest in any country but the United States.) Although its popular image in the West would begin to darken with the Suez Canal crisis that autumn, Israel in early '56 was still widely seen as a brave little European socialist outpost besieged by angry, unenlightened Arabs. And who could oppose the building of an orphanage?

In August a group of Hoffa supporters flew to Tel Aviv to lay the cornerstone of the planned James R. Hoffa Home for Children. A newspaper photo found among Gibbons' papers shows the twenty-nine junketeers posing for a group shot just before they boarded their plane. Among them are Hoffa; his seventeen-year-old daughter Barbara; Gibbons; Dick Kavner; Nick Blassie, the head of St. Louis' meat cutters' union and a political ally of Gibbons'; Allen Dorfman, described in the cutline as an "insurance executive," but in fact the middleman between Hoffa's Central States Pension Fund and Chicago's Outfit; and, in the back row, towering above the others (above even Gibbons) a person whom the cutline identifies as "John J. McCarthy, public relations director, Joint Council 13."[42]

Also aboard was one Hank Greenspun, publisher of the *Las Vegas Sun*. The trip to Israel got big play in the *Sun* (though apparently nowhere else, if the absence of other news clippings among Gibbons' papers is a clue), which was appropriate since the paper's namesake city was soon to receive great infusions of investment capital from the Central States Pension Fund. A page of pictures in the *Sun* shows Hoffa being thanked for his gift orphanage by various Israeli dignitaries, one of them an unsmiling Golda Meir, then foreign minister. According to one of McCarthy's press releases, Hoffa on leaving Israel would not head straight back to Detroit but, instead, "spend several weeks conferring with European trade union leaders in Rome, Paris and London."[43]

It all sounded very un–Hoffalike. Which was of course the whole point. For, a year later, in October 1957, officers of the nation's seven hundred Teamster locals gathered in Miami Beach to elect a new international president. Hoffa was the leading candidate. He was no longer unknown: Robert Kennedy and the McClellan Committee had in the previous months done their best to make him appear a public menace, a threat even to national security (see Chapter 15). The question now was whether that image would sink his chances for election to the IBT's presidency. Hoffa flew down to Florida fearing the worst.

Ted Schafers, who was in town to cover the convention for the *St. Louis Globe-Democrat*, caught a peek into Hoffa's state of mind. Hoping for a news story late one night, Schafers went up to Gibbons' room in the Eden Roc Hotel, the convention's headquarters. "I knocked on the door and Gibbons said to come in," Schafers recalled. "I go in and I find Gibbons on one twin bed and some broad on another." Gibbons sent the woman away. He and Schafers began talking. Then, "there's another knock. It's Hoffa. He comes storming in, furious, complaining about some guys who'd promised to support him but were now having second thoughts. He doesn't see me at first because I'm standing behind the door. Then he sees me. 'Who's this fuckin' guy?' he asks Gibbons. Gibbons calmly says that I'm a newspaper reporter from St. Louis. 'A *reporter!*' screeches Hoffa, and barrels out of the room even madder than when he came in."[44]

Hoffa had good reasons for being on edge. Outsiders like Robert Kennedy expected the vote to be a Soviet-style plebiscite, but they were mistaken. Gibbons and McCarthy, who were running Hoffa's campaign from the Eden Roc's lobby, knew that their man, whose delegate support was based in the Midwest and South, faced strong opposition from the two coasts, especially from big locals in New York City, New Jersey, California, and the Pacific Northwest.[45] In the end Hoffa received 1,208 votes as against 453 that were split among three other candidates. But the margin was deceiving. Many delegates, not entirely comfortable with Hoffa but unable to come together on a single opponent, wound up voting for the Detroit man after all.[46] McCarthy snorted at suggestions that the election was rigged. "If it was, I don't know why all of us in Gibbons' entourage worked so hard in that convention—leaflets, buttons, signs, autographed photographs, delegation charts in campaign headquarters rating Hoffa's votes against his three opponents [he said]. Gibbons and I wrote Hoffa's acceptance speech in an all-night session after the winning vote. If it was rigged, it would have been so much easier to write that speech at home and bring it to Miami Beach with us."[47]

Neither Gibbons' and McCarthy's efforts to make their client appear a great humanitarian, nor, on the other hand, Kennedy's to portray him as evil incarnate, appear to have figured much in Hoffa's triumph. Nor did the leaflets, buttons, signs, etc., distributed on the convention floor. Hoffa's Central Conference was by far the biggest and most populous of the IBT's four divisions, and members of the local unions constituting the conference, having prospered because of the contracts Hoffa had negotiated for them, remained solidly on his side (in St. Louis, for example, all fifty-five of the votes allotted to Joint Council 13 went to him).[48] That fact, plus the indecisiveness of his opponents, settled the issue in his favor.

President-elect Hoffa was bound for Washington. And Gibbons was going along.

15

Gibbons Goes to Washington

In January 1958 Jimmy Hoffa moved into what had been Dave Beck's presidential suite in the Teamsters Union's headquarters building at 25 Louisiana Avenue in Washington. Harold Gibbons, elected a vice president at the Miami Beach convention, took over a large adjoining office as Hoffa's executive officer.

The two men also moved into Beck's former Washington home: a large, $30-a-day apartment (expensive at the time) in the Woodner Hotel, overlooking the city's Rock Creek Park. John Bartlow Martin of the *Saturday Evening Post* visited them there one day. They were, he said, an "odd pair, Hoffa the bread-and-butter unionist, Gibbons the onetime Socialist. If they have a free evening, Gibbons is likely to sit up reading, Hoffa to watch television for an hour, then go to bed."[1]

Being the driven personalities they were, however, Hoffa and Gibbons spent far more time at 25 Louisiana than at the Woodner. Only three years old, the IBT building was Beck's baby. For much of the previous half-century the IBT had been directed from a cramped room in Indianapolis, which, in seasons when the treasuries of both AFL unions were thin, Beck's predecessor, Dan Tobin, had shared with John L. Lewis, president of the United Mine Workers. But Teamsters fortunes had since greatly improved. The new headquarters advertised the union's growing power and wealth. Ralph and Estelle James, whom Hoffa allowed to shadow him for six months in the early '60s, described the building as follows:

> Hoffa's glittering, white, five-story Washington headquarters is appropriately nicknamed the Teamsters' "marble palace." ... Elaborately decorated, the structure equals the most ostentatious corporate headquarters, with movie theater, penthouse terrace, private bathrooms and showers, plush carpets (one inch thick in the Executive suite), custom-designed drapes with the Teamsters' team and wheel emblem, finely carved furniture, wood paneling, and beautiful secretaries.... Hoffa's office provides a magnificent view of the Capitol, and boasts a 48-button intercom, private elevator, built-in TV-Hi-Fi and bar, and a full set of McClellan Committee hearings.

Hoffa added to Beck's Marble Palace a small gym and worked out there regularly. He encouraged staff members, especially the "more protuberant" among them, to use it but on most days he was the only person to do so.[2]

Like Gibbons, Hoffa wanted staffers who could "open an envelope." That wish evidently excluded associates from his own Local 299 in Detroit. According to Martin, the new president encouraged Gibbons to replace "the elderly, respectable businessmen around Beck" with "a hard-driving crowd that may produce profound changes in the comfortable old Teamsters Union."[3]

One early recruit was Yuki Kato, the young Japanese-American woman who had come to work for Local 688 out of a wartime "relocation" camp in Arkansas. "Gibbons told me I was going to go to Washington to be Mr. Hoffa's secretary," she recalled. "'I am?' I said. Well, I didn't have any roots in St. Louis, so I went along with him to Washington."[4]

Kato had for years been the keeper of Gibbons' secrets. "Yuki," writes David Salmon, "was the most likely person to know just where Gibbons actually was—and not where he was scheduled to be. She did not easily give away his location unless the reason was really important. She was far more aware of his movements than his wife Ann. She strove to protect him from other people, but not from himself."[5] A tiny, pretty, dryly unsentimental woman, Kato now began to do the same for Hoffa. "Hoffa was very good to me," she said. "He let me have the run of the place. Of course I never asked questions. I never repeated what I saw."

She liked Hoffa, and he seems to have liked and respected her. The Teamster boss was notoriously rough on subordinates. "But not me," said Kato. "He was the nicest guy to me. He wouldn't let anyone cuss in front of me. I remember the first meeting we had when they took over the international from Dave Beck. Here's this room full of Teamsters, and me the only woman there. Hoffa told them: 'Watch your language.'"[6]

Hoffa may also have respected Jake McCarthy, who came along to Washington to handle public relations, but he had little use for McCarthy's trade. Hoffa, McCarthy later said, considered public relations "so much hooey."[7] But it wasn't just PR that came between them. "Jake had a very difficult time getting along with Hoffa," recalled Kato. "With Hoffa you could not be negative, could not disagree with him to his face. Gibbons knew how to get around him. But Jake didn't. He'd come right out with it."[8]

McCarthy lasted three years in the Marble Palace. He resigned in 1961 "not because I thought Hoffa was corrupt as charged, but because he was too damn tough to work for. He could be severely abusive, especially in front of his fawning cronies. But when I left him he said, 'Thanks for everything,' and I could see in those piercing eyes and flexing muscles a desire to communicate some deep human feeling. I was sorry he never learned to do that."[9] McCarthy believed that Hoffa had been crippled by his upbringing, by his family's poverty and the savagery of industrial Detroit, and that as a result he was seriously deficient in trust and generosity. McCarthy later became a newspaper columnist. He wrote often about Hoffa, never failing to praise the latter's gifts as a labor leader, defending even his tactical alliance with Chicago's Outfit. "Hoffa could never control Chicago, still the nerve center of the mob, so he played his own political game in that town," McCarthy wrote in 1975. "The Central States Pension Fund, created by Hoffa, became a billion-dollar gold mine that a lot of shady faces had their eyes on. Some of them made money off finders' fees, insurance premiums and other things that good guys also get. Hoffa always said that if it was good enough for businessmen, it was good enough for his friends. But it never got looted, like Penn Central."[10]

Of Hoffa the man, however, McCarthy had had his fill. One evening in 1976, after downing several drinks, McCarthy remarked to a visitor something he would never have said in public. "Hoffa," he said, "had this deep need to make everyone around him feel like shit."[11]

Hoffa never bothered to hide his irascibility. According to Ralph and Estelle James, whom the IBT president allowed to closely observe him at work over a period of ninety days in 1961–62, "Hoffa's temper is the irrational, unsystematic part of his personality, a weakness which he seems unable or unwilling to correct. After a bad outburst he often says, in semi-apology to those around him, 'If I can't get mad at my friends, who can I get mad at?'" (To which the Jameses add: "His accompanying but unspoken thought may be, 'Otherwise, I might be forced to get mad at myself.'")[12]

Hoffa was roughest on Dick Kavner, who had come to Washington to serve the new president as a troubleshooter. Kavner and Hoffa were in many ways alike: They were both bright, intense, irritable, physical men. However, Kavner suppressed his irritability, etc., and tried hard to anticipate and satisfy his boss' every wish, indeed tried so hard that at one point he had to be hospitalized for exhaustion and then spent several months recuperating. Hoffa, write the Jameses, "often damned and belittled Dick Kavner, and even threatened to fire him, although Kavner was one of his brightest and hardest workers, as Hoffa boasted to others—when Kavner was not around."[13]

Gibbons had his own run-ins with Hoffa but, at least in the beginning, refused to let them get out of hand. "Gibbons had the knack of blowing it off," Yuki Kato said. "If he didn't agree with Hoffa, he'd tell him he didn't agree and then blow it off."[14]

Gibbons and Hoffa generally worked well together. Hoffa was socially awkward, suspicious, and instinctively conservative except in union matters, where he was a daring strategist. He was, as he liked to say, a meat-and-potatoes trade unionist, AFL to the core. Aside from his wife and children he had no interests but the IBT and his own role as its president. Gibbons, on the other hand, radiated an air of urbane, openhanded liberality. Hoffa felt most at ease with people like himself. Gibbons, according to his lieutenant David Salmon, had an "ability to adopt the speech and gesture patterns of almost any cultural group. He was comfortable in the in the company of workers, scholars, attorneys, preachers, street people, foreigners, and eventually the entertainment world. He learned to fit in far better than most union leaders."[15] Gibbons was frequently sent out to calm waters that Hoffa had roiled.

Gibbons was also valuable to his boss as an occasional scapegoat. In 1961, when Hoffa saw that he faced certain defeat in his effort to take control of the Western Conference's pension fund, he dispatched the St. Louisan to San Francisco to make the formal pitch to the Teamster leaders gathered there. As predicted, they voted Hoffa's proposal down. Hoffa, explaining the move later said, "If you are going to lose, you might as well lose real badly; then it's easier to pick up the pieces and put them together later. That's why I sent Gibbons instead of coming myself."[16]

Prickly though Hoffa could be, Gibbons had great respect for him. He admired Hoffa's courage, shrewdness, and ability to inspire those around him. The IBT president, he said some years later, "was an intense worker who knew the union from top to bottom. His working hours and demands on his staff were difficult to keep pace with. But he had a way of handling people which made them want to make the sacrifices. We didn't have as many problems as one would think we would, taking into consideration how different we were.

"But I always contended that labor unions were a movement; Jimmy viewed them as a business."[17]

As Gibbons saw it, his mission was to change the business-union-style Teamsters into something more like a social movement. During his early years in Washington he made progress toward that goal. Besides Kavner and the other St. Louisans, Gibbons brought into the Marble Palace Larry Steinberg and Joe Konowe. Steinberg, Gibbons' best friend from his RWDSU days, was a Russian-Jewish immigrant who had become boss of the Toledo, Ohio, Teamsters. Konowe, a New Yorker, also formerly of RWDSU, had given Hoffa particular fits in the late '40s during the struggle between that union and the Detroit Teamsters. Both men now became key members of the Hoffa administration. "It has been speculated," wrote John Bartlow Martin, "that the Gibbons-Kavner-Konowe axis may turn out to be the antimob faction in the union; indeed, this may be reason that Hoffa has raised it to prominence."[18]

Martin was wrong about that. Hoffa was relatively unconcerned about mobsters in and around the IBT. But he was determined to centralize the union. Like most AFL unions the IBT was a highly autonomous organization, each local conducting its own negotiations with employers and ratifying its own contracts. Hoffa, however, planned to develop and negotiate a single contract, like those negotiated by the big CIO unions such as the Auto Workers or

Steelworkers, covering the entire nation. In 1964 the IBT would approve such a "master" contract for its truck drivers. Among its other virtues, the master contract froze out those smaller-time mobsters and racketeers—like the Buster Wortman gang in St. Louis—who, after seizing control of Teamster locals, had worked out employer agreements that profited themselves rather than the locals' members. (The master contract did little damage to big, politically entrenched mobs such as Chicago's Outfit and those in Cleveland, New York, and New Jersey.) As for the "Gibbons-Kavner-Konowe axis," that group, composed almost entirely of left-wingers from the old CIO,[19] enthusiastically supported Hoffa's master-contract drive—because it made the IBT more like the CIO.

In the beginning at least, the Gibbons group may have been even less concerned than Hoffa about the presence of mobsters in the union. They envisioned a much bigger prize. "The concept of the [IBT] is changing," Joe Konowe told Martin. "We feel that our jurisdiction is not just trucking but distribution—warehousing, wholesaling, retailing and transportation." And what would be the point of that? "I think ultimately the Teamsters will play a role in national life much as the old CIO did," Konowe continued. "We who are interested in social and political objectives think the Teamsters have the economic power that makes it a good place to achieve them."[20]

Gibbons, in a conversation he had with the NBC newsman Chet Huntley, was more specific. The St. Louisan spelled out what he would do if he were elected the IBT's president:

"He said that sometime within the first hour of his administration he would get his union, and all of organized labor, into the works it should have been engaged in for all of these years. Gibbons says that labor should have led all the rest—federal government, state government, local government, insurance companies, and foundations—in undertaking the rehabilitation of cities, slum clearance, job training, war on poverty, juvenile delinquency, beautifying America, all the rest. That evening in Chicago, Hal Gibbons said, 'Let the Teamsters have Harlem for a few years and we could transform it.'"[21]

Gibbons was talking big, of course. Not even the most left-wing of the old CIO internationals had ever entertained so sweeping a vision. On the other hand, what Gibbons said to Huntley was essentially what he'd been saying for years in speeches to college classes, political meetings, and trade-union gatherings, including IBT gatherings. Now his dream seemed to be taking solid form. The Teamsters Union, soon to have two and a half million members, had become the nation's largest. Gibbons' old RWDSU and CIO friends were now Jimmy Hoffa's palace guard. And Gibbons himself sat at Hoffa's right hand.

* * *

15. Gibbons Goes to Washington

Ralph and Estelle James, describing Hoffa's presidential office in the Marble Palace, noted its private elevator, its 48-button intercom, its TV and hi-fi sets, and its complete, thirteen-volume record of testimony before the Select Senate Committee on Improper Activities in the Labor or Management Field—the McClellan (or "rackets") Committee, as it came to be known.

The father of the McClellan Committee was a man named Clark Mollenhoff. The product of a small farm community in Iowa, Mollenhoff was reared to hate wickedness and waste. In 1941, when he was twenty, he went off to college in Des Moines intending to study law. During his trip there he happened to notice carloads of apples sitting untended on railroad sidings. Those apples, young Mollenhoff learned, were from the Yakima Valley in Washington state, where Dave Beck of the region's Teamsters Union was directing a campaign to organize the apple growers' employees. As part of that campaign Beck had urged IBT members in other parts of the country to refuse to truck the fruit to local markets. In Iowa as elsewhere, Washington apples baked in the sun.

Young Mollenhoff, instead of practicing law, went to work as a reporter for the *Des Moines Register*. He made a name for himself covering labor scandals, particularly those involving the Teamsters. In the '50s, when he was attached to the *Register*'s bureau in Washington, D.C., he often encountered Dave Beck, who by then had become president of the IBT. One such occasion stirred within him an olfactory memory of Beck's role in the apple embargo of 1941.

"Apples rotted," Mollenhoff writes.[22]

Mollenhoff had long sought a senator or congressman willing to spearhead an investigation into what he saw as widespread trade-union corruption. But he hadn't had much success. Then, in late 1956, he began focusing on, not an elected official, but Robert F. Kennedy, the younger brother of a Massachusetts senator, John F. Kennedy. Mollenhoff later wrote: "Although I badgered Bob Kennedy relentlessly, I usually did it in a half-joking manner. I taunted him by questioning his courage to take on such an investigation. At other times I prophesied such an investigation could do for him what the Kefauver crime investigation did for" the Kefauver committee's chief counsel.[23]

Robert Kennedy was then at loose ends. Joseph P. Kennedy, the family patriarch, had for years dreamed of making one of his sons president: first Joseph Jr., who unfortunately died in the war, then John. He had no such grand plans for young Robert. The latter began his career working as a lawyer for Senator Joe McCarthy's committee hunting suspected Communists in government. In the summer of 1956 he managed his brother John's brief, abortive campaign to become the Democratic Party's nominee for vice president, a prize lost, ironically, to Estes Kefauver. That fall Robert rode the campaign train of Adlai Stevenson, the Democrats' presidential candidate, but became so disillusioned with Stevenson that he wound up voting for the eventual victor, the Republican Dwight Eisenhower.[24] Following the election, at Mollenhoff's urging, Robert traveled to Seattle to review evidence turned up by reporters there that Dave Beck of the Teamsters was a crook who had been stealing from his own members.

Robert then returned home to Massachusetts for Christmas. There he broached to his gathered family the idea of organizing a congressional investigation of the IBT. His father was appalled. Joseph Kennedy hastened to remind his sons that if John were one day to be elected president on the Democratic ticket he would require the support of the trade unions. "Such an investigation would be politically dangerous," Jean Kennedy Smith recalled her father saying. "It would antagonize labor and lead to nothing. He was really, deeply emotionally opposed."[25]

For once, Robert, ordinarily a dutiful son, went against his father's wishes. Two days after Christmas he conferred with Senator John McClellan, an elderly, influential Arkansas Democrat with whom young Kennedy had developed a nearly filial relationship. Within weeks McClellan and his colleagues had set up a special ("select") Senate committee charged with investigating labor corruption. The committee began its work on January 31, 1957.

Robert Kennedy became the committee's chief counsel. John Kennedy took a seat as a committee member, "reluctantly," his brother said.[26] That reluctance made sense. John Kennedy must have known his father was right. Not only did trade unions contribute millions of dollars to Democratic candidates, but union members were the most dogged and effective of Democratic ward workers. For a Democrat running for president, attacking unions looked like suicide.

But there was one union it might be safe to hit: the Teamsters.

True, old Dan Tobin, who led the IBT through most of the first half of the century, had been a Democrat. But Dave Beck was a Republican. (See Chapter 11.) In the autumn of '56 Beck had called a press conference on the White House lawn to announce that he was endorsing Eisenhower for reelection. And Jimmy Hoffa, after a period in which he first backed one party, then the other, in 1954 endorsed the GOP candidate for senator in a Michigan election. Following what he perceived as a generational shift in American politics, toward the GOP and away from the Democrats, Hoffa went on to form "a permanent alliance with the Republican Party."[27]

Not all IBT leaders agreed with this switch. Some believed it would have been, if not more profitable, at least less risky to emulate Tobin and stick with the Democrats. "At one time we were the bosses here in Detroit and Michigan, and, truthfully, we got a lot of governors elected," recalled one longtime Hoffa associate. "We put in prosecutors, judges, and everyone else.... Then Dave Beck got mixed up with Eisenhower, so the Democrats started chopping us up because we were too ignorant to get along with them."[28]

Robert Kennedy turned out to be the biggest chopper-upper of them all. In late January 1957, not long before the McClellan Committee got under way, Kennedy and George Meany, president of the two-year-old, now-combined AFL-CIO, sat down together for a long lunch in the dining room of the Senate Office Building. "The luncheon had been arranged," Kennedy later wrote, "so that we could explain to Mr. Meany the tremendous tasks we faced and so that we could try to understand the problems that our work would create for him."[29] According to Meany's biographer, the union chief was shocked to learn of the delinquencies of the IBT's Dave Beck, which Kennedy proceeded to lay out for him. Several days later, Meany called together the AFL-CIO's executive council and persuaded it to approve a resolution condemning any union leader who took the Fifth Amendment when appearing before a court or legislative body. Beck, present as a council member and expecting to be summoned soon by the McClellan panel, "angrily attacked the resolution, screaming and bouncing in his chair for more than half an hour."[30]

Meany had perhaps been more receptive to an investigation of the Teamsters than Kennedy expected. Tides were running in the labor movement. Public opinion, generally favorable to trade unions since the '30s, had recently soured a bit in the wake of news stories, magazine pieces, and even movies (*On the Waterfront*, for example) about infiltration of some unions by mobsters. That constituted a growing public-relations problem for the new boss of the AFL-CIO. Then too, according to the historian Thomas R. Brooks, Meany was not yet secure as head of the federation and felt threatened by certain leaders of the more dynamic member internationals, such as Walter Reuther of the UAW and Beck and Hoffa of the Teamsters. Meany especially feared that Hoffa might one day split the new federation as John L. Lewis had split the old AFL twenty years earlier. "Meany, in a sense, skillfully used the corruption issue as a tool to reshape the [AFL-CIO] into his concept of what the labor movement ought to be," writes Brooks. "What kept the merger from breaking up, ironically, were the McClellan revelations, which enabled George Meany and his supporters to convert what might have been a splintering off into a casting out of devils."[31]

Officially, the McClellan Committee Hearings lasted more than three years, from January 1957 to March 1960, though in fact it ran out of evils to investigate in September 1959. The committee probed a few businesses as well as unions. (A former Wurlitzer Co. vice president admitted that his firm paid mobsters in various cities to strong-arm reluctant restaurant and tavern owners into installing Wurlitzer jukeboxes in their businesses. Wurlitzer's man in St. Louis was Buster Wortman.)[32] And the committee investigated unions other than the Teamsters: the bakers, textile workers, meat cutters. But the primary program was Robert Kennedy versus the IBT.

Kennedy was allowed by Senator McClellan, the committee's chairman, to pick both the suspected misdeeds to be investigated and the witnesses whose testimony was likely to illustrate those misdeeds. Expected to be explosively dramatic, like the Kefauver crime hearings of 1950 and the Army-McCarthy hearings of 1954, the early McClellan Committee hearings were broadcast nationwide on network television. Millions of viewers found them fascinating. "It was a good television show," recalled a Republican who served on the panel. "The whole thing was like a good show. Prospective witnesses were screened in advance, and if they didn't seem able to put on a good act, they were never allowed to appear."[33]

Dave Beck went down first.

Beck was a garrulous fat man, a giant egg with a tiny human face. Just months before, he had enjoyed a reputation as a labor statesman, the friend of presidents, a frequent guest on the Sunday-morning TV talk shows. He expected to cruise to reelection as IBT president at the fall 1957 convention (the convention at which, as we have seen, Jimmy Hoffa would take office in Beck's place). Beck's troubles began when stories appeared in the Seattle press suggesting that he was an embezzler. In March of '57 he was subpoenaed to appear before the McClellan Committee. There, angered and frightened by the ferocity of Robert Kennedy's questions, Beck looked simply awful. He tried to take cover behind the Fifth Amendment—an action which (thanks to George Meany's engineering) cost him his seat on the AFL-CIO's executive council. Soon he'd be indicted for, and then convicted of, larceny and tax evasion. In less than a year Beck was through.

Then it was Hoffa's turn. He went before the committee for four days in August. The Kennedy-Beck show had been gripping television, but the one starring Kennedy and Hoffa was still more intense. Kennedy and Hoffa had already had several noisy run-ins: put together in a room, they inevitably set each other off like small male schnauzers. But Kennedy was better-looking. As one of Hoffa's biographers puts it, the hearings were carefully constructed to show "the young, handsome, articulate Kennedy … as the crusader for good against the squat, uneducated, deceitful Hoffa."[34]

The first day was unexciting, however. The Republican committee members tried to shield Hoffa by engaging him in long, vague politico-philosophical discussions. After that, Kennedy grilled the Teamster about several shady-looking but complicated financial deals, including a failed real-estate development in Florida and a Michigan trucking company he had put in his wife's name. Not very interesting for most viewers. If the committee had continued down this track, it would have lost its TV audience overnight.

Instead, Kennedy began to focus on Hoffa's mobster connections.

Had he wished, Kennedy could have asked similar questions of a number of his own colleagues, of Senator Paul Douglas of Illinois, for instance, a man who, though as close to a saintly reformer as could be found anywhere in American politics, nonetheless believed he had no choice but to trade favors with Chicago's Democratic machine—including the Outfit, an integral cog of it—that produced the votes that kept him in the Senate.[35] However, Kennedy's quarry was Hoffa. Perhaps the most memorable of Hoffa's mob associates was a certain John Dioguardi, better known as Johnny Dio.

Not a Teamster himself, Dio was a New York hoodlum with whom Hoffa, in his pursuit of the union presidency, had plotted to take over that city's IBT joint council. Dio had a record of many arrests and at least one spell in Sing Sing. (The novelist Budd Schulberg used him as a model for the brutal longshore boss Johnny Friendly in *On the Waterfront*.) "Suave, dark and well dressed, Dio came before the Committee August 8, 1957, some two weeks before Hoffa would appear," Kennedy recalled. Dio had little to say to the McClellan panel. But one day, leaving the hearings, he was ambushed by a group of newspaper reporters. As Kennedy describes the scene, Dio "lashed out at one of the photographers. Another cameraman caught the now famous picture of him swinging, his lips curled in an angry snarl, a cigarette dangling from the corner of his mouth."[36] In that instant Dio provided an image—reproduced on TV screens and in papers and magazines across the country—that proved to be invaluable to Kennedy and the McClellan Committee.

The year 1957 signaled a change in the way Americans saw professional criminals. Until then, organized crime had been viewed as a local matter, occurring primarily in immigrant neighborhoods of big cities. Anglo-Saxon types, feeling insulated from such crimes and their perpetrators, took little interest in them. Then, on November 14, 1957, three months after Johnny Dio testified before the McClellan Committee, police in the rural village of Apalachin, New York, stumbled upon a gathering of some one hundred well-dressed, city-dwelling Italians. These men turned out to be representatives of criminal organizations across the country, apparently acting as delegates to a kind of mobsters' convention. Their discovery in Apalachin came as a shock to the public (and to the FBI's J. Edgar Hoover, who had hitherto denied the existence of a national crime syndicate). The terms *Mafia* and *mafioso* began to pop up in everyday conversation. People no longer talked about gangs or mobs: they talked about The Mob.

In the beginning, though, few people had an idea what a mafioso might look like. Here the McClellan Committee hearings performed a public service by summoning Johnny Dio before it. For many, the furious, snarling Dio became the face of the Mob.

And because Robert Kennedy had no trouble establishing a connection between Dio and Jimmy Hoffa, the latter, whose ancestry was Dutch-Irish rather than Italian, came to look more and more like a mafioso himself.

The McClellan hearings brought Hoffa and Dio together in the public mind. It did the same thing even more vividly for the Kennedy brothers. Robert Kennedy was always the hearings' star. John tended to hang back a bit. He knew the hearings were risky for him, that old Joe Kennedy was correct in saying that if his sons were to anger the trade unions, John would never get the Democratic nomination for president in 1960, let alone be elected to the office. As it was, John Kennedy had little going for him at the time. By 1957 he'd been around Congress for a decade (six years in the House, five in the Senate) without ever doing anything particularly memorable. A former investigator for Robert Kennedy recalled that "Jack Kennedy had not been a very distinguished member of the House and was simply fluttering around in the Senate, where he was not really greatly respected except as a playboy."[37]

But, hazardous as they first appeared, the McClellan hearings turned out wonderfully for the Kennedys. If, write Robert Kennedy's earliest biographers, "the Battle of Waterloo was won on the playing fields of Eton, then it could also be said that the New Frontier was launched in the Senate Caucus Room. The nationally televised rackets hearings made Jack Kennedy a national hero. He was not as active in interrogation as a number of other members of the McClellan Committee, but he managed—with his brother coaching behind the scenes—to turn up at opportune moments to clash with the right witnesses. It was even a help to him in his later primary fights that many television viewers confused the two brothers and somehow regarded Jack as a composite of the tough, dogged counsel and the more aloof and courtly Senator."[38]

Without meaning to, Republicans on the committee handed the Kennedys a huge gift. In early 1958, when the panel was a year old, Senator Barry Goldwater, an energetic GOP member, began pushing for an investigation of a *Democratic* trade union, the United Auto Workers, then involved in a bitter Wisconsin strike. Strike leaders, the employer, and a group of international UAW leaders duly came to Washington to testify about the matter. John Kennedy, hitherto rather quiet, immediately leaped to the union's defense.

The UAW was the largest and one of the most liberal of the old CIO internationals. Of the candidates for the Democratic presidential nomination in 1960, the union's leaders were ideologically closest to Senator Hubert Humphrey, though they retained a sentimental attachment to Adlai Stevenson, the party nominee in '52 and '56. John Kennedy they viewed as a ladies' man with no taste for serious politics. But during this scuffle they saw they had been wrong. "Every time the UAW came under heavy fire from Goldwater.... John Kennedy would suddenly appear from out of nowhere," writes a historian. "Taking cues from his brother, Senator Kennedy would quibble and fence with Goldwater, inject some humor, ask a few tempering questions to deflate conservative, or anti–UAW, momentum, then leave before matters became too intense."[39]

The UAW bosses were impressed. Kennedy's performance, as two of his aides later noted, "brought a complete turnaround in their attitude toward him…. From then on, these tough-minded and demanding labor leaders, who exerted a strong influence within the Democratic party, respected Kennedy as a solid and intelligently grounded liberal. They backed him firmly at the 1960 convention against their former favorites, Adlai Stevenson and Hubert Humphrey. When the Republicans on the McClellan committee pushed the investigation of the UAW, thinking that it would bring a political embarrassment to Bobby Kennedy's brother, they were actually doing him a big political favor."[40]

Years later—after the assassinations of the Kennedy brothers and shortly before he himself was murdered and his body disposed of in a manner that will probably never be revealed—Jimmy Hoffa confessed, "I made two disastrous mistakes in my life. The first was coming to grips with Robert F. Kennedy to the point where we became involved in what can only be called a blood feud. The result was that I became John F. Kennedy's steppingstone to the White House."[41]

There's a good deal of truth in what Hoffa said. One could add, though, that the McClellan Committee's Republican members also turned themselves into steppingstones. Without trade union support John Kennedy never would have reached the presidency. But, with skill and no doubt great good luck, he and his brother performed an amazing pas de deux. Robert Kennedy alarmed the unions with his attack on the IBT. John Kennedy, by defending the UAW, not only calmed them down again but actually enlisted them in his cause.

* * *

Hoffa spent more hours testifying before the McClellan panel than any other witness. Harold Gibbons was the runner-up. Robert Kennedy disliked Gibbons, calling him "this bright, self-centered, arrogant man."[42] Kennedy "had a special thing for Harold," said a former Kennedy aide. "He kind of knew he was personally clean, but he couldn't stand the way Hoffa used Gibbons, the great liberal and intellectual, as his window dressing. He hated Gibbons, because he knew Gibbons could have done so much better for the union."[43] As for Gibbons, Patrick Gibbons says simply, "Father had zero love for the Kennedys."[44]

These animosities were only personal, so to speak. They didn't prevent Joseph Kennedy, in 1960, from summoning Gibbons down to Palm Beach, Florida, in an attempt to negotiate an endorsement by the Teamsters of his son John's presidential campaign. Nor did they, eight years later, keep

Robert from sending his brother-in-law Stephen Smith to Gibbons to seek the union's support for his own presidential bid.[45] Both efforts failed—the IBT endorsed the Republican Richard Nixon in 1960 and, briefly switching parties, the Democrat Hubert Humphrey in '68—but they showed that the Kennedys thought Gibbons was a reasonable man who just might be able to persuade Hoffa, whom they considered unreasonable, to agree to some kind of deal.

But Gibbons wouldn't have been quick to help Robert Kennedy. In a talk he once gave at the Brookings Institution in Washington, he described being questioned by Kennedy before the McClellan Committee. He said, "One of the great talents that Bobby displayed when I was up there was to take the most decent act you ever performed in your life, give it a slight twist, and dirty the whole thing up. This was his great chief stock in trade."[46]

Gibbons appeared before the committee for three straight days in early September 1958.

Robert Kennedy aside, Gibbons and the McClellan Committee were bound to misunderstand each other. The committee's charge was to ferret out "improper activities" in labor relations, which to the general public meant racketeering or corruption: that is, a union leader's use of his position to elicit unearned income from employers or his own members, or both. No one on the committee seriously accused Gibbons of that kind of impropriety. The committee did accuse him of "improper activities" in the sense of employing tactics that it considered overly aggressive. The keynote was struck on the first day of Gibbons' appearance by Senator Irving Ives, a moderate Republican. The two men were discussing the tendency of labor strikes to turn violent, and Gibbons said that, given the bitter feelings strikes often provoked, they couldn't help but be warlike. Ives protested the harshness of Gibbons' statement.

"The difference between what you are after and what happens in time of war … [is] as different as night and day," said the senator.

"In that, you and I would have to disagree," Gibbons replied.[47]

But the senators were gentle philosophers compared to their chief counsel. Robert Kennedy was a prosecutor. Uninterested in a truth-seeking dialogue, he had a case to prove. In Kennedy's version of the truth, the Teamsters Union under Jimmy Hoffa was not a legitimate trade union but rather a "conspiracy of evil."[48] Gibbons, he implied, was one of the conspirators.

Take, for example, the 1949 merger of Gibbons' CIO warehouse union and a separate AFL affiliate. As Kennedy chose to see it, the merger had in reality been the purchase by Gibbons' predatory group of three thousand hapless AFL members, as if they were shackled slaves (see Chapter 7). In Kennedy's presentation of the 1952–53 episode in which Gibbons and his staff acquired guns to defend themselves against a takeover by Buster Wortman's mob (Chapter 9), Wortman and the mobsters tended to vanish altogether, leaving Gibbons and his friends looking at best like vigilantes and at worst like mobsters themselves. Kennedy got great play from the taxi strike of '53, during which one of Gibbons' people drove a hijacked cab into the Mississippi (Chapter 10). As Gibbons should have known, it's usually the prosecution's attack, not parrying by the defense, that makes the headlines.

When Gibbons accused Kennedy of "dirtying up" virtuous acts, he probably had in mind the chief counsel's version of the wildcat cab strike of 1956. Gibbons had been determined that year to integrate St. Louis' Jim Crow cabbies' union. As a white fighter for what were then known as Negro rights, he was an eccentric figure, not just in Missouri but throughout the United States. Americans were just then learning the name Martin Luther King, Jr., a young clergyman leading a poorly understood bus boycott in Montgomery, Alabama. Congress was dominated by quite respectable white Democrats. Two McClellan Committee members, Senators Sam Ervin of North Carolina and Arkansas' John McClellan himself, became in 1956 signatories to the "Southern Manifesto," a protest by the great majority of Southern congressmen against the Supreme Court decision outlawing segregation in schools. Barry Goldwater, the strongest Republican voice on the McClellan Committee, would vote against the great Civil Rights Act of 1964. This is not to argue that McClellan, Ervin, and Goldwater were necessarily hostile to Gibbons because of his passion for black rights, only that they likely couldn't understand it.

In any case, Robert Kennedy in raising the wildcat taxi strike issue did his best to smother its central civil-rights aspects, whenever those aspects arose. On one hand, Kennedy downplayed the racism of the wildcatting cabbies and, on the other, focused sharply on the support Gibbons had admittedly received in the strike from Joe Costello, the ex-convict taxi-fleet owner, and the strikebreaking thugs he employed. When subpoenaed before the committee, Costello and his friends refused to testify under the Fifth Amendment. The chief wildcatter, by contrast, responded freely to Kennedy's gentle questions, maintaining that his group's motives in the strike had been not racist but purely economic. Given Kennedy, the McClellan Committee's makeup, and the atmosphere of the times, this was a debate Gibbons was bound to lose.

On September 3, 1958, a Wednesday, Gibbons' second day before the committee, Kennedy and several senators questioned him about his acquaintance with mobsters. Do you know Johnny Dio? asked Irving Ives. Yes, Gibbons said, he knew him, but only casually, in the course of carrying out assignments for the Teamsters. Ives repeated his question, adding that he was under the impression that Gibbons and Dio were in fact quite close. No, said Gibbons. "You're sure you were not?" pressed Ives.

"No," said Gibbons. "I am friendly at the point that Dulles and Eisenhower might be friendly with Ibn Saud."[49]

He probably meant to say: "No, I don't like Dio either, but just as America's secretary of state and president think it's expedient that they be nice to the autocratic but oil-rich king of Saudi Arabia, my boss Jimmy Hoffa (and therefore I as well) think it's expedient that we be nice to Johnny Dio." But that was too frank and so hadn't come out quite right.

Gibbons had a good reason not to like Dio. Two years before, a man had thrown acid into the face of a newspaper columnist named Victor Riesel, permanently blinding him. Dio, whom police believed to have ordered the attack, was arrested and charged with conspiracy. But the attacker was murdered before a trial could occur. The police having thus lost their witness, Dio went free.

Gibbons and Victor Riesel were friends. Riesel happened to be politically conservative and wrote for the conservative Hearst chain, but he admired Gibbons' trade unionism. Back in the early '50s, the Red Scare years, Riesel had written an impassioned Hearst column defending Gibbons against the charge of being sympathetic to communism. "Tall, slim, good-looking, and eloquent," Riesel wrote, "Gibbons rose fast [in the labor movement], taking on the Communists and the crooks in a running fight over the years.... So the mobs hate Gibbons." It was probably the warmest praise the St. Louisan would ever receive from a journalist.

As far as is known, Gibbons never discussed how he felt on the day when, responding to Irving Ives, he provided the queasiest possible endorsement of the man who hired the man who blinded Victor Riesel. But it must have gone like a swallowed chicken bone down into his soul.

16

The Split

On Friday, November 22, 1963, President John F. Kennedy was assassinated in Dallas.

Jimmy Hoffa happened that day to be out of town, in Miami. Harold Gibbons was in charge of the union's Washington, D.C., headquarters. When the news came in, Gibbons was winding up a late lunch at Duke Ziebart's Restaurant with the lawyer Edward Bennett Williams. He raced back to the Marble Palace to find that a tearful Larry Steinberg had already lowered the flag and sent employees home. Having approved Steinberg's actions, Gibbons wired a message of condolence to the Kennedy family and ordered the building closed for the funeral. Then he called Hoffa to fill him in.[1]

"He raised hell with me for having done it," Gibbons said years afterward. "He cursed the Kennedys—this was two hours after the guy had been shot—and he cursed me. And finally, after he screamed for a while, I told him, 'When you get back get yourself a new boy because I'm not going to be here. I'm resigning.' This for me was the last straw."[2]

It wasn't quite. Gibbons didn't actually leave IBT headquarters for another six weeks, and for years thereafter he and Hoffa would collaborate on projects from time to time. But nothing like their early, easy relationship would be restored until after Hoffa was released from prison in 1971, eight years later.

There were some who said Gibbons merely used the Kennedy assassination as a pretext for splitting from Hoffa. One such person was Ron Gamache, Gibbons' eventual successor as secretary-treasurer of Local 688. "He [Gibbons] realized he couldn't keep sitting across the desk from the man [Hoffa] he had been secretly working against," said Gamache.[3] Of course by the time Gamache said this, Gibbons, once his mentor, had become an enemy.

For five years, from 1958 to 1963, the Hoffa-Gibbons relationship had been functional enough to let the two not only work together in the Marble Palace but also live together at the Woodner Hotel. It wasn't surprising that the partnership eventually fractured. The interesting question is: how had they kept it working so well so long?

Gibbons often described Hoffa as a great labor leader, and he probably meant it. His model in that respect was John L. Lewis of the United Mine Workers. While in Washington, Gibbons' children said, he rarely missed an opportunity to drive out to Lewis' retirement home in nearby Alexandria, Virginia, to listen to the old man's reminiscences.[4] Gibbons admired Lewis for his role in creating the CIO, but even more, perhaps, for Lewis' insistence on calling a series of coal strikes in 1943, in the middle of the Second World War. Lewis was widely hated for it. Gibbons had spoken in praise of Lewis and the strikes at the time (see Chapter 4). Lewis, he saw, recognized no human authority higher than his own—not Congress', not even Franklin Roosevelt's.

Way back in 1958, when Hoffa was just starting to become something of a frightening figure to many in this country, Daniel Bell, *Fortune* magazine's labor expert, argued that such fear was groundless. Hoffa, like most once-fiery American union leaders, would grow tame after a while, Bell explained. "What ultimately will curb Hoffa is a craving for respectability, which is masked by the veneer of toughness."[5] Since Hoffa was only sixty-two when he vanished, we'll never know whether Bell's prediction was accurate—whether, that is, Hoffa might finally have turned into a lovable old goof whose twinkling eyes might one day appear on the cover of *People* magazine. But he hadn't softened when last heard from.

"Gibbons loved Jimmy," said a woman who became close to Gibbons in the 1970s. "I don't mean in a gay way. He just loved him."[6] Well, how do you analyze love, which, like wind, is invisible except for its effect on the lover? If Gibbons loved Hoffa, it may have been because the Teamster boss reminded him of John L. Lewis. It's a quality rarely seen in human beings, the willingness to be hated. Lewis had it, and Gibbons may have seen it in Hoffa too.

* * *

Still, the ties between Gibbons and Hoffa were fraying long before Kennedy was killed.

There were three main sources of friction. One certainly involved their personalities. Both men were near-religious trade unionists. On the other hand, both were also egocentric, autocratic, quick to anger, and often loudly profane when crossed. Like many other couples, they managed to stay together by spending much time apart. Hoffa was a monogamous teetotaler, whereas Gibbons loved barrooms and the company of pretty women. "Hoffa drove Father crazy when they lived together at the Woodner," said Patrick Gibbons.[7] "Father would get buggy if he had to stay in too many nights in a row," Larry Gibbons added. "He'd tell Hoffa, 'I'm going out for some cigarettes,' and then come back three days later."[8]

Then there was the petty pushing and shoving that males, even when friends, often do to each other. But Gibbons discovered that bosses usually get to push harder. When he and Hoffa took over the Marble Palace in 1958 the union provided each of them with a car. Hoffa, like Dave Beck before him, got a black Cadillac. Gibbons chose a Pontiac convertible. "Hoffa made [Gibbons] trade cars because he didn't like the big Cadillac," said Elizabeth Vasquez. "He thought the Pontiac was a lot more fun."[9] Something similar happened with Yuki Kato. She had been Gibbons' female right hand since the war years, but that changed in Washington. "I also worked for Gibbons, on the side," she said, "but my main job was with Hoffa."[10] At least Hoffa treated Kato with respect. Not so with Jake McCarthy and Dick Kavner (as noted in Chapter 15), whom Gibbons was unable to protect from Hoffa's scorn. That must have galled him.

Hoffa's mobster associates were a second source of tension. Hoffa himself made light of it, saying, "Twenty years ago the employers had all the hoodlums working for them as strike-breakers. Now we've got a few and everybody's screaming."[11] Unembarrassed by their presence, Hoffa allowed the racketeers to wander freely around the Marble Palace. Ralph and Estelle James sometimes encountered them while working on their book about Hoffa. "Lounging in the anteroom and sauntering in and out of Hoffa's office are individuals made notorious by the McClellan Committee," the Jameses write. "Some are personal friends valued for their companionship, others are seekers and sellers of influence."[12] Gibbons was uncomfortable around these visitors, a sentiment Hoffa seems to have understood. Larry Gibbons said, "Father told me that he'd be working with Hoffa on something, and they'd announce that some people had arrived, and Hoffa would say, 'Why don't you get out of here, Gibbons, because you don't want to be here when I deal with these guys.' And Father would leave the room and come back an hour later."[13]

Hoffa's underworld connections were clearly discomfiting to Gibbons and his former RWDSU friends. A certain amount of unacknowledged comedy resulted from this.

The Jameses, following Hoffa around the Marble Palace, were pleasantly surprised at his willingness to cooperate with their work—he even let them sit in on meetings of the Outfit-influenced Central States Pension Fund. But equally surprising, they write, was the stonewalling they received from some of Hoffa's aides:

> Hoffa's open attitude contrasted strongly with that of his executive vice president, Harold Gibbons, who urged us to concentrate on the International's monthly propaganda magazine, *The International Teamster*—which we could have done while remaining in a university library! This fear of exposure was also reflected in those particularly close to Gibbons. Larry Steinberg, Hoffa's "personal representative," and a long-standing friend of Gibbons, predicted, for example that we would do great harm to the Teamsters. Dick Kavner, one of Hoffa's best assistants and an old associate of Gibbons' from St. Louis, maintained that we would emerge with only a distorted, half-true picture.[14]

The Jameses found this interesting. They were like anthropologists who have come to study a tribe that still dresses in loincloths. Gibbons and his friends were like tribe members who have been to town once or twice and can sort of see things through the anthropologists' eyes. As a result, they keep trying to cover their fellows in T-shirts and shorts. After a while the anthropologists pack their notebooks and film and return whence they came. They say: Yes, the tribe was interesting, though those guys who seemed so nervous on the clothing issue were downright odd.

So, what about Jimmy Hoffa and his shadier friends? The people we've been calling racketeers and mobsters have been a problem for the labor movement practically since its inception. In his classic study *Labor Czars* the writer Harold Seidman describes how, after dramatic waves of 19th-century labor unrest—the big railroad strike of 1877, the Haymarket Riot in Chicago of 1886—U.S. employers retaliated by closing their doors to trade unions. This they did simply by firing union members and sympathizers. Unions responded by hiring what were known as "walking delegates." A walking delegate, since he is on the union's payroll, not the factory owner's, is free to travel around signing up new union members. Such men, Seidman writes, were "often illiterate, rough brawny men selected for their boldness rather than their intelligence and honesty; not all the walking delegates were equal to the responsibility. Sober and industrious workmen they might have been under the eyes of a taskmaster in the shop, but the sudden change from a position of servitude to one of authority frequently gave them exaggerated opinions of their own importance.... Nor was it long before the walking delegates learned that their new jobs provided numerous opportunities to pick up easy money.... Most of the walking delegates were honest, but others were not strong enough to resist temptation."[15]

And add this fact: the walking delegate's job was sometimes dangerous. Many were killed or crippled by gunmen hired by anti-union employers. To protect himself, a walking delegate might employ a gunman of his own. "In accordance with the general division of labor," wrote the left-wing sociologist C. Wright Mills, "violence thus became a specialty. The craftsman-as-worker ceased to use his fists, the craftsman-as-thug was hired to operate within this jurisdiction. In fact, the professional thug was one of the first professionals hired by the unions."[16]

Trade-union history has often been violent in America. Readers of this book will have picked up some clues as to why this is so. It helps to recall that, until the Supreme Court's *NLRB v. Jones & Laughlin* decision of April 1937, employees in this country had no legal right to form an organization that would enable them to bargain with employers. The law—local, state, federal—was *all* on the employers' side. In St. Louis (see Chapter 2), it was that court decision that kept warehouse owners from firing their union-

16. *The Split*

sympathizing workers wholesale. It should also be recalled that, in possessing the law, employers possessed a near monopoly (legal and not) on violence. In 1952 Harold Gibbons in St. Louis had good reason to arm himself against threats of assassination (see Chapter 9). Walter Reuther of the UAW, just four years earlier, had barely survived a shotgun blast fired through a window in his own kitchen. Victor Reuther lost an eye in a similar attack a year after that. Unionists suspected that an auto company had hired the would-be killers in both cases. The police in Detroit, where the Reuthers lived, were unable to either protect the brothers or later discover who shot them. Just as St. Louis' police couldn't do much to keep harm from befalling Gibbons.

In America, thugs and racketeers have found many opportunities to prosper. Gibbons, in one of his last newspaper interviews, was skeptical about a union leader's ability to eliminate them without serious assistance. "If the government, as powerful as it is, can't get the job done, how the hell do they expect an individual with no police power to achieve that?" he asked.[17]

Gibbons was likely thinking of Jimmy Hoffa's fate. Since union leaders had no police power, they sometimes tried to work out private understandings with mobsters. It was a kind of dance. Some unionists learned the steps and got good (and lucky) at dancing them. Hoffa, for instance, began his Detroit career reaching an accommodation with Angelo Meli, a mobster whose thugs ordinarily worked *for* businessmen *against* unions. He later reached accommodations with the Outfit and other big city mobs. But success may have caused him to overestimate his skills in mob-management, and that overestimation apparently led to his death in 1975.

* * *

Meanwhile, in 1963, the third cause of distress between Hoffa and Gibbons was the union's presidency. Gibbons' position as a Teamsters vice president was just as promising, and as awkward, as that of the typical vice president of the United States. Neither he nor Hoffa had a personal ambition larger than to be the IBT's top leader. But Hoffa *was* the leader, Gibbons merely the hopeful. That was the fundamental fact of the matter. Eventually it became obvious to Gibbons that, rather than winning a place as Hoffa's heir, he had spent years working himself into a tight, windowless box.

As has often been noted, Gibbons was an outsider in the AFL Teamsters. His natural home was the old CIO. No doubt some of the IBT's dozen or so other vice presidents held his origins against him. But Gibbons' problems in that regard may have been partly of his own making. "He wasn't altogether convinced of his acceptance" by other trade unionists, including members of the IBT brass, according to Jake McCarthy. "Gibbons was very assertive, fast-moving, verbal," McCarthy said. "But he wasn't a schmoozer. To relax he needed the company of cronies, but his cronies weren't the kind of people who could help him politically. In St. Louis, for instance, McCarthy said, "he ate lunch nearly every day at Al Baker's [restaurant] in Clayton—with his chauffeur."[18]

Hoffa had raised Gibbons to prominence in the Teamsters and, had he wished, could have made him a kind of caretaker-leader of the union, as he did with another man several years later (see Chapter 17). Without Hoffa's imprimatur, however, Gibbons' ascension to the top was impossible. The St. Louisan had a few influential champions: in the union's warehouse division, for instance, and among his former RWDSU friends working in the Marble Palace, and also in the person of the IBT's top lawyer, Edward Bennett Williams.[19] But he had not many in the Teamsters Union as a whole. As the Jameses concluded, "Many [IBT] members offer Hoffa an allegiance bordering on religious fervor."[20] A visitor once asked Tom Eagleton, who had cultivated relations with Missouri's Teamsters, why, given his ambitions, Gibbons had never broken completely with Hoffa. "There was no backing away from Hoffa in the Teamsters," Eagleton said. "Hoffa always had the members' support. If they'd been able, they would have voted to reelect him even when he was in prison."[21] Eagleton was probably right.

Not that Gibbons kept his ambition secret from Hoffa: they had been discussing it since the beginning of their friendship. And that friendship, with its highs and lows, would survive until Hoffa's death. But by 1963, after their five years together in the Marble Palace and the Woodner Hotel, Hoffa, who suffered from a chronic mistrust of people in general, seems to have mistrusted Gibbons most of all.

He may have had some grounds for it. At least once, Gibbons was tempted. In *The Teamsters*, his book about the union in the 1960s and '70s, Steven Brill tells a tale he heard from Joseph Rauh, a prominent Washington lawyer and ADA stalwart. One day when he and Gibbons were having lunch, Rauh said, he talked the St. Louisan into handing over to Robert Kennedy private papers that documented corruption in the Teamsters Union. "I'm going to prove to you and all my liberal friends that I've got nothing to hide," Rauh described Gibbons as saying. Unfortunately, Rauh added, he never heard from Gibbons again. "It's a tragedy," the lawyer concluded. "He was one of the great figures in the American labor movement. But he had a weakness for two-hundred-dollar suits, and for women; and I guess he just decided it wasn't worth giving that up. What a sad story."[22]

Other people believed that Gibbons' eventual decision not to break completely with Hoffa was the result of fear: fear that Hoffa's mobster friends might kill him. If so, it certainly wasn't in the Teamsters' world an entirely irrational fear, as would be demonstrated a decade later when someone, mobsters presumably, kidnapped and murdered Hoffa himself.

Gibbons, however, explained it this way: "Sure, there were a lot of things about Hoffa that I didn't like. But you know I came up with the guy, and I owed him. You have to factor that in in whatever you say about me."[23]

Fear, ambition, gratitude, $200 suits—which of these impulses (perhaps there were still others) led Gibbons to decide in Hoffa's favor? Probably he was like the rest of us, moved by not one but rather by a bundle of motives and never knowing for sure which predominates. But stick by Hoffa he did.

But that was in the long run. In the meantime, as the '50s became the '60s, Hoffa had grown increasingly hard to get along with. His touchiness was understandable. John Kennedy, whom the McClellan hearings had made famous and whose electoral campaign was to be aided by his father's money and his brother Robert's wolfish efficiency, was elected president in November 1960. He then appointed Robert attorney general. Once in office both Kennedys were distracted for more than a year by consequences of the April 1961 Bay of Pigs fiasco in Cuba. However, in December 1962, after the United States had ransomed back the émigrés captured in that disaster, Robert Kennedy was finally able to turn to what seems to have been for him a more interesting problem. "Now let's get Hoffa," he told an aide.[24] Thirty FBI agents and sixteen Justice Department lawyers were assigned to that project. Thirteen separate grand juries began considering indictments of the IBT boss.[25] Hoffa had five years earlier jumped into what he himself came to call a "blood feud" with Robert Kennedy. Now he was to pay the price.

By late 1963, as Steven Brill reports it, Gibbons' "relationship with Hoffa had not been good in recent months. Hoffa, under incessant pressure from the Kennedy Justice Department, had been more arrogant and moody than ever, frequently throwing temper tantrums that invariably featured bitter, humiliating tirades against any lesser personage (which meant everyone, including Gibbons) who happened to be in the room."[26]

Then occurred John Kennedy's murder, Gibbons' declaration that the union was officially in mourning, and Hoffa's telephone tirade.

Gibbons resigned as Hoffa's executive vice president. With him went Larry Steinberg, Dick Kavner, Yuki Kato, and Ferguson Keathley, a Local 688 staffer whom Kato had married.[27] Though he would often return to the city, for longer and shorter sojourns, this was the effective end of Gibbons' Washington career.

17

Hoffa Sets a Trap

"GIBBONS RETURNS HERE ON WEEK-END," was the *St. Louis Globe-Democrat*'s headline for December 14, 1963. "TIGHT-LIPPED ON SPLIT WITH HOFFA," said the sub-head. According to the paper, Gibbons "has been remarkably tight-lipped about his rift with the man he helped make president of the nation's largest and most powerful labor union. And unless he has a quick change of heart in the next 24 hours—which is unlikely—about the only voice being heard is that of Hoffa, who apparently can't stop talking. From the moment Mr. Gibbons' resignation became public, Mr. Hoffa has been on a continuous talkathon, obviously intended to lure everyone into believing nothing really serious has happened in the fight for control of the Teamsters Union."[1]

Hoffa simply denied that Gibbons had quit. He told a wire service reporter that the St. Louisan had "asked to be relieved of certain duties…. But he declared it was not true that he had resigned. He also dismissed as 'pure nonsense' reports that there was any connection with his statement after the murder of President Kennedy."[2] (Hoffa was reported by the press to have said that, with the president's death, Attorney General "Bobby Kennedy is just another lawyer.") Gibbons, in turn, also denied that he and Hoffa had fallen out. In a statement to the *Missouri Teamster*, a tabloid newspaper recently launched by Jake McCarthy for Joint Council 13, he said, "My personal relationships with President Hoffa have been excellent in the past, are now, and shall continue to be in the future."[3]

As 1963 came to an end, uneasiness in the IBT reflected that in the mourning nation at large. Hoffa's grip on the union seemed to have slipped. His ghoulish response to Kennedy's death had shaken many loyal Teamsters. And his own future now looked bleak. Hoffa had been tried in federal court, accused of taking a payoff (in the form of a truck-leasing business placed in the names of his wife and a friend's wife) from employers. No verdict was reached because the judge declared a mistrial based on his suspicion, soon elevated into an entirely new charge, that Hoffa had tampered with the jury.

This jury-tampering trial was to begin in Chattanooga in January 1964.[4] Hoffa also faced a second trial, to be held in Chicago later that year, on fraud charges growing out of the old Florida real-estate case. According to an article in the *New York Times*, a majority of the IBT's executive board—constituted by the union's president, secretary-treasurer, and thirteen vice presidents—was already unhappy with Hoffa for various other reasons. If he were to be convicted in Chattanooga, which seemed likely, that majority was ready, the paper said, to remove him from office and elect someone else in his place.[5]

The top candidates for Hoffa's job, the *Times* said, were Gibbons and Einar Mohn, chief of the Western Conference of Teamsters. A. H. Raskin, the *Times'* labor reporter, described Gibbons as the "probable front runner." But Gibbons carried a handicap, Raskin said. "He is an unusual blend of egghead and bon vivant and … comes out of the old C.I.O. All these attributes have made him something of an alien in the Teamster hierarchy, accepted solely on the basis of his sponsorship by Mr. Hoffa."[6]

Gibbons declared he had no interest in the union's presidency. He wasn't telling the truth. At practically the same moment Raskin filed his story, Dick Kavner was returning to St. Louis from Las Vegas, where he'd been sent to canvass support for a possible Gibbons candidacy among Western IBT leaders known to be unenthusiastic about Einar Mohn.[7] Mohn's people were very likely carrying out similar forays into Gibbons territory, the Midwest and South.

The stakes were raised in 1964 when Hoffa was found guilty in both the Chattanooga and Chicago trials and sentenced to eight years in prison. He immediately filed appeals. An IBT convention, at which a president would be elected, was scheduled for the summer of 1966. Both Gibbons and Mohn announced that they would immediately drop their own candidacies if Hoffa were to decide to seek reelection. That seemed doubtful, given the sentence hanging over him. Hoffa, now tied up in a series of appellate courts, wasn't saying whether he would run or not.

Given his notoriety, there was of course great speculation concerning a post–Hoffa Teamsters Union. People familiar with the IBT understood that Gibbons and Mohn represented two distinct tendencies—two Teamster parties, as it were. These were neatly summarized by a reporter for the *Wall Street Journal*:

> The Gibbons-Mohn contest has a significance beyond the immediate question of union leadership. Mr. Gibbons, though he has split from Mr. Hoffa, would nevertheless pursue the Hoffa course of seeking to centralize the leadership. This would mean concentrated control over contract negotiations with the trucking and warehousing industries, and an effort to shape more master agreements such as the one Mr. Hoffa forged for the long-distance and long-haul industries. Mr. Gibbons is currently working on a multicompany master agreement for the warehousing industry. In contrast, if Mr. Mohn were president, businessmen who negotiate with the Teamsters Union would find themselves talking more with the local and regional leaders.[8]

The IBT rank and file, had they been asked about it, would probably have approved the Hoffa-Gibbons drive toward centralization. As the *Wall Street Journal* writer noted, Hoffa had in 1964 signed a national "master" contract with the employers of long-distance truck drivers, a contract similar to those involving the CIO auto workers and steelworkers. According to an Associated Press story of the following year, thanks to the contract, "cross-country truck drivers, paid on a mileage basis, now make up to $15,000 a year. The lowliest Teamster warehouseman seldom makes less than $2.50 an hour, and Hoffa made a major breakthrough in abolishing lower wage differentials in the Southern states where most other unions find it a tough job just to get a toehold."[9] (What's more, centralization tended to freeze out racketeers dependent on contracts negotiated at the local level.) But most local and regional Teamster *leaders* still opposed centralization because it diluted their own authority.

Gibbons was well aware of local leaders' objections to his and Hoffa's line. In early 1965 Jake McCarthy worked up a draft campaign platform that, while admitting problems with centralized administration ("Our union is far too large to operate on the concept of intense centralization in the Washington office"), nevertheless saw no realistic alternative to it. The draft platform proposed, rather than a return to decentralized contract negotiations, institutional reforms such as an annual or semiannual meeting of joint council representatives—in effect another layer of meetings, a prospect unlikely to thrill the decentralizers.[10]

But the big problem for the Hoffa-Gibbons group in the IBT was that it had been split since the day John Kennedy was killed. On one hand, Hoffa no longer trusted Gibbons. "Gibbons was a smart man but he defied Hoffa after the Kennedy assassination on that lowering the flags deal," said a Hoffa associate. "'Too independent,' Jimmy said. 'He can't be controlled.'"[11] Another man, this time an ally of Gibbons', remembered discussing the question with Hoffa himself. "He said, well, he just wasn't sure about Harold," this man recalled Hoffa saying. "He didn't say why he wasn't sure. But I knew. Hoffa was the same as the other international Teamster leaders—afraid of Harold. Of his brain. That's what he was afraid of."[12]

In early 1964, though, Hoffa still badly needed Gibbons—he had bigger things to worry about than the other man's brain. Hoffa then faced the pair of federal trials and (though he couldn't yet know it) nearly three more years of appeals to higher courts. So he asked Gibbons to help him run the international.

Gibbons recalled the situation in his talks with Steven Brill. "Well, after trying through some emissaries to get me to stay, he came in to see me—I was still at headquarters clearing away some things—and said, 'You said you'd help out if I needed you. Well, I've got to go down South … for my [jury-tampering] trial. Will you at least stay until I get back?'" The St. Louisan agreed to do so but insisted that the relationship, previously a constitutional link between the union president and a subordinate vice president, become informal, one more befitting equals. "So I said I would [stay], but that I wouldn't take his money; I'd be paid by my St. Louis local."[13]

Thereafter Gibbons was constantly in and out of Washington, keeping an eye on things at the Marble Palace. In January 1964 he traveled with Hoffa to Chicago to negotiate the all-important "master" contract, setting wages and benefits for most of the nation's long-haul truck drivers. As Hoffa, soon convicted, began filing appeals, Gibbons flew around the country dealing with IBT problems that his former boss was increasingly too busy to handle. He also took these flights as opportunities to campaign quietly for himself as Hoffa's successor. He saw no contradiction between the two missions. Gibbons expected Hoffa to eventually decide against running for reelection and throw his support behind another candidate. That candidate, Gibbons was sure, would not be Einar Mohn, the leader of the IBT's decentralizing party. By process of elimination, if nothing else, Hoffa would be forced to back Gibbons despite possible lingering bad feelings. Years later the St. Louisan described to Steven Brill his thinking at this juncture. "Even after their falling-out over the Kennedy assassination, Gibbons still believed that this was likely as long as he didn't break with Hoffa totally."[14]

But Gibbons was wrong.

In early 1966 Hoffa announced that, after all, he *would* run for another term as IBT president. Not only that, but he also proposed—and the union accepted—an amendment to its constitution that created a new IBT office, the "general vice presidency," whose occupant would assume the duties of the president "in case of the death, resignation or removal of that officer."[15] Hoffa nominated for the post an IBT vice president named Frank Fitzsimmons.

Fitz, as he was known, was fifty-eight, a heavy, bespectacled, grandfather-like former road-repair worker and member of Hoffa's base organization, Detroit Local 299. For years he'd served Hoffa as a kind of valet. Fitz had neither powerful friends nor particular talents, nor even ambitions, as far as anyone knew. Hoffa would later describe him as "a guy I took off a 3-C Highway Company truck and hand-carried all the way from shop steward to general vice president."[16] He hadn't amount to much, was what Hoffa meant. Fitz *could* usually carry out orders, though, which was why Hoffa chose him. "Suspicious princes often promote the last of mankind, from a vain persuasion that those who have no dependence, except on their favour, will have no attachment except to the person of their benefactor," the historian Edward Gibbon wrote of a second-century Roman emperor who made a similar appointment.[17] Hoffa was determined to run the Teamsters Union from prison if necessary, and for that Fitz seemed the perfect tool.

Gibbons was shocked by Hoffa's move. (Which suggests that he didn't know his sometime friend as well as he thought.) "I've never seen him so down," an unnamed Gibbons associate told Steven Brill. "And, what made things worse was that Hoffa chose this guy, Fitzsimmons, instead. A total nincompoop. A guy who'd been a total nonentity in the union. It was humiliating."[18]

Gibbons decided to fight. In June 1966 he announced that he would oppose Fitz for the new post at the following month's IBT convention. (Einar Mohn now disclaimed interest in either of the union's top two offices.) Dick Kavner was already in the field—traveling to Seattle, Oakland, Los Angeles, Minneapolis, northern New Jersey—politicking for Gibbons among Teamster brass. In July, Jake McCarthy recalled, "we went down to a Miami [Beach] Teamsters convention laden with campaign materials on behalf of Gibbons' candidacy for the union's general vice presidency."[19]

Gibbons must have considered his chances pretty good. Except for Hoffa, he was the best-known Teamster in the country, and within the union itself he was widely admired, if not wholly trusted because of his CIO background and left-wing views. Fitzsimmons, on the other hand, was largely unknown and had only one serious backer, Hoffa.

But Hoffa was all he needed.

Hoffa had set a trap for Gibbons. He had included in his amendment to the union constitution a clause forbidding members of its executive board, all of whom faced reelection at each convention, to run for more than one board office at a time. This clause was the direct opposite of an amendment to the Texas constitution that that state's legislature had engineered in 1960. Texas' amendment allowed a candidate, in that case Lyndon Johnson, to run for both vice president of the United States and reelection as a U.S. senator. That way, should the Kennedy-Johnson ticket be defeated in that year's presidential election, Johnson would still retain his Senate seat. In the case of the Teamsters, though, a board member who happened to challenge Fitz for the general vice presidency would, if defeated, automatically *lose* his own vice presidency as well. If Gibbons were to persist in his folly, he might well be ejected from the executive board, falling back into the merely regional role from which Hoffa had raised him in 1953.

Of course there would be no ejection, no fall, if Gibbons rounded up sufficient votes for himself at the July convention. Unfortunately for the St. Louisan, the ardor with which some Teamster leaders had wanted to rid themselves of Jimmy Hoffa, in the months immediately following Kennedy's death, had now considerably cooled. Take, for example, the case of Pete Andrade, a Teamster boss in northern California. In December 1963 Andrade had, in a statement to Dick Kavner, "pledged his support and loyalty" to Gibbons. In May 1966, though, when Kavner again traveled in the West, Andrade gave him a different message to carry back to Gibbons: "He will not support you against Fitzsimmons, he so stated."[20] When, laden with campaign posters and buttons, Gibbons and his friends finally arrived in Miami Beach, they found that most of their erstwhile supporters had, like Andrade, absconded. Just days before the convention was to begin, Gibbons announced to the press that he would not after all be a candidate for general vice president. He understood that the votes weren't there. The posters and buttons had to be packed up and carted back to St. Louis, unused. In fact, in the interest of IBT unity, as he described it, Gibbons wound up nominating Fitz for the job he wanted for himself.

Eight months later, in March 1967, having finally exhausted his appeals but still president of the International Brotherhood of Teamsters, Hoffa entered the federal penitentiary at Lewisburg, Pennsylvania.

Fitz, in Washington, settled behind his absent master's desk.

18

Gibbons Relaxes

A July 1, 1966, editorial in the *Globe-Democrat* noted Gibbons' decision not to take on Frank Fitzsimmons for general vice president of the Teamsters Union. It went on to say:

> Thus the potential challenge of Harold Gibbons of St. Louis came to naught and we are sorry. Perhaps at some later date his efforts will be more successful, as they deserve to be. Mr. Gibbons would, in our opinion, make a first-rate leader of his union.... Although he has been endlessly investigated by Department of Justice agents, they have never come up with a single shred of evidence against him personally. Our feeling is that if there were any chicanery in his personal record, they would have long since discovered it and would not have been the least bashful about presenting it.... Because he is right and because Mr. Hoffa is wrong, we still have the feeling that someday Mr. Gibbons will head the Teamsters. We think it will be a better union when he does.[1]

Politically aware St. Louisans must have been stunned by these words. The *Globe* saying something nice about a labor leader? About a *Teamsters* leader? Gibbons later that day received a note from the city's mayor: "I find it somewhat unusual—especially for the Saint Louis Globe-Democrat—to canonize a person while he is still living. This morning's editorial did just that for you. In this one case, however, I would think Mr. Amberg was justified."[2]

Richard H. Amberg was the *Globe-Democrat*'s publisher. A Georgia native, he had been sent to St. Louis in 1955 by the Newhouse chain, the *Globe*'s owner, to perk up its circulation and advertising revenue—which he did, partly by changing a conservative paper into one that was provocatively right-wing. (Toward this end, Amberg hired the young Patrick Buchanan, later a popular columnist and speechwriter for Richard Nixon, to write editorials.) Dick Amberg was a throwback in several ways. "We all have our little quirks," recalled a former associate, "and one of Dick's was that he could not stand stop signs. He would not stop for them. He drove through without even slowing down."[3] Amberg was often in traffic court, just as the *Globe*'s lawyers were often in court defending the paper against libel lawsuits. (Amberg could be rough. For example: one wheelchair-bound local leftist was routinely described in *Globe* editorials as a "pudgy paraplegic.") Amberg especially disliked civil rights activists such as Bill Clay (about whom more later) and trade union bosses such as Larry Callanan of the Steamfitters, and vigorously sought with his newspaper to drive them from office or put them in prison, or both if practicable.

But he liked Gibbons. He kept this liking to himself at first. Larry Gibbons, Gibbons' younger son, remembered as a boy accompanying his father and mother to Amberg's home one Thanksgiving Day so that the publisher could present the Teamster boss with some *Globe*-sponsored award (Larry didn't recall what the award was for).[4] In those days, the later 1950s or early '60s, Gibbons' name was still poison to most of Amberg's business associates, and for that reason (Larry Gibbons believed) Amberg took care to keep the presentation a secret from news reporters, including his own.

Starting in such small ways, the relationship gradually became more public. The *Globe*, for example, began referring to the union boss in news stories and editorials as *Mister* Gibbons, a practice the *Post-Dispatch* adopted only some years later. And whereas the *Post* gave but perfunctory attention to Gibbons' Teamster benefit shows, the *Globe* not only publicized the shows in advance but also sent its drama critic to review them afterward, always positively. Before long Amberg and Gibbons were sharing the sponsorship of charities such as Dismas House, Morris Shenker's center for the rehabilitation of ex-convicts. By the time Amberg, only fifty-seven, died from a heart attack in 1967, he and Gibbons were leading seminars together at Washington University on employee-management relations. And in the meantime the *Globe* had run the July 1966 editorial in which Gibbons was "canonized."

So far as we know, Gibbons hadn't so much as met either of the two Pulitzers, Joseph II and Joseph III, who successively ran the *Post-Dispatch* during his years in the city, or any of Amberg's predecessors at the *Globe-Democrat* either. So his relationship with Amberg was something of a breakthrough. Odd as the Gibbons-Amberg friendship no doubt appeared to others, it was a sign of shifting winds in the city.

Some of these shifts were starkly material. In 1958, when Gibbons left for Washington and his work with Hoffa, St. Louis remained essentially what it had been at the turn of the twentieth century: a dark, cramped, brick-and-wood town, tightly girdled by the Mississippi on one side and largely rural St. Louis County (with its separate government) on the other. Since expansion outward was impossible, the city's modernizers—led by Mayor Raymond Tucker and the Forces for Progress faction of the Democratic Party—had been bent on reconstructing it internally, a plan that would first require the demolition of older neighborhoods and the removal of their inhabitants (see Chapter 8). This demolishing and removing they proceeded to carry out. Gibbons then returned five years later, in early 1964, to a landscape of scaffolding and cranes. On the waterfront there now slowly rose the great silver arms of Eero Saarinen's Gateway Arch. To the south, in what had been the warehouse district, Busch Stadium, the new home of the baseball Cardinals, was beginning to take shape. Ground was also being cleared for the Poplar Street Bridge, which, when completed, would greatly increase traffic between Missouri and Illinois along U.S. 40, which had itself been expanded from two lanes to four. The idea was to bring new people and new endeavors into the old city and by doing so refresh it.

Meanwhile another construction project was busy subverting the modernizers' plan. This was the federal interstate highway system. Work on the very first of those American superhighways, Interstate 70, had begun near St. Charles, Missouri, just twenty-five miles west of St. Louis, in July 1956. When it was finished, I-70 would draw energy *out* of the city.

Readers will recall that the city of St. Louis had in the nineteenth century legally separated itself from St. Louis County (see Chapter 8). This was done despite the fact that the county, enclosing the city on three sides as it did (the Mississippi took care of the fourth), thereby prevented St. Louis from expanding geographically. The city fathers of those days weren't interested in expanding. The city fathers of the 1950s, on the other hand, would have *loved* to expand—but, because of the old arrangement, couldn't. And worse was to come. With the completion of I-70 many of St. Louis' businesses, much of its capital (and therefore much of its tax base), and an ever-increasing part of its population, began moving west, north, and south—into villages and entirely new towns that, as a result of the transfer, would themselves become independent little cities (some indeed not so little) competing with St. Louis for political and economic significance.[5]

Of course all this had huge implications for the city. It had implications for Local 688 as well. Formerly city dwellers, many of Gibbons' Teamsters now moved into the new settlements to became suburbanites, owners rather than renters, county people with lawnmowers and mortgages. The vast majority of these Teamsters were, like their new neighbors, white. Although the law forbade racial discrimination in the real estate business, informal agreements among buyers and sellers worked to keep African Americans locked into the city. An exception was Levi Sanford, Local 688's vice president. Sanford had a growing family that was feeling cramped in its North St. Louis home. He was able to move to a larger house in a suburb called Olivette— but only because the owner happened to be Dick Kavner, who sold it to him.[6]

Few black St. Louisans had Kavners to help them, however. City Teamsters and county Teamsters were likely to respond to social and political questions in different ways. And, more's the pity, less likely to understand each other.

* * *

18. *Gibbons Relaxes*

Gibbons himself now seemed changed in some ways. His situation was certainly altered. We've been assuming that his central goal in life was to win the presidency of the Teamsters Union and then use the organization to pursue various reforms in society at large. If so, he had been thwarted, first, by his falling-out with Jimmy Hoffa after the Kennedy assassination in 1963 and, second, by Hoffa's choice of Frank Fitzsimmons as the union's caretaker leader

So Gibbons retreated to St. Louis, where, however, he was somewhat at loose ends because Local 688's heroic age was now behind it. The high drama of the early years had calmed. Partly this was due to the effectiveness—his enemies would say the ruthlessness—with which Gibbons had persuaded the city's employers that they could not afford to fight the unionization of their work forces. Partly it was the age, which persuaded employers that they no longer *needed* to fight unionization, because prices could usually be raised to cover increases in wages and benefits. Money had begun to flow during the late Eisenhower years, primed as it was by federal spending on the interstates and other construction projects, and would flow even more freely during the administration of Lyndon Johnson, following John Kennedy's death. Money in the 1960s relaxed tensions between capital and labor. "It was a wonderful time—big government, big business, big unions," recalled the St. Louis lawyer Tom Guilfoil, whose own specialty, then blossoming, was the negotiating of corporate mergers. "There seemed to be money for everyone."[7]

Local 688, with fourteen thousand members, was now the biggest local union in Missouri, one of the biggest in the entire Midwest. Dick Kavner, Gibbons' hard man, directed its day-to-day operations. Pete Saffo, Gibbons' talented diplomat, was secretary-treasurer of Joint Council 13, keeping the peace among the region's IBT leaders. The Teamsters, especially Local 688, remained important political players in the city's Democratic Party. Teamsters and members of the building trades unions—led by the Steamfitters—together provided much of both the manpower (Teamsters) and the money (Steamfitters) behind the party's Politicians faction. The relationship between the Teamsters and Fitters wasn't necessarily an easy one. Not only did both Gibbons and Larry Callanan, the Fitters' boss, possess large egos, which sometimes conflicted, but their respective organizations had dramatically differing views concerning the proper role of trade unions in society. A political scientist at Washington University described their differences this way:

> The Teamsters are the most active vocally and most controversial. They have a fairly fully articulated set of goals for St. Louis which include general expansion of services for low income groups and which emphasizes heavily the betterment of race relations and equality for Negroes. The militance of the Teamsters, with this ideological flavor, is in contrast to the unphilosophical bread-and-butter concerns of the Building Trades [including the Steamfitters] which seek jobs and contracts and find that extensive political alliances are of great assistance in securing these goals. They are not

interested in most of the program of the Teamsters, and the Teamster leaders sometimes express contempt for the unconcern with policy exhibited by the "pork chop" unions. Nevertheless, each group finds that under present conditions their channels of action bring them into working agreements with each other on political questions.[8]

In 1965 one such working agreement paid off in a big way. That spring Ray Tucker of the Forces of Progress faction ran for what would have been an unprecedented fourth term as the city's mayor. As usual he was supported by both of the city's newspapers, by its corporate leaders, and by most of its educated middle class. The Politicians faction—the Teamsters, Steamfitters and other construction unions, and a majority of Democratic ward committeemen—backed Alfonso J. Cervantes, a South Side alderman of Spanish extraction who also owned an insurance agency and a fleet of taxicabs. Cervantes was in addition the overwhelming favorite of the African American North Side, whose voters were still angry at Tucker for, as they saw it, driving them from their former homes in Mill Creek Valley. Cervantes defeated Tucker in the Democratic primary and then went on to swamp his Republican challenger in the general election. For the first time since its coming together in the early '50s, the Politicians faction had a friend in the mayor's chair.

In this friendlier atmosphere Gibbons himself seemed to relax—excessively, some people thought. He had, even in his early St. Louis days, alternated intense organizing activity with what an associate called periods of "ennui" —doldrums so deep that friends would ship him out of town on a Greyhound bus just to get him moving again (see Chapter 7). The pattern became more marked in the 1960s. "There would be stretches when he would be leading civil rights protests, anti-war stuff, [work for the peace candidate] Eugene McCarthy," recalled one local 688 staffer. At other times, this person said, Gibbons "got so wrapped up in the glamour and playing golf and that sort of stuff.... Involving himself with the entertainment crowd: Frank Sinatra, Dean Martin, Sammy Davis, Jr."[9]

Gibbons had come to golf belatedly, when he was nearly fifty. Patrick Gibbons, the elder son, has dated his father's passion for the game from the construction, in 1958, of the camp for Local 688 members outside the village of Pevely, Missouri. A union staffer named Ferguson Keathley (who would later marry Yuki Kato, Gibbons' longtime jack-of-all-trades) laid out the club's original nine-hole course. Once Gibbons had discovered the game, he had the course enlarged to eighteen holes. Few other members ever used it, but whenever Gibbons was in town he would drive down to Pevely and play at least one round with Keathley. "He went at the game like he did everything else," said Patrick Gibbons. "One hundred and ten percent."[10]

He became a pretty fair amateur golfer. Keith Payne—a young woman who, though born Nell Keith, had always been called by her middle name

("My mother knew when I was born that I'd be a tomboy," she said)—became Gibbons' personal golf instructor. He was, she said, "a kind, gentle, warm man who loved people and loved to laugh, a man who would do almost anything for his friends, who enjoyed fine food and wine—and who, most of all, loved to play golf." Of his skill at the game she said, "I gave him a half-decent swing that allowed him to score pretty well—for him. He broke ninety many times."

And Payne mentioned another, related Gibbons passion of the '60s. "He loved to have, and play golf with, celebrity friends."[11]

Gibbons had begun meeting show-business celebrities through the charity shows that Jake McCarthy and Pete Saffo produced for Joint Council 13 in the '50s. First there were the boxing matches, then, in the early '60s, when prizefighting went out of style, performances by stage and television stars such as Jimmy Durante and George Jessel. He met other celebrities on trips to Las Vegas. A chronic night owl, "Harold loved Vegas," recalled his son Patrick. "It ran on *his* time. He went to all the shows. He'd go to the first show, stay for the second and third, then go drinking with the stars. That's probably how he met Frank Sinatra."[12]

Sinatra was at the time interested in liberal politics, especially civil rights. He had gotten to know the Kennedy family because his friend the actor Peter Lawford had married Patricia Kennedy, Senator John Kennedy's sister. Sinatra became an active supporter of the senator's during the presidential campaign of 1960. That year, in an attempt to heal the breach between the Kennedys and the Teamsters Union, Sinatra brought together his new acquaintance Harold Gibbons and the family patriarch Joseph P. Kennedy at the latter's home in in Palm Beach, Florida. The elder Kennedy hoped thereby to win electoral support for his son from the Teamsters.[13] The talks failed because Hoffa, whose approval was needed for the deal, had by this time apparently come to hate *all* Kennedys. But Sinatra and Gibbons became good friends anyway.

That friendship thrived in a social scene in which the lady golfer Keith Payne was a participant. So, although she didn't meet Gibbons until a dozen years after the 1960 election, we ought to say something about her here.

Payne, born in 1950 in Atlanta, Georgia, was a slight, sandy-haired, athletic young woman who in the late '60s went to work as the golf pro at the Savannah Inn and Country Club, near the city of that name. The Teamsters' Central States Pension Fund then owned the hotel and club; it was run by Lou Rosanova, a representative of Chicago's Outfit. Rosanova, Payne said, introduced her to Gibbons. The Savannah Inn may also have been the place where Keith first met her friends Peter and Mary Epsteen. Peter Epsteen was an associate of Sam Giancana, an Outfit boss. Epsteen owned a Pontiac dealership in Chicago for some years, but later moved his car business to Palm

Springs in southern California. He seems also to have served Outfit functions in Las Vegas, such as introducing high-roller gamblers to stars who performed in the casinos there. Payne said she thought it was Epsteen who introduced Gibbons, not a high roller, to Sinatra.[14]

According to Payne, Epsteen put some effort into making Gibbons feel at home in Vegas. She suspected, she said, that Epsteen did this at the behest of Giancana and "the guys" (as she called them), because Gibbons was known to be close to Hoffa, whose Central States Pension Fund was pouring millions of dollars into Las Vegas real estate (see Chapter 12), and "the guys" wanted Hoffa and his fund to keep pouring. Payne said she once flew with Gibbons and Epsteen, on a plane the latter had chartered, to Las Vegas for the opening of a new show headlined by the pop singers Steve Lawrence and Eydie Gormé. After the show, they visited the two stars in their dressing rooms. Like most people, Gibbons enjoyed meeting celebrities. "I think Peter [Epsteen] was the one who arranged a lot of Gibbons' backstage visits," Payne said.[15]

The Gibbons-Sinatra relationship grew considerably past the dressing-room encounter stage, however. Aside from periodic quarrels, the most serious of which would occur in 1973, they remained drinking and golfing buddies to the end.

Sinatra was at the peak of his career in the mid-'60s. Gibbons would have liked to recruit him for one of the Teamsters' annual charity shows in St. Louis, but, according to his son Patrick, hesitated to ask because he thought it would be an imposition on the friendship. "But," Patrick Gibbons said, "one night when they were lying next to each other getting massaged in a Vegas spa, Sinatra suddenly said, 'You know, I ought to come do a show in your town.' And did. That was the start."[16]

Sinatra brought his show to St. Louis' Kiel Auditorium the next year, on Father's Day in June 1965. He was accompanied by Dean Martin, Sammy Davis Jr., Johnny Carson (then just a few years into his decades-long role as host of TV's *Tonight Show*), and two orchestras, one of them Count Basie's. Money collected from the ticket sale went to Dismas House, the halfway house for ex-convicts. The show was filmed by a CBS-TV camera crew and can be seen on a DVD.[17] It opens with brief footage of Gibbons, stiffly self-conscious but resplendent in a tuxedo, introducing the entertainers.

Sinatra returned two years later. For a show in February 1967 he brought along a much larger retinue, including Martin, Milton Berle (who served as emcee), the singers Connie Francis, Kaye Stevens, and Trini Lopez, a comic named Pat Henry, Herb Alpert and the Tijuana Brass, Nelson Riddle's Orchestra, and two groups of tap dancers. The movie actress Mia Farrow, Sinatra's wife at the time, was present but did not perform. Four thousand people crowded the Kiel Opera House for the show and hundreds more watched it via closed-circuit TV at St. Louis' Fox Theatre, Chicago's Congress Hotel, and New York's Americana Hotel. The combined audiences contributed $570,000, which was split among twenty St. Louis charities. (The Teamsters had raised but $10,000 in their first benefit, the prizefights of 1955.) Customers who had paid $150 and up for the choice seats were invited to a "champagne supper" after the show in the Chase Park Hotel's fancy Khorassan Room.[18]

Unlike the filmed '65 event, this second one seems to have vanished into the ether. We don't know what songs were sung or which jokes told. But there do survive photographs of the post-performance champagne supper at the Chase Park. In them the stars sit at a group of tables arranged in the midst of—but separate from—those of the larger crowd, the show-goers who had paid what was in those days a fairly steep price for both good seats at the show and a chance to hobnob with the celebrities at the post-performance supper. Surrounding the stars—like skirmishers around a wagon train—is a troop of uniformed Andy Frain ushers. So there couldn't have been much hobnobbing going on.

The scene in the Khorassan Room resembles that near the end of Proust's *In Search of Lost Time*. In the novel Madame Verdurin, formerly the patron of a small rural salon, has since married into the aristocracy and become so great a personage and attracted so many new followers that they must be accommodated in vast hotel banquet rooms rather than, as before, in her own parlor. The original salon members complain of the loss of intimacy but are "at heart delighted … to be a focus and an object of envy for the neighbouring tables."[19] The stars in the Khorassan Room are clearly not so delighted as Verdurin's guests. Indeed, they seem exhausted or bored or both. Berle sits alone contemplating his cigar. The vaudeville veteran George Jessel appears to sleep in his chair. True, Mia Farrow, sitting on a couch with Sinatra, is smiling at someone out of camera range, but her husband wears an abstracted look, as if remembering other evenings. Only Gibbons, facing the photographer from a squatting position behind the Sinatras' couch, wears a big grin. He's the one fan resourceful enough to slip through the Frain ushers and mix with the stars.[20]

"Sinatra was Gibbons' big show business benefactor," said Jake McCarthy.[21] Gibbons was strongly attracted to show-business people. A stockbroker acquaintance of Gibbons' put it less kindly: "He was starstruck."[22] But if Gibbons was drawn to Sinatra by his celebrity, what drew the singer to the labor leader?

Part of it was politics. Sinatra was a mild left-winger in those days. Within a few years he would swing right (and, after befriending Spiro Agnew, Richard Nixon's vice president, would endorse the Nixon-Agnew ticket for reelection in 1972), but he had started out in the '30s as an enthusiastic New Dealer and in the mid-'60s still thought of himself as a liberal Democrat. Gibbons was well-known as a labor intellectual and civil rights advocate.

There may have been other people who, in the wee Las Vegas hours, after the showgirls and liquor had begun to pall, could engage Sinatra, an intelligent man, in as lucidly a discussion of political economy in the United States as could Harold Gibbons, but they were surely very few.

Another possible basis for the friendship between Sinatra and Gibbons was suggested by Keith Payne, the latter's golf pro girlfriend. Payne said that Sinatra had for many years sought the respect of various mobsters ("the guys," in her phrase). Las Vegas in the '60s was a resort town run by "guys," particularly those from Chicago's Outfit, with their access to the Teamsters' Central States Pension Fund. Gibbons, Payne said, had "the guys'" respect whether he wanted it or not, whereas Sinatra, she believed, never could win it because to them he was just "a paid entertainer." Gibbons, she said, had encouraged Jimmy Hoffa to invest Teamster pension-fund money in Las Vegas. (Elizabeth Vasquez and Larry Gibbons disagreed. Larry said, "He firmly believed that the people who did that would go to jail or die.")[23] Whether it was true or not, the "guys" believed it, Payne said. "The guys don't forget things like that. Gibbons was one-on-one with members in high places of the underworld. Frankie just loved to be around them. He was their 'pet' in a way. Gibbons was *never* that."[24] Sinatra may have believed that hanging around Gibbons would cause the mobsters to take him seriously as well, though that didn't happen, Payne said.

Her argument was that, although an outsider would likely see the relationship between the universally famous Hollywood actor-singer Sinatra and the provincial labor boss Gibbons as representing social climbing on the latter's part, it was, in the world the two men shared—Las Vegas in the 1960s, where "the guys" often set the social tone—the other way around. Gibbons held the higher rank.

One could ask why, if Gibbons was made uncomfortable by the presence of mobsters in the IBT's headquarters in Washington (see Chapter 16), he was so willing to be seen as one of them in Las Vegas. The answer may be that he had lots of company. Among some men it was fashionable, especially in the first half of the decade. Sinatra personified the style (even if, as Payne said, real mobsters made fun of him for it). Another man who adopted not just the fashion but the way of life was the criminal defense lawyer Morris Shenker. In the '60s Shenker chucked his St. Louis life to acquire a partnership in the Dunes Casino in Vegas. This surprised his friends, including Tom Eagleton. The senator remembered asking, "Morris, why on earth would you give up your very successful law practice to run a gambling casino in Las Vegas?" Eagleton, making an attempt at the lawyer's East European accent, then quoted his reply: "'Because it's so *een*teresting!'"[25]

Las Vegas was interesting also for Gibbons.

The Sinatra-Gibbons friendship evidently was valuable to both men. In

1969 Gibbons spent $40,000 to buy a small house in the resort town of Palm Springs, which had become Sinatra's vacation home. (Such in any case the FBI was told by an informant, who added that Sinatra had loaned Gibbons the money for the purchase.)[26] Keith Payne strongly denied this, arguing that Gibbons might conceivably have borrowed money from Peter Epsteen, but would never have borrowed from the singer. "I think Gibbons would have been too proud to take from Frankie," she said.)[27] Gibbons' next door neighbor in Palm Springs was Jilly Rizzo, Sinatra's oldest friend. Next door to Rizzo's place was the home of Pat Henry, a comedian who warmed up audiences for Sinatra's shows. And Gibbons regularly played golf at the local Mission Hills Country Club, where Sinatra and his show-business pals had taken roost.

Wherever they crossed paths, Gibbons and Sinatra seem to have behaved like teenagers on a spree. Jake McCarthy remembered Gibbons coming into the Local 688 office one morning smiling broadly. He and Sinatra had been on the town the night before, Gibbons told him. But there had been a hitch: the singer knew no women in St. Louis. The union boss therefore got on the phone to hunt one up for him. "Imagine that," Gibbons said. "I had to go to *my* little black book to find a date for Frank Sinatra."[28]

Some of Gibbons' labor friends were dismayed by this side of him. Jerry Tucker, a young United Auto Workers leader, recalled going downtown to the CBS-TV affiliate one Sunday afternoon to appear with Gibbons on a public-affairs show. When the show's taping was completed, Gibbons invited Tucker to come home with him for a drink.

Gibbons had by then left the Chase Park Hotel and moved to a penthouse apartment atop Local 688's headquarters in Council Plaza on South Grand Avenue. His apartment had two approaches, one, public, was via an elevator in the building's lobby, the other, theoretically private, was by way of an outside staircase. The outside stairs were built, according to David Salmon, so that the union boss "could bring in women friends without using the elevator." As it happened, however, the staircase had been so constructed that it stood in full view of the two apartment towers put up for retired elderly people, and "some of the retirees waited [at] their picture windows … to see what women Gibbons was bringing in for that particular evening."[29]

Since the TV show occurred on a Sunday and Local 688's building was closed for business, Tucker and Gibbons presumably took the elevator. Arriving upstairs in the penthouse, they found a poker game in progress. Among the players were two of Sinatra's pals, the comedians Joey Bishop and Buddy Hackett. Also present were two young women, "somewhat scantily dressed but very attractive," Tucker recalled. These were showgirls who had "'come in with us from Las Vegas, just to keep us company and serve us drinks,'" Gibbons informed his young friend. "'What'll you have?'"

The players were happily raucous, Tucker remembered. "The comedians were, you know, funny. Quick one-liners. Unrehearsed stuff. Buddy Hackett was particularly funny, sticking it to the other guys around the table."

Gibbons asked Tucker if he would like to sit in. "And I looked, and these guys are betting five hundred dollars for openers and stuff like that," Tucker said. He recalled blanching at the thought. "'Aw, don't worry,' Gibbons told him. 'I'll give you a line of credit.'" Tucker said he'd rather just sit and watch for a while.

"I didn't stay too long," he recalled many years after the event. "I must have been there thirty, forty minutes. I figured that was just about enough exposure to the fast life of Harold Gibbons and went on home."[30]

* * *

In his memoirs, Jimmy Hoffa confesses to having made two "disastrous" mistakes in his career. First was getting into an unwinnable fight with Robert Kennedy. The second came in 1966 when, finally realizing that he could not avoid going to prison, he decided he must pick someone else to occupy the IBT's presidency until he came out to take it up again. He writes: "The choice came down to either Harold Gibbons, who for a long time had been one of my most loyal supporters, or Frank Fitzsimmons. I booted it. I picked Fitzsimmons."[31]

Hoffa went into Lewisburg Penitentiary in March 1967. From there he planned to continue running the union through Fitzsimmons, until then the humblest of servants. "The arrangement," recalled one of Hoffa's lawyers, "was that I was to take the orders from Hoffa during my visits [to Lewisburg] and deliver them to Fitz."[32] Fitz's job was to see that those orders were carried out. But by August 1968, according to an FBI informant inside the prison, Hoffa was saying "he was not satisfied with the independent attitude of Acting Teamster Head Fitzsimmons.... Fitzsimmons has not been following his orders and when Hoffa is released from Federal custody Fitzsimmons will probably get demoted to a lesser role in operating the union."[33]

To demote Fitz, though, Hoffa would first have to get himself out of prison. And, once out, he would then face other serious obstacles. One was Fitz's growing fondness for the president's job and the perks that went with it. Another was the union's dozen or so vice presidents. By tradition an IBT president sat quietly behind his desk, letting the vice presidents and lesser officials run their particular fiefdoms as they wanted (the Teamsters were the most decentralized of trade unions). Hoffa had briefly changed that setup. As the journalist Murray Kempton, a longtime Hoffa watcher, described it, Hoffa's

> major achievement as an organizer was to convert the Teamsters Union from a confederation of regional barons to a monarchical structure obedient to every command from national headquarters. The construction of this monument was not quite com-

plete when he went to jail; and the endemically anarchic impulses of Teamster habit soon enough wrecked its foundations. Every professional went back into business for himself, delighted to be free of Hoffa's overbearing interferences and unable to regard his return from prison as other than the gravest of perils to the independence of subordinates, who, having wept to see him go, found themselves rejoicing to have him gone.[34]

In short, although Fitzsimmons and other IBT hierarchs at first noisily petitioned the government to get Hoffa's sentence reduced, they did so with a rapidly dwindling sense of urgency. Hoffa was always popular with the union's rank and file, but he had no real friends among its bosses. They were content to let him sit in jail.

The exception was Gibbons. Despite their falling-out over John Kennedy's murder, despite the choice of Fitz rather than Gibbons as the union's caretaker, the St. Louisan remained a Hoffa loyalist. As we'll see, this turned out to be costly for him.

* * *

Meanwhile, as Gibbons partied with celebrities, a formidable young rival was learning the political ropes on St. Louis' North Side. William L. Clay, an African American born in 1931, grew up in a city very different from that which Harold Gibbons had made his adopted home. St. Louis' black population, a little over a tenth of the whole in 1941, had by the 1960s become a third. Most black people lived in the formerly Irish neighborhoods north of Delmar Boulevard, where their nucleus had moved after the destruction of Mill Creek Valley under Mayor Ray Tucker. Concentrated there, they eventually paid Tucker back by voting him out of office. Mill Creek, Bill Clay would write in his memoirs, was "an unconscionable transgression of the property rights of black home owners. However, in terms of political assessment, it greatly expanded the political base of our people."[35]

Clay had been in politics of one sort or another most of his life. He started out in the youth auxiliary of St. Louis' NAACP, whose president was Ernest "Cab" Calloway, Gibbon's house intellectual. Calloway became Clay's mentor. "He was an astute politician with an analytical mind," Clay writes. "We developed most of our campaign ploys by bouncing them off him and evaluating his reactions."[36]

The Calloway-Clay relationship hit its first bump in 1958 when the NAACP's youth group engaged the folk singer Pete Seeger to perform at a fundraising concert. Seeger had once been close to the Communist Party. The young people apparently weren't aware of that fact, but Calloway, an old-fashioned, anti–Communist socialist, certainly was. The older man "red-baited" the youth group and canceled the concert, Clay writes.[37] Angered by Calloway's interference, Clay dropped out of the NAACP and became active in CORE instead.

Clay worked briefly in real-estate and insurance before taking a job as a business agent for a public employees' union, the American Federation of State, County, and Municipal Employees. In this role he got a chance to take on Gibbons himself. At first the two men merely skirmished a bit. "In 1961 Local 688 raided the … union I was associated with, public employees—street and parks department workers," Clay said. "Then we raided them and got our members back—plus some of theirs."[38]

But Clay was an enormously competitive man. His real opportunity to deliver "payback," as he put it, came in 1962. As might have been foreseen, it involved the city's chronically unhappy taxicab drivers. Teamsters Local 405, the cabbies' organization, had by then been under Gibbons' trusteeship for nearly a decade, meaning that its officers were Local 688 people appointed by him rather than elected by Local 405's own membership. The wildcat strike of 1956 had only increased Gibbons' reluctance to ease his grip on the cabbies. Five years after the wildcat, the National Labor Relations Board finally ordered an election. In what turned out to be drawn-out campaign for the right to continue representing the taxi drivers, Gibbons' Teamsters found themselves opposed by a land-based department of the Seafarers Union. Bill Clay, an outsider (and indeed an officer of still a third union, the public employees), cast his lot with the Seafarers. That union had built a following among Local 405's white members. The largest African American cab company in town was Marcella, whose drivers had previously shown no particular desire to leave the Teamsters. Clay went to work on them. "Well, I knew a lot of those cab drivers," he said later, "and when the … election was held the Seafarers won by two hundred votes."[39] So Gibbons, who had long taken pains to insist on the desegregation of a Jim Crow taxicab local, now lost the cabbies of *both* races to an integrated campaign against himself.

Clay had earlier become a public official. In 1959, by which time the population of the 26th Ward, in St. Louis' northwest, had clearly tilted African American, he and several others began jockeying for the Democratic nomination for alderman of the ward. Through a combination of brashness and charm Clay won secret financial support from Jordan Chambers, boss of the North Side's black Democrats. Until then Chambers had backed white, usually Irish, politicians, in return for patronage jobs that he doled out among his followers. (Chambers' money was delivered to Clay by the white, one-legged war veteran Joe Ames, a former Gibbons lieutenant and CORE activist—see Chapter 6.)[40] With Chambers' help Clay won both the primary and general elections. The city woke to find itself with twenty-seven white aldermen—and, for the first time in its history, a black one.

But the really big moment in Bill Clay's life came in the late summer of 1963. CORE had begun a campaign against the Jefferson Bank and Trust Co., on Washington Boulevard, on the city's near North Side. Although the bank

18. Gibbons Relaxes

had many African American depositors, its owners and employees were all white. CORE demanded that the bank hire four black tellers, threatening to hold protest demonstrations if it refused. On Friday, August 30, a circuit judge issued a restraining order against actions that might interfere with bank business. To add muscle to his order he also issued an injunction against nine specific CORE leaders. Clay was one of the nine.

On the afternoon of the 30th, several hundred demonstrators carrying signs appeared on the bank's sidewalk. Some went into the building and sat on the floor, blocking access to tellers' cages. Soon police and sheriff's deputies appeared. There then occurred a certain amount of confusion, some pushing and shoving, tripping and stumbling, but no real trouble. And no arrests. The arrests began in the evening. The nine CORE leaders were charged with contempt of court for failure to obey the judge's orders, and within a few days all were in jail.

Clay would later write that, from the start of the bank campaign, "the landscape of the civil rights movement in the city underwent radical change.... The passive, condescending behavior of established Negro leaders with whom the power structure customarily dealt was replaced by an aggressive, uncompromising—and in many cases angry—new black leadership."[41]

The white establishment's response to the bank campaign helped shape that "radical change." CORE was energetically denounced by Missouri's governor, by Mayor Ray Tucker, by the conservative *Globe-Democrat*, even by the liberal *Post-Dispatch*. Sharpest of all was the *Globe*, which said, "The efforts of this infinitesimally small but boisterous segment of the St. Louis community will disgust and revolt all of those who—like this newspaper—have been working so long to open new opportunities to Negroes to improve the status of the race."[42] It's likely, however, that few black North Siders were disgusted by CORE's actions. In those days North Siders who had jobs were cooks, maids, janitors, many of whom nursed the hope that their children might grow up to become, say, bank tellers. Now the Jefferson Bank had all but said that their dream wouldn't come true.

But military defeat can sometimes blossom into political victory. In Ireland, in April 1916, for example, a small band of armed rebels seized and briefly held sections of the city of Dublin. The English, who had ruled the island for centuries, first suppressed the rebellion and then quickly courtmartialed and shot fifteen rebel leaders. The Irish public, hitherto annoyed by and even contemptuous of what it saw as the rebels' pretensions, was outraged by the executions. Rallying belatedly to the rebel side, the Irish spent the next six years driving the English from their shores.

Jefferson Bank was Dublin without the shooting. CORE's campaign continued for another seven months, until, in March 1964, the bank hired a halfdozen African American white-collar employees. Other previously all-white businesses began hiring blacks as well. Apparently they were afraid not to. "They felt we would come to them next," said Norman Seay, a CORE leader.[43]

Meanwhile public attention had shifted from Jefferson Bank jobs to the fate of the CORE Nine. Accused of "criminal contempt of court," the Nine went on trial in the autumn of 1963. To try the case, the judge appointed as special prosecutor a man who also happened to be the Jefferson Bank's lawyer, and such were the times then that few white people seem to have thought that appointment odd. Each of the defendants was found guilty. They were sentenced to terms ranging from 60 to 270 days in the city jail. Clay and another man, CORE's chairman, received the 270-day sentences.

Clay was thirty-two that year, a slim man with close-cropped hair and a small, neat beard. He was prominent among the Nine, and especially disliked in some (mainly white) quarters because as an alderman he was a public official who had openly defied another public official, the judge. In his case, it was felt, "criminal contempt" was more than just a legal phrase. Thanks to the court system, Clay's fame grew. The Jefferson Bank protesters' case climbed through a series of appeals till it reached the U.S. Supreme Court (which refused to hear it, thereby letting the convictions stand), and with each new verdict Clay's name and photo appeared again in the press. It wasn't until the spring of 1967 that the case was finally concluded. For many people in South St. Louis (especially among *Globe* readers) the dark face seen again and again in the newspapers was that of a villain. Not so in the North.

In the 1920s, after the English had finally given up and gone home, survivors of the 1916 Rebellion often found themselves elected to the government of the newly independent Ireland. Something similar occurred in North St. Louis. At election time, it became an advantage for a candidate there to portray himself or herself as a veteran of the Jefferson Bank campaign. Some such claims were more credible than others. But no one could doubt Bill Clay's.

19

Calloway for Congress

"Calloway was the idea guy," Mike Ryan said. "He planted ideas with Gibbons and then created ways to implement them."[1]

The idea in this particular case was the Tandy project.

Tandy is a five-acre park in North St. Louis. It was named for one Charlton Hunt Tandy, a free black man who raised and led a militia company for the North in the Civil War and was for fifty years afterward a power in the local Republican Party. Tandy Park forms the heart of the Ville, one of St. Louis' oldest African American settlements. In 1966, when Local 688 launched what it called the Tandy Area Council, the Ville was home to Ernest "Cab" Calloway and his wife DeVerne.

Since the turn of the century, the Ville had belonged to the city's black bourgeoisie—physicians, lawyers, merchants, and at least one millionaire: Annie Malone, a manufacturer of hair-care products. Members of the black middle class settled there because then-legal restrictive covenants barred them from many other parts of North St. Louis, most of which had been settled by people of Irish and German descent. In 1948 the Supreme Court declared the covenants unconstitutional. As it happened, the period of the covenants' collapse was also that when the city's African American population, until then rather small, more than doubled, rising from about 13 percent of the total to nearly a third.[2] The newcomers were not middle-class. They were mostly poor Southerners, rural people, ill-educated farm laborers and sharecroppers displaced by the mechanization of agriculture. History funneled them into North St. Louis, where they joined the city's internal refugees, equally poor former residents of the now-flattened Mill Creek Valley (see Chapter 8). Meanwhile the Irish and Germans fled.

An observer of this process wrote: "In the 1950s the area of the city open to black residents increased from 500 to 650 square blocks, but all 150 of these new blocks had already been designated as deteriorating or blighted by the City Plan Commission before blacks moved in. Loan agencies refused to extend credit to whites for purchases in these areas, further encouraging white flight.

Unscrupulous realtors exploited the black demand for housing (as well as white hostility to blacks) by "blockbusting"—frightening white homeowners about declining property values in order to panic them into selling houses at low prices that realtors could then resell to blacks at inflated prices."[3]

The writer is describing an exchange of populations, a phenomenon that often occurs between two countries at the end of a war. In this case, blacks wound up occupying neighborhoods from which they had previously been barred. Whites moved to newer suburban developments in the north and west. The problem for the North Side was that whereas most of the Irish and Germans, although not wealthy, had at least possessed decent jobs, few of the African Americans had any but the most menial occupations. Nor were they likely to get decent-paying jobs, given white employers' refusal to hire blacks. So the housing stock, already blighted (according to the City Plan Commission), could only continue deteriorating. General poverty festered and spread.

The Calloways, who had watched the impoverishment of the North Side practically from the start, were determined to do something about it, each in his or her own way. In 1962 DeVerne Calloway was elected as a Democrat—and the first African American woman—to Missouri's legislature. There she served for twenty years, focusing primarily on measures to help the poor, especially women and children.[4]

Ernest Calloway spent the late '50s as president of the city's NAACP. In the mid-'60s he was appointed by St. Louis Democrats to the board of the local Office of Economic Opportunity, the main engine of the Johnson administration's War on Poverty. He was initially attracted by the OEO's "community action" programs, which sent volunteer social workers into impoverished neighborhoods to show residents how to tackle their problems. But he soon became disillusioned with those efforts; they seemed to him intended to placate angry poor people, not rouse them to serious action. Or, as Calloway put it, the OEO's real aim was not so much to reduce poverty as "to contain the 'poor' without disturbing traditional economic and political balances in the urban complex."

What was needed, Calloway decided, was a "trade union oriented war on the slums." And the person to wage such a war was "the Negro trade unionist," who, he wrote, would instinctively apply the lessons learned "during the eight-hour period where he works to the sixteen-hour period in the community where he lives."[5] No doubt Calloway was thinking of Local 688's old community stewards program (see Chapter 8). That program seems to have fallen into disrepair in the late '50s, partly because many of the local's members were beginning to move from city wards, where the program had originated, to the suburbs. But those leaving were mainly white members. Calloway had his eye on the black Teamsters left behind.

He calculated that there were some five-hundred African American Local 688 members living on the North Side of St. Louis. Under the original Local 688 program, which was ward-based, any city ward containing at least twenty-five of the local's members could elect a "community steward." The steward's job was to pressure the appropriate ward alderman or Democratic party committeeman to install stoplights at dangerous intersections, improve trash collection, and perform whatever other tasks that residents wanted done. (In return, the alderman or committeeman could usually count on receiving those votes in the next election.) If twenty-five activist Teamsters could change a neighborhood, what might not *five hundred* accomplish on the North Side? With such forces Calloway hoped (in the words of a writer friendly to his project) to apply "the strategic insights of trade unionism to the realm of community organizing."[6]

Thus in 1967 the Tandy Area Council (TAC) was born. Gibbons enthusiastically agreed to support Calloway's project. But Ernest Calloway, one of nature's professors, was not himself an activist. Formal leadership of TAC was assigned to Jim Pace, a young Methodist minister from Brownsville, Texas, who had spent nearly a decade working in church-sponsored Peace Corps–type projects in Latin America. Gibbons had brought him into Local 688 as its political director, replacing Sid Zagri. (Zagri—see Chapter 8—had gone to Washington with Gibbons in 1957, but then stayed on with Hoffa after the 1963 split). Whereas Zagri had seen his job mainly as a vehicle for funding friendly political candidates, Pace, viewing it through the lens of his Latin-American experience, wanted to return to grass-roots organizing.

If, however, Calloway was too donnish in manner to conjure crowds in North St. Louis, Pace the Texan was far too white to even try it. He therefore recruited two talented young black Local 688 organizers, Claude Brown and Levi Sanford, to work the streets. Brown and Sanford rented a storefront at the intersection of Grand Boulevard and Hebert Street, a location about a mile northeast of Tandy Park, to serve as TAC's headquarters.

Since its chief expense was Brown's and Sanford's salaries, TAC was a relatively cheap operation. (Which Gibbons surely appreciated, since he was beginning to take heat from more conservative Local 688 members who disliked what they saw as his detours from straight meat-and-potatoes trade unionism.) Fortunately, as far as TAC was concerned, high spirits were more necessary than money in the early days, and high spirits were plentiful. Brown and Sanford soon attracted numerous bright volunteers, including North Side Teamsters such as Leroy Graham and Frank Boykin, independent street agitators like Ivory Perry, and members of other leftish unions, especially the United Auto Workers. The late Jerry Tucker, then a militant young UAW leader at the Carter Carburetor plant, several blocks up the street, heard about the Tandy Area Council soon after it was inaugurated. As he recalled it, "I walked into [TAC] one day and said, 'Hey, I'm here to find out what's going on. Our local union is up on North Grand ... and maybe we can help you in some way.'"7

The TAC fish spawned many minnows. One group patrolled the aisles of North Side supermarkets to make sure the prices were no higher and the meat and produce no less fresh than those in the white suburbs. A second group helped single mothers sign up for Aid for Dependent Children benefits, and a third encouraged landlords to keep their rental properties in good repair, picketing the landlords' homes if they failed to do so.

An especially bright memory for Tucker was the occasion on which TAC, the UAW, and local supporters of the California-based United Farm Workers combined to pressure North Side supermarkets into discontinuing the sale of non-union California grapes. Several hundred marchers gathered one Saturday morning to picket the Kroger and A&P stores in the Water Tower neighborhood of North Grand. Cheers went up when, after a mysterious, chauffeur-driven car pulled alongside the marchers, Gibbons and the Farm Workers' Cesar Chavez popped out to join the picket.

Whether Calloway was present Tucker didn't say. Always an undramatic figure, he was nonetheless much respected by the young people around TAC, Tucker remembered. "He was sort of their guru, their mentor."8

Mike Ryan, a wearer in those day of various Local 688 hats, including TAC's, described a voter-registration drive conducted by the council. "We registered lots and lots of people to vote," he said. First, though, the rules first had to be changed. To register under the old rules, a prospective voter had to make his or her way downtown to the registrar's office—and do so on a work day, because the office was closed on weekends. "But we [Local 688] placed people on the city's board of election commissioners," Ryan said. The reconstituted board of commissioners purchased a fleet of vans, which were then used to carry assistant registrars "to union functions and into the community to register voters. During business hours," Ryan added. "And on Saturdays and Sundays too."9

* * *

As the North Side's racial composition changed, so did its politics. For years its leading public officials—aldermen, state representatives, state senators—had been white male Democrats whose patrons were white, usually Irish, political bosses. As noted, this tradition was broken in 1962 when DeVerne Calloway (backed, as it happened, by an Irish patron) was elected to the legislature. After that the whites, both candidates and bosses, fell one by one until 1968, when Raymond Howard of CORE, a veteran of the Jefferson Bank campaign, unseated Mike Kinney in a contest for the state senate. Kinney, ninety-three years old, a remnant of the old Egan gang, had been in the senate since 1912. Jelly Roll Hogan, whose own clan once fought the Egans with pistols and tommy guns, had lost his state senate seat a few years earlier. (See Chapter 8.) An ancient order was passing.

But 1968 was also the year of an even bigger political event. Black St. Louis got its own congressman.

Until then Missouri's 13th Congressional District, in which most of the city's African Americans then found themselves, included many more white voters than black, so victory there seemed out of reach. But politics, like unhappiness, is always aboil. In 1964 Democrats from Missouri's five-county rural Bootheel region (the stub protruding into northeastern Arkansas), feeling disregarded by the party's then-dominant Kansas City faction, came north looking for friends. One summer evening a group of Bootheelers attended a barbecue in the back yard of the North Side home of Joe Ames, the one-legged former aide to Harold Gibbons. Ames had a decade earlier left Local 688 for a job with the American Federation of State, County and Municipal Employees. More importantly, he had become the white lieutenant of the North Side's African American political boss, Jordan Chambers. Chambers had since died, but not before electing Ames a state legislator from a black district.[10] ("Elected him, hell! Chambers *appointed* Joe Ames," said the lawyer-politico Tom Guilfoil.)[11] Ames was thus poised to broker a deal between black and white party factions. For his barbecue he brought the Bootheelers—representatives of cotton planters whose political and social views differed in no way from their Arkansas planter neighbors: they were dixiecrat segregationists—face to face with the North Side's insurgents, including Bill Clay. Over steaks and whiskey certain understandings were reached.[12]

Ames, talking about the barbecue many years later, didn't specify what these understandings were. But one can guess. Warren Hearnes, the Bootheelers' leader, was that fall elected Missouri's governor, with North Side help. Tom Eagleton, a young St. Louisan with whom Hearnes had formed an alliance a few years earlier, became lieutenant governor.[13] Then, in 1967, a handful of Bootheel Democratic legislators and their allies joined the Republican minority in redistricting a large chunk of North St. Louis and St. Louis County, thereby giving African Americans a congressional district in which they would be predominant.

Ernest Calloway had a hand in this operation as well. The legislature's vote to redistrict came as the result of a decision of the U.S. Supreme Court, and Calloway was one of several North Side plaintiffs whose lawsuits eventually led to that decision.

However, the new 1st Congressional District (as it was named) was no more than a vague idea until someone actually determined its boundaries. That job fell to Calloway, with the assistance of Mike Ryan. The job was done on weekends. Ryan drove the car while Calloway peered out the window and totted up the households. "It was us and an adding machine," Ryan recalled. "Calloway would say, 'We need to go count Negroes in such and such a neighborhood.' So I would drive and absorb Calloway's wisdom. And we would look at whether we could snatch this piece of property and fit it into the vote line, and whether it was contiguous, and all the other things you have to do."[14]

Elections for the new congressional seat were scheduled for 1968, the party primaries in August, the general in November. Calloway, perhaps feeling that he deserved the seat, having done so much to bring it to birth, announced that he would run as a Democrat.

Other black North Siders considered campaigns of their own. A white man, a professional politician named Milton Carpenter, was also a Democratic candidate. Carpenter wasn't popular among black people in St. Louis: his Howard Johnson's restaurant had been Jim Crow until civil rights laws forbade the practice. Although the new congressional district had a black majority, it continued to possess thousands of whites, and Carpenter banked on their support—and banked as well on multiple black candidates splitting the black vote. And besides Calloway, there *was* another, very serious black hopeful.

Bill Clay, the hero of the Jefferson Bank campaign.

Clay had been busy since the bank episode. He had relinquished his alderman's position to become the 26th Ward's Democratic committeeman. A ward's committeeman, being the person who doled out the ward's patronage jobs and was accordingly in charge of its political machinery, was usually more powerful than its alderman. That was certainly soon true of Clay and the 26th. Clay, moreover, had become associated with Steamfitters' Local 562. The Fitters had been an all-white organization, but Clay persuaded John "Doc" Lawler, the union's political genius, who in turn persuaded his boss, Larry Callanan, that with African Americans rapidly replacing the Irish as the majority population on the North Side, it behooved their union to cultivate allies among rising black politicians—especially Bill Clay. In 1966 the Steamfitters took in fifteen black members, journeymen and apprentices. Clay was hired by the union to supervise their induction.[15]

Getting into Callanan's union was one thing, Clay found; winning Callanan's support for his candidacy for Congress was another. The Fitters' boss had intended to remain neutral. Clay says (in his autobiography, unblushingly titled *Bill Clay: A Political Voice at the Grass Roots*) that he changed Callanan's mind by tricking Harold Gibbons into bragging to a newspaper reporter that, with Teamster help, Ernest Calloway was certain to win the election. Callanan, Clay writes, exploded angrily when he heard about Gibbons' boast. He told the Fitters' treasurer: "Write Clay a check for what he needs now and for whatever he needs on a daily base."[16]

Magic words! Although the Steamfitters were a much smaller organization than Local 688, they were wealthier, especially in what they collected for their political fund. Each of Local 688's thirteen thousand Teamsters paid perhaps fifty cents a month into a political fund—but the one thousand members of Callanan's union put *a dollar per job* into theirs. Clay estimated that the Fitters took in as much as $300,000 annually to spend on political interests. "Could you imagine how much printing, canvassing, telephoning, newspaper ads, and radio time could be bought from the [Fitters'] money machine?" he asks in his memoirs.[17] One can imagine *him* imagining it with great delight.

Ernest Calloway was fifty-nine that year, Bill Clay thirty-seven. Calloway was a principled racial integrationist. He often said, "When I become a Negro first and a trade unionist second, I will have failed in my life."[18]

"He was the real thing," Tom Eagleton said,[19] meaning that Calloway was an American radical of the vintage type. Calloway had spent years tracing the careers of St. Louis' banking, industrial, and merchant leaders, noting their memberships on each other's boards of directors, explaining how those boards' apparently narrow *business* decisions often turned out to be *political* decisions as well, affecting not just the business itself but the whole city, sometimes in unfortunate ways. (The destruction off Mill Creek Valley, which Calloway saw as engineered by real-estate interests, was his frequent example). Calloway's choices as co-chairmen of his congressional campaign illustrated his faith in racial integration: Theodore McNeal, a former Pullman porter who had become the first African American member of the state senate (having unseated Jelly Roll Hogan), and Charles Oldham, a white CORE leader. Calloway, at the rally with which he kicked off his run, called for an interracial movement of the city's mostly white trade unions and its mostly black North Side against what he termed the "local nobility."[20]

If in the primary campaign Calloway took the civil-rights high road, Bill Clay took another. Clay knew that the district's white voters, fearful of their rapidly multiplying black neighbors, were sure to line up solidly behind the erstwhile segregationist Milton Carpenter. Still, he would win, Clay believed, as along as black voters were just as solid for him. But what if blacks split their votes among two or more black candidates? In fact, there were several other black Democrats seeking the party nomination. Calloway seems to have been the one he took most seriously. What if Calloway were to pull enough votes to tip the election to Carpenter? To prevent that, Clay launched an assault whose gist was captured in a headline in a popular North Side weekly: "Clay Charges Calloway with Vote Splitting." In the accompanying article, Clay was quoted as describing Calloway as "part of a conspiracy which involves Harold Gibbons, international vice-president of the Teamsters Union, and has as its aim the defeat of a Negro for Congress in the 1st District."[21] Yes,

Clay was saying, Calloway is himself a black man, but in this instance a black man willing to act as bait in a plan devised by his crafty white master.

Clay seems to have believed this. He repeated it in his 2004 autobiography and said it again in an interview not many years ago: "It was apparent that Calloway had no chance to win. He was running as a spoiler."[22]

Clay was probably wrong. Calloway wasn't running as Gibbons' spoiler. No one who knew Ernest Calloway could imagine him pretending to be something he wasn't—certainly not bait. Clay seems to have been wrong about Gibbons too. Mike Ryan, asked whether the union boss was behind Calloway's campaign for Congress, said, "No, no, that was Calloway's idea. And Gibbons wasn't all that helpful, let alone encouraging of the campaign."[23] David Salmon agrees. Gibbons responded unenthusiastically to Calloway's congressional effort, Salmon writes, possibly out of jealousy, "because he could not stand the thought of Ernest Calloway becoming a challenging public figure."[24]

In fact, Gibbons had been less than happy with the redistricting itself. According to Ryan, Gibbons had been "close to" the area's former congressman, a white, liberal, pro-labor Democrat who had decided after much of thought not to take his chances in the new 1st District's primary and dropped out of the race.[25]

Gibbons then *did* support Calloway, to an extent. On his recommendation, Local 688's Shop Stewards' Council gave Calloway's campaign $5,000, an amount that went much further in 1968 than it would today. But for this race it was nowhere enough. On July 1st, a little over a month before the August primary, Calloway asked Gibbons for an additional $22,500, in order to compete for the support of North Side ward committeemen who were already, he claimed in a memo, going to the "highest bidder."[26] Gibbons' papers don't indicate whether this second wish was granted or not.

There probably wasn't time for counter-bidding anyway. However he did it, Clay already had the North Side committeemen, and thus their organizations, sewed up. But then, lack of money wasn't Calloway's big problem. The problem was that Calloway, the former NAACP president, the elder statesman, was admired on the North Side—but Clay had been the *star* of the Jefferson Bank affair. Calloway was a wise counselor—but Clay was *exciting*. Jerry Tucker, the UAW leader, knew both men well. He had worked with Calloway in the Tandy Area Council and had walked picket lines with Clay outside Milton Carpenter's segregated Howard Johnson's. About '68 he said, "I was torn back and forth. But later I told Clay, 'You know, in the final analysis—and I don't just tell you this to blow smoke—much as I like Calloway, I felt that you would be the guy to go *shake 'em up!*'"[27]

The North Side obviously agreed. Clay won the August 6 primary with 45 percent of the vote. Carpenter, the white innkeeper-politician who had gambled on a fractured field of African American opponents, took only 32 percent. Calloway, on whom Carpenter's hopes had perhaps chiefly rested, wound up with a disappointing 12 percent.[28] Three other black candidates divided up the remaining 11 percent.

Clay, who in November's general election handily defeated his Republican opponent, went on to represent the 1st District seat for thirty-two straight years. Then, in 2000, he more or less bequeathed it to his son Lacey Clay, who has held it since.

* * *

Calloway's big triumph occurred the year after his run for Congress, in 1969.

It began with a stoppage. In the early winter of that year, after the St. Louis Housing Authority announced that it was raising rents in public housing, some tenants began withholding not only the increase but the basic rent itself. Individual protests grew quickly into a mass movement. By spring three thousand public housing tenants were refusing to pay rent. They were, they said, on a "rent strike."

The strike would last nine months. During those months it became the source of great municipal uneasiness, in part because the withheld rent money threatened to bankrupt the Housing Authority, which had been in fiscal trouble to start with. More important was the fact that, although the city had so far escaped the inner-city riots that in the later years of the decade burned sections of Harlem, Watts, Newark, Detroit, Washington, D.C., and other Northern cities, many citizens, both white and black, feared the rent strike would be the spark that finally set St. Louis ablaze.

Local 688—or at least a significant part of it—became deeply involved in the strike. An account of the local's participation can be found in Robert Bussel's 'A Trade Union Oriented War on the Slums': Harold Gibbons, Ernest Calloway, and the St. Louis Teamsters of the 1960s," which appeared in the journal *Labor History* in 2003. Bussel, himself a trade unionist turned academic, admired the work of the two Teamster leaders. "Integrating the identities of 'worker' and 'citizen' was," he writes, "fundamental to Gibbons and Calloway's vision of an engaged social unionism that would allow union members to become full-fledged participants in the life of the community." Bussel especially liked their approach to race. "Steeped in the inclusive ethos of industrial unionism, fearing that racial division could be used to undermine labor's hard-won gains, and drawn to the political potential of an alliance between St. Louis' growing African-American population and the labor movement, Harold Gibbons and Ernest Calloway fought for racial integration, both within the Teamsters and throughout the broader community."[29]

In Bussel's telling of the rent strike story, Gibbons and Calloway are a team of brilliant commanders, like Lee and Longstreet in Civil-War Virginia or the Reuther brothers in Depression-era Detroit. Bussel mentions the two men always in tandem: Gibbons and Calloway did this, Gibbons and Calloway did that. But that doesn't really seem to have been the case.

In fact, the decisions that brought that brought Local 688 into the rent strike were probably made by neither man. Gibbons was by then the chief executive of an organization with more than thirteen thousand members,[30] most of whom he didn't know and who didn't know him. The local was no longer what it had been in the '40s and early '50s, when officers and members lived in each other's pockets. Because he found himself increasingly out of touch with the activities of his own union, Gibbons from time to time dropped in on its various departments seeking information. One of his favorite sources was the shop stewards' school at the camp in Pevely. "He would want to know what kind of stuff we were into," recalled Mike Ryan, then an instructor there. "He'd want to pick up what details he wasn't getting from whatever method of reporting [Dick] Kavner was using. That's how he found out about things like the rent strike."[31]

Calloway certainly would have learned about it sooner than Gibbons. He was mentor to the Tandy Area Council's staff, including Claude Brown, Leroy Graham, and Frank Boykin. These men, themselves community organizers with many friends and acquaintances among the rent strikers, seem to have been pulled into the movement practically from its start. Calloway was thus drawn in almost immediately too.

Calloway had at that time no prominent role in the official Local 688 hierarchy; he was carried on the payroll as a researcher and writer. David Salmon, whom Gibbons had made manager of the Central Conference of Teamsters headquarters in Council Plaza, worked from an office next door to the older man's. There Calloway sat alone, turning out *Missouri Teamster* articles and manuals for shop stewards. Salmon admired Calloway's cheery disposition, but also felt sorry for him. "I was more successful in building a career around my official job than was Cab," Salmon writes.[32] He believed that Calloway, having somehow lost Gibbons' confidence, had arrived at a dead end in his career in Local 688.

Salmon was wrong about the dead end. If Calloway had little formal power in Local 688, he nevertheless remained quietly influential. His authority was exercised primarily via the noon-hour political seminar he regularly conducted in Council Plaza's restaurant and in cafes and lunchrooms up and down Grand Boulevard. To his table came not only the Tandy Area Council organizers but also Jake McCarthy, Jim Pace, Levi Sanford, Mike Ryan, and others whom Ryan has described as leaders of the union's "social concern wing."[33] As the name implies, these men were believers in the idea Gibbons had picked up in Wisconsin in 1932: that some institutions (universities, say, or trade unions), although designed primarily for one function (educating the young, representing laborers' economic interests), might also serve as a kind of base from which participants could on occasion sally out into the wider world and combat evils there. Having accepted this point of view, the "social concern wing" also slid easily into supporting the rent strike.

According to Ryan, it was Jim Pace, the Methodist minister-turned-missionary-turned Local 688's political director, who decided to take the union into the strike (though no doubt after clearing the move with Gibbons).[34] Under Pace's direction the union provided the strikers with money, office facilities in Council Plaza, and, unquestionably most important, the full-time assistance of its Tandy Area Council organizers.[35] This however was done somewhat stealthily (much like the union's backing of the CORE sit-ins a generation earlier), in an effort to avoid alienating conservative members. Gibbons himself made no public statement about the strike until June, five months after it began.

The stealth seemed necessary because the "social concern wing" of the union had its opponents. Among some white Local 688 members there had long been complaints that Gibbons was excessively solicitous of black members and black people generally. Such murmurs were first heard in 1945 when he took the friendless black taxicab drivers into the union. The grumbling was repeated in the late '40s and early '50s when he sponsored the CORE chapter that desegregated downtown businesses; in 1956 when he crushed the white cabbies' wildcat; and again in the mid–'60s when the union launched the Tandy Area Council. But in the late '60s the complaints grew angrier and louder.

Gibbons had in the fall of 1968 spoken at a large North Side rally protesting the beating by police of two black nationalists. In his speech he pledged Teamster support for a drive against police brutality. After all, he reminded the audience, the labor movement had itself suffered such violence "before the police discovered Negroes."[36] Soon after his speech, according to an FBI informant, a group of St. Louis-area Teamsters held a meeting to protest the protest. The informant reported that 4,000 IBT members had signed petitions rebuking Gibbons—and defending the police. The informant didn't say whether any of the petition campaign's originators and signers were from Local 688, though it seems certain that some were.[37]

Gibbons, during the rent strike of the following year, asked Mike Ryan and Claude Brown to conduct what we would today call focus-group discussions among the union's shop stewards, hoping thereby to learn members' opinions on a number of topics. Ryan and Brown did so with eleven such groups, reporting that many griped about rising taxes. This of course made them no different than other Americans. Much more disconcerting, however, was their finding that "the white membership feels that all of the taxes are caused by the 'niggers' and Gibbons is a bastard for helping them because this causes their [the whites'] taxes to be increased."[38]

Some of this racist feeling undoubtedly fed support for the union's "business wing," the faction, according to Ryan, that opposed the Calloway-led "social concern wing."[39] But the "business wing" was not at its core racist. Its key adherents were business agents, union staff people who represented members in practical, nuts-and-bolts matters: contract negotiation, filing grievances, collecting dues. The leader of the "business wing" faction was Ron Gamache. A large, balding man, a former Marine and Korean War veteran, Gamache had been brought into the union back in the '50s by Gibbons, who liked the aggressiveness the younger man displayed as an organizer. And Gamache respected many of Gibbons' qualities. "He [Gibbons] taught me a lot," he said. However, although he agreed with some of Gibbons' and Calloway's ideas concerning reforms in the larger community, he believed those ideas often diverted energy and resources from what he saw as the union's primary mission, bringing in hitherto unorganized shops and renegotiating good contracts with organized ones.[40]

"Gamache was my best friend," said Levi Sanford, the onetime African American vice president of Local 688. Gamache had earlier helped ease Sanford's rise in the union's hierarchy. "Whenever some business agent would hold a party in his home—and they were all white except for me—Ron always took me along," Sanford said.[41]

Later, after he succeeded Gibbons as boss of Local 688—and had cleaned out many of the more prominent "social concern" people, including Sanford—Gamache proved to be a competent if unimaginative trade-union leader. But by then the union was very different.

Meanwhile, in 1969, the rent strike dragged on. Begun in winter, negotiations between the strike leaders and the Housing Authority continued through spring and into summer. In June, at a session whose participants included Mayor Alfonso Cervantes, Jake McCarthy happened to announce that the Teamsters were "one thousand percent behind the rent strike." Cervantes responded to McCarthy's remark as if he were a pike going for a fly. One cause of the strike's prolongation had been the inability of its leaders to agree on goals. What they needed, Cervantes believed, was to speak with a single voice. Would the Teamsters negotiate for the strikers? Cervantes asked McCarthy. Would Harold Gibbons take charge?

McCarthy said he would ask. Returning to Council Plaza, he apologized to Gibbons for being so quick to speak for him. "Harold," he said, "I may have put you in a corner on this strike." "Hell, no. I'll step in and settle it," Gibbons replied. "But I'm going to have to run the show."[42]

The strikers agreed to let him do this, though evidently only after a certain amount of debate. "Nothing is going to take place in public housing through Mr. Gibbons that the striking tenants do not want," Jean King, one of the strike leaders, promised her comrades. "If you know anything at all about Mr. Gibbons, you know that he *will* get the job done."[43]

Cervantes, representing the Housing Authority, began meeting with Gibbons at City Hall. The two knew each other well. Colleagues in the Politicians faction of the local Democratic Party (see Chapter 8), they had in 1965 worked together with Larry Callanan of the Steamfitters and the lawyer Morris Shenker to drive Ray Tucker from the mayor's office and replace him with Cervantes himself. But Cervantes and Gibbons were probably not friends. An insurance agent, Cervantes had years earlier taken possession of the Laclede Taxi company from a customer who couldn't pay his insurance premiums. One result of acquiring the business was that Cervantes then had to negotiate periodically with Gibbons about increases in his cabbies' wages and benefits. That can't have been fun.

In discussing a possible rent strike settlement, the two men made little progress. Cervantes, in his memoirs, spells out why: "Gibbons was asking me to sign away my authority as mayor to appoint commissioners to the board of the [Housing Authority]. That power … was henceforth to be vested in the Civic Housing Alliance—in other words, Harold Gibbons."[44]

But Cervantes found himself cornered. The Civic Housing Alliance he mentions was a coalition thrown together to supersede the municipal government, including, as he says, Cervantes himself, in the city's public housing. Though apparently Gibbons' idea, the Civic Alliance was supported by some of St. Louis' most powerful bankers and industrialists, among them August A. Busch, Jr., boss of the Anheuser-Busch brewery and owner of the St. Louis Cardinals. Such a grouping would have been unthinkable at any other time— Gibbons being disliked, even hated, by many of these businessmen—but the strike was now eight months old and, as one of them said, "a damn explosive situation."[45]

Then there was HUD, the U.S. Department of Housing and Urban Development. Nineteen-sixty-nine was the first year of the new Nixon administration, which, difficult though it is to believe now, contained a number of surprisingly liberal Republicans. One was HUD's boss, George Romney, the former governor of Michigan (and father of Mitt Romney, the GOP's presidential candidate in 2012). That summer, with the protracted St. Louis rent strike making national TV news, Romney sent several teams of observers to St. Louis to investigate the situation. One Romney lieutenant hinted publicly that HUD might reduce or even cease federal subsidies to the city if the strike were not soon settled. Another HUD team, impressed on one hand by the haplessness of the Housing Authority and on the other by the success of Local 688's own experiments in housing—namely, the two towers of retirees' apartments in Council Plaza—suggested to Cervantes that "full consideration be given to the possibility that the management and operation of the total [city] housing program be turned over to the Teamsters Union."[46]

By late October, it was clear that some sort of deal like that was inescapable. Only Cervantes still held out. Then he too surrendered, following a private meeting in Gibbons' office at Council Plaza. Gibbons said he told the mayor he had forty-five days to get an agreement, because after that the Housing Authority would be bankrupt and forced to shutter the housing projects. "If that happens, you're going to have the biggest riot any city ever had, and I personally will lead the blacks out to [the upper-middle-class suburbs] Clayton and Ladue."[47]

A settlement was finally signed on October 29, 1969. Effective management of the city's public housing was turned over the new Civic Alliance. Gibbons became the new organization's president. A creature of state law, the old Housing Authority remained in existence, but in order to make sure that it wasn't used to make mischief, Frank Boykin of Local 688 and the Tandy Area Council was installed as chairman of its board. The Civic Alliance, writes Bussel, thus operated "largely under the aegis of Local 688."[48]

The non–Teamster, non-tenant members of the Civic Alliance seem to have agreed to this setup for two reasons. First, the old Housing Authority was broke and, as Gibbons had maintained since joining the strike, public housing simply could not survive in St. Louis without federal money. That needed money, if it was available, would have to come through HUD, which at the time looked favorably on Gibbons and his union. Second, none of the other Alliance members had any idea how to get the city's public housing system functioning again. Gibbons' union—or at least one of its members—was pretty sure he did know how.

It was at this point that Ernest Calloway came into his own.

The Alliance had quickly spawned a variety of subsidiary groups, including something called the Social Goals Committee. Calloway, chief theoretician of Local 688's "social concerns wing," became the theoretician of the Social Goals Committee.

As Calloway saw it, public housing in the United States was a system run by government bureaucrats who had little sympathy—and often more than a little contempt—for their clients in public housing. He considered the system psychologically poisonous because it tended to demoralize public housing tenants and make them contemptuous of themselves. To break out of this psychic trap, Calloway believed, tenants should launch some concerted, confidence-building action—a rent strike, for example. But victory in a strike wouldn't be enough. Neither would merely frustrating the bureaucrats who ran public housing. Tenants must take over and exercise the bureaucrats' powers and responsibilities themselves.

Calloway was a syndicalist to the bone, a radical democrat who believed that trade unionism was the answer to all serious labor questions—that even in questions not specifically involving labor, some sort of trade union-like organization was probably the best bet. He proposed turning St. Louis' nine public housing projects into union-like *associations*. Each association would elect its own officers and collect monthly dues from its resident-members, like a union local. With these dues the associations would employ lawyers, accountants, managers, maintenance workers, security guards. (Calloway hoped to use HUD subsidies to train tenants to fill some of these roles.) All this—the strike, the victory, the new structures and roles for public housing residents—Calloway dubbed "creative self-determination."[49]

Approved by the Civic Alliance, Calloway's plan was set in motion in February 1970. Within a month, a thousand tenant households had enlisted in his associations.[50]

But there was resistance as well. A strike leader at the huge Pruitt-Igoe housing project complained that "the Teamsters are pushing around us residents and want to make us an arm of their already powerful organization."[51]

Even more ominous was growing resistance to the project inside Local 688. During the rent strike, Robert Bussel writes, "it became apparent that a significant number of stewards and rank-and-file members of Local 688 were reluctant to enlist in Gibbons and Calloway's 'trade union oriented war on the slums.'"[52] For Calloway and his "social concern wing," one, seriously steep price of success in the rent strike was new growth for the opposition "business wing."

Local 688, the institution with which Gibbons had long hoped to cure or at least calm some of the surrounding society's ills, was itself showing serious symptoms of those ills.

20

"This Stupid War"

Harold Gibbons was a longtime critic of the United States' war in Vietnam. This put him at odds with most other Teamster leaders—and also with many members of his own local union.

He signed antiwar petitions, gave antiwar speeches, helped organize big antiwar demonstrations, and published a union newspaper, the *Missouri Teamster*, which regularly editorialized against the war. Late in the Vietnam era he was asked by a reporter if he wasn't out of step with the other IBT brass, who, with Frank Fitzsimmons, increasingly agreed with the policies of the administration of Richard Nixon, including its prosecution of the war. "Oh yes," he replied, "I'm in disagreement with President Nixon on the war as sure as I was with President Johnson, as I was with Eisenhower and as I was with Kennedy."[1]

As early as November 1968 Gibbons was forced by his colleagues in Joint Council 13 to replace Jake McCarthy, the *Missouri Teamster*'s antiwar editor. Arguments flared over the war even in Local 688's headquarters at Council Plaza. Adherents of the local's "business wing" generally supported the war effort, whereas those of the "social concern wing" joined Gibbons in antiwar work. According to Mike Ryan, one Christmas the local's officers were told one to send each other greeting cards, the exchange intended to sooth factional animosities. "My wife and I sent peace cards," Ryan said. Business wing partisans responded by "throwing them back on my desk."[2]

But the antiwar Gibbons possessed at least one influential ally: Nixon's national security adviser, Henry Kissinger. Kissinger had for years been quietly dubious about the Vietnam adventure. When, in November 1963, the South Vietnamese military, with encouragement from the Kennedy administration, overthrew the government of South Vietnam's president, Ngo Dinh Diem (and murdered Diem), Kissinger saw the coup as very likely fatal to the whole enterprise. Kissinger believed the coup had wrecked the rudimentary political structures the anti–Communist South would require if it were to have any hope of preserving its independence from the North. Kissinger planned to state this belief publicly. But in his memoirs he says, "I was in the process of writing an article along these lines, predicting a drastic deterioration in Vietnam, when President Kennedy was assassinated. I decided it would be in bad taste to proceed."[3]

By the winter of 1972 Nixon as well as Kissinger had come to believe that the United States could not win the war in Vietnam. Neither, however, should it appear to lose. Defeat, they believed, would dismay other allies whom we had vowed to defend against communism; it would also alienate the administration's conservative political base. What was needed, Nixon and Kissinger thought, was an understanding with North Vietnam that would allow American forces to leave Indochina without *seeming* to have been forced to do so. What was needed was a deal.[4]

Such a deal would be very difficult to pull off. Since no one else could be trusted, it would require subtle conversations between the antagonists at the highest possible level: between Kissinger himself and North Vietnam's chief negotiator, Le Duc Tho. Unfortunately, the two men had broken off a series of clandestine talks in Paris the previous November. How might Kissinger let his opposite number know that he was ready to begin again?

It was at this point that Gibbons came into the picture. Kissinger and Gibbons had first met at Pebble Beach, California, in either the fall of 1966 or the winter of '67. The occasion was one of those long weekends during which business or government executives are brought together to relax, play golf, and (as a kind of penance) listen to a hired academic talk for an hour or so on some possibly relevant topic, trade with Ecuador, say, or Finnish ceramics. On this weekend the academic was Kissinger, then a political science professor at Harvard. His topic was Vietnam. Hundreds of thousands of U.S. soldiers and marines were by then in that country trying to buck up the South Vietnamese generals and their dispirited troops. Kissinger urged his Pebble Beach audience to support the war, because, he said, defeat would be bad for America's international image. In a question period following his talk, a man in the back of the room asked why defeat should be so awful. France had been driven from its former colony in Algeria, but now the French and Algerians were getting along fine, weren't they? The man in the back was Gibbons. After the session Kissinger sought him out, the two men repaired to the bar, enjoyed several drinks together, and became friends.[5]

In April 1967 Kissinger, recalling "our conversation at Pebble Beach with warmth," invited Gibbons to address a seminar at Harvard's Center for International Affairs, of which he was a founder. Seminar speakers were not assigned topics, he wrote. Gibbons "should feel free to talk about whatever is on your mind."[6]

No record of Gibbons' talk to Kissinger's seminar survives, but it must have been well received because he was invited to return the following year.

(In a scribbled outline for his 1968 talk Gibbons argues that the mainstream labor movement is no longer a force for reform in the United States. Indeed, though "some unions" remain progressive, most act as "an arm of the establishment." His hopes for social change, he writes, rest on a coalition of "business, labor, church, intellectual, and civil rights movement.")[7] In 1969 Kissinger left Harvard to join the new Nixon administration. Gibbons began, when in Washington, to visit him at the White House or meet him for drinks at Duke Ziebert's restaurant, then one of that city's most popular watering holes.

Kissinger, planning for Nixon's groundbreaking trip to China in February 1972, included Gibbons and his hard man Dick Kavner in the presidential entourage. We don't know why Kissinger did this or why he thought he could get away with it—Gibbons was by this time on the White House's "enemies list." We do know that Gibbons and Kavner expected to go.

The China trip was originally scheduled for August 1971, a month after an exploratory visit to Beijing by Kissinger, the first by an American government official since the Communist seizure of power in 1949. For Nixon's trip Kissinger envisioned a U.S. contingent of 252 people; Gibbons was to travel as the chairman of the entourage's Labor Committee, with Kavner his "executive assistant."[8] The great adventure was first postponed from August to October, then from October to.... At this point Gibbons' old colleague Victor Riesel, the blinded labor journalist, takes up the story. Kissinger, Riesel writes, "began talking about including Gibbons, who was Hoffa's house intellectual, in the contingent accompanying President Nixon to China. There were protests, and Dr. Kissinger, whom some had accused of being too coy, too cute, too winning too often, promised a friend that Gibbons would not go to Peking and that he would not be welcomed in Dr. Kissinger's headquarters."[9]

So in February 1972 Nixon and Kissinger went to China. Gibbons and Kavner stayed home.

Who was Riesel's source? The "too winning too often" phrase suggests William Rogers, Nixon's secretary of state who, time and again, was overshadowed by the national security adviser, Kissinger. Rogers, as we'll see, helped kibosh a later journey Gibbons planned for Asia, so he may have had a hand in this one too.

But the more likely culprit was Charles W. Colson, the presidential aide assigned to romance Frank Fitzsimmons of the Teamsters. In this Colson was successful. He arranged for Fitzsimmons to be placed on blue-ribbon commissions, to be taken into the Oval Office for occasional chats with Nixon, and invited to White House soirées. Years later Mrs. Fitzsimmons said, "I can't tell you how much Fitz and I loved it, or how much we miss it now that those [Jimmy] Carter people are here." As for Fitz himself, John Dean told Steven Brill, "I remember seeing Colson leading him around like a new prize puppy."[10] Colson, doing another favor for Fitz, may have kept Gibbons, Fitzsimmons' enemy, off the plane to Beijing.

Meanwhile, although Gibbons failed to accompany Nixon to China in February, he did make it to Hanoi just weeks afterward. Kissinger figured in this trip too. But the prime instigator was a man named David Livingston.

Livingston was about as "old Left" as you could get in the 1970s. Five years younger than Gibbons, he had begun his labor career during the Depression organizing warehouse workers in New York City. Like Gibbons' local union in St. Louis, Livingston's Local 65 was in the '40s affiliated with the Retail and Wholesale and Department Store Union international. But Livingston and a number of other New York RWDSU leaders were Communists or at least under Communist discipline. In the Montgomery Ward walkout of 1944–45 (see Chapter 4) Livingston and his political brethren did what they could to break the strike. Thereafter a deep enmity existed between Communist trade unionists like Livingston and anti–Communists like Gibbons.

The U.S. Communist Party, beset by government prosecution and its own dishonesties, disintegrated in the early 1950s. That freed its trade union leaders to sink or swim on their own without reference to the Soviet Union. Many sank. A few, like Livingston (and Harry Bridges of the West Coast longshoremen), prospered because they were tough, talented unionists who kept their members' loyalty by winning good contracts. Livingston's Local 65 actually grew much larger in the following decade, absorbing other cast-off RWDSU locals and renaming itself District 65. Minus the Russian connection, District 65 and Gibbons' Local 688 were actually rather similar. District 65 recruited heavily among New York's African American and Puerto Rican populations, raising their members into leadership positions, and led civil rights and antiwar protest movements. In later years District 65 became part of the United Auto Workers. Livingston himself joined the Democratic Socialists of America, Michael Harrington's mildly radical remnant of the old Socialist Party.

But in the minds of many union leaders of his and Gibbons' generation, Livingston remained a "Stalinist." In the winter of 1972 Livingston was invited, presumably through old political connections, to visit North Vietnam and to bring other American labor leaders along with him. Gibbons agreed to join the delegation. Word of the planned trip quickly got around in the United States. "Emil Mazey of the UAW summoned me to Detroit," recalled Ron Borges, a Gibbons lieutenant. "He told me, 'Harold's going to Hanoi with Livingston. Those guys are outside the mainstream.'"[11]

Whatever Livingston's politics had once been, though, they clearly no longer much troubled Gibbons. (Mazey would soon relent as well.) The delegation's sole aim, he told a reporter, was "to see what we can do to end this immoral and senseless war."[12]

Not that Gibbons was willing to be seen as unpatriotic, especially by Teamsters. According to another newsman—Jake McCarthy, who in 1970 had left Local 688 to become a columnist for the *Post-Dispatch*— "informed sources [!] said that Gibbons had been reluctant to accept the invitation until he was assured that it would not conflict with United States efforts to end the war. He received briefings from Kissinger and others."[13]

We don't know what went on between Kissinger and Gibbons in these briefings, but we do know the premises each man was operating from. In Gibbons' view, the war was entirely bad. "There is no moral cause in Vietnam," he once told an antiwar rally. "We are not fighting for freedom, we are suppressing it; we are not raising their standard of living, we are destroying their homes, villages, children, fields, their lives.... And we are in a war that cannot be won."[14] In Kissinger's view the war wasn't bad, but prolonging it was undesirable.. Kissinger preferred to focus his energies on Communist Russia and China, not on their small-fry client state North Vietnam. "The Nixon administration," he writes in his memoirs, "saw it as its task to lay the foundation for a long-range foreign policy, even while liquidating our Indochina involvement."[15]

Hence "liquidation" of the war became the goal for both Kissinger and Gibbons. But whereas Gibbons wanted the United States out of Vietnam as soon as possible, and hang the consequences, Kissinger insisted that this withdrawal be one that could be portrayed as a kind of victory—"peace with honor" was the administration's slogan. For this, North Vietnamese cooperation was necessary. But the North Vietnamese weren't cooperating.

Kissinger was hopeful about his next move, however. He had been warned by U.S. intelligence that North Vietnam was planning to launch a large-scale spring offensive. Expecting it to fail, he believed that the North Vietnamese would then be more open to negotiations. He appears to have urged Gibbons, as a labor leader and man of the Left, to recommend to Hanoi a renewal of the clandestine talks that had been broken off in Paris six months earlier.

Gibbons' and Livingston's journey began March 12, 1972. Cliff Caldwell, an official of the meat cutters' union, became the third member of what was termed a "labor mission to Hanoi."[16] Gibbons kept a journal of the trip. The three pilgrims had arranged to meet at New York's JFK International. Livingston, Gibbons writes, arrived with a large "entourage." Gibbons had come to the airport earlier with his own well-wishers: Ed McMahon of TV's *Tonight Show* and Pat Henry, a nightclub comic and pal of Frank Sinatra's. They seem to have spent the wait in the lounge. "A congenial hour of jokes and champagne," the journal says.[17]

Gibbons and Livingston sat together on the flight to Los Angeles and discussed going on to China after concluding their business in North Vietnam, though they later dropped the idea. Livingston slept on the leg from California to Hawaii. Gibbons, ever the night owl despite being "tired and weary … read for an hour articles by I. F. Stone in the New York Review, March 9th and February 24th issues. Finished up on Salsbury, 'Behind the Lines Hanoi.'"[18]

This was truly a journey to the East. The pilgrims' itinerary was to take them from Hawaii to Tokyo and then Hong Kong via Pan American, from Hong Kong to Vientiane, Laos, via the Malaysian airline MAS, and from Vientiane to Hanoi on Aeroflot, the Soviet line. Gibbons and Livingston each saw their mission differently. (Caldwell, the expedition's junior member, is mentioned infrequently in Gibbons' journal.) Livingston intended to act as a cheerleader, bringing the North Vietnamese moral support from the peace movement back in the United States. Gibbons, having met with Kissinger and various State Department officials before embarking, was to some extent an envoy of the U.S. government. The trio discussed these differences on the morning they flew from Hong Kong to Vientiane. "Talked about who should be head of delegation—no decision [the journal says]. Talked about approach to N.V. Disagreed with Dave—re: praising N.V. and condemning U.S. Cliff and I are in agreement. Dave appeared to be reluctant to approach the question of negotiations. Was in favor of requesting prisoner release to our delegation because it would strengthen our role in U.S. peace movement. I told Dave I was insisting on discussion of current negotiations in the hope that some movement be achieved or new meetings set up."

In neutral Laos they were met by Ted Koppel and a camera crew from ABC-TV, "after which we boarded a four engine Turbo Prop Russian plane for the hours [sic] ride to Hanoi." There they were greeted by a delegation of North Vietnamese trade unionists, led, as Gibbons noted, by "four lovely girls carrying huge bouquets.... The warmth of the people we have been bombing for all these years was very touching." It was impossible, he told his journal, to imagine the shoe on the other foot: an American crowd greeting North Vietnamese visitors with similar friendliness.

The pilgrims traveled from the airport to downtown Hanoi in "heavy" Russian cars, riding through a heavily bombed landscape. "On the way we passed workers strengthening a huge dike along the river. Long sticks were being used to pack the dirt on the side of the dike. Dirt was being passed from worker to worker in small wicker baskets. Women were repairing the street with hot asphalt. The primitivness [sic] of the tools and methods was unbelievable."

Gibbons and his friends spent a week in the city, staying at the Unification Hotel, a formerly luxurious French hostelry that was now showing its age. They were taken to museums, shown war damage, entertained and lectured by a variety of Communist Party officials. One day they were allowed to talk to two American POWs. They could talk to them but, contrary to Livingston's wishes, could not bring them back to this country. The Vietnamese complained that prisoners released earlier had been used by the U.S. government for propaganda purposes. "They said that when and if they ever got to the point of considering the release of any individuals they would perhaps communicate with us," Gibbons writes.

On their last day they had a two-and-a-half-hour meeting with the country's chief negotiator, Le Duc Tho. In his memoirs Kissinger admits worrying that the North Vietnamese, who had unhorsed Lyndon Johnson with the Tet offensive of 1968, might refuse to renew negotiations until after the U.S. presidential election in November 1972, hoping that Nixon would lose to the antiwar Democratic candidate George McGovern, who would very likely then settle the conflict on easier terms than would Nixon.[19] Gibbons, no doubt at Kissinger's urging, warned Le Duc Tho not to count on getting a better deal from a different American president. "I told him that as of right now Nixon will probably be reelected." The North Vietnamese should take advantage of a pre-election window of opportunity, he suggested. "Told him that between now and November Nixon is anxious [to] settle war."

Le Duc Tho complained to his visitors about the chief of the formal U.S. delegation to the Paris peace talks, a career diplomat named William Porter. "'Porter has a bad attitude. Very provokative [sic],'" Gibbons quotes the Vietnamese as saying. Gibbons said not to worry about Porter, that he was a stalking horse who in the end would be of no consequence in the peace talks. "Told him that when settlement is reached it will be negotiated by Mr. Kissinger."

Gibbons, Livingston, and Caldwell returned to the United States on March 28. In Washington the pilgrims spent an hour with Kissinger and also testified in closed session before the Senate Foreign Relations Committee. They asked officials of the three big television networks to allow them report to the country about their trip to North Vietnam, especially their conversation with Le Duc Tho; the networks turned them down.[20] Undeterred, the three men began laying the groundwork for a new project, a congress of antiwar trade union leaders scheduled to meet in St. Louis in June.

* * *

Back in St. Louis, Gibbons contemplated a reply to a letter from the parents of a missing naval airman. Their son, Lieutenant Bernard Rupinski, had been the navigator of a plane shot down during a bombing run over North Vietnam. Learning of Gibbons' visit to in Hanoi, his parents wrote to him, asking if he perhaps had news of Bernard. In answering, Gibbons confesses that he's had trouble deciding what to say to them, "because the news I have is not good." It so happened that one of the POWs whom Gibbons, Livingston, and Caldwell had been allowed to interview in Hanoi was the pilot of the plane in which Rupinski had flown. The pilot, Gibbons writes, had been able to bail out more or less safely. Unfortunately, Rupinski didn't jump and was in the plane when it crashed.

"I can only tell you that I regret much having to forward this information," Gibbons writes to the parents, "but do so in the hope that it may bring some relief."

Another writer might have stopped right there. Or he might have closed by saying that the parents should be proud of the son who gave his life for his country. But frustration with the war seems to have suddenly boiled over in Gibbons. He writes: "I have for the past eight years spent time, energy, money and effort to convince our Government to get out of this stupid war which is spending the lives of our young people and the resources of our Nation for no discernible reason. Nothing in Indo China affects the security of our Nation and we have no business being over there."[21]

Meanwhile, as the result perhaps of the message from Kissinger to Le Duc Tho that Gibbons carried to Hanoi, the two principals agreed to resume on May 2 the secret talks in Paris that had been abandoned six months before. The new talks did not go well. In fact, as Kissinger tells it in his memoirs, he found the refusal of the North Vietnamese to give ground highly irritating.[22] On the other hand, the two sides *were* talking again.

* * *

North Vietnam's long-awaited spring offensive began April 1, just days after Gibbons and his friends had left for the States. It was repelled, which was a great relief to Kissinger. In July the Democratic presidential campaign was all but wrecked by the revelation that McGovern's running mate, Missouri's own Tom Eagleton, had a history of hospitalizations for depression. The Eagleton news, Kissinger says, came in turn as a relief to Nixon, who decided that he no longer needed to hurry into negotiations with North Vietnam.[23] There would be no new Tet. The Democrats were wounded, perhaps mortally. But not everything was going Nixon's way. A month before the Democratic convention, White House-directed burglars were caught breaking into Democratic headquarters in the Watergate office-and-apartment complex in Washington. Although no one could guess it at the time, the Vietnam war, having ended Lyndon Johnson's career, was soon to claim a second presidential casualty.

Meanwhile Jimmy Hoffa stewed.

Hoffa had been released from prison six months earlier, just before Christmas 1971. He was met at the gates of Lewisburg prison by Gibbons and Robert Crancer, a steel executive who had married Hoffa's daughter Barbara. They boarded a Learjet owned by Joint Council 13 and flew to St. Louis, where the Hoffa family had gathered at the Crancer home to await Jimmy's arrival. According to a reporter who saw him that day, Hoffa wore "a baggy charcoal-gray suit, blue tie, brown shoes, and dark coat."²⁴ His wardrobe would improve in time, but his luck wouldn't.

Hoffa, who supported Richard Nixon for president in 1968, had expected the new Republican president to free him from the penitentiary. But for three years, despite the lobbying of influential friends, nothing happened. One such friend was William Loeb, publisher of the very conservative *Union-Leader* newspaper in Manchester, New Hampshire. The *Union-Leader* had received several big loans from the IBT's Central States Pension Fund, and Loeb was determined to express his gratitude for them. In a September 1970 letter to Gibbons he said he had arranged the ghostwriting and publication of *The Trials of Jimmy Hoffa*, the jailed man's first memoir. "I persuaded [the ghost Donald] Rogers to do the job and [the conservative Chicago publisher] Regnery to publish the book because I am convinced that the true picture of Jim should be put out so many misconceptions can be corrected." Loeb said he had pleaded Hoffa's case directly with Nixon and Vice President Spiro Agnew. The publisher and his wife had "dined with the President and Mrs. Nixon in the White House at the state dinner for [Indonesia's president] Suharto last June and I have received very friendly cordial letters from the President and the Vice President, addressed to 'Dear Bill' and signed 'R. N.' and 'Ted,' but as a practical matter that doesn't get Jim out of jail."²⁵

By early 1971 Nixon had finally decided it was time to free Hoffa from prison. An election year was coming up, and Jimmy Hoffa was still popular with many of his union's members. But releasing him was going to be a tricky business for the presidential aide put in charge of it, Charles Colson. A freed Hoffa would inevitably be a threat to Frank Fitzsimmons, at the time still the IBT's caretaker leader—and a threat to Fitz would be one to Colson, Fitz's man in the White House. How could Colson turn Hoffa loose and yet keep Fitzsimmons safe?

What Colson came up with was a three-cornered deal involving Hoffa, the Justice Department, and Fitzsimmons. With a Justice official named Will Wilson, he spent the early summer negotiating with Hoffa's representatives, his son James P. Hoffa and his St. Louis lawyer Morris Shenker. Colson and Wilson promised the elder Hoffa a parole if he would, first, agree not to run for reelection and, second, resign from all of his union posts, including the presidency of Local 299, his base in Detroit. The suspicious Teamster boss resisted initially, but in the end Colson and Wilson persuaded the son and the lawyer that the government's word could be trusted. Shenker and young Hoffa then persuaded the father to put his agreement in writing. That was in June.²⁶

Hoffa's approval of the deal failed to satisfy Fitz, however. He did get part of what he wanted. In July, at an executive board meeting in Miami Beach, Fitzsimmons announced Hoffa's retirement, after which he himself was sworn in as the IBT's president—no longer the general vice president, a mere caretaker. Immediately after the swearing in, a door behind the podium opened and in swept the president of the United States, Richard Nixon, to personally bestow his blessing on Fitz as "my kind of labor leader."[27]

But even that wasn't quite sufficient for Fitzsimmons. The big White House gift to him was delivered two days before Christmas. Nixon signed an order of commutation freeing Hoffa from Lewisburg—but the order included a clause, concocted by Colson and John Dean, forbidding him to seek any office in the Teamsters until March 1980, eight years down the road.[28] To Hoffa, who, having given up all his union jobs and titles, had intended to head straight back to Detroit and start campaigning for the IBT presidency, the clause must have come as an extremely unpleasant surprise.

* * *

Hoffa had counted on receiving an outright pardon, not a commutation. Released from prison, he found himself restricted by his parole board to travel between Detroit and Miami, where he had a condo. In the spring of 1972 he was living in Miami. In order to carry on sensitive business outside those two cities—in New York and Europe, for example—he was relying on a man named William L. Taub.

Taub was and remains today a mysterious figure. A small, dark man, sixty at the time, he seems to have made a living as a professional networker, though that word wasn't yet in general currency. Forming an acquaintance with one wealthy (and often powerful) person he would use it to meet others, then still others, until he had spun an international web of acquaintances. Among these he counted two popes, Marilyn Monroe, President Eisenhower, Madame Mao Zedong, Aristotle Onassis—and Jimmy Hoffa. For such people he might perform errands, including serving as their representative in business deals, some perhaps of doubtful legality. Whether he actually knew Madame Mao and the others can probably never be established. But he must have been acquainted with some wealthy people because he was usually able to live in high style himself. The *New York Times* and *Life* magazine, after his adventure with Hoffa, pronounced Taub a con man and a fraud.[29]

Years later Taub published a memoir with the characteristically ambiguous title *Forces of Power*.[30] In it he says almost nothing about his background, save only that his father was once paralyzed because of a fall and would have died if Eleanor Roosevelt hadn't sent FDR's own neurosurgeon to keep him alive. "Later, when I called the hospital inquiring about his bill, which I hadn't received, I was told there would be no charge, 'at the request of President Roosevelt.'"[31] It's the sort of remark that will shrivel the confidence of almost any reader, and Taub writes similarly about other famous and infamous persons. On the other hand he provides, in the last third of his book, the only extant full narrative of his exploits with Hoffa in the summer of '72. Although he may not have been able to resist fictionalizing some of its details, Taub tells a story that in its general outline has been confirmed by other sources. Fantastic as it sounds, it seems to be true.

Taub writes in *Forces of Power* that he found Hoffa that spring to be angry, anxious, and suspicious of everyone but his immediate family. The cause of his unhappiness was John Dean's clause in Nixon's commutation order, preventing him from having anything to do with the Teamsters. Hoffa was a man of rather spectacular narrowness: life outside the union and its politics was a kind of hell for him. He may have felt more imprisoned in his Miami condo than ever in his cell in Lewisburg. How could he get that clause dropped?

Taub had a plan.

The plan went like this: Hoffa would travel to Hanoi. The North Vietnamese, thrilled to have the famous American labor leader among them, would hand over a dozen or fifteen American prisoners of war. Hoffa would then return with the POWs to the United States, there to be acclaimed by a grateful nation as a hero, much too popular to be bound by the small print in a presidential order. The hated clause would be abrogated or simply forgotten. Hoffa, whirlwind of energy and cleverness that he was, would soon return to the presidency of the IBT. And who knew? There might be a collateral prize. The dramatic repatriation of the returned POWs might deliver the jolt that finally got Americans and North Vietnamese talking peace seriously.

Taub took his plan to Miami where Hoffa's response was, unsurprisingly, explosive. "'Is this what you wanted to talk to me about?' he yelled. 'This crazy idea?'"[32]

It wasn't so crazy sounding, however, as to make Hoffa forbid the little man to try it out.

Thus, Taub writes, on June 11 and 12, 1972, he traveled to the North Vietnamese embassy in Choisy-le-Roi, a suburb of Paris, to meet Le Duc Tho and discuss with him a visit to Hanoi by the deposed Teamster boss. Taub also had a later conversation on the topic with Le Duc Tho in Sofia, Bulgaria.

We know this because of the FBI. The bureau learned about these meetings from a French informant (described as *"a very good source to be protected"* [emphasis in the original]), perhaps a member of that country's intelligence services.[33] The French informant described not only the meetings but the plan to take Hoffa to Hanoi. He also named Harold Gibbons as a participant in Taub's project. Taub seems to have sold himself to the North Vietnamese as representing both Hoffa and Gibbons. Gibbons was vital to Taub's idea for two reasons. First, the Vietnamese knew him from his visit to Hanoi three months earlier. Second, Gibbons was a friend of Henry Kissinger's. To even leave the United States legally, let alone make it to Hanoi, Hoffa was going to require highly placed help in getting permission from his parole board and a passport from the State Department. Kissinger, if Gibbons could talk him into it, could solve those problems.

Although Gibbons was vital to Taub's plan, Taub confesses in his book that he neglected to inform the St. Louisan of the role assigned to him.[34] Imagine then Gibbons' surprise when he received this cablegram:

> Gladly invite James Hoffa comma Harold Gibbons and William Taud [sic] for one week stop Arrival Hanoi July first or second desirable stop Visas may be obtained in Vientiane or Paris stop.
> Hoang Quoc Viet
> President Vietnam Tradeunion [sic][35]

* * *

Meanwhile Gibbons had other things on his mind. One, scheduled in St. Louis for June 23–24, the last weekend of the month, was a national congress of antiwar trade unionists. The congress was intended as the christening of a new organization, Labor for Peace, which Gibbons, Livingston, and Caldwell had formed in March after their return from Hanoi. For it, according to the *Post-Dispatch*, 900 delegates from 35 international unions gathered in Joint Council 13's auditorium at Council Plaza. "They represented a cross-section of the labor movement," the paper said, "older organizers who were active in the 1930s, young workers barely out of school, women and blacks."[36] Coretta Scott King, Martin Luther King's widow, and Mike Gravel, a liberal Democratic senator from Alaska, were the featured speakers. After listening to them and others denounce the war, the delegates turned to a discussion of ways they might help bring it to an end.

The proposal eliciting the most enthusiasm, especially among the younger delegates, was for calling a one-day national strike against the war. Staughton Lynd, a New Left historian and writer, defended the strike idea in a stemwinder of a speech that brought roars of applause from the audience. Opposition to the proposal, mostly from older union leaders, was almost as loud. Jerry Tucker, recalling the moment, said, "I agreed with Staughton, internally."[37]

He meant that he didn't actually say the words. Tucker, the United Auto Workers officer who was his union's liaison with Gibbons' Teamsters, didn't want to offend Emil Mazey, secretary-treasurer of the UAW, who co-chaired the congress with Gibbons. Mazey, normally one of the most outspoken left-wingers at a trade union meeting, hoped for calm deliberation at this one. Although dead set against the war, Mazey didn't particularly care what actions the congress voted to take as long as that action was arrived at more or less through consensus. A noisy split was what he feared.

Even a "Stalinist" consensus apparently would have seemed, to Mazey, better than a split. Harry Bridges bailed him out. This was rich, considering that in the spring Mazey had been shocked by Gibbons' going to North Vietnam with David Livingston, a former Communist. No labor Communist was more notorious than Bridges.

Bridges' appearance was an event in itself. He was in fact much better known than Livingston because the federal government had tried strenuously to deport him on several occasions to his native Australia, but always failed. The longtime leader of the West Coast longshoremen, Bridges had been, if not an actual party member, very close to the Communists in the '30s and '40s, hewing to the party line in, for instance, the breaking of the Montgomery Ward strike. Old anticommunist CIO radicals like Gibbons remained wary of him. But to younger unionists Bridges was a star of sorts, living labor history. And at the antiwar congress, Tucker said, "It was Harry Bridges who got up and cut the baby in half."[38]

Bridges in his speech reminded the delegates that, numerous though they seemed in that crowded auditorium, they represented but a fraction of American labor. Not many of the 900 delegates, although members of 35 internationals, could be said to represent the actual wishes of those internationals concerning the war. Because the congress' delegates were so relatively few, Bridges argued, the proposed one-day strike would be ineffective—or, worse, comic. Bridges advised them to drop the national strike idea and instead go back to their home organizations and proselytize against the war there in whatever fashion they chose. The delegates wound up voting as Bridges had suggested. As Tucker put it, "He was so respected with his left-wing background that everybody kind of found that to be the acceptable compromise."[39]

One other question troubled the congress' two co-chairmen. They had hoped that the presence of at least one international, the United Auto Workers (the nation's largest after the IBT), would demonstrate real political muscle to the country at large. Many, perhaps most, of the UAW's leaders, were known to oppose the war. Leonard Woodcock, Walter Reuther's successor as the international's president, had not long before joined Gibbons on the platform at an antiwar rally in New York. Now, according to Tucker, Woodcock and the other members of the UAW's executive board had promised to attend the St. Louis gathering.

No doubt the most hopeful of the congress' organizers was Emil Mazey. The UAW's secretary-treasurer had been a bitter critic of the war since 1965, the year President Johnson sent the first large contingents of U.S. troops to South Vietnam and began bombing the North.[40] For years he was a lonely voice on his union's executive board because most other members, whatever their own misgivings about the war, had gone along with Reuther, who had in turn gone along, in both domestic and international politics, with Johnson, his friend and ally. Now Reuther was dead and Nixon was president. Mazey was fervently hoping that the St. Louis congress would reveal a UAW united against the war.

It wasn't to happen.

Tucker, Mazey's aide during the congress, spent most of it at the older man's side. As he recalled it, the trouble began Friday morning, when the delegates were to arrive in town. The office phone rang. It was, Tucker said, Leonard Woodcock's secretary, who reported that the international's president was tied up in important union business in Denver and wouldn't be able to make it to St. Louis. "Emil went ballistic," Tucker said. "'Them fuckers!'" Mazey was heard to exclaimed. "'Now I'm gonna get a call in the next half hour from …'" and then, Tucker said, Mazey listed one by one the more conservative members of the union's executive board. Woodcock's call had evidently served as a signal that they need not attend the congress either. "And, sure enough," Tucker said, "everyone Mazey named, the right wing within the board of the UAW, failed to show up."[41]

The more leftish members of the board *did* come to town and did participate in the congress, and that was gratifying. Even so, Tucker said, "Emil was hopping mad because he had projected having a unified UAW on this the whole question. I knew he was seething inside. He tucked it in, but I could tell he was a very unhappy guy about that."[42]

Tucker remembered a single Teamster official, a mid–level leader from, he thought, California, attending the congress. That wasn't counting Gibbons himself, of course, nor the members associated with Local 688's social concern wing.

Tucker also recalled Mazey apologizing to Gibbons for the poor showing of UAW brass. "Harold just shrugged and said, 'What the hell, look what I *don't* have here. You're lucky you've got what you've got.'"[43]

* * *

When the congress ended, June 25, Gibbons had six days to pack his bags to pack his bags and get to Hanoi with Hoffa and Taub. As it turned out, there was no rush because the July 1 arrival scheduled by the North Vietnamese had to be scrubbed. The papers Hoffa needed to travel abroad were still not available to him. How were they to be gotten? The blinded columnist Victor Riesel described what happened next.

"On July 5, [William L] Taub and the Teamsters['s] fourth vice president, big, husky, graying Hal Gibbons, lunched with none other than Dr. Henry Kissinger," Riesel reported, "—and in San Clemente, no less."[44] San Clemente, then known as the "Western White House," was President Nixon's California home.

This wasn't fiction. Ron Ziegler, Nixon's press secretary, owned up to the San Clemente meeting when the whole Hoffa-to-Hanoi story finally broke in the news later that summer.[45] And Kissinger's office has left a daily record of his conversations with people; that for July 5–14, 1972, says: "HAK, William Taub, Harold Gibbons, et al."[46] The later dates probably represent follow-up phone calls after the July 5 meeting.

Who were the "et al."? Hoffa wasn't there; everyone seems agreed on that. Taub says that Nixon did sit in, though he let Kissinger do most of the talking for the administration. Taub spoke for Hoffa. (According to Taub, Gibbons had little to say as well). The White House, once the story had broken, maintained that Nixon was not only not present at the San Clemente luncheon but had been kept completely in the dark about Taub's plan.[47]

In *Forces of Power* Taub moves from the San Clemente episode to one in which Hoffa runs him around the country carrying messages to Frank Fitzsimmons and Alan Dorfman, the man whom Hoffa had years earlier put in charge of the IBT's Central States Pension Fund. None of these tasks have to do with the Vietnam war; rather, they involve the usual double-crosses of internal Teamster politics. The errands, Taub decides, are mainly pointless, the messages mainly lies. Soon, however, he is back negotiating with government figures about the Hanoi trip, though the double-dealing he describes here is apparently not much different than that practiced among top Teamsters.

Kissinger, Taub writes, had promised in San Clemente to enthusiastically endorse Taub's project when he met next with Le Duc Tho. But that's not what happened. On July 19, 1972, two weeks after the San Clemente meeting, Kissinger was again in Paris negotiating with the North Vietnamese. A transcript of those talks was acquired by the Associated Press twenty years later, in 1993. The AP article based on the transcript noted "an attempt by former Teamster boss Jimmy Hoffa to go to Hanoi to negotiate the release of American prisoners" That effort, the AP said, "was shot down at the Paris peace talks by none other than Henry Kissinger."

According to the AP, Kissinger said to Le Duc Tho, "We have been harassed by a Mr. Taub who is a lawyer for Mr. Hoffa. He [Hoffa] is a convict, he has just been in a penitentiary and is on probation. Therefore he is still under sentence. I cannot believe you would have us release a convict in order to release prisoners to him."[48]

We don't know what Kissinger hoped to achieve with this double-cross of Taub, Hoffa, Gibbons—and also, perhaps, his boss Nixon. More may be learned once his papers are opened to the public, although that may take a while because the former secretary of state has directed that those papers be sealed until five years after his death.

In any case, Kissinger did not succeed in "shooting down" the Hoffa-to-Hanoi plan. Le Duc Tho, a professional revolutionary who had served two prison sentences under the French, was apparently undisturbed by the news that Hoffa was a former jailbird. The invitation to Taub, Hoffa, and Gibbons stood. And finally, after Kissinger tried to sabotage the Hoffa trip, a second highly placed sponsor appeared: Attorney General Richard Kleindienst.

Kleindienst had recently succeeded John Mitchell, who, like Charles Colson, would soon serve time in prison for Watergate crimes. The new attorney general came to the project, Taub says, because Nixon told him to. Nixon, Taub theorized, no longer feared losing the coming November election to the Democrat George McGovern. Now he wanted to crush the Democrats utterly. To that end he hoped to win the votes of tens of thousands of IBT members, most of whom normally voted Democratic but would be grateful to him if he enabled Hoffa to rehabilitate himself by journeying to North Vietnam and returning with liberated American POWs. The Nixon administration was thus split on the project, as Taub describes it. Kissinger, Secretary of State William Rogers, and Colson, Frank Fitzsimmons' man in the White House, opposed the Hoffa trip. Nixon and Kleindienst were *for* it.

On their first meeting, Taub writes, Kleindienst told him, "There must be no word of this to Mr. Rogers at the State Department or to Mr. Kissinger."[49]

That summer the North Vietnamese kept setting new dates for the three Americans to arrive. All had to be scotched because the permits for Hoffa to travel, promised—first, Taub says, by Kissinger, then by John Dean—somehow never arrived. Hoffa, Taub writes, became increasingly anxious and suspicious of everyone involved. Finally Kleindienst assigned a deputy attorney general, Ralph Erickson, to smooth the project's path. Erickson helped Hoffa get permission from his parole board to leave the country. Gibbons booked seats for himself, Hoffa, and Taub on a Pan American flight to Paris, whence they would transfer to a chartered plane bound for Vientiane, Laos; they would then proceed to Hanoi on a Russian plane, as Gibbons had done in March. The three were set to depart the United States on Thursday, September 7.

On Wednesday the sixth they arrived in Washington to have their passports validated and receive visas for travel to North Vietnam. That went smoothly, again thanks to Erickson of the Justice Department. "The American consulates along our route had received coded messages from the Justice Department, acting under Nixon's orders, alerting them to our passage," Taub writes. "They were to assist us along the way. The consulates in Paris, Bangkok, and Vientiane must have been wondering why the message came from Justice instead of State."[50]

But the next morning things began to fall apart. The phone in Taub's hotel room rang. A reporter from the *Detroit Free Press* had somehow gotten the gist of the story and was looking for details. Taub was able to fob him off, realizing however that the trip was no longer a secret. Gibbons, who perhaps had a premonition, had fallen ill and was forbidden by his doctor to travel. At the same time, panic began to infect various government offices around the city. Erickson called after a meeting with Nixon at the White House. "He said to tell you to get Mr. Hoffa out of the country and on his way to Hanoi if you have to chloroform him," Taub writes.[51] Meanwhile, Secretary of State Rogers cabled "urgent instructions" to the U.S. embassies in Paris, London, Moscow, Stockholm, and Vientiane "to check airline arrivals in the event that Hoffa and Mr. Taub turned up next week. If they did, he ordered, the officials should seek recovery of the passports long enough to eliminate the validation."[52]

Taub and Hoffa hurried out of town, taking a commuter plane to New York, where they were to catch the 7 p.m. Pan Am flight to Paris.

In New York the project imploded.

"I'm not going," Hoffa suddenly told Taub. He didn't trust the Justice Department, which, as he saw it, had railroaded him into prison in the first place. "I don't like it, that's all," he said of what would be his first journey overseas. "I don't like the smell of it. If I go, I'll never get back into the country. I'll never have my family around me again."[53] He also confessed to having been the saboteur of Taub's project—it was Hoffa himself who leaked the story to the *Detroit Free Press*, thereby igniting the panic in Washington.

The fuss there lasted several days. As the *New York Times* reported: "Confusion and recrimination between Government agencies mounted over who was responsible for the idea of a Hoffa visit to Hanoi to 'negotiate' release of American prisoners of war. Reliable sources said that Mr. Rogers, Attorney General Richard Kleindienst and Henry A. Kissinger, the President's assistant for national security, were all involved to varying degrees. Relations between their offices have become strained in recent days, these sources added. Mr. Rogers was reported to have been irate on learning that subordinates had validated the passports of Hoffa and Mr. Taub."[54]

Taub flew on alone to Paris and once there said only, "No comment." Hoffa and Gibbons slipped off to Detroit and St. Louis, respectively, where they had nothing to say at all. Kissinger and Kleindienst both admitted meeting with Taub but denied helping him in any way. The North Vietnamese professed ignorance of the whole business. The press, frustrated by its inability to dig out more information about the affair, soon lost interest. As noted earlier, the *Times* and *Life* wound up portraying Taub as a kind of zany scofflaw.

But the columnist Victor Riesel, who clearly possessed a knowledgeable source, had asked the right questions: "Who is Taub? Who is his principal? How could he get to Le Duc Tho so easily?"[55]

Taub remained out of public notice until the publication of *Forces of*

Power seven years later, after which, since the book got few reviews, he seems to have disappeared completely.

In his book Taub admits that he was initially furious at Hoffa for having wrecked the project. Later, however, he says the former Teamster boss may had good reason for his actions. "His last-minute refusal to get on the plane had exasperated me at the time, but now I was beginning to think he had been instinctively right."[56] Hoffa suspected he might be assassinated once he had gone abroad. Even worse, he feared that once he was out of the country his enemies—among whom he was by then including Nixon, Kleindienst, Erickson, maybe even Taub and Gibbons as well—might scheme to prevent his returning.

For Americans of a certain age, Hoffa's great fear brings to mind "The Man Without a Country," Edward Everett Hale's 1863 story about a young army lieutenant who, having cursed his own country in a thoughtless moment, is sentenced to permanent exile from it. The lieutenant is placed on a naval vessel which, although he is treated like a gentleman passenger, is for him a seagoing prison. As it sails around the world, he is prevented from disembarking at any U.S. port. The crew is forbidden to bring him news of events back in America. Years pass. The lieutenant is transferred from one naval vessel to another, then to still others. Having long since repented his curse, he longs for at least a sight of his native land. But not even at the end is he to be released. He dies and is buried at sea.

Hale intended "The Man without a Country" to inspire strong patriotic feeling in the North during the Civil War. It proved to be enormously popular then and for decades afterward. Generations of American children learned the story in school. The chances are excellent that Hoffa was once one of those kids.

* * *

In Paris, on January 27, 1973, Henry Kissinger and Le Duc Tho signed an agreement to end the Vietnam War. It had been a long haul. American administrations began edging into Vietnam with the defeat of French colonialism by the Communist-led Viet Minh in 1954. President Eisenhower, who only the year before had extricated his countrymen from the war in Korea, sent the French and their native allies tons of war materiel, but no troops. Kennedy sent several thousand troops. Johnson and Nixon sent tens, then hundreds of thousands. But regret soon overtook the latter three presidents. Memoirs and biographies show that not long after each of the three inherited Vietnam from his predecessor, he began looking for a way to escape it. Though few saw it at the time, three puzzled American administrations, on one hand, and an increasingly fierce American antiwar movement, on the other, shared the same underlying goal: getting out.

They differed only—though often violently—in how and when to pull that off. Kissinger and Gibbons were among the handful who could see that their interests, if not their politics, coincided and as a result could work together for a while. For a while.

The Hoffa-to-Vietnam project finished as farce. It wasn't facial just because Hoffa himself stamped his foot and refused to proceed, but also because throughout that summer various high officers of the Nixon administration had kept popping up to help or hinder—or first help, then hinder—the project, as if they were frantically adulterous men and women popping in and out of bedroom doors.

That, anyway, seems to be the way Gibbons saw it. The cablegrams sent between him and the North Vietnamese can be found in his papers, and so can the Victor Riesel column, but he appears to have held onto no other evidence of the episode. Nor did he talk about it with family and friends. Incomprehension showed on the faces and in the voices of Gibbons' children when they were told of the bungled Hoffa trip to Hanoi. Gibbons' former colleagues at Local 688 reacted in the same way.

A man who usually loved describing his adventures to others, Harold Gibbons kept this one to himself.

21

The Fall

When Harold Gibbons came to grief, literally, in the spring of 1973, it was partly because so many of his old Local 688 crew had preceded him into new endeavors, retirement, or death. He was like the last green pea upon a brown stalk. Though he mightn't have admitted it even to himself, he must have felt very vulnerable.

Pete Saffo was probably the most important of the old gang to go. Pete, the quiet man, the diplomat, the fixer, had been in ill health for several years. He died in the fall of 1970, the victim of a diseased cardiac valve. "What he died from, today is nothing," said Harland Horn, Saffo's successor as secretary-treasurer of Teamsters Local 610 in St. Louis, a delivery-drivers' union. "They operate, completely cure it. But in those days they just kept you alive till you died."

Saffo was fifty-three. For thirty years, no matter what other roles they might fill on the side (running Local 610, for example), he and Dick Kavner had served as Gibbons' palace guard. As Horn put it, their real job was "protecting Gibbons' rear end. That was their main purpose. Always."[1]

Phil Reichardt, Bill Latal, Max Voras, and the other founders of St. Louis' warehouse union were by then also gone. Lou Berra, one of the few founder still living, had come out of prison (see Chapter 11) to manage the elderly people's apartments in Council Plaza, work that he continued in the '70s; but he had long since given up participation in serious union affairs. Ernest "Cab" Calloway had retired from the union and traveled the few blocks north on Grand Boulevard to become professor of urban studies at St. Louis University. Jake McCarthy, after leaving the editorship of the *Missouri Teamster*, had become been Gibbons' administrative assistant but was "squeezed out" of Local 688 by Kavner in 1970. "Kavner was jealous of me," McCarthy said. He didn't say how the squeezing had been done.

"Gibbons and I were flying back from Washington and I told him I'd turned in my resignation," McCarthy said. "Well, it turned out he already knew that. He just said maybe it was all for the best." In recalling this scene years later, McCarthy sounded disappointed, as if he still wished Gibbons had stood up for him against Kavner.[2] McCarthy went downtown in '70 to work for the *Post-Dispatch*, where he was a popular columnist for a number of years.

Kavner himself retired in January 1972 after having a heart attack—although, as we'll see, he continued to find things to do around Council Plaza. Gibbons let him use a small room upstairs in the main office building. In that room, as McCarthy, who remembered Kavner as "abrasive, opportunistic and ruthless," put it, the local's hard man "remained an irritant within the union."[3]

The gradual phasing out of Local 688's veteran leaders resulted in a natural loosening of fraternal bonds. So too did the geographical dispersion of the local's membership. Though members had once lived packed together into the city's downtown neighborhoods, many were now suburbanites. Jim Pace, in a memo to the union's leaders in December 1968, estimated that no more than 46 percent of the membership remained in city wards, whereas 53 percent then made their homes in either St. Louis County, Jefferson County, or across the river in Illinois. What's more, Pace calculated that more than half of those members remaining in the city proper were North Side residents—meaning that they were very likely either African Americans trapped there because of segregated housing practices or whites desperate to sell their homes and join their relatives and friends in suburbia.[4]

This general loosening of ties was made vivid, maybe for the first time, during a series of special shop stewards' meetings in August 1969. These sessions, probably the idea of Jim Pace, Local 688's political director, were intended to gauge morale among the union's fifteen thousand members, the theory being that since stewards were the union officers closest to the rank and file, they would know best what the rank and file really felt and thought concerning hot issues. Eleven groups of stewards participated in these talks. Mike Ryan and Claude Brown (of the Tandy Area Committee) took turns chairing the discussions and then writing up synopses of them afterward. Later still, Ryan produced a four-page, single-spaced report in which he tried to interpret what he and Brown had heard the stewards say.[5]

Ryan and Brown gathered in lots of complaints. As noted in Chapter 20, some of this unhappiness was racist—gripes, for example, that the local's leaders were overly concerned with black people's problems and insufficiently so with those of whites. Some was ideological: a group of ten stewards declared that the *Missouri Teamster* was "a nasty Communist paper" that glorified "known Communists like Martin Luther King" and featured articles that were "a bunch of socialistic ideas attempting to lead the members into socialism."[6] Other grievances were by comparison relatively low-key. They ranged from the quality of services offered by the Labor Health Institute to bullying and/or indifference on the part of certain union officers; from the prices charged for drinks in Council Plaza's restaurant and cocktail lounge to the availability of carts on the golf course at the Pevely camp.[7] Ryan tried in his report to make sense of the cloudier, less easy-to-read outbursts. What he thought he saw beneath the anger and resentment was actually a kind of sadness, nostalgia for the union's pioneering days. "Twenty years ago," he wrote, "it was necessary for Gibbons, Kavner, Saffo … and the staff to spend a great deal of time together—not because they enjoyed attending so many meetings but[,] because they were groping to build a local union, they didn't know what they were going to do from day to day."[8] In the early years members had seen their leaders on a frequent basis, not just at rallies and on picket lines but also on those numerous occasions when Gibbons and the others would turn up on the shop floor itself to make sure the boss hewed to the contract's terms, that there was no cheating going on.

But all that was now institutionalized, Ryan wrote. On one hand, shop stewards had been trained to enforce contracts themselves; and, on the other, employers had learned that it was generally more economical to follow the wording of contracts closely than to try to cheat on them. Both sides had become more rational and professional. But in a sense, Ryan thought, Local 688 members seemed to *miss* employers' attempts to cheat, because those attempts had made work more *interesting*. At one of his and Brown's meetings, Ryan wrote, "the stewards called for inspirational speeches from Gibbons, wildcat strikes, bosses living in terror of the business agent and the union."[9]

Was Gibbons even available for such combat in 1969? Ryan's notes show a sense of abandonment on the part of the stewards themselves. One group of them called for Gibbons, Kavner, and other leaders to attend more shop meetings. Gibbons' presence especially was missed. "Gibbons should be seen more by the rank and file in order to spark new life and concern in the union," these stewards said. Ryan heard a similarly plaintive note throughout the meetings. He wrote, "Many members feel Gibbons has lost interest in Local 688 because he does not attend any shop meetings or steward council meetings."[10]

And of course Gibbons did have interests other than Local 688, among them the public housing strike, which happened to be going on in the same summer as Ryan and Brown's special stewards' meetings. Other non–Local 688 interests included his efforts to end the Vietnam war; to free Jimmy Hoffa from prison and return him to the IBT presidency; to come out a winner on other IBT political questions, in Central Conference politics, and in Joint Council 13 politics; and to play golf and drink and relax with show business friends. Ryan himself may have begun as far back as the special stewards' meetings of 1969 to share the sadness he heard in those meetings. He was certainly ready, decades later, to blame Gibbons to a certain extent for the troubles Local 688's boss brought down on himself and on the union. "Gibbons sort of lost his focus," Ryan, looking back, said in an interview in 2005. "He got so wrapped up in the glamour and playing golf and that sort of stuff, and he was chasing the broads."[11]

"He spread himself thin and lost touch with 688," was the way Jake McCarthy put it.[12]

* * *

There are basically two versions of how Gibbons was overthrown, Jake McCarthy's and one belonging to Ron Borges.

Borges had come to St. Louis in the spring of 1969, hired by Gibbons to serve as research director for the Central Conference of Teamsters. Gibbons had found him working for the AFL-CIO in Washington. Gibbons told him, Borges recalled, "Build a staff, but hire someone to do the actual [research]. I want you to travel, conduct negotiations, serve the conference's member unions." But even that was partly a blind, Borges said. Gibbons had never entirely surrendered the idea of running against Fitzsimmons for IBT president. Borges' real job would be to facilitate that campaign, if and when it ever came off.

Borges was twenty-nine, an eager young man who bore a physical resemblance to the actor Marlon Brando. Gibbons fascinated him. "He had a lot of contradictions in his life," Borges recalled. "He was a socialist but he loved the good life. He was always broke because he spent money like crazy—he *destroyed* money. He was the original 'limousine liberal.'"

Gibbons tried the younger man out as a late-night, pub-crawling companion. "He had the worst diet in the world," Borges said about Gibbons. "He started drinking soon after he got up in the morning and drank all day. He smoked until [in his seventies] he developed a lip cancer. He stayed up until two or three in the morning." Borges remembered a morning when, feeling bad after a night on the town with Gibbons, he was sent by a Labor Health Institute doctor to a hospital for a checkup. Gibbons visited him there, playing doctor, noisily trying to take over the diagnosis and prescription of care himself. Ann Gibbons brought Borges soup. "Don't try to keep up with him," she said, speaking of her husband. "He'll kill you."

Borges, who had attended a Rhode Island college before going to the AFL-CIO, was a novelty around Council Plaza: a trade unionist with a bachelor's degree. At some point while he was settling into his St. Louis job, he said, he was told by Gibbons and Kavner that he would be groomed to take over Local 688 as secretary-treasurer after Gibbons retired.[13] This seems to have been true. Jake McCarthy later wrote in a *Post-Dispatch* article that Borges had been "considered Gibbons' hand-picked successor and was viewed as an outsider by veteran [Local 688] business agents."[14] Gibbons' son Larry recalled the episode just a little differently. "Dick [Kavner] liked Ron and was grooming him to eventually hold a higher office in 688," Larry Gibbons said. "I think that was part of the motivation those low-level guys had when they made their deal with Fitzsimmons: they saw that Ron had been placed above them."[15]

Thus the situation stood as the 1970s began. In Borges' version of what was about to happen, the good guys were Gibbons, Kavner, and Borges. These three found themselves opposed by a group of small-minded conservative Teamsters intent on hijacking Local 688 and stripping it of its glamour and sheer contrarian, utopian élan.

Jake McCarthy's version was different. For one thing, it began back in the '50s when Gibbons, then moving into the national spotlight, "relied on two longtime associates to mind the store for him—Pete Saffo and Dick Kavner. They feathered their own nests pretty well, but wound up leaving Gibbons with an empty bag." Saffo's and Kavner's main goal had *not* been "protecting Gibbons' rear end," as Harland Horn put it, but rather protecting their own. This they did by making sure that no one else got near the union's levers of power. "If a Local 688 business agent began to think or speak for himself, Kavner would shunt him out of sight," McCarthy wrote. "Gibbons always acquiesced." Here McCarthy offered a recent example: "Ron Gamache, a soft-spoken and competent man, was shifted to organizing duties with the Joint Council."[16]

Gamache we've met, of course. He was the burly, sad-faced, former Marine, at one time one of Gibbons' favorite organizers, who then later developed a number of complaints about Gibbons' leadership and, as a result, had become a spokesman for Local 688's "business wing" (see Chapter 20). As Gamache saw it, the older man's fundamental sin was neglecting traditional bread-and-butter trade unionism in favor of exotic social experiments—opposing wars or tackling poverty in the ghetto, for example. As a result of such wastefulness, in Gamache's opinion, "by 1973 the money in Local 688's treasury was gone. There were un-negotiated contracts [with employers] that were as much as nine months overdue." Gamache also considered Gibbons deficient in good sense when it came to Teamster politics. "Gibbons went against Fitz—and with a man [Hoffa] you could see wasn't going to get in again."[17]

In Borges' story about Gibbons' fall, Gamache was a villain. In McCarthy's he was, if not the hero, at least a grownup, a man acting out of a strong sense of responsibility for the local.

* * *

Local 688 had a number of sobering experiences in the early '70s. One had to do with the Civic Alliance, the mechanism set up to conclude the rent strike and reorganize St. Louis' public housing. In theory, the Civic Alliance was a partnership between Gibbons' local and St. Louis' business leaders. In fact the real partnership was between the "social concern wing" of Gibbons' local union and the U.S. Department of Housing and Urban Development (HUD) in the administration of President Richard Nixon.

The HUD connection was crucial. Public housing tenants had quit paying rent in February 1969 partly because the city's seven housing projects—most of them thrown up in gimcrack fashion to begin with—were in dire need of maintenance and repair (see Chapter 20).[18] The city "lost" the rent strike because its housing department was nearly broke and couldn't have made the repairs even if it had wanted to. Gibbons and his friends "won" because they were backed by the promise of federal money—by, that is, by George Romney, the secretary of HUD. An auto industry magnate, Romney represented a wing of the Republican Party that has since become nearly extinct: he favored civil rights legislation and opposed the war in Vietnam. In 1969, at the dawn of the Nixon years, Romney could see no reason why, just because Lyndon Johnson's Democrats had lost the election, the government should abandon Johnson's policies vis a vis poor people. Nixon disagreed.[19] It took him some time to squelch Romney, however, and during that period the combination of HUD money and Teamster management went some distance to actually improve public housing in St. Louis.

Unfortunately, the HUD money eventually dried up, the Alliance's business members lost interest once the threat of rioting had passed, and the tenants—much to Ernest Calloway's sorrow—refused to adopt a trade-union-like discipline that would enable them to manage the projects themselves. For all these reasons the Civic Alliance for Housing disbanded in May 1972 and direction of the public-housing system reverted to the city's old Housing Authority, where it has remained ever since.

Although the Civic Alliance brought Gibbons and his union a certain amount of prestige and political influence in St. Louis, it also proved costly in at least two ways. Over its brief existence, the Alliance deprived both Local 688 and the Tandy Area Council of some of the union's most talented black organizers. As a result Tandy weakened, never to recover. At the same time the Alliance *strengthened* Gibbons' internal union critics, especially those who argued that the local's forays into community organizing diverted it from what should have been its primary function, representing members' interests on the shop floor. Robert Bussel, in his article about the rent strike, quotes a newsletter put out by Rank-and-File Teamsters (RAFT), a group of Local 688 dissidents: "Harold Gibbons and the kind of union thinking he represents have been inadequate in meeting the needs of workers in the shop concerning such issues as job security, speedup, safety, racism, abuse by supervisors, and inadequate, lengthy, and cumbersome grievance procedures."[20] Bussel, who is elsewhere enthusiastic about Gibbons' attempts to stretch the parameters of traditional trade unionism, admits here to seeing some justice in RAFT's complaints.

RAFT was a small group with a short life, but because it happened to be loosely associated with some local college Marxists it developed a reputation as *left-wing*. This occurred despite the fact that its criticism of Gibbons "and the kind of union he represents" brought it very near the position held by what we described in Chapter 20 as Local 688's "business wing"—which members of the local's opposition "social concern wing," understanding themselves to be leftists, saw as *right*-wing. All this is no doubt confusing, and probably wouldn't be worth mentioning except that, for Gibbons, the convergence of these two apparently differing ideological tendencies within his own organization should have been taken as a worrisome sign.

Also ominous, for those who could see it, was Local 688's creation of a separate *new* union, a kind of step-child, called Local 102.

Although, as we've noted, Local 688 began life as a warehousemen's organization, it soon became "miscellaneous," meaning that it acquired, along with warehousemen, members who bagged coffee beans, baked pasta, typed letters in offices, sold clothing in retail shops, drove taxis, and practiced one of a number of other trades. Their wages varied according to their particular trades, but all Local 688 members were eligible for the same fringe benefits, including medical care through the Labor Health Institute. Or at least they were until the early '70s, when the cost of these benefits—especially the cost of medical care—began a long, historic climb upward. When that happened, small, marginal employers became increasingly unable to handle the union's benefits package. What was Local 688 to do then with the men and women working in these small shops? Abandon them? Or find them a new trade union home?

Levi Sanford, Local 688's vice president in those days, cited an example of the problem. In Fenton, a St. Louis suburb, he said, a small company employed four or five people in the manufacture of plastic ballpoint pens. One year at contract time, the owners argued persuasively that, yes, they could give a wage increase but not the full range of benefits. For a while, Local 688 sent the ballpoint pen makers and others like them to a small leather-workers' union that, though not affiliated with the IBT, had its offices in Council Plaza.[21'] Then, in 1972, Gibbons, Kavner, and their friends established this brand-new local union, Local 102. The ballpoint pen makers and other marginal groups left the stopgap leather-workers' local to join the new organization, which had some three hundred members.[22]

Sanford was elected or appointed (it isn't clear which) the local's president, at the same time retaining the vice presidency of Local 688. Neither he nor the new union's other officers were paid, he said, though Dick Kavner, by then officially retired from the Teamsters, received a retainer to serve Local 102 as a consultant.

Now here's an interesting historical twist. Local 102 soon became affiliated with something called the International Distributive Workers of America. The Distributive Workers had been formed in New York in 1969—mainly out of what had been David Livingston's old District 65. Readers will recall that Livingston was a former Communist. As we've seen, their mutual dislike of the Vietnam war enabled Livingston and the anti–Communist Gibbons to put aside years of bitterness to work together against the war. Local 102's creation and affiliation with the Distributive Workers was apparently also part of this reconciliation. In fact, Local 102 and District 65 seem to have been the new international's *only* constituent entities. By the early '70s, whatever their past political quarrels, Livingston and Gibbons were singing from the same mildly leftish hymnal.

Either just before or just after Local 102 joined the Distributive Workers, Gibbons and Kavner sent Levi Sanford to New York to spend two weeks getting familiar with the bigger organization. Sanford enjoyed his stay. "They had some of the same things we had here in St. Louis," he said, mentioning in particular the Distributive Workers' health care program, which was similar to the Labor Health Institute back home. He was also impressed by the energy and aggressiveness of the New York leaders."[23] And best of all, Sanford must have thought, the Distributive Workers were going to help Local 688 solve its sticky benefits problem.

* * *

But the Local 102 gambit made things worse instead of better.

First, some Local 102 members, already unhappy about losing their benefits as well as their identity as Teamsters, complained that the switch had been done without their getting to vote on it.[24] They seem to have felt as would a pet taken from a comfortable home and left on a country road in the middle of the night.

Second, some members of Local 688 itself began to talk about "dual unionism." The term refers to one of the blackest sins in the trade-union lexicon: two different labor organizations competing for the same body of workers, a situation which, dividing as it does the forces potentially united against an employer, is bound to give him a valuable advantage over them. "Small employers liked the idea [of Local 102] because it dodged the benefits issue," Sanford said.[25] Of course they did; they saved money that way. The problem was that when other employers of Local 688 members heard about Local 102, they too wanted their workers to switch unions so that they also could dodge the benefits issue. The parent union, Local 688, soon found itself *competing* with Local 102, the step-child. This led Ron Gamache, though now exiled to the Central Conference, to charge that the creation of Local 102 alongside Local 688 constituted dual unionism. Levi Sanford said, "Gamache and others complained [about it] to Fitzsimmons," meaning of course Frank Fitzsimmons, president of the international.[26]

There remains some disagreement concerning which of Gibbons' actions finally caused Fitzsimmons to drive him from his own union. One was surely the St. Louisan's trip with David Livingston and Cliff Caldwell to North Vietnam in March 1972. Mike Ryan believed that the trip was the last straw for Fitz. Whereas the Teamsters were on record as supporting the U.S. effort in Vietnam, Gibbons, an IBT vice president, flew into the enemy capital "in the Jane Fonda mode!" as Ryan put it. "He went in to visit with the folks in Hanoi to figure out how to end the war. It infuriated Fitzsimmons. *Infuriated him!*"[27]

Worse was coming, though. Four months later, in mid–July, the IBT's executive board gathered at the luxurious La Costa Hotel and Country Club, overlooking the Pacific in southern California. According to Steven Brill's *The Teamsters*, the primary reason for the meeting "was the union's endorsement of Richard M. Nixon for reelection. It was to be Fitzsimmons' big gift for his friend, the President. The way the talk was going [on the eve of the meeting] the board's unanimous vote for Nixon the next day was being taken for granted."[28]

But one board member was holding out: Gibbons. He had, several weeks before, warned Local 688's Stewards' Council that he was "1000 percent" against endorsing Nixon.[29] Gibbons was accompanied to La Costa by his aide Ron Borges. On the evening before the endorsement vote, another IBT vice president pulled Borges aside and, speaking of Gibbons, said, "'Listen, take him up to Los Angeles early tomorrow—that way he won't have to cross Fitz.'" The theory being that if Gibbons were somehow absent from the board's vote, Fitzsimmons could still claim it had been unanimous for Nixon. "I strongly advised the same thing," Borges said, "but Gibbons insisted on staying and voting no."[30]

Another Teamster claimed to have heard Gibbons and Fitzsimmons screaming at each other in the hallways that evening. "Everybody in the joint could hear the whole argument," this man writes. "Harold was really pissed. Fitz had sold out to Nixon and was trying to turn the whole union over to him. Harold says, 'Under no conditions will I ever endorse Richard Nixon for anything, including dogcatcher. You can stick Nixon straight up your ass if you expect me to support him.'"[31]

The actual vote came early the next day—sixteen for Nixon; Gibbons, sticking to his guns, saying no. Afterward all seventeen men piled into a fleet of limos and sped the few miles up the coast to San Clemente, Nixon's home, to present him, in person, with their not-quite-unanimous endorsement. The president handled the occasion gracefully. Of course he already knew about Gibbons' vote. Smiling, he entertained his guests with drinks and a barbecue lunch and autographed golf balls for them. Afterward he led the Teamster heavies out to his private three-hole course. There Nixon picked up a club and hit a ball onto the green. Then, turning to—of all people—Gibbons, he invited him to do the same.

"He hit one on [to the green] and I hit one on," Gibbons recalled. "And then Fitz and a bunch of the others took turns. But they were all missing it. They just kept missing, and Nixon and I kept hitting it on. It was so funny."[32]

But not so funny for Fitz. Borges said he knew then that his boss was in serious trouble. "To vote against Nixon was to vote against Fitz," he said. "That vote gave Fitzsimmons the opportunity to kick him out."[33]

And Fitz had still other reasons to resent Gibbons. With all his faults, his promiscuousness, his weakness for fine clothes and the company of celebrities, Gibbons seems to have been with most people a kind man. But he wasn't kind to Fitz. Hoffa had long treated Fitzsimmons with unconcealed contempt; and Gibbons, having watched him do it, seems to have picked up the habit himself and passed it on to his own associates. Gibbons, according to his son Patrick, routinely referred to Fitzsimmons as "Mumbles."[34] "Pete Saffo called Fitz 'Cabbagehead,'" recalled Harland Horn. "He said he was the dumbest son of a bitch that ever was born."[35] It's possible that Fitzsimmons was more painfully stung by the use of such epithets than by Gibbons' rebelliousness on political matters. In any case, it all added up. Fitz must have yearned for years to swat the St. Louisan as if he were a fly.

And by the winter of 1972–73 Fitzsimmons may have had a practical reason for such a swatting. Gibbons, alone among the IBT's vice presidents, remained an ally of Jimmy Hoffa. Hoffa was now the founder of an organization called the National Alliance for Justice, and under its aegis was traveling around the country giving speeches that called for the reform of America's prisons. The National Alliance for Justice also sought justice for Hoffa personally, as Hoffa saw it: the organization filed a suit in federal court asking the judge to set aside the hated restriction in his commutation order so he could jump back into Teamster politics. That prospect must have seriously worried Fitz.

* * *

In mid–December 1972 Fitzsimmons announced at a press conference that he was removing Gibbons as director of the Central Conference of Teamsters. Fitz "vigorously denied" that, in doing so, he was punishing the St. Louisan for refusing to join IBT executive board members in endorsing Richard Nixon for reelection as president. "This is just the culmination of a disappointing series of jobs Harold has done as an administrator," Fitzsimmons said.³⁶ Ron Gamache of Local 688's "business wing" was named to replace Gibbons as the conference's boss. Conference offices were moved from Council Plaza to Chicago.

On May 10, 1973, Fitzsimmons presided over a banquet in Washington. Gibbons was not present. The dinner's theme was "Bonds for Israel," but according to a *Post-Dispatch* reporter who later talked to some of those who attended, it could have been called "Knives for Gibbons." An unidentified Teamster leader from St. Louis described the atmosphere this way: "His own guys, the guys he sponsored over the years for some of the big jobs in Local 688—[they] were cutting him up that night."³⁷

According to Keith Payne, the lady golfer with the man's name, the banqueters were entertained that evening by Gibbons' erstwhile friend Frank Sinatra.³⁸ Gibbons was saddened but not angered to learn of this, she said. Sinatra, a fierce political liberal during the Kennedy years, had moved rightward in the Nixon years, partly as the result of having become a golfing friend of Nixon's vice president, Spiro Agnew.

As noted earlier (see Chapter 18) Payne and Gibbons met in late 1972 at a nightclub in Savannah. She was twenty-three, he almost forty years older. A nurse, she was trying to launch a new career as a golf pro at the country club to which the nightclub was attached. He was a duffer who loved the game but needed help with his swing. She seems to have been a nearly irresistible combination for him: an attractive young woman who could teach the game. He soon began calling long-distance to offer her the pro's job at the course at Local 688's camp in Pevely, which she finally agreed to take on. Payne moved to St. Louis in, she thinks, early '73. Gibbons seems to have become her most frequent pupil. "The rest [the non-golfing part of the relationship] just happened," she said. "We just fit somehow."³⁹

Payne was thus present that spring of 1973 to witness Gibbons' downfall. Like others, she saw it coming—and was amazed that Gibbons seemingly did not. Harland Horn, Pete Saffo's protégé, said, "When he got in trouble with Fitzsimmons and the international, when they took the Central Conference away from him, all these so-called friends that Gibbons had, they were leaving him in droves. I said, 'Harold, you pick your friends really bad.' I said, 'You ought to be better at picking your friends.'"⁴⁰

Payne would have agreed. She recalled an evening earlier that year when a pair of prominent St. Louis Teamster leaders dropped by Gibbons' house in Palm Springs for dinner. Payne cooked the food and served the guests, but not happily because she thought she had caught them exchanging looks and making little jokes at their host's expense. After they had gone she tried to tell Gibbons that the two men weren't real friends. He just laughed the idea off, she said.⁴¹

On Friday, May 18, 1973, Michael Dunn, an associate of Ron Gamache's, rose before Local 688's seven-man executive board, meeting in the conference room in Council Plaza, to charge the union's top leaders with several "infractions," including sponsoring a form of dual unionism with Local 102. Dunn had been one of the union's ambitious types whom Gibbons had tried to slow by transferring him to a different organization, in Dunn's case to Joint Council 13. Jake McCarthy described Dunn as "outspoken, aggressive."[42] Ron Borges described him as a "goon."[43] The meeting was long and cacophonous. By its end, though Gibbons was allowed to keep his job as secretary-treasurer, he had to "agree to devote more time to the affairs of Local 688, the warehousemen's union, and less to travel and nonunion matters." Levi Sanford was forced to resign as the local's vice president; the board elected Dunn to replace him. Also, Borges was forced to resign as recording secretary. And the retired Dick Kavner was forced to abandon the small office Gibbons had lent him. "Kavner's desk was cleaned out and vacated Friday," the *Globe-Democrat* reported.[44]

Dunn denied that the IBT had had anything to do with the shakeup in Local 688. "We don't need Mr. Fitzsimmons or anyone else to tell us what to do," he said.[45]

It sounded at first as if, with Sanford, Borges, and Kavner gone, Dunn planned to run the local as Gibbons' partner. But Dunn had apparently crossed messages with Fitzsimmons, because within days the word came down that Gibbons would have to go as well.

Or it might have been that Fitzsimmons himself was just bring careful. There had been a time when Gibbons could have pulled his members together, fired them up with a rousing speech, and defied the whole international. After all, he had done exactly that in January 1948 when, after a vote in the Stewards' Council, he had marched his union straight out of the Retail, Wholesale and Department Store Union. A similar performance, ending this time with the membership's rejection of the Teamsters Union, wouldn't have seemed an attractive prospect to Fitz.

Fitz probably needn't have worried. Marcus Albrecht can remember, that year, sensing an anti–Gibbons mood seep through Joint Council 13 like a fog. Albrecht had been befriended by Gibbons as the result of antiwar work they had done together. The younger man was a member of Local 600, a freight drivers' union, one of the council's largest. Local 600 was almost completely white and pretty conservative as well, he said. Albrecht described a big rally that the local held at Kiel Auditorium in preparation for a drivers' strike. "Gibbons came and gave the most unbelievable speech," he said. "It gave me goosebumps. He had that deep voice, a deep beautiful voice, and he talked about how we were all Teamsters, and how all the other Teamster locals were going to stick with us, and we were going to see this thing [the strike] through.

"He was a fabulous speaker. But his speech wasn't well received. Not well received at all. Everyone was glad to hear that the other locals were with us, but my guess is that Gibbons wasn't their choice of somebody to deliver that message."[46]

Gibbons seems to have understood that he could no longer elicit roars of approval from any Teamster group, not even his own. As Jake McCarthy said, "At the end he realized he couldn't take it to the members."[47]

But Fitzsimmons was apparently taking no chances. On Wednesday the 23rd, Ron Borges was in Chicago looking for a new job. "I tried a couple of times to call Harold," he said, "but couldn't get through because he was in a meeting with two Teamster vice presidents, Bobby Holmes from Detroit and Ray Schoessling from Chicago. Schoessling was thought to be Gibbons' friend—but it turned out that he wasn't. He and Holmes had come to St. Louis to confront Gibbons."[48]

Jake McCarthy described that confrontation in an article that appeared a few days later. Clearly his source was Gibbons himself. Fitzsimmons insisted, through his two representatives (whom McCarthy did not name), on having Gibbons' resignation. If Gibbons were to refuse to resign—if, for example, he tried to rally Local 688's members to resist Fitz and the IBT—Fitz would still prevail in the end, and many other staff members, beside Gibbons himself, Borges, and Sanford, would lose their jobs. "Fitz would have put the local in trusteeship, run by outsiders, and a lot more local heads would roll," McCarthy wrote.

So Gibbons made a deal. "'Keep everybody on the staff for three years and I'll step out. I don't want this local torn apart,'" McCarthy quoted Gibbons as saying. "'I've given it too much of my life to mess it up now. If I'm the guy who has to go, I'll go.'"

Gibbons announced his decision that evening at an emergency meeting of the local's Stewards' Council. "'My belly was on fire,'" he told McCarthy afterward. "'I had to stop a couple of times before I could go on.'"[49]

Gibbons resigned not just the secretary-treasurer's office in Local 688 but also the presidencies of Joint Council 13 and the Missouri-Kansas Conference of Teamsters, and the top positions in the Labor Health Institute, the Council Plaza management group, the Pevely camp board, and other union offices. He resigned everything except the vice presidency of the international. Fitzsimmons let him keep that, restrained perhaps by other IBT vice presidents who feared that if Fitz were allowed to take the position from Gibbons he might one day do the same to them too.

Ron Gamache was elected the new secretary-treasurer of Local 688, and with his elevation the Gibbons era in St. Louis came to an end. It ended practically without public notice, even in the city. Friday, May 18, 1973, the day that Mike Dunn accused Gibbons and his friends of being guilty of "infractions" against the union also happened to be the day the TV networks began broadcasting sessions of the special Senate Committee on Watergate matters. In the days to follow the nation would be busy acquainting itself with Sam Ervin, John Dean, John Ehrlichman, Bob Haldeman, and the others and with their deeds and crimes. Who could compete with a show like that?

22

Out to Grass

Harold Gibbons died November 17, 1982, at the age of seventy-two. He had been in Oklahoma City playing in a golf tournament and was on a plane returning to his home in Palm Springs, California, when he suffered a ruptured abdominal aneurysm. Emergency surgery at a hospital in Inglewood, California, could not save him.

"Gibbons had two aneurysms that he knew of," recalled his onetime lieutenant Ron Borges, "one behind a knee, and one behind his heart. He was fatalistic about it. He knew he'd lived hard and was ready to pay for it."[1]

"Harold Gibbons stipulated in his will that Calloway was to give his funeral eulogy," DeVerne Calloway told a visitor a few months after Gibbons' death. Her husband Ernest "Cab" Calloway, sitting nearby, grinned at her words. He knew what was coming next. Cab Calloway had lost the power of speech as the result of a stroke suffered the year before. DeVerne Calloway, a tiny woman recently retired from Missouri's House of Representatives where she'd been a member for nearly twenty years, lit a cigarette and glanced over at her husband. About the eulogy, she said, "It may be just as well. He'd probably still be talking."[2]

"When Mr. Gibbons died, I thought in my naiveté that the whole city would shut down," said Marcus Albrecht, a former St. Louis Teamster who is now the regional director of a teachers' union in southern Illinois. "That's the way I viewed him, as that kind of figure. They had a crummy little funeral in Council Plaza. Later his second wife had a service up at the cathedral. But I had expected something like a civic holiday. It was so understated, a lack of acknowledgment of everything this guy had done. How could it be so little?"[3]

Gibbons certainly experienced many ups and downs in the nine years left to him after his removal, in the spring of 1973, as boss of Teamsters Local 688. The worst of the downs might have come the night of the removal. He had spent it at the apartment of Keith Payne, the lady golfer.

"The actual night of the ousting is a most painful thing to relate," Payne said. "I held him all night as he slept—and then as he woke up and cried, then fell asleep again, many times." Payne urged him to leave the Teamsters Union altogether and just enjoy life. Gibbons seemed horrified by that idea, she said. If he weren't a vice president of the Teamsters he would be a "nobody," he told her. "'No one will play golf with me if I am a nobody,'" he added. "He was *serious*," Payne said. "It was probably the most intimate thing he had ever confided to me." Payne tried to tell him that, title or no, his friends would still love and respect him. "But he also feared that he would lose his celebrity friends, that he would no longer be comped at casinos in Vegas, or be able to go backstage at shows.

"I honestly believe he would have quit [the union] if not for all that. At the time he was almost completely whipped," Payne said.[4]

Gibbons suddenly found himself to be a relatively poor man as well as one stripped of most of his posts and honorifics. Though he continued to receive the $18,000 a year due an IBT vice president, he no longer got the additional salaries that accompanied the secondary titles (presidency of the Missouri-Kansas Conference of Teamsters, for instance), nor did he, as before, have access to Local 688's expense account. This was severely restricting for a man who had long spent money as if he were a Rockefeller. "All of a sudden, he didn't have all his salaries and he ran out of money rapidly each month," Payne said. "I would usually have to pay the last couple of weeks."[5]

Wanda Koss, a former secretary at Joint Council 13, mentioned Gibbons' impoverishment too. She noticed, one wet winter day when he visited the joint council office, that he wore on his feet nothing more substantial than "thin shoes." Koss had recently bought her husband a pair of Red Wing work shoes, she said. She got another pair and left them with the desk clerk at the Chase Park Hotel, where Gibbons was then living again, possibly on the charity of Morris Shenker, the criminal defense lawyer who was the hotel owner's brother-in-law. "The next time Gibbons came down to the council office he was wearing those shoes. Good Teamster boots!" Koss said.[6]

More trouble was on the way. Having audited his tax returns for 1970 and '71, the Internal Revenue Service ordered him to pay $800 in back taxes. Not that $800 was a huge amount of money, but the order came when Gibbons was least able to pay it. Testimony in the Watergate hearings later revealed that Charles Colson of the White House staff had suggested the audit because Gibbons was considered an "enemy" by the Nixon administration.[7]

During these straitened times, on June 26, 1974, Ann Gibbons died of uterine cancer.[8] Her marriage to Harold had been an odd one by all accounts. He had been flagrantly unfaithful to her for years, at least since his move to Washington with Jimmy Hoffa in 1958. Yet in *The Teamsters* Steven Brill writes, "Harold and Ann Gibbons had somehow been an extraordinarily close couple."[9]

She clearly served as his ethical adviser and political conscience. He rarely went to sleep at night, no matter where he was staying, without first calling Ann to review the day's events. (Keith Payne can remember sometimes dialing the phone number for him.)[10] Often their conversations were about politics or business. Ron Borges said, "Harold told me once that Ann had chided him because she knew the details of some contract the autoworkers or steelworkers had just signed, and he didn't."[11] At other times they might talk about books or art. "He relied on her for all his guidance," a family friend said. "I mean, with him spending all day with people like Hoffa or the others who didn't have his background or share his social beliefs, she was his one outlet and the one person he shared everything with—except, of course, the affairs."[12]

The world without Ann lost depth for him. Six months or so after her mother's death, Elizabeth Vasquez visited her father in Washington, where he was then staying in a hotel. "He immediately began telling me about a speech he'd just given, letting me know he'd done a wonderful job," she said. "He described the speech's themes, how important they were, how responsive the audience had been. Then he said, 'You know, when I got back to my room, before I realized what I was doing I'd picked up the phone and dialed your mother's number.' Because he had to tell her," Vasquez continued. "Because until *she* knew, he hadn't had the real audience yet."[13]

Not long before Gibbons himself died, he told Vasquez a story that may be quite revealing. When he was fourteen, he said, he had fallen in love with his teacher. The teacher was only sixteen—but this was back in the days when, upon graduation, a small country school's ablest pupil often took over the teacher's job herself, and Gibbons was already six feet tall, therefore a semi-plausible suitor. Gibbons told his daughter, "I don't know what she thought, but I was completely in love. I arranged to have a date with her." The date involved going over to the teacher's house after school let out. There the teacher introduced Gibbons to her mother—who asked if he were related to a certain Joe Gibbons. Yes, he replied, Joe Gibbons was his uncle. "Well," the mother said, "when Joe Gibbons ran for a seat on the school board some years ago, it was the first time a Catholic had ever been on the ballot for anything in this area. And since this was before women were allowed to vote, I dressed up in overalls to look like a man and went down and voted for him."

"Now there's a story that captures a whole era," Vasquez said.[14]

Of course she's right. But the story is also interesting in itself, especially in the way it begins with a crush on a young girl but then leaves her behind to fasten on to the mother, a resourceful woman with a firm grip on her religious and political identity. From his own mother, bossing her huge brood of twenty-three children, to his older sister Annie, who did the actual raising of him, to Lillian Herstein and her socialist-Progressive friends, who introduced him to the Chicago labor movement, to Ann Culter Gibbons who, whatever her own troubles, functioned for years as his reality-principle-over-the-telephone, Gibbons had always, when push came to shove, looked to strong women for the answers he needed. Ann's death nearly did him in.

His relationship with Keith Payne seems to have begun to dwindle not long after Ann's death. He was in southern California with Payne when Ann died. They had planned to drive north up the coast, "playing every decent course along the way," Payne remembered. The news of Ann's death scrubbed that plan. "We never made our trip," Payne said.[15]

In the spring of 1977, when Gibbons was sixty-six, he married again. The bride was Antoinette "Toni" Stein, the former owner of a St. Louis modeling agency. "She was striking, young, very much younger than him," said Mike Ryan. "I was surprised at him marrying, settling so suddenly. There had been so many others who traipsed through the place."[16]

Although Gibbons' family and friends tended to be divided in their opinion of Toni Stein, they agreed that she had ended his sexual wandering. "I thought Toni sort of infantilized him," Vasquez said. "She would pack his bags and make sure he had socks. He might buy her a teddy bear. Around her he acted like some dotty old guy, which he'd never been before. But what Toni did was—what I felt when I saw them together—she made him happy. He was happy in her presence."[17]

The wedding was held in Palm Springs. Frank Sinatra, Ed McMahon, and other movie and TV stars put on a show for the guests at a reception following the ceremony. (So any political rift in the Gibbons-Sinatra friendship appears to have been healed by the time of Gibbons' second marriage.) Gibbons and Toni now spent most of their time in California. Gibbons grew a small white beard to cover a scar left by the removal of a lip cancer. Toni Gibbons enjoyed lunching with society ladies. They still had to watch their pennies. Gibbons was able to spend much time on the golf course, but only, Vasquez said, because Sinatra and other friends paid his greens fees.[18]

* * *

After he was driven from Local 688 in May 1973, Gibbons had only his vice-presidential responsibilities in the Teamsters Union to concern himself with, and those responsibilities were limited to IBT business in, as Wanda Koss, the secretary at Joint Council 13, put it, "North and South Dakota."[19] And there wasn't all that much IBT business in the Dakotas.

It wasn't the relative poverty of his new life that so depressed the St. Louisan. "The worst part was not the money, but having three years [1973 through 1975] with no job," he told Steven Brill. "You just can't imagine what that does to you."[20]

In 1976 Frank Fitzsimmons gave him a job. According to unidentified St. Louis Teamsters who talked to a *Globe-Democrat* reporter, Fitzsimmons had planned earlier in the year to drive Gibbons from his IBT vice presidency, stripping him of his one remaining union office. But then came the trouble in California. Cesar Chavez's United Farm Workers found themselves locked in a bitter battle with that state's Teamsters, who had lately decided they would compete with Chavez's organization to represent agricultural laborers. (Talk about "dual unionism"!) Because Chavez had by then become something of a national folk hero, like Robin Hood, this aggression against his union by the California Teamsters was embarrassing to Fitz. Gibbons, he recalled, was famously a friend and supporter of Chavez's (see Chapter 20). Aware that the St. Louisan was desperate for almost any kind of assignment, Fitzsimmons sent him to California to solve the problem. "If anyone can cope with Chavez, it's Harold," the *Globe* reporter was told.[21]

Although Gibbons spent much of '76 in California trying to somehow reconcile the two unions, he finally had to give it up as a failure. (Or maybe he failed on purpose, so he wouldn't have to seriously hurt Chavez.) In the end, after Gibbons departed from the fray, the United Farm Workers triumphed over the California Teamsters and wound up the dominant agricultural workers' organization in the state despite the IBT's best and worst efforts.[22] Meanwhile Gibbons held on to the vice presidency and even seems to have restored himself sufficiently in Fitz's good graces to be put back on an expense account. The worst of the poverty was over.

Of course the big event in this stretch of Gibbons' life occurred on July 30, 1975, when Jimmy Hoffa, still trying to reclaim the IBT presidency from Fitzsimmons, disappeared from a restaurant near his home in suburban Detroit. Gibbons' interpretation of that event seems to have been pretty much the same as everybody else's: Hoffa had been kidnapped and murdered by persons close to, if not members of, the IBT. Whom did he consider responsible? "I once asked Daddy if he thought that Frank Fitzsimmons was responsible for Jimmy Hoffa's death," Elizabeth Vasquez said. "And he said, 'Frank Fitzsimmons didn't *have* to have anything to do with Hoffa's death. But somebody benefited from Frank Fitzsimmons being [the union's] president. They did it [killed Hoffa] without ever having to have a conversation about it.'"[23]

For a short time newspaper and TV reporters parked outside Gibbons' door. When he asked why, one said, "Well, frankly, Mr. Gibbons, we figure you may be the next to go."[24]

Gibbons seems to have worried about that himself. Wanda Koss, the joint council secretary, said he once told her he had been staying in a hotel in Wisconsin the day Hoffa disappeared. A fire broke out in the hotel that night. Gibbons wondered if the fire was deliberately set, intended to kill him, Koss remembered.[25] In the end, according to Ron Borges, Gibbons said he had received a phone call from Mickey Cohen, a once notorious Los Angeles mobster, who essentially promised that what had happened to Hoffa would not happen to him. Gibbons seemed to stop worrying about it then, Borges said.²⁶

Hoffa's body was never found, of course, and few of the questions surrounding his disappearance were ever satisfactorily answered. But because his destruction occurred in such a spectacularly public way, it seemed to lend fresh energy to the government agencies already devoted to cleaning up the culture that had produced him. In 1977 the U.S. Labor Department and the IRS took over management of the Central States Pension Fund. In 1989 the Justice Department used the Racketeer Influence and Corrupt Organizations (RICO) Act of 1970 to establish a government trusteeship over the Teamsters Union itself. That trusteeship lasted more than a quarter of a century, until a federal judge ended it in a ruling of February 17, 2015. According to a news story on the ruling, the long trusteeship had "resulted in the removal of more than 200 Teamster officials ... including 50 local union presidents.... Four of the union's last seven presidents were indicted in office and the Justice Department spent decades investigating mob ties."²⁷

Frank Fitzsimmons managed to die unindicted, in 1981, but two of his successors, Roy Williams of Kansas City, who admitted in court to taking orders from the Chicago Outfit, and Jackie Presser of Cleveland, became government informants in attempts to stay out of prison. Meanwhile Congress' deregulation of over-the-road trucking in 1980 brought thousands of nonunion firms into the industry. Nonunion firms were happy to hire nonunion drivers, and within a few years the number of drivers who carried Teamster membership cards had dropped by nearly a quarter of a million.²⁸ The IBT eventually inherited in 1998 by James P. Hoffa, Jimmy's lawyer son, was significantly smaller, less powerful, and considerably less belligerent than his father's version.

* * *

In 1980 Harold Gibbons, the lifelong socialist, joined the other members of the IBT's executive board in endorsing the Republican candidate Ronald Reagan for president. His explanation seems to have been that because Reagan had once been president of the Screen Actors Guild, a labor union of sorts, he deserved the support of other unionists. But his real motive was probably tactical in nature. In January 1981, just days before Reagan's inauguration, Gibbons submitted to the new president's transition team an application to be appointed director of the U.S. Mediation and Conciliation Services.²⁹ There was no chance he'd get the post. The liberal Arizona congressman Morris Udall, whom Gibbons had asked for a letter of reference, tried to tell him this gently, reminding the St. Louisan that it was unlikely the new administration would listen to either of them, both being Democrats.³⁰ Of course Udall was right, and Gibbons was soon attacking Reagan as if the endorsement had never happened, describing the new president's economic program as one "a child can recognize as kind of stupid."[31]

* * *

Council Plaza is gone now. Gibbons' little nine-acre socialist city-within-a city came to resemble one of those old newsreel favorites, the hilltop mansion carried away by a slow-motion mudslide. In this case the mud slid for decades. The project had had a weak foundation. Gibbons had hoped to bring together there, with his own Local 688, the headquarters of all the other joint council members. However, according to David Salmon, only two or three small locals (including the non–IBT leather workers) agreed to move their offices to the Plaza. None of the other big IBT locals—the construction drivers, over-the-road and local freight drivers, beer truck and dairy drivers—ever joined in. "The leaders of those locals were most reluctant to come under Gibbons' tutelage," Salmon said.[32] Even worse was the Plaza's financing. This involved a tangle of mortgagees and mortgagors who, once Gibbons had been ousted, went at each other with lawsuits. Meanwhile the tenants vanished. The buildings stood mostly empty for years until, only recently, the tower apartments, built by the Teamsters for retirees but now under private ownership, have become homes for students at nearby St. Louis University. The Plaza's onetime gas station is today a taco stand.

Local 688 hung on in the Plaza until 2006. Mike Goebel, the union's former secretary-treasurer, finally directed the breakaway. His predecessor, a Gibbons loyalist who was, Goebel said, "nostalgic about past glories," had long refused to move.[33] Goebel moved; he took the local into a one-story brick building, a former bank, on Woodson Road near Lambert-St. Louis International Airport, where it remains today.

With some eight thousand members, Local 688 continues to be one of the biggest IBT local unions in the nation. It still has its Labor Health Institute, though the LHI is now an ordinary health maintenance organization rather than a medical clinic. The local remains dedicated to political as well as economic activism, and is still leftish. (The IBT itself, which for half a century had backed Republicans, endorsed the Democrats Barak Obama for president in 2008 and 2012 and Hilary Clinton in 2016.) Local 688 continues to follow a tradition begun back in the 1940s when, following Gibbons' advice, it began running its own members for public office. In recent years the local has placed liberal Democratic members on St. Louis' board of aldermen and in Missouri's legislature. A member of Local 688 until recently served as Missouri's state treasurer.

The problem for today's Local 688 is that although the union itself remains in many ways what it was when Gibbons was its leader, the surrounding social and political terrain has changed dramatically. Take Missouri, for instance. The state's rural heartland, stretching from the Bootheel in the southeast to St. Joseph in the northwest, usually voted Democratic until the 1970s, but since then has slowly become Republican.³⁴ Republicans now outnumber Democrats 2–1 in the Missouri's House of Representatives and 3–1 in its Senate. In 2015 GOP majorities in the legislature approved anti-labor "right-to-work" measures that failed of enactment only because they were vetoed by a Democratic governor. In November 2016 a Republican was elected governor. Right-to-work legislation now appears inevitable.³⁵ For at least the foreseeable future Local 688 and other Missouri unions and their allies are likely to remain on the defensive politically, not at all the positive force they often were in Gibbons' time.

Today twenty-seven states have right-to-work laws; they include Michigan and Wisconsin, where unionism used to be strong. As a social institution the American trade union, in the late twentieth and early twenty-first centuries, has contracted like a drying sponge. It wasn't just the Teamsters who lost members. Thirty-five percent of the nation's workforce belonged to unions in 1950, the period when Gibbons took his independent St. Louis warehousemen into the IBT.³⁶ Since then, the path has gone steeply downhill. In 1980 20 percent of the workforce were members of unions; 13.5 percent were members in 2001, and only 11.3 percent in 2014.³⁷ The trade unionist, at this rate of attrition, may one day become as rare as the farmer.

* * *

Among the American industries that experienced the great surge of unionization in the 1930s—mining, steel, automobiles, electrical parts, transportation, the needle trades—many are much less healthy today because firms in other countries can produce those goods more cheaply than can ours. Globalization, has sapped the strength of many a once-powerful union, along with that of the industry in which the union's members labor. The trend is not new. Gibbons' Local 688 had a run-in with it fifty years ago. The company involved, a Portsmouth, Virginia-based firm called Abex, manufactured brake shoes for railroad cars at a plant in a St. Louis suburb. In 1967 Local 688, which had been signing up the plant's employees, called a strike intended to force the company to recognize the union. But the strike stalled because Abex was what we now know as a "multinational" corporation. Although the union did manage to shut down the St. Louis plant, it was helpless to do the same with Abex's facilities in Germany, France, England, and Sweden.³⁸

Also destructive to industrial workforces has been automation, the replacement of human labor by machines, especially computers. Bayard Rustin came to St. Louis to talk about this trend in 1964. The occasion was one of Local 688's City Wide Shop Conferences; Rustin was the keynote speaker. Ernest Calloway introduced him to the conference delegates, describing him as "the Tom Paine of the Civil Rights Movement."

Rustin, more modest, called himself an "angelic troublemaker." He had grown up in a family of poor black Quakers and as a young man sang ballads in Harlem nightclubs. In the '30s he joined, then left, the Communist Party. In the late '40s he studied satyagraha with Gandhi's movement in India. Later he became the strategic thinker behind Martin Luther King Jr.'s anti–Jim Crow campaigns in the American South. A conscientious objector during World War II, Rustin had spent a term in Lewisburg Penitentiary. Two years before he went to jail, he served as a mentor to Bernice Fisher and her Chicago friends in the founding of CORE.

So, in St. Louis in the fall of '64, he was closing a kind of a circle.

Rustin began his talk by reminding the conference that the great, 250,000-person March on Washington of a year earlier had originally been designated a "March … for *Jobs* and Freedom [italics added]." In bringing so many people to the nation's capital, the march's planners (including its chief architect, Rustin himself) had hoped to inspire federal legislation that would, first, outlaw Jim Crow in public accommodations and, second, create a national public works program aimed at putting the nation's many unemployed—whites as well as blacks—to work again. The march turned out to be a great success. Jim Crow was soon outlawed. But there had been no very serious public works program, Rustin said. Indeed, most people soon forgot that the march had called for one.

Rustin was concerned about its absence because he knew automation was coming like a freight train. He had earlier that year added his signature to "The Triple Revolution," the manifesto of a group of left-wing intellectuals and futurists who believed that a world in which labor was increasingly taken away from humans and performed by machines—a process just then beginning to seem inevitable—would be a catastrophe.[39]

To illustrate his point, Rustin reminded his listeners of the old story about Captain John Smith and the company of Englishmen who founded the Jamestown settlement in Virginia in 1607. The New World had appeared to those Englishmen as one shock after another—naked aborigines, bears, panthers, poisonous snakes. An even graver threat soon appeared amongst the settlers, some of whom considered themselves gentlemen. As gentlemen, they were accustomed to having things done for them by servants. When told that they must help clear land and plant and cultivate the colony's food, they rebelled. But Captain Smith announced: "He that will not work shall not eat." His words cleared the gentlemen's minds and they went into the fields to work.[40]

Here Rustin paused his tale to point out that, because of automation, the great socioeconomic problem of the future is likely to be the exact opposite of seventeenth-century Jamestown's. Captain Smith's world had more work to be done than it had people to do it. Our own new world, Rustin said, will have more workers than work.

Automation was still relatively new and unsophisticated in America in the 1960s, when Rustin first became alarmed by it. Today, however, a half century later, robots commonly perform the assembly-line tasks formerly done by men and women. Auto manufacturers now experiment with driverless cars. Driverless trucks are sure to follow. Who will need Teamsters then?

Rustin said: "When the Virginia colony was founded Captain John Smith said, 'No work, no eat.' I would have voted with him out there in the wilderness. But a society which willfully builds up machinery to rob men of work has no right to say, 'No work, no eat.'"

Rustin finished his talk by echoing the call once made by the philosopher William James for a "moral equivalent to war." "Because of the large number of jobs which will be lost," he said, "a moral equivalent, a redefinition of *work* is needed [italics added]."[41]

Rustin offered no clue as to what a moral equivalent to work might be. (For humans there is probably no moral equivalent to work, just as there is none to food or oxygen or companionship.) However, he did suggest some *jobs* that a society more enlightened than his own would insist be done: the construction, if necessary by the government, of "schools, hospitals, roads, child care centers."[42] Those aren't shocking notions, of course. They are what we nowadays call infrastructure, and have been part of every liberal-labor program proposed in American politics for the past seventy or eighty years.

But the infrastructure has gone unbuilt. And many of the nation's industrial jobs have gone, period. At the time of Gibbons' death, for example, St. Louis was home to some thirty-five thousand autoworkers. Then in 1981 General Motors moved its Corvette plant, which had been at the corner of Union Boulevard and Natural Bridge Avenue, to a town in Kentucky. Ford closed its plant in the northwest suburb of Hazelwood in 2006. Chrysler, which had operated two plants in the southwest suburb of Fenton, closed both in 2009.[43] These troubles weren't St. Louis' alone, of course. In that last year, 2009, General Motors and Chrysler themselves survived only because the Barack Obama administration pumped enough federal money into them to keep them afloat.

As things stand, the future looks bleak for industrial jobs that pay decent wages. If history is any guide, the disappearance of those jobs is likely to cause considerable turmoil in American society. Turmoil isn't always a bad thing, however.

Troubled times can be dangerous—they are certain, for example, to generate movements composed of people driven by fear and suspicion of others. During the Great Depression some frightened Americans signed up with fascist organizations such as the Black Legion, Silver Shirts, and Ku Klux Klan. But those years also brought us the CIO, the trade union federation that from its birth in 1935 was insistently and famously egalitarian. There seem to be two reasons the CIO unions were egalitarian. One was tactical: a labor organization that refuses to exclude anyone on the basis of race, ethnicity, religion, or other invidious form of discrimination is much less vulnerable to strikebreaking than organizations that do exclude. The other reason was moral. It was based on the Parable of the Good Shepherd (Matthew 18:12–14) in the New Testament. *Which of you,* the Parable asks, *if ninety-nine of your hundred sheep are safe, will rest until you have gone back into the night and found the sheep that is lost?*

The Europeans who formed history's first trade unions were often irreligious, sometimes even atheist. Still, they were usually moved, if only unconsciously, by the impulse represented by the Parable. The CIO unions were moved in the same way.

It's conceivable that mass joblessness resulting from globalization and automation could revive the trade union movement in the United States. Or *reinvent* is perhaps the word. The insurgent unionization of the Depression years occurred as basic industries, the demand for their goods on the rise, began to hire workers again. In post-industrial America, a reinvented labor movement will have to make its own demand—that the nation construct those "schools, hospitals, roads, child care centers," and other pieces of infrastructure that Bayard Rustin called for fifty years ago.

* * *

For such to happen, trade union veterans will have to remember why their movement came into being in the first place. And, at the very least, they will have to be tireless bearers of the Word.

Patrick Gibbons, Harold's eldest son, remembers one of the last times he saw his father. Patrick is perhaps the most rebellious of Gibbons' three children, but he's a Left-winger's offspring who rebelled from the Right. Whereas Harold opposed the Vietnam war, Patrick enlisted in the air force and was sent to Vietnam to help fight it. Whereas Harold always described himself as a socialist, Patrick is a strong believer in capitalist economics.

But he admired his father. On the day he recalls, Gibbons was scheduled to give a talk at one of the colleges in San Antonio, Texas, where Patrick today makes his home. Patrick drove over to the campus to see him. "I was directed to a big, crowded room but at first I didn't see Harold in it. I finally found him sitting on a couch in the corner talking to two old ladies about the importance of trade unions.

"He loved people, loved being around them, loved talking to them, loved persuading them. He would talk to two people as if they were a hall of Teamsters," Patrick said.[44]

Sinner though he was, Harold Gibbons went to his grave bearing the Word.

Chapter Notes

Introduction

1. Ernest Calloway, note to the author of February 1983.
2. Harry Vernon Ball, "Case History of a Labor Union: The United Distribution Workers," MA Thesis, Washington University, St. Louis, 1950, vol. 2, p. 521.
3. Steven Brill, *The Teamsters*, Simon & Schuster, New York, 1978, p. 341.
4. Ball, vol. 2, pp. 390–391.
5. Author's telephone interview with Joseph Ames of October 16, 2007.
6. Author's interview with Marcus Albrecht of October 13, 2005.
7. Author's telephone interview with Jake McCarthy of February 1983.
8. Author's interview with Ron Gamache of February 1983. The papers Gamache couldn't find in 1973 are today stored in the library archives at Southern Illinois University, Edwardsville.
9. Sheila Michaels, emails of February 7, 2007.

Chapter 1

1. Author's interview with Elizabeth Vasquez and Larry Gibbons of November 13, 2005. Unless otherwise noted, information concerning the Gibbons family comes from this series of interviews. The source for Kennedy's question is McClellan Committee Hearings, September 2, 1958, Part 39, p. 14,559.
2. Shawn Murphy, e-mail of December 30, 2005. Murphy is a historian of the Scranton area.
3. John O'Hara, "The Doctor's Son," in *The O'Hara Generation*, Random House, New York, 1969, p. 10.
4. Sally Bixby Defty, "Teamster Boss," *St. Louis Post-Dispatch*, May 11, 1969, p. 1G. If the idea of a Welsh "patch" seems unlikely, consider that in the early twentieth century the Scranton area possessed the largest concentration of Welsh people (many of whom were anthracite miners) outside Wales and England. See William D. Jones, in *Wales in America: Scranton and the Welsh 1860–1920* (University of Scranton Press, Scranton, 1993, p. xvi).
5. Vasquez and Gibbons.
6. Defty.
7. *A Dick Keefe Profile*, KMOX-TV, St. Louis, April 23, 1978. A tape of this show can be found in Box 4, Folder 1, Gibbons papers.
8. O'Hara, p. 14.
9. Author's telephone interview with Patrick Gibbons of February 2, 2008.
10. Author's telephone interview with Larry Gibbons of January 18, 2006.
11. Author's interview with Elizabeth Vasquez and Larry Gibbons of December 22, 2005.
12. Harold sometimes had trouble recalling the names and faces of much older siblings. He was accosted once in Chicago by a woman who asked, "Aren't you one of the Gibbons boys?" He said he was. "I thought so," the woman exclaimed. "I'm your sister Margaret" ("The Gibbons Clan," *St. Louis Star-Times*, August 6, 1947). This brief newspaper clipping is attached to an August 15, 1947, FBI memorandum by an agent who had apparently been sent to Chicago and Madison, Wisconsin, to look into Gibbons' background.

13. Sidney Lens, *Unrepentant Radical,* Beacon Press, Boston, 1980, p. 111.
14. Steven Brill, *The Teamsters,* Simon and Schuster, New York, 1978, p. 339.
15. "School for Workers: Education for a Democratic Workplace," at http://schoolforworkers.uwex. edu/about.cfm.
16. Brill, p. 341.
17. Defty.
18. Brill, p. 341.
19. Edward N. Doan, *The La Follettes and the Wisconsin Idea,* Rinehart & Company, New York, 1947, p. 14.
20. Quoted in Brigid O'Farrell and Joyce L. Kornbluh, *Rocking the Boat: Union Women's Voices, 1915–1975,* Rutgers University Press, New Brunswick, pp. 17–18. O'Farrell and Kornbluh devote a chapter to Lillian Herstein.
21. See Steven Fraser's *Labor Will Rule: Sidney Hillman and the Rise of American Labor* (Free Press, New York City, 1991), especially Chapter 3, for a description of the lively intellectual cross-fertilization between upper-class Progressive women and socialist women trade unionists, particularly in Lilian Herstein's Chicago. Much of modern American liberalism came out of this mix.
22. O'Farrell and Kornbluh, pp. 22.
23. O'Farrell and Kornbluh, pp. 25–26.
24. For the EEP, see Joyce L. Kornbluh, *A New Deal for Workers' Education: The Workers' Service Program, 1933–1942,* University of Illinois Press, Urbana, 1987, especially pp. 25–30.
25. O'Farrell and Kornbluh, p. 26.
26. Lillian Herstein, letter to Harold Gibbons of September 28, 1971, Box 28, Folder 5, Gibbons papers.
27. Richard Rose, "Teamsters' New Boss?" *The Nation,* March 23, 1957, p. 253.
28. Thomas F. Eagleton, e-mail of August 18, 2005.
29. O'Farrell and Kornbluh, p. 282.
30. O'Farrell and Kornbluh, p. 27.
31. FBI memo of April 15, 1953; Barbara Warne Newell, *Chicago and the Labor Movement,* University of Illinois Press, Urbana, 1961, p. 224.
32. O'Farrell and Kornbluh, p. 26. Newell, p. 37.
33. Lens, p. 77.
34. Defty.
35. Newell, p. 109. On the strike, see Newell, pp. 107–110. The taxi drivers, who had intended to form a CIO union, wound up as the result of a political compromise in the AFL Teamsters.
36. FBI memo of September 3, 1946.
37. Brill, p. 342.
38. Peter Wyden, "Labor Boss," *St. Louis Post-Dispatch,* March 30, 1952, p. 3H.
39. Defty
40. Patrick Gibbons.
41. Rose. Under a union-shop contract, all workers in a shop would be forced to join the union.
42. FBI memo of August 1, 1950, quoting a *Louisville Courier-Journal* news item of May 18. 1938. Orr had served in Spain with volunteers from Britain's Independent Labour Party, to which George Orwell also belonged. In fact, Orr recalled welcoming Orwell to revolutionary Barcelona in 1937. See Adam Hochschild, "Orwell: Homage to the 'Homage,'" *New York Review of Books,* December 19, 2013, p. 62.
43. Vasquez and Gibbons, November 13, 2005. This is the version of how their parents met that Larry remembers being told by their mother. Elizabeth recalls another version: Harold and Ann met on the campus of Louisville University, where both had spoken at an antiwar rally. Gibbons's FBI file contains a *Louisville Times* item of April 30, 1938, mentioning the rally and the presence of the two speakers. Of course both versions could be substantially true.
44. Author's telephone interview with Larry Gibbons of October 4, 2006. "In later years Aunt Lois lost interest in politics and became first a Quaker, then a Buddhist, among other things."
45. Vasquez and Gibbons.
46. FBI memo of September 25, 1959.
47. Patrick Gibbons.

Chapter 2

1. James Neal Primm, *Lion of the Valley: St. Louis, Missouri,* Pruett Publishing Co., Boulder, 1981, p. 351.
2. Author's telephone interview with Ted Schafers of July 9, 2007.
3. Schafers.
4. Ernest Calloway mentions Penney's pay scales in *Ten Years of Trade Union Democracy in Action* (Local 688, St. Louis, 1951, p.

11), a sixty-six-page publication commemorating the union's tenth anniversary under Gibbons' direction. Information about wages at Brown Shoe and other warehouse employers can be found in Box 40, Folder 10, Gibbons papers.

5. The early warehouse union had a public-relations man named Joe Reynolds. Sometime in the late 1940s he suggested that the union make a movie illustrating its history. A two-scene sketch, written for the movie and called "A Shoe Warehouse Packing Room," can be found in this file. In one scene John Naber, a founding member of the union, plays a worker complaining to a fictional foreman named Mac about having his work hours extended. Irritated by Naber's temerity, Mac decides to teach him a lesson. A second scene shows him saying, "Well, John, looks like I've got some bad news for you. Starting Monday we have to lay you off." The movie was apparently never made (file labeled "Joe Reynolds," Box 40, Folder 10, Gibbons papers).

6. Harry Vernon Ball, Jr., "Case History of a Labor Union: The United Distribution Workers" (master's thesis, Washington University, 1950), vol. 1, p. 8. The CIO organizer who talked to Kid McCoy and his friends was Ralph Shaw, a Communist who later became secretary of the Missouri CP. Unless otherwise noted, information in this book concerning the warehouse union's formative years is taken from Ball's thesis.

7. Ball, p. 10, says the Penney's election was in June. Calloway, p. 11, reproduces an NLRB notice setting July 8 as the date. In November Penney's laid off 135 warehousemen, all union members; as a result of NLRB pressure the workers eventually got their jobs back, though in some cases that took as long as nine months.

8. "Strikers Evacuate Emerson Plant after 53 Days," *St. Louis Post-Dispatch*, April 29, 1937, pp. 1A, 3A.

9. Calloway, p. 38; David W. Salmon, *Recollections: Part Five: Establishing a Career and Family in St. Louis, 1948–1953,* privately printed, Provo, 2003, p. 351.

10. Arnold M. Rose, *Union Solidarity: The Internal Cohesion of a Labor Union,* University of Minnesota Press, Minneapolis, 1952, p. 11.

11. Calloway, p. 11.

12. Harry Vernon Ball, Jr., pp. 4–5 of "Conclusions," a typescript found in Box 40, Folder 11, Gibbons papers. "Conclusions" may have been an early draft of the last chapter of Ball's master's thesis, "Case History of a Labor Union."

13. Salmon, p. 212. Ball died in 2006. His obituary can be seen at *www.sociology.hawaii.edu/ events/obitball.*

14. Ball, "Case History of a Labor Union," p. 22.

15. The uncredited Pittsburgh photograph is on p. 12 of Calloway.

16. On warehousemen and their unions, see Robert D. Leiter, *The Teamsters Union: A Study of Its Economic Impact,* Bookman Associates, New York, 1957, pp. 62, 100–102.

17. See George G. Kirstein, *Stores and Unions: A Study of the Growth of Unions in Dry Goods and Department Stores,* Fairchild Publications, New York, 1950, pp. 56–58, 75–79. The international was originally called the United Retail and Wholesale Employees of America. It has been known as RWDSU since shortly after the end of World War II.

18. Kirstein, p. 58.

19. Interview with Moe Foner, Columbia University Libraries Oral History Research Office, Session 18, June 12, 1986 (*columbia.edu.cu/_1web/indiv/oral /foner/transcript18*).

20. Kirstein, p. 78.

21. Ball, pp. 28–29.

22. Ball. p. 33.

23. Ball. p. 34. Why should Gibbons have gotten in trouble for participating in a left-wing caucus during the convention of a generally left-wing union? Sidney Hillman, president of the Amalgamated Clothing Workers as well as the real power in the Textile Workers, had resigned from the Socialist Party in 1936 in order to back Roosevelt, rather than the SP's Norman Thomas, in that year's presidential election. Many of his associates became New Deal Democrats too. They would not have looked kindly upon a continuing Socialist caucus in either the Amalgamated or the Textile Workers.

24. Ball.

Chapter 3

1. David W. Salmon, *Recollections: Part Six: I Joined Teamsters Local 688,* privately printed, Provo, 2003, p. 322.

2. Wyden.
3. Ball, p. 33.
4. Salmon, p. 298. Emphasis in original.
5. Defty.
6. Ball.
7. Rose, p. 253. In fact Hillman, who died in 1946 at the age of fifty-nine, had neither sufficient time nor health to pay much attention to RWDSU and its young officers. Even so, he seems to have served Gibbons as a distant father figure. For Hillman and the early retail and warehouse workers' union, see Fraser, pp. 345–346, and Kirstein, p. 75.
8. Author's interview with Levi Sanford of March 28, 2006.
9. Calloway, p. 18. The following year, 15 warehouse union members—10 men and 5 women—attended a two-week session of the School for Workers. Members were sent for similar sessions every year until 1947, when "heavy post-war strike expenses forced a curtailment of the program."
10. Ball, p. 35.
11. Fraser, p. 114.
12. Ball, "Conclusions," p. 19. In Harry Ball's opinion, Gibbons' "amalgamation" of St. Louis' separate warehouse locals was a mistake because it replaced direct democracy with representative democracy, an inferior thing.
13. Lon W. Smith, "An Experiment in Trade Union Democracy: Harold Gibbons and the Formation of Teamsters Local 688, 1937–1957" (PhD diss., Illinois State University, Normal, 1993), pp. 61–62. For a time the locals kept their separate identities, but since their treasuries had been gathered up by the Joint Board, their independence was purely formal.
14. Ball, p. 38.
15. Salmon, p. 293.
16. Ernest Calloway, "Who Runs St. Louis?: Flow of Economic Power and Decision-Making in St. Louis," Center for Urban Programs, St. Louis University, 1980, p. 28.
17. Ball, pp. 125–126.
18. Vasquez and Gibbons.
19. Author's interview with Yuki Kato of July 11, 2008. Kato is today the widow of a man named Ferguson Keathley. However, since she is far better known by Local 688 veterans by her maiden name, I have consistently used it here. Incidentally, she holds no grudge against the U.S. government for "relocating" its Japanese citizens during the war. She said, "I think one of the greatest things that happened as a consequence of being put in the camps, at least for my generation, was being scattered all over the country." If not for the internment, "I would have been still in California living in my little Japanese community." "Relocation," though brutal, showed her a bigger world.
20. Calloway, *Ten Years of Trade Union Democracy in Action*, p. 62.
21. Robert H. Zieger, *The CIO: 1935–1955*, University of North Carolina Press, Chapel Hill, 1995, pp. 165–169.
22. Salmon, p. 311.
23. Ball, p. 168; Calloway, p. 26.
24. Nathan Simon and Sanford Rubushka, "Membership Attitudes in the Labor Health Institute of St. Louis," *American Journal of Public Health*, June 1956, p. 716.
25. Ball, pp. 175–176.

Chapter 4

1. Calloway, p. 23.
2. Ball, p. 134.
3. Ball, pp. 136, 138.
4. Ball, p. 96.
5. Ball, p. 97.
6. On Sentner, see Rosemary Feurer, *Radical Unionism in the Midwest, 1900–1950*, University of Illinois Press, Urbana, 2006; also Feurer, "William Sentner, the UE, and Civic Unionism in St. Louis," in Steve Rosswurm, ed., *The CIO's Left-Led Unions*, Rutgers University Press, New Brunswick, 1992, pp. 95–117.
7. "Missouri: 1; Texas: 0," *Time*, June 11, 1945. Emerson's new CEO was Stuart Symington, later a U.S. senator from Missouri.
8. Dwight Macdonald, *Politics Past* (originally published in 1957 as *Memoirs of a Revolutionist*), Viking Compass, New York, 1970, p. 17. A former Trotskyist, Macdonald estimated the number of his comrades at eight hundred.
9. Author's telephone interview with Wanda Koss of July 7, 2006. Koss, a retired secretary at St. Louis' Teamsters Joint Council 13, says Gibbons once told her that in 1934 he made a special trip from the Wisconsin

School for Workers to Minneapolis to meet the leaders of the Teamster strike.

10. FBI memo of February 25, 1943. The memo, the first in Gibbons' extensive bureau dossier, says: "A review of St. Louis file 100-5238 reveals that the above mentioned subject is already in line for investigation in regard to his activities concerning the Trotsky Party..."

11. Ball, pp. 109–110.

12. Ball, p. 117.

13. "Union Hits Ward Strike," *New York Times*, December 19, 1944, p. 16A. The article describes a meeting at which representatives of New York's RWDSU Local 65 voted to condemn its own international's strike against Montgomery Ward.

14. Lens, p. 16.

15. Lens, pp. 110–111.

16. Feurer, *Radical Unionism*, pp. 186, 200.

17. Feurer, p. 196.

18. FBI memo of July 20, 1948.

19. See the FBI memo of February 28, 1945, which noted that Herbert Benjamin, then the Communists' leader in Missouri, had recently criticized UE's representatives on St. Louis' Industrial Union Council for losing a council vote to Gibbons' warehousemen, thereby, he said, threatening to "let a bunch of [deleted] Trotskyites take over the CIO here."

20. Farrell Dobbs, *Teamster Rebellion*, Monad Press, New York, 1972, pp. 24–25.

21. James R. Hoffa and Donald I. Rogers, *The Trials of Jimmy Hoffa: An Autobiography*, Henry Regnery, Chicago, 1970, p. 107.

22. Hoffa and Rogers, pp. 134–135.

23. "Wildcat Strike of 300 Ties Up Trucking Firm," *St. Louis Post-Dispatch*, November 14, 1946, p. 1A; "300 AFL Rebels Close 6 Truckers after Expulsion," *St. Louis Post-Dispatch*, December 9, 1946, p. 1A; "Union Asks for Firing of Drivers in Illegal Strike, for Injunction," *St. Louis Post-Dispatch*, December 10, 1946, p. 1A, 6A.

24. "Union Asks for Firing of Drivers," p. 6A.

25. January 10, 1947, memo from J. Edgar Hoover to the SAC, St. Paul, Minnesota.

26. Dunne's letter is quoted in an undated FBI memo, presumably of January 1947, describing an anonymous informant's report. The memo says only that the informant was a woman. The "party" mentioned in the letter was the Socialist Workers Party, formed by the Trotskyists in 1938, after their expulsion from the Socialist Party.

27. "Six Drivers Expelled over Wildcat Strike, 25 on Probation," *St. Louis Post-Dispatch*, January 9, 1947, p. 1A.

28. December 8, 1948, memo from FBI's SAC, St. Paul, Minnesota, to the SAC, St. Louis. The memo's wording suggests that it was based on the transcript of a recording. The St. Paul SAC describes Dunne's visitor as "a man believed to be Gibbons." It certainly sounds like him.

29. FBI memo of January 2, 1953.

Chapter 5

1. Quoted in Ball, vol. 2, p. 288. Browder was the party's leader in the late 1930s and '40s.

2. Ball, p. 289.

3. Ball, pp. 294–295.

4. Sanford. Sanford, who joined the union several years after this episode, is reconstructing the fateful Gibbons-Kavner conversation from stories the two men told him.

5. Ball, p. 330.

6. Sanford.

7. Arnold M. Rose, *Union Solidarity*, p. 26.

8. FBI memo of January 8, 1949, quoting *St. Louis Star-Times* articles of December 4, 1947, and January 17, 1948; Ball, p. 353; Calloway, p. 32.

9. Calloway.

10. Author's telephone interview with Gladys W. Gruenberg of January 29, 2007.

11. Author's telephone interview with Ron Borges of July 21, 2008.

12. Vasquez and Gibbons, November 13, 2005.

13. Quoted in Con Kelliher, "Powerful Boss of St. Louis Teamsters Is One of City's Most Controversial Figures," *St. Louis Globe-Democrat*, August 25, 1956.

14. "4 Arrested in Fight on New Picket Line," *St. Louis Post-Dispatch*, July 28, 1948, p. 11A; "Grady Pickets Arrested, Beat Picture Taker after Release," *St. Louis Post-Dispatch*, July 29, pp. 1A, 3A, 1D; Ball, p. 423.

15. Author's telephone interview with Joe Ames of March 7, 2007.

16. Author's telephone interview with Marvin Rich of February 16, 2007.

17. Sanford.
18. Patrick Gibbons.
19. Vasquez and Gibbons.
20. Author's interview with Elizabeth Vasquez and Larry Gibbons of May 7, 2006.
21. Ames.
22. Borges.
23. Sanford.
24. Salmon, pp. 302–303.
25. *Unrepentant Rebel,* p. 146.
26. Joe Miller, "Labor's New Strong Man," *New Republic,* August 1, 1949, p. 16.
27. Ball, p. 353; Box 40, Folder 17 ("Research Department: Wages—Miscellaneous, 1950–1951"), Gibbons papers.
28. Ball, p. 383.
29. Sidney Lens, *Left, Right and Center: Conflicting Forces in American Labor,* Regnery, Chicago, 1949, p. 427.
30. Ball, p. 388.
31. Salmon, p. 308. Arnold Rose agreed, concluding that the shop-floor meetings were "favored by only a minority of the members" (*Union Solidarity,* p. 152).
32. Ball, pp. 463–464.
33. Salmon, p. 308.
34. Ball, vol. 1, p. 194.
35. Rose, pp. 25–26.
36. Rich.
37. Rose, p. 104.
38. See note 7.
39. Rose, pp. 109, 111. It wasn't that white working people were more prejudiced than the general white population: 86 percent of the latter said black people shouldn't be allowed to live on the same block as whites.
40. Rose, pp. 114, 116.
41. Patrick Gibbons.
42. Annetta Dieckmann, "Union Makes Use of the Social Scientist," *Journal of Educational Sociology,* February 1952, pp. 344–345. Dieckmann, like Lillian Herstein, had been a Gibbons patron in Chicago's worker-education movement of the early 1930s. Her article describes Rose's study and some of its consequences.
43. Ball, vol. 2, p. 514.
44. Rich.

Chapter 6

1. Harold J. Gibbons, "Why the Union Is Concerned," *St. Louis Post-Dispatch,* February 28, 1952, p. C2. This was a letter to the paper's editor explaining why a trade union would involve itself in the school desegregation controversy.
2. The union itself claims to have no data concerning members' racial backgrounds. Writing in the early '50s, Arnold Rose noted that "Negroes are present at all union meetings and at stewards' meetings in significant numbers" (Rose, p. 105). Mike Goebel, the local's recent secretary-treasurer, estimated the "minority" portion of its membership to be about 40 percent (author's interview with Goebel of February 6, 2008).
3. Program for the funeral of Bernice Fisher, Concord Baptist Church of Christ, Brooklyn, New York, May 4, 1966.
4. James Farmer, *Lay Bare the Heart: An Autobiography of the Civil Rights Movement,* Arbor House, New York, 1985, p. 75.
5. Author's telephone interview with George Houser of August 29, 2007.
6. Author's telephone interview with James Robinson of August 27, 2007.
7. Mary Kimbrough and Margaret W. Dagen, *Victory without Violence: The First Ten Years of the St. Louis Committee on Racial Equality (CORE), 1947–1957,* University of Missouri Press, Columbia, 2000, pp. 19–21. The book is dedicated to the memory of Bernice Fisher.
8. Marvin Rich.
9. Ames.
10. Salmon, p. 211.
11. Kimbrough and Dagen, p. 24.
12. Quoted in Brill, pp. 343–344.
13. August Meier and Elliott Rudwick, *CORE: A Study in the Civil Rights Movement,* University of Illinois Press, Urbana, 1975, p. 55.
14. Author's telephone interview with Joe Ames of April 27, 2007.
15. Richard Dudman, "St. Louis' Silent Racial Revolution," *St. Louis Post-Dispatch,* June 11, 1990, p. 3B.
16. Kimbrough and Dagen, pp. 44, 90. See also Meier and Rudwick, pp. 49–55, 93, and "Lunch Counter Demonstrations," at www.umsl.edu/virtual/stl/phase2/1950/events/woolworthsdem.
17. Brill, p. 344.
18. Ball, pp. 468 and 521. Meanwhile Gibbons was about to become a member of

CORE's National Advisory Committee. See Joe Ames' letter to Gibbons of June 12 and the latter's reply of June 20, 1950, in Box 2, Folder 1, Gibbons papers.
19. On Peurala see O'Farrell and Kornbluh, p. 261.
20. Marvin Rich. Early St. Louis CORE had within its ranks a number of talented people, including, beside Leon Higginbotham, Huston Smith, a historian of the world's religions; the sociologist Arnold Rose; Charles Oldham, who would move to New York to become CORE's national chairman; Rich, who would go along with Oldham to direct the organization's public relations; and Ames, who would become a vice president of the American Federation of State, County and Municipal Employees.
21. Ames.
22. Ball, pp. 397–399.
23. Brill, p. 344. A similar union initiative involved sewers. Many warehousemen lived in tenement neighborhoods and were among the city residents most plagued by pooling raw sewage and its accompanying diseases. A citizens' campaign to create a public sewer system encompassing both St. Louis and St. Louis County had stalled for lack of the manpower needed to collect signatures on petitions. Joe Ames and Marvin Rich went to Gibbons to suggest that Local 688 adopt the project. "He thought about it for no more than a few minutes," said Ames, "and gave us the okay and also a little money." (Author's telephone interview with Joe Ames of October 16, 2007.) The labor was provided by union volunteers. After sufficient signatures were gathered, a February 1954 referendum approved what would become the Metropolitan Sewer District.
24. Ball, p. 467.
25. Author's telephone interview with Evelyn Rich of August 28, 2007.
26. Bernice Fisher, letter of March 25, 1962, to Ernest Calloway (Series 1, Folder 2, Calloway papers.)
27. "Bernice Fisher, 49, a Founder of CORE," *New York Times*, May 3, 1966, p. 47A.
28. Author's interview with Mike Ryan of October 19, 2005.
29. Jake McCarthy, "Before It Was Fashionable," *St. Louis Post-Dispatch*, April 9, 1973, p. 3A.

30. Ernest Calloway, "To Sleep, Perchance to Dream on a Ridge in the Mexican Sierras," *St. Louis American*, March 26, 1981.
31. Ernest Calloway, "Why I Cannot Serve in the Jim Crow Army," December 23, 1940. This is Calloway's statement to his draft board (Series 1, Folder 4, Calloway papers).
32. Gordon Burnside, "Calloway at 73," *St. Louis*, March 1983, p. 112.
33. Ryan.
34. Author's interview with Ernest Calloway of February 1983. A stroke had earlier deprived him of his power of speech. He laboriously picked these words out on a toy typewriter. His wife DeVerne answered many of the questions put to him. For others, she fetched various old articles by or about him.
35. Committee on Democratic Rights of Members, "Planning for an Integrated School System in St. Louis," Warehouse and Distribution Workers Union, St. Louis, December 15, 1951.
36. Marvin Rich.
37. Committee on Democratic Rights, p. 1.
38. Salmon, *Recollections: Part Six*, p. 338.

Chapter 7

1. Vasquez and Gibbons, May 7, 2006.
2. Patrick Gibbons, February 2 and 18, 2008. When speaking of his father in these interviews, Patrick sometimes called him by his first name. Ann, he added, usually called her husband "Gibbons," as did the children when they were young. "He never seemed to mind that we called him by his last name," said Patrick. Meanwhile friends from the '30s and '40s often referred to Gibbons as "Hal," whereas those from later years generally preferred "Harold."
3. Vasquez and Gibbons, November 13, 2005.
4. Vasquez and Gibbons, May 7, 2006.
5. Patrick Gibbons, February 2, 2008.
6. Author's telephone interview with Patrick Gibbons of July 7, 2008.
7. Salmon, p. 332.
8. Vasquez and Gibbons, November 13, 2005.
9. Salmon, p. 303.
10. Author's interview with Jerry Tucker of December 8, 2005.
11. Ball, p. 417; Calloway, p. 33.

12. "Communists Said to Plan Labor Unit," *New York Times*, September 15, 1948, p. 27. For an interesting reading of this still-murky episode in U.S. Communist history, see Judith Stepan-Norris and Maurice Zeitlin, *Left Out: Reds and America's Industrial Unions*, Cambridge University Press, Cambridge, 2003, pp. 297–327.

13. Lens, *Unrepentant Radical*, pp. 146–147. The AFL international within which Lens and Gibbons hoped to establish their "special department" was the Building Service Employees. That organization's president admitted the existence of the plan (whose failure he blamed on "a variety of jurisdictional problems") in testimony before a congressional committee (see "11 Unionists Face Contempt Charges," *New York Times*, October 7, 1948, p. 1A).

14. Lens, p. 147.

15. Brill, p. 351. Gibbons was threatened by gangsters in the early '50s. "Well, we didn't know a goddamn thing about hoodlums," he recalled. "But Dick [Kavner] knew Hoffa.. .. So we went over to Detroit and talked to Hoffa."

16. Calloway, p. 15. Camie, in Calloway's words, "a veteran organizer and teamster of the old horse-dray days," was in 1941 appointed by Teamsters Joint Council 13 to organize the smaller St. Louis warehouses that were as yet untouched by the CIO union.

17. McClellan Committee Hearings, August 26, 1958, Part 38, p. 14,239.

18. Calloway, p. 33.

19. Vasquez and Gibbons, November 13, 2005.

20. Robert F. Kennedy, *The Enemy Within*, Popular Library, New York, 1960, p. 131.

21. McClellan Committee Hearings.

22. William M. Blair, "AFL Teamsters Raid CIO Local in St. Louis, Add 6,000 Members," *New York Times*, January 27, 1949, p. 14A.

23. Larry Gibbons, October 4, 2006.

24. Vasquez and Gibbons.

25. "To Friends of the United Distribution Workers Union and Its Personnel," January 27, 1949 (quoted in Calloway, p. 66).

26. Lens, pp. 135–136.

27. Lens, *Left, Right and Center*, pp. 337–338.

28. Ball, p. 423.

29. Ball, vol. 1, p. 16.

30. Smith, p. 128.

31. Ball, p. 420.

Chapter 8

1. Quoted in Sidney Lens, *The Crisis of American Labor*, Sagamore Press, New York, 1959, p. 52.

2. For the separation of St. Louis City from St. Louis County, see Lana Stein, *St. Louis Politics: The Triumph of Tradition*, Missouri Historical Association Press, St. Louis, 2002, pp. 3–4.

3. Kimbrough and Dagen, p. 43.

4. Robert H. Salisbury, "The Dynamics of Reform: Charter Politics in St. Louis," *Midwest Journal of Political Science*, August 1961, pp. 262–263.

5. Donald Janson, "Civic Gain Linked to Smog Control," *New York Times*, June 5, 1957, p. 37A.

6. Ball, p. 404. St. Louis, like other Northern cities after World War II, saw a marked increase in its African-American population, the result of emigration from the South. The city had 93,580 black residents in 1930, just over 10 percent of its total population. By 1950 it had 153,766 blacks, or 18 percent (Ernest Calloway, "The Negro Social and Economic Thrust," in *Who Runs St. Louis?*, Center for Urban Programs, St. Louis University, 1980, p. 28).

7. Ball, p. 408. Until it died in June 1951 the *St. Louis Star-Times* competed with the *Post-Dispatch* and the *Globe-Democrat*. The *Globe* died in 1983.

8. "Slum and Sewer Bonds, Firemen's Work Cut Beaten," *St. Louis Post-Dispatch*, November 3, 1948, p. 1A. The sewer and fire department bonds were separate referendum questions.

9. Joseph Heathcott and Maire Agnes Murphy, "Corridors of Flight, Zones of Renewal: Industry, Planning, and Policy in the Making of Metropolitan St. Louis, 1940–1980," *Journal of Urban History*, January, 2005, p. 160.

10. Heathcott and Murphy, p. 163.

11. The best-known of these tower complexes was called (to commemorate a white politician and a black war hero) Pruitt-Igoe.

12. Kenneth E. Gray, *A Report on Politics in Saint Louis*, Center for Urban Studies, Cambridge, Massachusetts, 1961, pp. V-11 and V-12.

13. Con Kelliher, "Powerful Boss of St. Louis' Teamsters Is One of City's Most Controversial Figures," *St. Louis Globe-Democrat*, August 26, 1956, quoted in Smith, p. 168.
14. Brill, p. 344.
15. Gray, pp. V-9 and V-10.
16. Gray, p. V-9.
17. Ryan.
18. Arnold Rose, pp. 81–82. Rose's survey-takers asked specifically about voting in the presidential election of 1948.
19. Kelliher.
20. Gray, p. II-5
21. Stein, p. 79.
22. Some St. Louisans considered John L. "Doc" Lawler, the Fitters' business agent and Larry Callanan's chief lieutenant, to be the union's real political mastermind. See Jake McCarthy, "Looking Back at Doc Lawler," *St. Louis Post-Dispatch*, February 2, 1972, p. 3A.
23. Denny Walsh, "A Two-Faced Crime Fight in St. Louis," *Life*, May 29, 1970, pp. 28–29.
24. "Carroll Glues St. Louis to Its TV Screens; Grand Jury Tries to Link Him to Handbook," *New York Times*, March 23, 1951, p. 13A.
25. Eagleton.
26. Author's telephone interview with Joe Ames of August 31, 2007.
27. The twenty-eight wards weren't the only factor complicating St. Louis politics. Following the separation of the city from St. Louis County in 1876, the city was assigned a dozen "county" offices as well as the usual municipal ones. After 1950 these "county" offices, a rich source of patronage, were usually held by members of the Politicians group (see Stein, especially pp. 72–73). But to keep the story simple, I've focused here on ward politics.
28. Quoted in John M. McGuire, "Dowd: The Stan Musial of the Bench," *St. Louis Post-Dispatch*, May 30, 1990, p. 3D.
29. Author's interview with Thomas Guilfoil of June 4, 2007.
30. See D. R. Fitzpatrick, *As I Saw It*, Simon and Schuster, New York, 1953, pp. xi, 59, 197. A collection of original Fitzpatrick drawings can be seen in the Western Missouri Manuscript Collection, Jefferson Memorial Library, University of Missouri at St. Louis.
31. "Bakewell or Schendel," *St. Louis Post-Dispatch*, March 4, 1951, p. 2B. Alongside this editorial was a Fitzpatrick cartoon of a sad-looking donkey chained outside a building labeled "Shenker, Callanan & Co." The editors liked the cartoon so much they used in during another election campaign the following year.
32. Harry B. Wilson, "Between the Lines," *St. Louis Globe-Democrat*, October 23, 1951, p. 3A.
33. "A Review of the 1951 Municipal Election with Special Emphasis on the Race for President of the Board of Aldermen," Box 41, Folder 37, Gibbons papers. The report's authors were Robert Pentland, Pete Saffo, and Joe Ames.
34. *St. Louis Post-Dispatch,* August 6, 1952, p. 2B.
35. Ames, April 27, 2007.
36. Guilfoil.
37. Ames, March 7 and April 27, 2007.
38. In 2013 St. Louis regained legal control of its police department for the first time since the Civil War.
39. See Daniel Waugh, *Egan's Rats,* Cumberland House, Nashville, 2007, for the story of the Hogan and Egan gangs.
40. "Police Shake-Up Makes Chapman Detectives Chief," *St. Louis Post-Dispatch,* March 17, 1953, pp. 1A, 3A.
41. Kinney had the year before survived a primary election challenge by Doc Lawler, Larry Callanan's lieutenant. Information concerning Chapman's association with Kinney comes from the author's interview of May 8, 2008, with a St. Louis police veteran named Melburn Stein. Mel Stein was the officer who, with a partner, foiled the Southwest Bank robbery of 1953, a once well-known St. Louis incident later made into a movie starring Steve McQueen.
42. Salisbury, p. 268.
43. Salmon, p. 338.
44. Kelliher.
45. Wilson. In fact, the union was celebrating its tenth anniversary since Gibbons' arrival in 1941. It had been formed, as we've seen, in the spring of 1937.
46. Wyden.
47. Wilson.

Chapter 9

1. James B. Jacobs, *Mobsters, Unions, and Feds: The Mafia and the American Labor*

Movement, New York University Press, New York, 2006, p. 9. Tom Guilfoil happened to say something similar about St. Louis. Tom Eagleton, he claimed, was "sheltered from the realities" and "never understood the connections between the Democratic Party, organized labor, and organized crime. He never understood the results." What were the results? "We won a lot of elections" (Guilfoil).

2. Carl R. Baldwin, "Buster Wortman's Quiet Departure," *St. Louis Post-Dispatch,* August 11, 1968, p. 1G.

3. Quoted in Brill, pp. 351–352.

4. For this incident, see Brill, pp. 30–31; Dan E. Moldea, *The Hoffa Wars: Teamsters, Rebels, Politicians and the Mob,* Paddington Press, New York, pp. 43–44; and Thaddeus Russell, *Out of the Jungle: Jimmy Hoffa and the Remaking of the American Working Class,* Knopf, New York, 2001, pp. 173–174.

5. Lens, *Unrepentant Radical,* pp. 97–99, 101–103.

6. Ames, April 27, 2007.

7. Captain Thomas L. Moran, testimony before the McClellan Committee, Part 38, August 21, 1958, pp. 14,258–14,259.

8. David Witwer, *Corruption and Reform in the Teamsters Union,* University of Illinois Press, Urbana, 2003, pp. 173–174.

9. Moran, p. 14,261.

10. Harold Gibbons, testimony before the McClellan Committee, Part 39, September 2, 1958, p. 14,647.

11. Gibbons testimony.

12. Both statements and the lawyer's remarks about them are in McClellan Committee Hearings, Part 40, September 11, 1958, p. 14,986.

13. Author's interview with Jake McCarthy of February 1983.

14. Kato. The "other guys," she said, were Tom Flynn, a vice president of the IBT, and Bert Brennan, Robert Holmes, and Rolland McMaster of Hoffa's own Detroit local. Their visits seem to have been brief. Gibbons' older brother Larry, a former Chicago policeman, also showed up in St. Louis at this time. Gibbons' brother "used to escort me home every night after work," said Kato. According to Elizabeth Vasquez, the brother came to town intending to personally guard Harold and his family, but was soon shown the door by Ann Gibbons, who disapproved of his profane and occasionally racist language (Vasquez and Gibbons, November 13, 2005).

15. Quoted in Ralph C. James and Estelle Dinerstein James, *Hoffa and the Teamsters,* Van Nostrand, Princeton, New Jersey, 1965, p. 66.

16. "Teamster with Heft: Robert Bernard Baker," *New York Times,* August 21, 1958, p. 15A.

17. Ames, April 27, 2007. Baker, testifying before a Senate investigating committee in 1958, was asked about a Des Moines gangster to whom he had at one time made many phone calls. Baker said he made the calls because he was friend of the gangster's family. Well, then, tell me, a senator said, how many children does this man have? Five or six, Baker replied. And what are their names? "I just call them darling," said Baker. "They're all darlings to me" (Barney Baker, testimony before the McClellan Committee, Part 37, August 21, 1958, p. 14,092).

18. Schafers.

19. Ames. According to a former Baker girlfriend who subsequently testified before a Senate committee, the belly-bumper worked in the late '40s as a bouncer in a Miami casino owned by Jake Lansky, Meyer Lansky's brother. The girlfriend was at that time employed by Max Caldwell, the Chicago mobster whom, a few years earlier, Sid Lens had driven out of his grocery clerks' union (Ruth Ann Braugher, testimony before the McClellan Committee, Part 37, August 19, 1958, pp. 14,041–14,045). Small world.

20. According to the FBI, the house cost $11,500. In 1959, when the bureau researched the transaction, Gibbons was making monthly mortgage payments of $82. He was then earning $6,500 a year as secretary-treasurer of Local 688, or a little less than $2,000 more than he had been earning in 1948 (FBI memo of September 8, 1959). Gibbons wasn't getting rich off his members.

21. Vasquez and Gibbons, November 13, 2005, and December 22, 2005. Local 688 used to hold annual Christmas parties, complete with a Santa Claus who handed out gifts to children. Larry Gibbons was later told that, one year when he was still small, he asked Santa, "Are you Barney Baker?"

22. Ames, August 31, 2007.

23. Sanford.

24. "Gangsters' Grab at City Locals of Teamsters Union under Inquiry," *St. Louis Post-Dispatch,* March 6, 1953, p. 4A.
25. Ames, April 27, 2007.
26. Joe Ames, letter to the author of November 27, 2007.
27. "Teamsters Drop Two Ex-Convicts from Council Local," *St. Louis Post-Dispatch,* March 29, 1953, p. 3A.

Chapter 10

1. Rick Stoff, "Harold Gibbons Takes a Look Back," *St. Louis Globe-Democrat,* September 23–24, 1978, p. 24A.
2. "Teamsters' Local Acts to Rid Union of Gangsters," *St. Louis Post-Dispatch,* March 19, 1953, p. 1A.
3. "International Union Takes Over Taxicab Local," *St. Louis Post-Dispatch,* March 28, 1953, p. 3A.
4. Captain John L. Dougherty, testimony before the McClellan Committee, Part 37, August 19, 1958, p. 14,009.
5. "Warrant Is Refused for Weapons Charge," *St. Louis Post-Dispatch,* May 8, p. 14A.
6. "Warrant Is Refused for Weapons Charge"; "Dowd Criticizes Police, Defends Refusal to Issue Two Warrants," same paper, May 9, 1953, p. 3A. The prosecutor, Edward L. Dowd, was himself a former police officer and the scion of an Irish-Catholic St. Louis family that produced several generations of Democratic cop-politicians.
7. Sanford interview.
8. Guilfoil. In 1959 a St. Louis police captain described an attempt by the owner of a Wortman-connected cigarette-machine company to move into territory dominated by the Sicilian mob. The Wortman man was shot nine times (Captain Richard J. Hackmeyer, testimony before the McClellan Committee, Part 46, February 10, 1959, p. 15,579). Despite brief periods of cooperation with Wortman, the Sicilians and Syrians seem to have usually encouraged him and his people to stay east of the Mississippi.
9. "Larry Callanan, Top Aide Indicted in Labor Racket Inquiry, Sought by FBI," *St. Louis Post-Dispatch,* May 16, 1953, p. 1A; "Callanan, Lawler to Surrender Tomorrow, Their Attorney Says," same paper, May 17, 1953, pp. 1A, 8A. Callanan was convicted and sentenced to a dozen years in prison. Lyndon Johnson pardoned him in 1964.
10. "Building Supply Delivery Halted by Strike of 1200 Truck Drivers," *St. Louis Post-Dispatch,* May 19, 1953, p. 1A.
11. "Building Supply Delivery Halted by Strike of 1200 Truck Drivers."
12. Flynn and his driver were both seriously hurt. Originally bound from St. Louis to Chicago, they languished together for weeks in a hospital in Joliet, Illinois. The driver was Gibbons' older brother Larry, a former Chicago policeman. No one emerged from this incident smiling. According to David Salmon, "Flynn blamed Larry.... Larry was left crippled and unhappy that the union did not take care of him financially. He was a constant, unhappy critic of his brother" (Salmon, *Recollections,* Part 6, pp. 347–348).
13. "Civic Needs Group Says Aldermen Promote Decay with Spot Zoning," *St. Louis Post-Dispatch,* June 16, 1953, p. 3A. See Lana Stein, *St. Louis Politics: The Triumph of Tradition* (Missouri Historical Press, St. Louis, 2002, p. 93) for the origins of Civic Progress and its membership in 1953.
14. "Mayor Calls Union, Concrete Men in Effort to End Strike," *St. Louis Post-Dispatch,* June 30, 1953, p. 3A.
15. "Mayor Tucker's Proper Role," *St. Louis Post-Dispatch,* June 30, 1953, p. 2B.
16. Ames telephone interview of April 27, 2007.
17. "Hottest July 31 on Record, No Relief in Sight," *St. Louis Post-Dispatch,* July 31, 1953, p. 6A. The temperature that day was 101.4.
18. *St. Louis Post-Dispatch,* July 29, 1953, p. 17A.
19. "Jobless Workers' Wives Join Woman's Drive to End Strike," *St. Louis Post-Dispatch,* July 31, 1953, p. 1A. A Mrs. Eva Homeyer of suburban Kirkwood, a member of Mrs. Miller's group, confided to a reporter, "The department store called this morning and wanted our TV set back. I told them to come and get it. You can't get blood out of a turnip" ("'I Want Truck Strike Settled,' Mayor Tells Both Factions," *St. Louis Post-Dispatch,* August 11, 1953, p. 1A).
20. "Mayor Demands Arbitration in Building Tie-up, Return to Jobs," *St. Louis Post-Dispatch,* July 17, p. 1A. A second local station,

KTVI-TV, took to the air two weeks after the mayor's broadcast.

21. *St. Louis Globe-Democrat,* August 5, 1953, p. 9A.
22. "One Truck Group Settles, Other Drivers Reject Mayor's Demands," *St. Louis Post-Dispatch,* July 18, 1953, p. 1A. The group that settled was not among the thirty-five cement, sand, and gravel dealers.
23. Edward F. Woods, "Losses in Building Industry Pile Up as Truck Drivers, Concrete Men Continue Fight," *St. Louis Post-Dispatch,* July 19, 1953, p. 3A.
24. "Drivers Again Reject Proposal to Arbitrate in Secret Vote," *St. Louis Post-Dispatch,* August 7, p. 3A. Accompanying the article was a photo of Mrs. Miller watching the strikers cast their ballots.
25. "Time to Quit Stalling," *St. Louis Post-Dispatch,* August 10, 1953, p. 2C.
26. "Truck Strike Settled, Union Accepts Terms Ending 13-Week Walkout," *St. Louis Post-Dispatch,* August 12, 1953, pp. 1A, 3A.
27. "Strike's Lesson," *St. Louis Globe-Democrat,* August 13, 1953, p. 8A.
28. "Truck Strike Settled."
29. Kelliher.
30. "Yellow Cab Drivers Assaulted in Strike," *St. Louis Post-Dispatch,* December 5, 1953, p. 8A
31. McClellan Committee, Part 39, September 2, 1958, p. 14,573.
32. Guilfoil.
33. "Harold Gibbons Arrested on Cab Violence Charge," *St. Louis Post-Dispatch,* December 5, 1953, p. 3A. Yellow Cab's owner was arrested the same evening after police stopped the taxi he was driving and found him to be carrying two pistols.

Chapter 11

1. Guilfoil.
2. Bender is quoted in Sally Bixby Defty, "Gibbons Kept Cool under Senate Fire," *St. Louis Post-Dispatch,* May 12, 1969, p. 3D.
3. "U.S. Attorney Here Rejects Offer of Racket Fighter," *St. Louis Post-Dispatch,* December 3, 1953, p. 1A.
4. Brill, p. 354.
5. Salmon, p. 300.
6. Lou Berra, statement of March 23, 1954, in Box 40, Folder 25, Gibbons papers.
7. Kato.
8. Salmon, p. 353.
9. Ames interview of April 27, 2007.
10. "Unionist Armed against Thugs, Attorney Says," *St. Louis Post-Dispatch,* April 6, 1954, p. 3A.
11. "Grand Jury Case 1954–1955." The file contains a transcript of Goldschein's interrogation of Berra before the grand jury. The checks mentioned, written to Berra by the contractor, covered a four-year period, 1949–1952. Berra refused to discuss them, claiming his Fifth Amendment right not to incriminate himself.
12. Salmon.
13. Author's interview with Jerry Tucker, December 8, 2005.
14. St. Louis police kept tabs on all three—Gibbons, Baker, and Costello—in these years. See Dougherty, testimony before the McClellan Committee, Part 37, August 19, 1958, pp. 14,011–14,012, 14,014.
15. Callanan spent six years in prison before being released on parole in 1960. In 1964, on the recommendation of Attorney General Robert Kennedy, his sentence was commuted by President Lyndon Johnson.
16. Moran testimony, McClellan Committee, Part 38, August 26, 1958, p. 14,258.
17. "Text of U.S. Grand Jury Report Assailing Some Union Practices," *St. Louis Post-Dispatch,* June 9, 1954, p 7E.
18. Daniel Bell, "St. Louis Blues," *Fortune,* July 1954, p. 36.
19. The remarks by Smith and Hoffman are quoted in an article by Robert S. Ball that appeared in the *Detroit Press* of November 28, 1953, and was later reproduced in the McClellan Hearings, Part 37, pp. 13,967–13,968.
20. See Clark R. Mollenhoff, *Tentacles of Power: The Story of Jimmy Hoffa,* World, Cleveland, 1965, pp. 50–51. Ironically, from Gibbons' point of view, Hoffa had in the previous summer worked through the St. Louisan to hire Ratner in the first place. Gibbons' lieutenant Dick Kavner was sent (with the belly-bumping Barney Baker) to Topeka to put the former governor on the IBT payroll.
21. Joseph A. Loftus, "Leader in Kansas Aided Hoffa in '53," *New York Times,* August 14, 1958, p. 1A. Ratner was then testifying before the McClellan Committee.

22. "Hoffman Balked by Committee in Labor Inquiry," *St. Louis Post-Dispatch,* July 15, 1953, p. 2A.
23. Thaddeus Russell, *Out of the Jungle: Jimmy Hoffa and the Remaking of the American Working Class,* Knopf, New York, 2001, p. 170.

Chapter 12

1. John Bartlow Martin, *Jimmy Hoffa's Hot,* Fawcett/Crest, Greenwich, CT, 1959, p. 32. This was a collection of articles Martin had written for the *Saturday Evening Post.*
2. Sanford.
3. Murray Kempton, "The Pessimist," *New York Review of Books,* February 22, 1979.
4. Quoted in Moldea, p. 25.
5. Russell, p. 23.
6. Ralph and Estelle James, *Hoffa and the Teamsters,* Van Nordstrand, Princeton, New Jersey, 1965, pp. 1–2.
7. Quoted in Moldea, p. 122. The leader of the CIO union was John L. Lewis' younger brother Denny.
8. Jimmy Hoffa, letter to Thomas Flynn of May 15, 1946, quoted in James and James, p. 78.
9. Russell, p. 84.
10. James and James, p. 79.
11. Russell, p. 104.
12. Martin, pp. 33–34.
13. Martin, p. 32.
14. Saul Bellow, "Cousins," in *Collected Stories,* Janice Bellow, ed., Penguin, New York, 2001, p. 195.
15. Author's telephone interview with Jake McCarthy of February 1983.
16. Martin, p. 23.
17. See, for example, FBI memo of January 2, 1953.
18. James and James, p. 116.
19. Brill, p. 358.
20. Calloway interview. But Calloway didn't *like* Hoffa. During the 1983 interview, his wife DeVerne happened to remark that Ann Gibbons "couldn't stand" Hoffa. "And neither could he," she added, nodding toward her mute husband. Ernest Calloway just grinned.
21. Gibbons and Vasquez interview of December 22, 2005.
22. Patrick Gibbons, telephone interview of February 18, 2008.
23. "Missouri-Kansas Conference—Kavner's Reports, 1954," in Box 53, Folder 11, Gibbons papers.
24. Arnold H. Lubasch, "Ex-Teamster Chief Tells Jury Mafia Controls Union Leaders," *New York Times,* June 2, 1987, p. 1A. See also Wallace Turner, "Union Loans: Mob's Hold on Casinos," *New York Times,* April 3, 1986, p. 22A.
25. McCarthy.
26. Turner.
27. Vasquez and Gibbons, November 13, 2005.
28. Jake McCarthy, "Teamster Corruption Story," *St. Louis Post-Dispatch,* April 2, 1976, p. 3A.
29. Adam Cohen and Elizabeth Taylor, *American Pharaoh: Mayor Richard J. Daley: His Battle for Chicago and the Nation,* Little, Brown, Boston, 2000, p. 192. "The 1st Ward's alderman and ward committeeman, John D'Arco, was a well-known front man for [Anthony] Accardo and Sam Giancana. And many of the 1st Ward Democratic Organization's patronage jobs went to notorious Mafia foot soldiers" (p. 190).

Chapter 13

1. Quoted in James Deakin, *A Grave for Bobby: The Greenlease Slaying,* Morrow, New York, 1990. Deakin, who later became the *Post-Dispatch*'s White House correspondent, had been a student of David Salmon's at Washington University.
2. Schafers.
3. Such anyway is what Mollie Baker, by then Baker's former wife, told the McClellan Committee two years later. See Part 37, August 19, 1958, pp. 13,997. Ted Schafers of the *Globe-Democrat,* offering a third theory, said Costello didn't in fact wound himself, either deliberately or accidentally, but rather was shot by his wife during a domestic dispute (Schafers interview).
4. "Striking Taxicab Drivers Vote to Form Own Union," *St. Louis Post-Dispatch,* August 19, 1956, p. 1A.
5. "Strikers Seek Recognition of New Cab Union," *St. Louis Post-Dispatch,* August 20, 1956, p. 3A.
6. "Union Agent, Ex-Convict, in City Again; Denies Role in Cab Strike," *St. Louis Post-Dispatch,* August 22, 1956, p. 2C.

7. "Union Agent, Ex-Convict, in City Again."
8. Vasquez and Gibbons, November 13, 2005.
9. "Union Agent, Ex-Convict, in City Again."
10. "Four Suspects Arrested after First Violence of Cab Strike," *St. Louis Post-Dispatch,* August 23, 1956, p. 3A.
11. "Union's Trouble-Shooter Shortens Visit after Cold Police Welcome," *St. Louis Post-Dispatch,* Friday, August 24, 1965, p. 3A.
12. "Mr. Gibbons Flexes His Muscles," *St. Louis Post-Dispatch,* August 25, 1956, p. 4A.
13. "Taxicab Service Back to Normal; Cab Strike Ends," *St. Louis Post-Dispatch,* August 30, 1956, p. 3A.
14. McClellan Committee hearings, Part 38, August 26, 1958, p. 14,388.
15. McClellan Committee hearings, September 2, 1958, p. 14,602.
16. McClellan Committee Hearings, September 2, 1958, pp. 14,603–14,605. Shoulders and Sanders remained active in St. Louis' underworld for many years. Shoulders was killed by a car bomb in 1972, the victim of a war between two wings of St. Louis' "Syrian" mob over control of a local of the Laborers Union.
17. McClellan Committee hearings, September 2, 1958, pp. 14,600–14,601.
18. Howard B. Woods, "Harold Gibbons," *St. Louis Argus,* January 17, 1958. A facsimile of Woods' piece is included in an undated FBI report concerning Gibbons.
19. Deakin, p. 222.

Chapter 14

1. McCarthy. Unless otherwise noted, all quotes from McCarthy are from the February 1983 interview.
2. *St. Louis Post-Dispatch,* March 8, 1954, p.11A.
3. W. J. McGoogan, "36 Rounds of Boxing Tonight; Miceli Opposes Rawlings," *St. Louis Post-Dispatch,* April 21, 1955, p. 5B; and "Lombardo and Miceli Win; 3464 Applaud Polio Fight Show," *St. Louis Post-Dispatch,* April 22, 1955, p. 5C. The fights brought the polio foundation $10,000, less the cost of Goldstein's shirt and shoes. A biographer, Nick Tosches, author of *The Devil and Sonny Liston* (Little, Brown, Boston, 2000), writes that the future champ was in his early career controlled by John Vitale, a leader of St. Louis' Sicilian mob.
4. Jake McCarthy, "Harold Gibbons, Idealist: A Reminiscence," *St. Louis Post-Dispatch,* November 21, 1982, p. 2C.
5. Vasquez and Gibbons, December 22, 2005.
6. Paul Harris, "Former Post-Dispatch Writer Jake McCarthy Dies," *St. Louis Post-Dispatch,* August 27, 2000, p. 11C; Bill McClellan, "Columnist Was Rare Breed: Writer Who Never Lost Idealism," *St. Louis Post-Dispatch,* August 28, 2000, p. 1D; Ray Hartmann, "A Good Jake," *Riverfront Times,* August 30, 2000; Hank Vogt, "Jake McCarthy: Change in Image," *UMSL Currents,* February 3, 1972.
7. Vasquez and Gibbons, November 13, 2005.
8. Vasquez and Gibbons.
9. The information concerning Gibbons' 1957 salary is from Arnold Rose. According to the Department of Commerce, the average salary that year for a man working full-time was $4,700 ("Average Income Rose Slightly in 1957 Despite Increased Unemployment," *Current Population Reports: Consumer Income,* May 1958, p. 1).
10. Richard Rose. Richard Rose was a reporter for the *Post-Dispatch.*
11. Kelliher.
12. Author's telephone interview with William L. Clay of July 31, 2008. Clay immediately began to hedge on the word, adding, "Or perhaps I should say 'confident.'" He had a right to be confident. Both he and Ernest Calloway were brilliant men." But 'conceited' was the first adjective he had come up with.
13. Vasquez and Gibbons, December 22, 2005.
14. Vasquez and Gibbons, May 6, 2006.
15. Vasquez and Gibbons, December 22, 2005.
16. See James and James, pp. 21–22. In what would be known as the Test Fleet case, Hoffa was charged in 1962 with accepting payment from an employer in return for quashing a Teamster strike. A hung jury allowed him to go free, but that trial led to another in which he was convicted of jury tampering in the first case. Sentenced to prison, Hoffa lost effective control of the IBT.
17. Author's telephone interview with Wanda Koss of July 14, 2006. Koss, who asked

Gibbons the question about investments, worked for many years as a secretary at Joint Council 13.
18. Brill, p. 363.
19. Vasquez and Gibbons.
20. Schafers.
21. FBI memo of August 25, 1950.
22. Lens, *Unrepentant Radical,* p. 146.
23. Vasquez and Gibbons, November 13, 2005.
24. Brill, p. 356.
25. Salmon, p. 332.
26. Vasquez and Gibbons, December 22, 2005.
27. J. Edgar Hoover, memo of August 31, 1959, to SAC, St. Louis; FBI memo of September 8, 1959.
28. Vasquez and Gibbons.
29. Irving Howe, "In the American Grain," *New York Review of Books,* November 10, 1983.
30. Brill, p. 343.
31. Salmon, p. 323.
32. Defty, "Teamster Boss." Lou Berra, who had served a prison term as a result of the grand jury probe of 1954, became manager of the Council Plaza apartments towers.
33. *Officers' Report: Twenty Second City Wide Shop Conference,* Local 688, St. Louis, 1970, p. 3.
34. Author's interview with Norbert Hewlett of June 14, 2008.
35. Salmon, pp. 326–327. Salmon, seeing Council Plaza as evidence of Gibbons' increasing grandiosity, soon left St. Louis to take an IBT job in California.
36. Kelliher.
37. McClellan Committee hearings, Part 39, September 3, 1958, p. 14,680.
38. "Hoffa Ally Wins Narrow Victory," *New York Times,* January 17, 1958, p. 30A. The carnival workers remained part of Local 688 in 2008. Michael Goebel, the union's secretary-treasurer, had in his office a framed photo of himself, James P. Hoffa (the IBT president, Jimmy Hoffa's son), and a group of costumed performers, all Local 688 members, at the headquarters of the Ringling Bros. and Barnum & Bailey Circus in Sarasota, Florida.
39. The Harvard lecture was probably McCarthy's idea. Three years later, when Hoffa was all too well known as a result of the McClellan Committee hearings, McCarthy suggested in a memorandum that Hoffa keep out of the limelight during a six-month "quietus." He should, however, at the same time "avail himself of as many high-level speaking engagements as possible: Yale University, University of Virginia, etc..... The net effect would remove him from the area of day-to-day sniping.. ." (McCarthy to Gibbons, memo of September 9, 1959, in Box 1, Folder 13, Gibbons papers).
40. Mollenhoff, p. 118.
41. Richard Rose, p. 252.
42. The photo is in a file labeled "'Teamster Trip to Israel," Box 2, Folder 8, Gibbons papers.
43. "Teamster Trip to Israel.."
44. Schafers. "Gibbons didn't like me at first because I worked for a Republican paper," said Schafers. "And I didn't have a particularly high opinion of him then either. But I was impressed because I could see he was a coming power in the union."
45. File labeled "Summary of Election Results for General President, IBT, 1957," Box 60, Folder 10, Gibbons papers.
46. Martin, p. 65.
47. Jake McCarthy, "Reminiscences of Hoffa," *St. Louis Post-Dispatch,* August 4, 1975, p. 3A.
48. McCarthy.

Chapter 15

1. Martin, p. 94.
2. James and James, p. 42.
3. Martin, p. 96.
4. Kato.
5. Salmon, p. 346.
6. Kato.
7. Jake McCarthy, "Reminiscence of Hoffa II," *St. Louis Post-Dispatch,* August 6, 1975, p.3A
8. Kato.
9. Jake McCarthy, "Reminiscence of Hoffa," *St. Louis Post-Dispatch,* August 4, 1975. p. 3A.
10. McCarthy, "Reminiscence of Hoffa II." The June 1970 bankruptcy of the Penn Central Railroad was at the time the largest in U.S. history. Several owners were accused of plundering the road for personal gain.
11. Author's interview with Jake McCarthy of December 1976.
12. James and James, p 60.

13. James and James, p. 58.
14. Kato.
15. Salmon, p. 298
16. James and James, p. 303.
17. Dan E. Moldea, *The Hoffa Wars*, Paddington Press, New York, 1978, p. 67.
18. Martin, p. 94.
19. The AFL and CIO merged in 1955.
20. Martin, p. 96.
21. Chet Huntley, "Hoffa and the Teamsters," an NBC Radio show broadcast December 9, 1965. A copy of the script is in Box 66, folder not numbered, Gibbons papers.
22. Clark R. Mollenhoff, *Tentacles of Power: The Story of Jimmy Hoffa*, World, Cleveland, Ohio, 1965, p. 157.
23. Mollenhoff, p. 124. Rudolph Halley, Kefauver's chief counsel, who became well-known as a result of the committee's televised hearings, later parlayed that fame into some success in local New York politics.
24. Evan Thomas, *Robert Kennedy: His Life*, Simon and Schuster, New York, 2000, p. 74.
25. Quoted in Thomas, p. 75.
26. Robert Kennedy, *The Enemy Within*, Popular Library, New York, 1960, p. 33.
27. Russell, p. 170.
28. Quoted in Moldea, p. 419.
29. Kennedy, p. 204.
30. Joseph C. Goulden, *Meany*, Atheneum, New York, 1972, p. 236.
31. Thomas R. Brooks, *Toil and Trouble: A History of American Labor*, Delacorte, New York, 1964, p. 234.
32. Milton H. Hammergren, testimony before McClellan Committee, February 10, 1959, Part 46.
33. Quoted in Robert E. Thompson and Hortense Myers, *Robert Kennedy: The Brother Within*, Dell, New York, 1962, pp. 194–195. Asked whether he discussed the committee's schedule with its members, Kennedy replied, "No, I pretty well decide it and I have consultations with the Chairman" (Arthur M. Schlesinger, Jr., *Robert Kennedy and His Times*, vol. 1, Houghton Mifflin, Boston, 1978, p. 178). Clark Mollenhoff, long acquainted with the IBT as he was, advised Kennedy in the selection of cases and witnesses. In return, Kennedy made Mollenhoff privy to committee documents withheld from other reporters, thereby enabling the Iowan to publish a series of scoops that later brought him a Pulitzer Prize. See Donald A. Ritchie, *Reporting from Washington: The History of the Washington Press Corps*, Oxford University Press, New York, 2005, p. 224.
34. Russell, p. 194.
35. See Mollenhoff, p. 100.
36. Kennedy, p. 79.
37. Quoted in Peter Collier and David Horowitz, *The Kennedys: An American Drama*, Summit, New York, 1964, p. 507. It was only in helping to draft a bill based on McClellan Committee findings, writes Theodore Sorenson, John Kennedy's longtime aide and speechwriter, that Kennedy "truly mastered the legislative process" (*Kennedy*, Harper and Row, New York, 1965, p. 53).
38. Thompson and Myers, pp. 192–193.
39. James W. Hilty, *Robert Kennedy: Brother Protector*, Temple University Press, Philadelphia, 1997, p. 120.
40. Kenneth P. O'Donnell and David Powers, *Johnny, We Hardly Knew Ye: Memories of John Fitzgerald Kennedy*, Little Brown, Boston, 1970, p. 137.
41. James R. Hoffa and Oscar Fraley, *Hoffa: The Real Story*, Stein and Day, New York, 1973, p. 13.
42. Kennedy, p. 94.
43. Quoted in Brill, p. 355. Brill doesn't name the aide.
44. Patrick Gibbons, February 18, 2008.
45. Vasquez and Gibbons, November 13, 2005. According to Vasquez and Gibbons, Robert Kennedy telephoned their father just before the June 4, 1968, Democratic primary in California, hoping to persuade him to persuade Hoffa to make the endorsement. Nothing came of it because Kennedy was murdered on election night.
46. File labeled "Speech before Brookings Institute," Box 5, Folder 54, Gibbons papers. These are notes, probably made by Jake McCarthy during Gibbons' speech and a subsequent question-and-answer session. Though the notes are undated, internal evidence suggests that the speech was delivered in late 1959.
47. McClellan Committee Hearings, Part 39, September 2, 1958, p. 14,573.
48. Kennedy. p. 159.
49. McClellan Committee Hearings, Part 39, September 3, 1958, p 14,654.

Chapter 16

1. Arthur A. Sloane, *Hoffa,* MIT Press, Cambridge, 1991, pp. 279–280, offers the most detailed account of this frequently described scene.
2. Brill, p. 361.
3. Author's interview with Ron Gamache of February 1983.
4. Vasquez and Gibbons, November 13, 2005.
5. Daniel Bell, "The Capitalism of the Proletarians," in *The End of Ideology,* Collier, New York, 1961, p. 223.
6. Author's telephone interview with Keith Payne of November 30, 2012.
7. Patrick Gibbons, February 18, 2008.
8. Author's telephone interview with Larry Gibbons of December 6, 2005.
9. Vasquez and Gibbons, December 22, 2005.
10. Kato. The FBI kept a watch on the Hoffa-Gibbons ménage at the Woodner Hotel. An informant reported visits to their suite by Gibbons' "Chinese girlfriend," presumably Yuki Kato (FBI field report of July 31, 1959).
11. Quoted in Schlesinger, vol. 1, p. 173.
12. James and James, p. 44.
13. Vasquez and Gibbons, December 22, 2005.
14. James and James, pp. 8–9. Dick Kavner, the most verbally abused of Hoffa's aides, asked the Jameses not to report it. "Kavner... defended his boss at this point. Hoffa's temper should not be mentioned in the book, he stressed, for it would make him appear emotionally unbalanced" (p. 6).
15. Harold Seidman, *Labor Czars,* Liveright, New York, 1938, pp. 6–7. Seidman's "walking delegate" is nowadays called a "business agent."
16. C. Wright Mills, *The New Men of Power: America's Labor Leaders,* Harcourt, Brace, New York, 1948, p. 127.
17. Rick Stoff, "Gibbons: The Hoffa Years," *St. Louis Globe-Democrat,* September 25, 1979, p. 13A.
18. McCarthy, February 1983.
19. Williams, one of his generation's foremost criminal defense lawyers, had kept Hoffa out of jail on at least one occasion, but there was little love lost between them. See Murray Kempton, "The Mercenary," in *America Comes of Middle Age,* Little, Brown, Boston, 1963, pp. 366–368.
20. James and James, p. 47.
21. Eagleton.
22. Quoted in Brill, p. 358.
23. Brill, p. 360.
24. Quoted in Collier and Horowitz, p. 303.
25. Schlesinger, vol. 2, p. 291.
26. Brill, p. 360. In early 1962 Hoffa physically assaulted a Marble Palace employee named Sam Baron. Hoffa had learned that Baron was in fact a spy for Robert Kennedy. (See Baron, "I Was Near the Top of Jimmy's Drop Dead List," *Life,* July 20, 1962, p. 68.) Baron, a former Socialist and RWDSU official, had been brought into the Teamsters by Gibbons, a circumstance that couldn't have increased Hoffa's affection for the St. Louisan.
27. After leaving the Marble Palace in 1963, Kato retired from trade union work and settled with her husband and children in Pevely, Missouri, where Keathley managed Local 688's camp for members.

Chapter 17

1. Ted Schafers, "Gibbons Returns Here on Week-End," *St. Louis Globe-Democrat,* December 14–15, 1963, p. 12A.
2. Kenneth Jacobson, "Hoffa-Gibbons Alliance with Teamster Union Reported to Have Ended," *St. Louis Post-Dispatch,* December 6, 1963 pp. 1A, 5A.
3. Quoted in Walter Sheridan, *The Fall and Rise of Jimmy Hoffa,* Saturday Review Press, New York, 1972, p. 307. Sheridan, a former FBI agent, commanded the Kennedy Justice Department's "Hoffa Squad."
4. Hoffa's chief counsel in the Chattanooga trial was Morris Shenker, the St. Louis-based criminal-defense wizard and Gibbon's ally in the Politicians faction in St. Louis politics.
5. A. H. Raskin, "Hoffa Facing a Palace Revolt," *New York Times,* December 15, 1963, p. 6E. The jury-tampering charge, a felony, grew out of what in the earlier case had been only a misdemeanor.
6. Raskin.
7. Memo titled "Summary of Trip to Las Vegas, December 13, 1963," in a file labeled "Gibbons—Campaign for Presidency," Box 3,

Folder 2, Gibbons papers. The anonymous author of this report (perhaps Jake McCarthy) had been sent—just weeks after John Kennedy's assassination—to weigh possible support among Western IBT leaders for Gibbons versus Einar Mohn in a campaign for the IBT presidency in 1966. Gibbons clearly assumed that Hoffa either wouldn't run for reelection or, if he did run, could be beaten. (Incidentally, Dick Kavner seems to have been used cautiously in these matters: the memo's author recommended that he be kept away from the IBT bakery drivers' division, where he "is thoroughly disliked."

8. John A. Grimes, "Maneuvering for Hoffa Post Becomes Open as Teamsters' Western Head Bids for the Job," *Wall Street Journal,* November 9, 1965, p. 6.

9. Neil Gilbride, Associate Press. McBride's article appeared in the *Houston Post* of November 14, 1965. See the file labeled "Newspaper Clippings about Hoffa's Sentence and Potential Successor 1965–1966," Box 66, Folder 4, Gibbons papers.

10. "Platform 1966 (Gibbons for President," Box 66, Folder 4, Gibbons papers. With this document is a January 27, 1965, memo from McCarthy to Dick Kavner saying, "The attached is in response to your request that I draft some thoughts about platform and campaign in the event a vacancy should exist in the office of General President."

11. Quoted in Moldea, p. 182.

12. Author's interview with Harland Horn of October 30, 2007. Horn, a protégé of Pete Saffo's, was secretary-treasurer of IBT Local 610, a truck drivers' group in St. Louis.

13. Quoted in Brill, 361.

14. Brill, p. 362.

15. Article VI, Section 8, *Constitution Adopted by the Miami Beach, Florida Convention, July 4–7, 1966,* p. 27–39.

16. James R. Hoffa and Oscar Fraley, *Hoffa: The Real Story,* Stein and Day, New York, 1975, pp. 13–14.

17. *Gibbon's Decline and Fall,* D. M. Low, ed., Harcourt, Brace and Company, New York, 1960, p. 50. Commodus was the emperor, Cleander the would-be tool.

18. Quoted in Brill, p. 362.

19. Jake McCarthy, "Harold Gibbons, Idealist: A Reminiscence," *St. Louis Post-Dispatch,* November 21, 1982, p. 2C.

20. "Summary of Trip to Las Vegas"; Kavner memo of May 16, 1966, titled "HJG vs. Fitzsimmons at the Convention," in folder labeled "Campaign for Presidency," Box 3, Folder 2, Gibbons papers.

Chapter 18

1. "Mr. Hoffa and Mr. Gibbons," *St. Louis Globe-Democrat,* July1, 1966, p. 10A. Gibbons had indeed been "endlessly investigated," as the editorial noted. In a directive of June 4, 1959, written in the wake of McClellan Committee headlines, the FBI's J. Edgar Hoover ordered his agents to closely investigate five "Top Hoodlums": Murray Humphreys of Chicago's Outfit, Bill Bufalino of Detroit, and Bill Presser and Babe Triscaro of Cleveland—all labor racketeers, sure enough—and Gibbons. The extensive Gibbons probe, described in Chapter 14 of this book, led nowhere. Then, in 1960, Gibbons and several St. Louis Teamster associates were tried and acquitted in federal court on charges that they had violated the law concerning political contributions. Between 1972 and 1976, Gibbons was investigated on different grounds by four separate Department of Justice strike forces. For thirty years, from World War II through the end of the Vietnam War, from Harry Truman's administration to Gerald Ford's, Gibbons may have been the most exhaustively investigated non-Communist in the United States.

2. Box 3, Folder 6, Gibbons papers. The mayor was Alfonso Cervantes.

3. G. Duncan Bauman and Mary Kimbrough, *Behind the Headlines,* Patrice Press, Tucson, Arizona, 1999, p. 47.

4. Vasquez and Gibbons, November 13, 2005.

5. See Colin Gordon, *Mapping Decline: St. Louis and the Fate of the American City,* University of Pennsylvania Press, Philadelphia, 2008, pp. 40–41. "By 2000, the twelve-county metro area [comprising both Missouri and Illinois counties] boasted 233 incorporated municipalities...; 91 were in St. Louis County alone" (p. 45).

6. Sanford.

7. Guilfoil.

8. Robert H. Salisbury, "St. Louis Politics: Relationships among Interests, Parties, and

Governmental Structures," *Western Political Quarterly,* June 1960, p. 499.
  9. Ryan.
  10. Patrick Gibbons, telephone interview of February 8, 2008.
  11. Keith Payne, e-mail of December 6, 2012.
  12. Patrick Gibbons.
  13. Peter Collier and David Horowitz, *The Kennedys: An American Dream,* Summit, New York, 1984, p. 246. Collier and Horowitz interviewed Gibbons in September 1979.
  14. Keith Payne, e-mails of December 2, 6, and 12, 2012.
  15. Payne, e-mail of December 2, 2012.
  16. Patrick Gibbons.
  17. "Live and Swingin'," Reprise Records, 2005. The DVD is accompanied by a CD of a separate, unrelated floor show that Sinatra, Martin, and Davis staged in a Chicago-area nightclub in 1962.
  18. "Teamsters Charity Show Raises about $570,000 for 20 Groups," *St. Louis Post-Dispatch,* February 9, 1967, p. 3D; Bob Goddard, "Teamster Show Brings Truckload of Entertainment," *St. Louis Globe-Democrat,* February 9, 1967, p. 3F.
  19. Marcel Proust, *Finding Time Again,* Ian Patterson, trans., Penguin, London, 2003, p. 40.
  20. These pictures can be seen at the Thomas Jefferson Library, University of Missouri, St. Louis. The Local 688 photograph collection there is numbered 559.
  21. Jake McCarthy, "Harold Gibbons, Idealist: A Reminiscence," *St. Louis Post-Dispatch,* November 21, 1982, p. 2C.
  22. Author's telephone interview with Gordon Hoener of May 24, 2007. Besides selling stocks and bonds, Hoener had a mind-reading act that he performed in St. Louis nightclubs.
  23. Vasquez and Gibbons.
  24. Payne, e-mail of December 6, 2012.
  25. Eagleton. Shenker was under federal indictment for tax evasion when he died in 1989. He might well have beaten that charge, just as he had earlier thwarted his sometime partners in the Outfit. In 1979 the FBI secretly recorded a Chicago conversation between Shenker and the Outfit's Joey "the Clown" Lombardo. Lombardo claimed that the lawyer owed him and his friends $2.5 million.

Shenker denied it. Listen, Lombardo said, you're 72 now; if you don't pay up, you won't see 73. "So what?" Shenker replied (Ronald J. Lawrence, "Mob Threatened Shenker with Death, Tapes Reveal," *St. Louis Post-Dispatch,* February 24, 1983, pp. 1A, 5A). Pneumonia killed the old lawyer ten years later. So far as is known, he never paid. Lombardo, found guilty of a murder, was sentenced to life in prison in 2007.
  26. FBI memo of August 19, 1969.
  27. Payne, e-mail of December 2, 2012.
  28. McCarthy, "Harold Gibbons: Idealist."
  29. Salmon, *Recollections: I Joined Teamsters Local 688,* p. 327. In 1968 Salmon left Local 688 to work for the Western Conference of Teamsters in Los Angeles. He was by then, he writes, disillusioned with Gibbons, partly because of what he saw as the Teamster boss' neglect of his wife Ann, whom Salmon and his wife had befriended.
  30. Author's interview with Jerry Tucker of December 8, 2005.
  31. Hoffa, *Hoffa: The Real Story,* pp. 13–14
  32. Quoted in Brill, p. 74. The lawyer was William Bufalino, one of J. Edgar Hoover's five "Top Hoodlums" and later a suspect in Hoffa's disappearance and presumed murder.
  33. FBI memo of August 28, 1968.
  34. Murray Kempton, "The Jumper," *New York Review of Books,* February 11, 1993.
  35. William L. Clay, *Bill Clay: A Political Voice at the Grass Roots,* Missouri Historical Society Press, St. Louis, 2004, p. 144.
  36. Clay, pp. 18–19.
  37. Clay, pp. 75–76.
  38. Author's telephone interviews with William L. Clay of July 31 and August 5, 2008.
  39. Clay interviews. See also "Cabbies Join Seafarer Union," *New York Times,* February 23, 1962, p. 14A.
  40. Clay, p. 43. "Ames, a white labor leader, funneled money for canvassers, signs, and election day workers into the campaign."
  41. Clay, p. 127.
  42. Quoted in Lana Stein, p. 131.
  43. Quoted in Lorraine Kee, "Jefferson Bank Demonstrations Are Remembered as 'Catalyst for Change,'" *St. Louis Post-Dispatch,* December 13, 2003, p. 29A. Ten other people were arrested and charged in subsequent Jefferson Bank demonstrations; so in the end the original nine became nineteen.

Chapter 19

1. Ryan.
2. Calloway, *Who Runs St. Louis?*, p. 28.
3. George Lipsitz, *A Life in the Struggle: Ivory Perry and the Culture of Opposition*, Temple University Press, Philadelphia, 1988, p. 68.
4. DeVerne Calloway's political patron was Jack Dwyer, the longtime, white chairman of the city's Democratic Central Committee. Dwyer was, moreover, a leader of the party's Forces of Progress faction. The fact that DeVerne, married to a leader of the opposition Politicians faction, could nevertheless work closely with Dwyer suggests that factional lines were fairly elastic, depending on the issues and personalities involved.
5. Quoted in Robert Bussel, "'A Trade Union Oriented War on the Slums': Harold Gibbons, Ernest Calloway, and the St. Louis Teamsters in the 1960s," *Labor History*, vol. 44, no. 1, 2003, p. 55. In 2015 Bussel published *Fighting for Total Person Unionism: Harold Gibbons, Ernest Calloway and Working-Class Citizenship* (University of Illinois Press, Urbana), a fuller treatment of the Gibbons-Calloway partnership.
6. Bussel.
7. Tucker, December 8, 2005.
8. Tucker.
9. Ryan.
10. For more about Chambers, see Mary Weleck, "Jordan Chambers: Black Politician and Boss," *Journal of Negro History*, October 1972, pp. 352–369. Ames said of Chambers that he "had more natural leadership ability than any other man I've ever known. I've done a little public speaking myself and know from experience that any good speaker can, every now and then, get a crowd to where it will follow him to the barricades. Chambers did it every time" (Ames, March 7, 2007).
11. Guilfoil.
12. Ames.
13. Eagleton e-mail of August 18 and interview of August 23, 2005. Tom Eagleton was the son of Mark Eagleton, the mayoral candidate defeated by Raymond Tucker in the Democratic primary of 1953. In 1960, when he was St. Louis' circuit attorney, the younger Eagleton and several friends parleyed with the Bootheelers at The Brass Rail, a Hill restaurant owned by Louis "Midge" Berra, the longtime Democratic committeeman of the 24th Ward. The two groups agreed to support Hearnes for secretary of state and Eagleton for attorney general. Both men won their races in that year's November election.
14. Ryan interview. Calloway's map was amended in still later court decisions, but not greatly. Ryan, after leaving Local 688, became a political consultant who specialized in redistricting efforts. "So this first work with Calloway became very important [to me]," he said.
15. Clay, *Bill Clay*, p. 102. Clay's wooing of Callanan is described on pp. 99–104 and 163–165. The fifteen black Steamfitters (ten journeymen and five apprentices) were selected by a small group of North Side political figures, including Clay. The new Fitters thus became patronage workers, each beholden to the organization of the man who chose him. *Bill Clay: A Political Voice at the Grass Roots* is unusually and refreshingly forthright on the realities of American retail politics.
16. Quoted in Clay, p. 165.
17. Clay, pp. 99, 165.
18. Quoted in Salmon, p. 334.
19. Eagleton interview.
20. Ernest Calloway, untitled campaign speech dated March 20, 1968, in "Calloway for Congress," Box 23, Folder 1, Gibbons papers.
21. *St. Louis Argus*, July 18, 1968. The clipping is in "Calloway for Congress," Box 22, Folder 1, Gibbons papers. Ryan.
22. Author's telephone interview of Bill Clay of July 31, 2008.
23. Ryan.
24. Salmon, p. 318.
25. Ryan.
26. Harold Gibbons, memo of May 10, 1968, to John Naber, Local 688's president; Ernest Calloway, memo of July 1, 1968, to Harold Gibbons, both in "Calloway for Congress," Box 23, Folder 1, Gibbons papers. In the second memo Calloway, aware that the law forbade the local from donating the $22,500 directly, suggests setting up paper organizations to do so.
27. Tucker.
28. Manuel Chait, "Clay, Crawford, Symington, Scott Nominated in House Races," *St. Louis Post-Dispatch*, August 7, 1968, p. 6A; Clay, *Bill Clay*, p. 165.

29. Bussel, pp. 51–52.
30. Salmon, p. 355. In 1968 Salmon left St. Louis to work for the IBT on the West Coast. At that time, he writes, Local 688 had 13,293 members, 40 percent in manufacturing, 26 percent in warehousing, 18 percent in sales and services, 10 percent in office work, with the rest described as miscellaneous.
31. Ryan.
32. Salmon, p. 333.
33. Ryan.
34. Ryan.
35. Bussel, pp. 59, 62. Bussel says that assigning the most skilled Tandy Area Council organizers to the rent strike project crippled TAC and led to its demise.
36. Timothy Bleck, "U.S. Asked to Investigate Police," *St. Louis Post-Dispatch*, September 18, 1968, p. 1.
37. FBI memo of November 29, 1968.
38. Mike Ryan, memo to Harold Gibbons and Dick Kavner, of September 4, 1969, in a file labeled "Stewards' Council Meetings," Box 44, Folder 11, Gibbons papers.
39. Ryan interview.
40. Author's interview with Ron Gamache of February 1983.
41. Sanford.
42. McCarthy, "Harold Gibbons, Idealist: A Reminiscence." McCarthy in '69 had time to involve himself in the rent strike. He had the previous fall left the *Missouri Teamster* to become Gibbons' administrative assistant (Harold Gibbons, interoffice memo of September 16, 1968, in file labeled "Jake McCarthy," Box 76, Folder 20, Gibbons papers). McCarthy later said he was "pressured out as editor because his views were not conservative enough to suit the Teamsters" (Hank Vogt, "Jake McCarthy: Change in Image," *UMSL Current*, February 3, 1972). The *Missouri Teamster* was the organ of Joint Council 13, most of whose leaders probably shared the views of Local 688's "business wing." McCarthy's ouster was a sign that Gibbons was losing political ground in his own organization.
43. Quoted in Bussel, p. 59.
44. Alfonso J. Cervantes, *Mr. Mayor*, Nash Publishing, Los Angeles, 1974, p. 59.
45. Bussel, p. 60.
46. Quoted in Bussel.
47. Joel L. Fleischman, "Not without Honor: A Prophet Even in His Own Country: A Case Study of the Resolution of the St. Louis Public Housing Tenants' Strike of 1969 (Role of H. Gibbons)," Ford Foundation Dispute Resolution Project, p. 52. Fleischman interviewed Gibbons in 1978. A copy of his 72-page typescript is in Box 1, Folder 44, Gibbons papers. It's not clear whether the paper was ever published.
48. Bussel.
49. Ernest Calloway, ed., *Public Housing Rent Strike in St. Louis,* Local 688, St. Louis, no date but probably spring 1970. This is a mimeographed collection of articles and working papers, most of them by Calloway, about the strike, its goals, and its aftermath.
50. Ernest Calloway, "The New St. Louis Housing Tenant," in *Public Housing Rent Strike in St. Louis.*
51. Quoted in Bussel, p. 61.
52. Bussel, p. 62.

Chapter 20

1. File labeled "Today Show, March 30, 1972," Box 2, Folder 17, Gibbons papers. This is a transcript of the interview of Gibbons by NBC's Frank McGee.
2. Ryan.
3. Henry Kissinger, *White House Years*, Little, Brown, Boston, 1979, p. 231.
4. See Robert Dallek, *Nixon and Kissinger: Partners in Power* (HarperCollins, New York, 2007), especially pp. 263, 396, 431, and 454–455, on Nixon's and Kissinger's hints to the North Vietnamese that if they were to allow a "decent interval" of time to pass after U.S. forces sailed for home, they would have a more or less free hand in defeating the South Vietnamese and reuniting their country.
5. Patrick Gibbons, interview of February 2, 2008. The younger Gibbons, who, years later, attended a seminar in New York run by Kissinger's consulting firm, Kissinger and Associates, was told this story by the former secretary of state.
6. Henry Kissinger, letter of April 17, 1967, to Harold Gibbons, in Box 28, Folder 3, Gibbons papers.
7. Harold Gibbons, outline for 1968 Center for International Affairs presentation, in Box 28, Folder 3, Gibbons papers. Gibbons has written "ALA" in red ink in the margin of

the outline. The letters stood for Alliance for Labor Action, a brief joint endeavor by the Teamsters and the United Auto Workers to work among the urban poor. According to Walter Reuther's biographer, "the Reutherites were particularly pleased that [Frank] Fitzsimmons had chosen the lone radical on the Teamster executive board, the ex-Socialist Harold Gibbons, to play a leading role in the ALA," (Nelson Lichtenstein, *Walter Reuther: The Most Dangerous Man in Detroit*, University of Illinois Press, Champaign-Urbana, 1997, p. 431.) The ALA, formed in 1968, petered out after Reuther died in a plane crash in 1970.

8. China Goodwill Mission, press release of July 14, 1971; Dick Kavner, letter of July 23, 1971, to the People's Republic of China, via the China Goodwill Mission, requesting visas for Gibbons and himself. (Both the press release and Kavner's letter are in a file labeled "China Trip," Box 1, Folder 62, Gibbons papers.) China and the United States had no formal diplomatic relations in '71. Arrangements were therefore made through the China Goodwill Mission, Mercer Island, Washington State. The mission was the brainchild of Amos Heacock, a onetime sympathizer of the U.S. Communist Party who, at the time of the Nixon trip, was evidently working for the Chinese. For Heacock, see "Airman Denies He Was Red," *New York Times*, May 15, 1953.

9. Victor Riesel. "Gibbons Has Big Role in Hoffa Power Play," *St. Louis Globe-Democrat*, September 20, 1972, p. 14A.

10. Brill, p. 91. In early 1973, after he left the White House, Colson became general counsel for the Teamsters Union, replacing Edward Bennett Williams, a Democrat. Colson's new career was short-lived because he was convicted of Watergate crimes in 1974.

11. Author's telephone interview of Ron Borges of July 16, 2008.

12. Seymour M. Hersh, "Gibbons One of Three on Mission to Hanoi," *St. Louis Post-Dispatch*, March 18, 1972, p. 1A. Hersh's article, which carries a Hanoi dateline, originally appeared in the *New York Times*.

13. Jake McCarthy, "Gibbons: Hanoi Doubts U.S. Desires Peace," *St. Louis Post-Dispatch*, March 28, 1972, p. 1A.

14. Harold Gibbons, untitled speech, in "Vietnam Moratorium Day Speech, November 15, 1969," Box 5, Folder 38, Gibbons papers.

15. Kissinger, *White House Years*, p. 65.

16. David Livingston, Harold Gibbons, and Clifton Caldwell, "Labor Mission to Hanoi," *The Nation*, April 24, 1972.

17. File labeled "Hanoi Diary—March 12–27, 1972, III," Box 1, Folder 27, Gibbons papers. Unless otherwise noted, the quotations that follow in this section are from Gibbons' twenty-seven-page journal, several copies of which are in the folder.

18. The book Gibbons mentioned was Harrison E. Salisbury's *Behind the Lines—Hanoi*, an account by a *New York Times* editor of a 1966 trip to North Vietnam. Gibbons also notes that during the layover in Los Angeles he talked to Louis Goldblatt, secretary-treasurer of the International Longshore and Warehouse Union, about a "merger." Whether this merger was to be between the IBT and the ILWU, or to involve some other arrangement, Gibbons doesn't specify. Like Livingston's District 65, the West Coast longshoremen were a formerly Communist-led organization.

19. See Kissinger, *White House Years*, pp. 1,305–1,308.

20. Elmer W. Lower, president of ABC News, letter of May 4, 1972, to Gibbons, Livingston, and Caldwell, in file labeled "Itinerary—Hanoi Trip 1972," Box 1, Folder 25, Gibbons papers. Lower denied their request, saying that the Ted Koppel interview with them in Laos in March had satisfied ABC's interest in their expedition. Officials at NBC and CBS apparently wrote similar replies.

21. Harold Gibbons, letter of April 20, 1972, to Mr. and Mrs. Frank Rupinski, in file labeled "Hanoi Trip, March 12–27, 1972, V.," Box 1, Folder 30, Gibbons papers.

22. See Kissinger, pp. 1,169–1,174.

23. Kissinger, p. 1,308. Fearful that the news about Eagleton's psychiatric care would damage their electoral chances, the Democrats replaced the Missouri senator with Sargent Shriver, a Kennedy in-law and former head of the Peace Corps. It didn't help. The Nixon-Agnew ticket coasted to victory in a great landslide. McGovern and Shriver carried only Massachusetts and the District of Columbia.

24. Quoted in Moldea, p. 294.

25. William Loeb, letter of September 9, 1970, to Harold Gibbons, in file labeled "Hoffa," Box 28, Folder 13, Gibbons papers.
26. Arthur C. Egan, Jr., "Hoffa Victim of Double-Cross on Parole," *Manchester Union-Leader*, September 13, 1971, p. 1., in Box 28, Folder 13, Gibbons papers. Hoffa's son was the source for Egan's story. The federal parole board denied Hoffa's parole petition in August; hence the suspected "double-cross." Nixon finally released Hoffa on a clemency plea four months later. See also Brill, p. 96.
27. Quoted in Brill, p. 90.
28. Brill, p. 95. Dean admitted to Brill that he was the person who added the clause to the commutation order. According to Brill, Hoffa had been aware of the clause—had in fact agreed to it *verbally*, thinking he could easily renege on it once he was out of jail. The surprise came when he discovered that Dean's changes *on paper* left him legally bound.
29. Fred P. Graham, "Official Chagrined by Hoffa's 'Lawyer' in P.O.W. Incident," *New York Times*, September 12, 1972, pp.1, 13; "White House Mystery," *New York Times*, September 16, 1972, p. 28; Paul O'Neill, "The Unknown Man Who Knew Absolutely Everybody," *Life*, September 29, 1972, pp. 78–80.
30. William L. Taub, *Forces of Power*, Grosset and Dunlap, New York, 1979.
31. Taub, p. 100.
32. Taub, p. 149.
33. FBI memo of September 22, 1972.
34. Taub, pp. 162–163. Taub and Gibbons had probably met twenty years earlier. In 1951 Taub was the manager of a U.S. concert tour by the St. Louis-born but long expatriated African-American entertainer Josephine Baker. One of her stops was at Kiel Auditorium in St. Louis, where her show was sponsored by Local 688.
35. The cablegram, which bears no date, is in a file labeled "Telegram Hanoi Trip No. 2, 1972," Box 1, Folder 31, Gibbons papers. Since it calls for the American visitors to arrive on or about July 1, it must have been sent fairly soon after Taub's and Le Duc Tho's meeting in Paris.
36. "Labor Leader Rejects Call for Peace Strike," *St. Louis Post-Dispatch*, June 25, 1972, p. 14A.
37. Tucker. Tucker served as a general gofer during the congress, arranging travel schedules, reserving block of hotel rooms, and so forth. He later rose in his union hierarchy to become director of the region comprising UAW-organized plants in Missouri, Kansas, Texas, and Colorado. His chief mentors were Mazey and Victor Reuther, longtime leaders of the union's Left. Tucker died in 2012.
38. Tucker.
39. Tucker.
40. Lichtenstein, p. 405.
41. Tucker. "Probably not," Tucker said, when asked if the presence at the congress of the former Communists Harry Bridges and David Livingston explained why the more right-wing UAW board members stayed away. The real reason, he thought, was intra-union politics. Following Walter Reuther's death in a plane crash in 1970, Tucker said, the board's conservatives chose Leonard Woodcock as the union's new president. "Now these are conservative on scale," he added. "[Woodcock] wasn't as conservative as George Meany—he was a flaming *radical* compared to George Meany. But in terms of the internal workings of the UAW, Leonard was considered more conservative than" other candidates. The conservatives didn't necessarily favor the U.S. effort in Vietnam, Tucker suggested; they simply disliked the union's left-wingers more than they disliked the war.
42. Tucker.
43. Tucker.
44. Riesel.
45. David E. Rosenbaum, "Hoffa Plans a Hanoi Trip; U.S. Later Cancels Permit," *New York Times*, September 8, 1972, pp. 1–2.
46. Presidential/HAKMemCons, 1026, at http://nixonlibrary.gov
47. Riesel. Riesel adds that "President Nixon knew nothing of this."
48. Associated Press, "Kissinger Put End to Hoffa's POW Proposal." This version of the AP story appeared in the *Deseret News*, Salt Lake City, Utah, November 11, 1993. See http://www.deseretnews.com/article/320138/kissinger-put-end-to-Hoffas-pow-proposal.
49. Taub, p. 189.
50. Taub, p. 193.
51. Quoted in Taub, p. 196.
52. Benjamin Welles, "Hoffa Lawyer Sought Deal on Trip, Kleindienst Says," *New York Times*, September 9, 1972, pp. 1, 9.
53. Quoted in Taub, p. 197.

54. Welles.

55. Riesel. In his book Taub says he made contact with Le Duc Tho by way of his (Taub's) Parisian lawyer, a woman who was a friend of Bulgaria's female minister of justice, who in turn had connections inside North Vietnam's government. He also hints that he had help from Jiang Quing, the wife of Mao Zedong. But who knows?

56. Taub, p. 200.

Chapter 21

1. Author's interview with Harland Horn of October 30, 2007.

2. McCarthy phone interview of February 1983.

3. Jake McCarthy, "Behind the Gibbons Ouster," *St. Louis Post-Dispatch*, May 30, 1973, p. 3A.

4. Jim Pace, December 20, 1968, memo to Gibbons, Kavner, Saffo, and Local 688 President John Naber, in "Community Action Committee," Box 43, Folders 3, 15, and 16, Gibbons papers.

5. Mike Ryan, report of September 4, 1969, concerning shop stewards' complaints, in "Stewards' Council Meetings," Box 44, Folder 11, Gibbons papers.

6. Mike Ryan and Claude Brown's focus group notes of August 19, 1969, in "Murray Hines' Shop Steward Meeting," Box 44, Folder 11, Gibbons papers.

7. Claude Brown's focus group notes of August 28, 1969, in "E. Smith's Shop Steward Meeting," Box 44, Folder 11, Gibbons papers.

8. Ryan, report of September 4, 1969.

9. Ryan and Brown's focus group notes of August 7, 1969, in "Levi Sandford's Shop Steward Meeting," Box 44, Folder 11, Gibbons papers.

10. Ryan and Brown's focus group notes of August 7, 1969.

11. Ryan.

12. McCarthy phone interview.

13. Author's phone interview with Ron Borges of July 16, 2008.

14. Jake McCarthy, "Gibbons Quits Teamsters Post," *St. Louis Post-Dispatch*, May 24, 1973, pp. 1A, 5A.

15. Vasquez and Gibbons, December 22, 2005.

16. Jake McCarthy, "Behind the Gibbons Ouster," *St. Louis Post-Dispatch*, May 30, 1973, p. 3A.

17. Gamache.

18. See John Herbers, "The Case History of a Housing Failure," *New York Times*, November 2, 1970, pp. 1, 36. Herbers' focus is on St. Louis' notorious Pruitt-Igoe complex, about which one housing official said, "It was like building a battleship that would not float. The damn thing sank."

19. Nixon didn't like Romney anyway. According to Richard Reeves' *President Nixon: Alone in the White House* (Simon and Schuster, New York, 2001, p.71), Romney was "a man used to being listened to, who casually interrupted the president at meetings." Nixon told aides, "Just keep them away from me"— *them* being the extroverted Romney, Vice President Spiro Agnew, and Secretary of Transportation John Volpe.

20. Quoted in Bussel, p. 63. For more on RAFT, see George Lipsitz, "Beyond the Fringe Benefits: Rank & File Teamsters in St. Louis," *Liberation*, July-August 1973, pp. 30–45, 53.

21. Levi Sanford, telephone interview of August 29, 2006. Unless otherwise noted, the information here about Local 102 comes from the Sanford interview. The leather-workers' local was a Cold War relic. In 1950 the St. Louis local of the Fur and Leather Workers Union split from its Communist-led international. Gibbons took the rebels under Local 688's wing and gave them rent-free office space for several years. In 1973 the leather workers were still in Local 688's headquarters building, though they had by then become paying tenants (see "Re: American Legion Award 1954," Box 2, Folder 5, Gibbons papers). Following his ouster from Local 688, Sanford became president of the leather workers local.

22. Robert H. Teuscher, "Gibbons Ouster Linked to Rival Union," *St. Louis Globe-Democrat*, May 25, 1973, p. 1A. At its first Convention, in September 1971, according to Teuscher, the International Distributive Workers of America declared that the union's purpose was to organize the "working poor, black workers, Spanish-speaking workers and other minority groups."

23. Sanford interview. On the Distributive Workers see Vanessa Tait, *Poor Workers' Unions: Rebuilding Labor from Below*, South End Press, Cambridge, Massachusetts, 2005,

pp. 67–70. In 1979 the Distributive Workers were taken into the United Auto Workers as (once again) District 65. In 1993 District 65 declared bankruptcy and its members were absorbed by other UAW locals.

24. See Lipsitz, p. 36.
25. Sanford phone interview. This was the beginning of the end of Local 688's benefits structure, Sanford said. "Employers began picking and choosing the benefits they'd pay for." Members also lost interest in the question, he said, coming to prefer health insurance coverage over the actual medical care they had received from the Labor Health Institute, for example. Today the LHI is a health maintenance organization like all the others, rather than a clinic.
26. Sanford phone interview.
27. Ryan.
28. Brill, p. 366.
29. Stewards' Council meeting notes of June 21, 1972, Box 44, Folder 11, Gibbons papers.
30. Author's telephone interview with Ron Borges of July 16, 2008.
31. Joe Franco and Richard Hammer, *Hoffa's Man*, Dell, New York, 1987, p. 330.
32. Quoted in Brill, p. 368.
33. Borges.
34. Patrick Gibbons, telephone interview of February 2, 2008.
35. Harlan Horn.
36. Harry Bernstein, "Gibbons Fired from Teamsters Union Post," *St. Louis Globe-Democrat*, December 14, 1972, p. 1.
37. Robert J. Wehling, "Key Incidents Are Cited in the Fall of Gibbons," *St. Louis Post-Dispatch*, May 25, 1973, pp. 1C, 4C.
38. Keith Payne, e-mail of December 6, 2012.
39. Payne.
40. Horn.
41. Payne, e-mails of December 6 and 20, 2012. The two visitors, whom Payne suspected of engineering Gibbons' ouster from behind the scenes, went on to enjoy long careers in the St. Louis union.
42. McCarthy, "Behind the Gibbons Ouster."
43. Author's telephone interview with Ron Borges of July 21, 2008.
44. "New Leader Denies Anti-Gibbons Move in Teamster Ousters," *St. Louis Globe-Democrat*, May 21, 1973, p. 14A. The "new leader" of the headline was Dunn.
45. "3 Are Forced Out; Setback for Gibbons," *St. Louis Post-Dispatch*, May 20, 1973, pp. 1A, 30A.
46. Author's interview with Marcus Albrecht of October 13, 2005.
47. Jake McCarthy, telephone interview of February 1983.
48. Author's telephone interview of Ron Borges of October 2, 2008. Although he had by this point been stripped of his office as Local 688's recording secretary, Borges remained a business agent for the union. Dunn and the others hoped to "freeze him out" by giving him "crappy jobs," he said. He represented bakery workers, for example, which required getting up at three in the morning to make shop visits. He'd gone to Chicago seeking a new job.
49. McCarthy, "Behind the Gibbons Ouster."

Chapter 22

1. Ron Borges, telephone interview of July 16, 2008.
2. Gordon Burnside, "Calloway at 73," *St. Louis*, March 1983, p. 112.
3. Albrecht.
4. Keith Payne, e-mail of December 2, 2012.
5. Keith Payne, e-mail of December 6, 2012.
6. Author's telephone interview with Wanda Koss of July 14, 2006.
7. "Memo Typical of White House—Gibbons," *St. Louis Globe-Democrat*, June 28, 1973, p. 2.
8. "Mrs. Ann Gibbons," *St. Louis Globe-Democrat*, June 27, 1974, p.14A.
9. Brill, p. 369.
10. Keith Payne, e-mail of November 20, 2012).
11. Borges.
12. Quoted in Brill, p. 369.
13. Elizabeth Vasquez and Larry Gibbons, November 13, 2005.
14. Vasquez and Gibbons.
15. Keith Payne, e-mail of November 30, 2012.
16. Ryan.
17. Vasquez and Gibbons.
18. Vasquez and Gibbons. Keith Payne, on the other hand, vehemently denied that Gibbons would have let Sinatra pay his greens fees.
19. Author's telephone interview with Wanda Koss of August 11, 2006.

20. Quoted in Brill, p. 370.

21. James L. Morice, "Fitzsimmons Reportedly Drops Plan to Oust Gibbons," *St. Louis Globe-Democrat*, June 3, 1976, p. 10A. Another unnamed St. Louis Teamster suggested to Morice that Fitz, uneasy about a possible federal investigation of the Central States Pension Fund, wanted to keep Gibbons inside the IBT tent rather than drive him out. So there many have been several motives.

22. For Gibbons' adventures in California, see Brill, pp. 373–376.

23. Vasquez and Gibbons.

24. Quoted in Brill, p. 372.

25. Koss.

26. Ron Borges, phone interview of July 21, 2008.

27. David Shepardson, "Judge Approves End to U.S. Decree Overseeing Teamsters," *Detroit News*, February 17, 2015.

28. William Serrin, "Nonunion Rivals and Dissent Are Troubling the Teamsters," *New York Times*, May 16, 1982, p. 1A. Within a decade, over-the-road truck drivers had come to constitute less than 10 percent of the union's membership; warehouse workers made up 25 percent (Peter T. Kilborn, "As Teamsters Vote, the Only Certainty is Change," *New York Times*, December 10, 1991, p. 16B.)

29. William C. Lhotka, "Gibbons Considered for Federal Mediation Post," *St. Louis Post-Dispatch*, January 14, 1981, p. 3A. A copy of the application is in Box 1, Folder 49, Gibbons papers.

30. Morris Udall, note to Harold Gibbons, undated but presumably from early 1981, in "Correspondence 1979–1982," Box 1, Folder 17, Gibbons papers.

31. Undated *St. Louis Post-Dispatch* clipping, in "Newspaper Articles re Gibbons," Box 1, Folder 3, Gibbons papers. The article describes a speech Gibbons gave to the Press Club of Metropolitan St. Louis. Gibbons was particularly critical of the Reagan administration's championing of deregulation of trucking and airlines. He said, "Established trucking firms are being undercut by 'fly-by-night' operators who routinely ignore safety regulations in doing business."

32. Salmon, p. 326.

33. Author's interview with Mike Goebel of February 6, 2008.

34. "Thirty-two percent of Missourians are born-again [Christians]," said the late Tom Eagleton, who witnessed the change occur during his years in Missouri politics. Evangelical Christians tend to be active Republicans, he pointed out. "That's the difference," he said. "They get out the vote" (Eagleton interview).

35. In early 2017, the GOP-dominated legislature passed and the new Republican governor signed a right-to-work law. It was, however, overturned in a referendum of August 2018.

36. Gilbert J. Gall, *American Workers, American Unions*, John Hopkins University Press, Baltimore, 2002, p. 202.

37. U.S. Bureau of Labor Statistics, Union Members Summary, January 28, 2016, at www.bls.gov/news.release/union2.nr0.htm.

38. Notes from Local 688's Stewards' Council Meeting of March 20, 1968, Box 44, Folder 11, Gibbons papers. In 1968 Gibbons went to Europe to try to persuade European unions to strike Abex shops there. Apparently he had little luck. Disease, not trade unions, finally defeated Abex. The company manufactured brake shoes containing asbestos. Lawsuits claiming that the asbestos had given employees mesothelioma forced it to close in 1978 (see www.asbestos.com/companies/abex-corporation.php.).

39. The text of "The Triple Revolution" can be found at scarc.library.oregonstate.edu/coll/pauling/peace/papers/1964p.7–01.html.

40. The Captain Smith story is charming, at least for white people. But it was in fact a metaphor for the big economic problem facing colonial America: Who will perform the labor underlying capital accumulation in the soon-to-be new nation? The answer, in the long run, was African slaves. See Edmund S. Morgan, *American Slavery, American Freedom*, Norton, New York, 1975.

41. Bayard Rustin, untitled of speech of September 27, 1964, in file labeled "City Wide Shop Conferences 1964, 1966," Box 43, Folder 11, Gibbons papers.

42. Rustin.

43. Steve Giegerich, "Loss of Corvette a Turning Point for St. Louis Manufacturing," *St. Louis Post-Dispatch*, July 10, 2011.

44. Patrick Gibbons.

Bibliography

Books and Articles

Along with the books and articles listed here, I've consulted articles that appeared in the *New York Times, St. Louis Globe-Democrat, St. Louis Post-Dispatch, Missouri Teamster,* and other periodicals.

Alinsky, Saul D., *John L. Lewis: An Unauthorized Biography.* New York: Vintage, 1970.
Andrew, John A., III, *Power to Destroy: The Political Uses of the IRS from Kennedy to Nixon.* Chicago: Ivan R. Dee, 2002.
Baldwin, Carl, "Buster Wortman's Quiet Departure." *St. Louis Post-Dispatch,* August 11, 1968.
Ball, Harry Vernon, "Case History of a Labor Union: The United Distribution Workers." Masters's thesis, Washington University, St. Louis, 1950.
Baron, Sam, "I Was Near the Top of Jimmy Hoffa's Drop-Dead List." *Life,* July 20, 1962.
Bauman, G. Duncan, and Mary Kimbrough, *Behind the Headlines.* Tucson: Patrice Press, 1988.
Bell, Daniel, *The End of Ideology.* Glencoe, IL: Free Press, 1960.
_____, "St. Louis Blues." *Fortune,* July 1954.
Brill, Steven, *The Teamsters.* New York: Simon & Schuster, 1978.
Brooks, Thomas R., *Toil and Trouble: A History of American Labor.* New York: Delacorte, 1964.
Burnside, Gordon, "Calloway at 73." *St. Louis,* March 1983.
_____, "The Good Teamster." *St. Louis Weekly,* July 13 and July 20, 1983.
Bussel, Robert, "'A Trade Union Oriented War on the Slums': Harold Gibbons, Ernest Calloway, and the St. Louis Teamsters in the 1960s." *Labor History* 1, 2003.
Calloway, Ernest, "Creative Self-Determinism." *Missouri Teamster,* August 23, 1969.
_____, "The Negro Social and Economic Thrust." In Calloway, *Who Runs St. Louis?* St. Louis: Center for Urban Programs, St. Louis University, 1980.
_____, *10 Years of Trade Union Democracy in Action.* St. Louis: Teamsters Local 688, 1951.
Cervantes, Alfonso J., *Mr. Mayor.* Los Angeles: Nash Publishing, 1974.
Clay, William L., *Bill Clay: A Political Voice at the Grass Roots.* St. Louis: Missouri Historical Society Press, 2004.
Cohen, Adam, and Elizabeth Taylor, *American Pharoah: Mayor Richard J. Daley: His Battle for Chicago and the Nation.* Boston: Little, Brown, 2000.

Collier, Peter, and David Horowitz, *The Kennedys: An American Drama*. New York: Summit, 1964.
Deakin, James, *A Grave for Bobby: The Greenlease Slaying*. New York: Morrow, 1990.
Dieckmann, Annetta, "Union Makes Use of the Social Scientist." *Journal of Educational Sociology*, February 1952.
Dobbs, Farrell, "Hoffa and the Teamsters." *International Socialist Review*, Summer 1966.
_____. *Teamster Rebellion*. New York: Monad Press, 1972.
Dubovsky, Melvyn, and Warren Van Tine, *John L. Lewis: A Biography*. New York: Quadrangle, 1977.
_____, "John L. Lewis." In *Labor Leaders in America*, edited by Dubovsky and Van Tine. Urbana: University of Illinois Press, 1987.
Farmer, James, *Lay Bare the Heart: An Autobiography of the Civil Rights Movement*. New York: Arbor House, 1985.
Feurer, Rosemary, *Radical Unionism in the Midwest, 1900–1950*. Urbana: University of Illinois Press, 2006.
_____, "William Sentner, the UE, and Civic Unionism in St. Louis." In *The CIO's Left-Led Unions*, edited by Steve Rosswurm. New Brunswick: Rutgers University Press, 1992.
Fine, Sidney, *Sit-Down: The General Motors Strike of 1936–1937*. Ann Arbor: University of Michigan Press, 1969.
Fleischman, Joel L., "Not Without Honor: A Prophet Even in His Own Country: A Case Study of the St. Louis Public Housing Tenants' Strike of 1969 (Role of H. Gibbons)." Cambridge, Ford Foundation Dispute Resolution Project, 1978.
Foner, Moe, interview. New York, Columbia University Libraries Oral History Research Office, June 12, 1986.
Fraser, Steven, *Labor Will Rule: Sidney Hillman and the Rise of American Labor*. New York: Free Press, 1991.
Franco, Joe, and Richard Hammer, *Hoffa's Man*. New York: Dell, 1987.
Gall, Gilbert J., *Pursuing Justice: Lee Pressman, the New Deal, and the CIO*. Albany: State University of New York, 1999.
Gibbons, Harold J., interview by Dick Keefe, *A Dick Keefe Profile*. KMOX-TV, St. Louis, April 23, 1978.
_____, interview by Patrick Emory, *At Ease*. KSD-TV, St. Louis, June 3, 1978.
_____, "The Poor Must Find Dignity, Security in Housing." *Missouri Teamster*, September 19, 1969.
_____, "Why the Union Is Concerned." *St. Louis Post-Dispatch*, February 28, 1952.
Gordon, Colin, *Mapping Decline: St. Louis and the Fate of an American City*. Philadelphia: University of Pennsylvania Press, 2008.
Gray, Kenneth, *A Report on Politics in St. Louis*. Cambridge: Center for Urban Studies, 1961.
Heathcott, Joseph, and Maire Agnes Murphy, "Corridors of Flight, Zones of Renewal: Industry, Planning, and Policy in the Making of Metropolitan St. Louis." *Journal of Urban History*, January 2005.
Hilty, James W., *Robert Kennedy: Brother Protector*. Philadelphia: Temple University Press, 1997.
Hodgson, Godfrey, *America in Our Time*. Garden City, NY: Doubleday, 1976.
Hoffa, James, and Donald I. Rogers, *The Trials of Jimmy Hoffa: An Autobiography*. Chicago: Henry Regnery, 1970.
_____, and Oscar Fraley, *Hoffa: The Real Story*. New York: Stein and Day, 1975.

Howe, Irving, and Lewis Coser, *The American Communist Party: A Critical History.* Boston: Beacon Press, 1957.

International Brotherhood of Teamsters, *Constitution Adopted by the Miami Beach, Florida, Convention, July 4–7, 1966.*

Jacobs, James B., *Mobsters, Unions, and Feds: The Mafia and the American Labor Movement.* New York: New York University Press, 2006.

James, Estelle, "Jimmy Hoffa: Labor Hero or Labor's Own Foe." In *Labor Leaders in America,* edited by Melvyn Dubovsky and Warren Van Tine. Urbana: University of Illinois Press, 1987.

James, Ralph, and Estelle James, *Hoffa and the Teamsters.* Princeton: Van Nordstrand, 1965.

Kempton, Murray, *America Comes of Middle Age.* Boston: Little, Brown, 1961.

———, "The Friends of Jimmy Hoffa." *New York Post,* July 9, 1977.

———, "The Jumper." *New York Review of Books,* February 11, 1993.

———, *Part of Our Time: Some Ruins and Monuments of the Thirties.* New York: Simon & Schuster, 1955.

———, "The Pessimist." *New York Review of Books,* February 22, 1979.

Kennedy, Robert, *The Enemy Within.* New York: Popular Library, 1960.

Kenny, Kevin, *Making Sense of the Molly Maguires.* New York: Oxford University Press, 1998.

Kimbrough, Mary, and Margaret W. Dagen, *Victory without Violence: The First Ten Years of the St. Louis Committee on Racial Equality (CORE), 1947–1957.* Columbia: University of Missouri Press, 2000.

Kirschten, Ernest, *Catfish and Crystal.* Garden City, NY: Doubleday, 1960.

Kirstein, George G., *Stores and Unions: A Study of the Growth of Unions in Dry Goods and Department Stores.* New York: Fairchild Publications, 1950.

Kissinger, Henry, *White House Years.* Boston: Little, Brown, 1979.

Leiter, Robert D., *The Teamsters Union: A Study of Its Economic Impact.* New York: Bookman Associates, 1957.

Lens, Sidney, *The Crisis of American Labor.* New York: Sagamore Press, 1959.

———, *Left, Right and Center: Conflicting Forces in American Labor.* Chicago: Regnery, 1949.

———, *Unrepentent Radical.* Boston: Beacon Press, 1980.

Lipsitz, George, "Beyond the Fringe Benefits: Rank & File Teamsters in St. Louis." *Liberation,* July-August, 1973.

———, *A Life in the Struggle: Ivory Perry and the Culture of Opposition.* Philadelphia: Temple University Press, 1988.

Livingston, David, Harold Gibbons, and Clifton Caldwell, "A Labor Mission to Hanoi." *The Nation,* April 24, 1972.

Macdonald, Dwight, *Politics Past: Essays in Political Criticism.* New York: Viking Compass, 1970.

Martin, John Bartlow, *Adlai Stevenson of Illinois.* Garden City, NY: Doubleday, 1976.

———, *Jimmy Hoffa's Hot.* Greenwich, CT: Fawcett, 1959.

McAdams, Alan K., *Power and Politics in Labor Legislation.* New York: Columbia University Press, 1964.

McCarthy, Jake, "Behind the Gibbons Ouster." *St. Louis Post-Dispatch,* May 30, 1973.

———, "Harold Gibbons, Idealist: A Reminiscence." *St. Louis Post-Dispatch,* November 21, 1982.

———, "Reminiscence of Hoffa—I." *St. Louis Post-Dispatch,* August 4, 1975.

———, "Reminiscence of Hoffa—II." *St. Louis Post-Dispatch,* August 6, 1975.

Meier, August, and Elliott Rudwick, *CORE: A Study in the Civil Rights Movement*. Urbana: University of Illinois Press, 1975.
Mills, C. Wright, *The New Men of Power: America's Labor Leaders*. New York: Harcourt, Brace, 1948.
Moldea, Dan E., *The Hoffa Wars: Teamsters, Rebels, Politicians and the Mob*. New York: Paddington Press, 1978.
Mollenhoff, Clark, *Tentacles of Power: The Story of Jimmy Hoffa*. Cleveland: World, 1965.
Newell, Barbara Warne, *Chicago and the Labor Movement*. Urbana: University of Illinois Press, 1961.
O'Donnell, Kenneth P., and David Powers, *Johnny, We Hardly Knew Ye: Memories of John Fitzgerald Kennedy*. Boston: Little, Brown, 1970.
O'Farrell, Brigid, and Joyce L. Kornbluh, *Rocking the Boat: Union Women's Voices, 1915–1975*. New Brunswick: Rutgers University Press, 1996.
O'Hara, John, "The Doctor's Son." In *The O'Hara Generation*. New York: Random House, 1969.
O'Neill, Paul, "The Man Who Knew Absolutely Everybody." *Life*, September 29, 1972.
Pensoneau, Taylor, *Brothers Notorious: The Sheltons, Southern Illinois' Legendary Gangsters*. New Berlin, IL: Downstate Publications, 2002.
Pearson, Drew, *Drew Pearson's Diaries: 1949–1959*. Edited by Tyler Abell. New York: Holt, Rinehart and Winston, 1974.
Primm, James Neal, *Lion of the Valley: St. Louis, Missouri*. Boulder: Pruett Publishing, 1981.
Riesel, Victor, "Gibbons Has Big Role in Hoffa Power Play." *St. Louis Globe-Democrat*, September 20, 1972.
Ritchie, Donald A., *Reporting from Washington: The History of the Washington Press Corps*. New York: Oxford University Press, 2005.
Rose, Arnold, *Union Solidarity: The Internal Cohesion of a Labor Union*. Minneapolis: University of Minnesota Press, 1952.
Rose, Richard, "Teamsters' New Boss?" *The Nation*, March 23, 1957.
Royko, Mike, *Boss: Richard J. Daley of Chicago*. New York: Dutton, 1971.
Russell, Thaddeus, *Out of the Jungle: Jimmy Hoffa and the Remaking of the American Working Class*. New York: Knopf, 2001.
Salmon, David, *Recollections: Part 5: Establishing a Career and a Family in St. Louis, 1946–1953*. Provo: privately printed, 2003
———, *Recollections: Part 6: I Joined Teamsters Local 688*, Provo: privately printed, 2003.
Salisbury, Robert H., "St. Louis Politics: Relationships among Interests, Parties, and Government Structures." *Western Political Quarterly*, June 1960.
Schlesinger, Arthur M., Jr., *Robert Kennedy and His Times*. Boston: Houghton Mifflin, 1978.
Seidman, Harold, *Labor Czars*. New York: Liveright, 1938.
Sheridan, Walter, *The Fall and Rise of Jimmy Hoffa*. New York: Saturday Review Press, 1972.
Simon, Nathan, and Sanford Rubushka, "Membership Attitudes in the Labor Health Institute of St. Louis." *American Journal of Public Health*, June 1956.
Sloane, Arthur A., *Hoffa*, Cambridge: MIT Press, 1991.
Sorenson, Theodore, *Kennedy*. New York: Harper and Row, 1965.
Smith, Lon W., "An Experiment in Trade Union Democracy: Harold Gibbons and the Formation of Teamsters Local 688, 1937–1957." Ph.D. diss., Illinois State University, Normal, 1993.

Stein, Lana, *St. Louis Politics: The Triumph of Tradition*. St. Louis: Missouri Historical Society Press, 2002.
Stepan-Norris, Judith, and Maurice Zeitlin, *Left Out: Reds and America's Industrial Unions*. Cambridge: Cambridge: University Press, 2003.
Taub, William L., *Forces of Power*. New York: Grosset and Dunlap, 1979.
Thomas, Evan, *The Man to See*. New York: Simon & Schuster, 1991.
_____, *Robert Kennedy: His Life*. New York: Simon & Schuster, 2000.
Thompson, Robert E., and Hortense Myers, *Robert F. Kennedy: The Brother Within*. New York: Dell, 1962.
Tosches, Nick, *The Devil and Sonny Liston*. Boston: Little, Brown, 2000.
Velie, Lester, *Desperate Bargain: Why Jimmy Hoffa Had to Die*. New York: Reader's Digest Press, 1977.
Walsh, Denny, "A Two-Faced Crime Fight in St. Louis." *Life,* May 29, 1970.
Waugh, Daniel, *Egan's Rats*. Nashville: Cumberland House, 2007.
Wehrle, Edmund F., *Between a River and a Mountain: The AFL-CIO and the Vietnam War*. Ann Arbor,: University of Michigan Press, 2005.
_____, "'Partisan for the Hard Hats': Charles Colson, George Meany, and the Failed Blue-Collar Strategy." *Labor* 3, 2008.
Weleck, Mary, "Jordan Chambers: Black Politician and Boss." *Journal of Negro History,* October 1972.
White, Theodore H., *The Making of the President 1960*. New York: Pocket Books, 1961.
Williams, Edward Bennett, *One Man's Freedom*. New York: Atheneum, 1977.
Witwer, David, *Corruption and Reform in the Teamsters Union*. Urbana: University of Illinois Press, 2003.
Zieger, Robert H., *The CIO, 1935–1955*. Chapel Hill: University of North Carolina Press, 1995.

Interviews

The people interviewed for this book, and the dates of the interviews, are as follows.

Marcus Albrecht, October 13, 2005.
Joseph L. Ames, March 7, April 27, August 31 and October 16, 2007.
Ronald Borges, July 16 and 21 and October 2, 2008.
Ernest Calloway with DeVerne Calloway, February 1983.
William L. Clay, July 31 and August 5 and 31, 2008.
Sally Bixby Defty, February 1983.
Martin Duggan, May 25, 2007.
Thomas F. Eagleton, August 18 and 23, 2005.
Ron Gamache, February 1983.
Lawrence Gibbons, November 12 and December 6 and 22, 2005, January 18, May 7 and October 4, 2006, and May 2, 2007.
Patrick Gibbons, January 31, February 2, 18 and 28, 2008.
Michael Goebel, February 6, 2008.
Gladys W. Gruenberg, January 29, 2007.
Thomas J. Guilfoil, June 4, 2007.
Gordon Hoener, May 24, 2007.
Harland Horn, October 30, 2007.

George Houser, August 29, 2007.
Dick Kavner, February 1983
Yuki Kato Keathley, July 11, 2008.
Wanda Koss, July 14, 2006, and July 19, 2007.
John J. "Jake" McCarthy, December 1976, and February 1983.
John M. McGuire, May 21, 2007.
Sheila Michaels, February 7, 2007.
Shawn Murphy, December 29, 2005.
Keith Payne, November 30 and December 2 and 6, 2012, and January 11, 2013.
Evelyn Rich, August 22 and 23, 2007.
Marvin Rich, February 16, 2007, and May 18, 2010.
James Robinson, August 27, 2007.
Michael Ryan, October 19, 2005.
Levi Sanford, March 28 and August 29, 2006.
Ted Schafers, July 9, 2007.
Melburn F. Stein, May 8, 2009.
Jerry Tucker, December 1 and 8, 2005.
Elizabeth Gibbons Vasquez, November 12 and December 22, 2005, May 7, 2006, and May 2, 2007.

Documents

Harry Ball's "Case History of a Labor Union: The United Distribution Workers" is in the John M. Olin Library, Washington University, St. Louis.

Ernest Calloway's papers are in the Western Missouri Manuscript Collection, Thomas Jefferson Library, University of Missouri at St. Louis.

Harold Gibbons's papers are in the Louisa H. Bowen University Archives and Special Collections, Lovejoy Library, Southern Illinois University, Edwardsville, Illinois.

McClellan Committee transcripts are in Hearings before the U.S. Select Committee on Improper Activities in the Labor or Management Field, Washington, D.C., Government Printing Office, 1957–60. See Parts 13, 32, 37, 38, 39, 46, and 59 for testimony by Harold Gibbons, Barney Baker, Joe Costello and others mentioned in this book.

Index

Ace Cab Co. 129
Agnew, Spiro 235
Albrecht, Marcus 8, 236–237, 239
all-city shop conferences 37
Amalgamated Clothing Workers (ACW) 71
Amberg, Richard H. 176–177
American Federation of State, County and Municipal Employees (AFSCME) 188
American Federation of Teachers (AFT) 17
Americans for Democratic Action 96
Ames, Joseph 6, 60, 63, 92, 93, 96, 97, 195; raid on joint council 98
Anheuser-Busch 103
Apalachin meeting 157
"Archibald Patch" 12; see also Taylor, Pennsylvania
Aubuchon, Michael 103, 104, 105, 106
automation 246–248

Baker, Barney 95–97, 130, 132; arrest by police 100–101, 119; guarding Gibbons family 96–97
Ball, Harry Vernon: "Case History of a Labor Union: The United Distribution Workers" 10, 24, 55
Beck, Dave 64, 72–73, 97, 117, 122, 153, 154, 156
Bell, Daniel 115–116; see also *Fortune* magazine
Bender, Fred 110
Benson, Ezra 117
Berle, Milton 182, 183
Berra, Lou 23, 25, 39, 111–114, 225
Bishop, Joey 185
Bittner, Van 18

Blassie, Nick 145
Bootheel Region of Missouri 195
Borges, Ron 8, 209, 228–229, 236
Boykin, Frank 193, 200
Bridges, Harry 27, 40, 218; see also Communist Party; International Longshore and Warehouse Union; Montgomery Ward strike
Brill, Steven: *The Teamsters* 10, 15, 168, 344n23
Brookings Institution 160
Brown, Claude 193, 200, 201, 226–228; see also 1969 focus groups
Brown, Ed 32, 112
Brown Shoe Co. 23
Brownell, Herbert, Jr. 110, 117
Bryn Mawr College 16
Busch, August A., Jr. 203
"business wing" of Local 688, 202, 231
Bussel, Robert: "A Trade Union Oriented War on the Slums: Harold Gibbons, Ernest Calloway, and the St. Louis Teamsters of the 1960s" 199–200, 204–205, 230; see also Calloway, Ernst; Gibbons, Harold; housing strike
Butler Brothers Co. 23

Caldwell, Cliff 210
Callanan, Larry 81–82, see also Clay, William, L.; "politicians"; Steamfitters Local 562
Callanan, Tom 87
Calloway, DeVerne 8, 65, 67, 192, 239
Calloway, Ernest ("Cab") 8, 65, 96, 192–193, 195–196, 239, 246; appearance 66; candidate for Congress 196–199; and Clay 187; as Gibbons' "idea guy" 65; and

283

housing strike 199–205; president of St. Louis NAACP 68; recruitment by Gibbons; 67; "a trade union oriented war on the slums" 192; work on school desegregation plan 67; youth 66
Camie, Larry 43; merger of AFL and CIO warehouse unions 72–73; St. Louis truck wildcat 43–45
Carpenter, Milton 196, 198
Carson, Johnny 182
cement drivers' strike 102–107
Central Conference of Teamsters 122, 234
Central States Pension Fund 126–127, 145, 181, 244
Cervantes, Alfonso J. 133, 180, 202–03; *see also* "politicians"
Chambers, Jordan 60
Chapman, James 87, 111, 113, 132, 133; *see also* St. Louis Police Department; Stein, Melburn
Chase, Stuart 16
Chase Park Hotel 183
Chavez, Cesar 194, 243
Chicago Federation of Labor 16, 17
city charter referendums 87; *see also* "forces of progress"; Local 688; "politicians"; "urban renewal" in St. Louis
Civic Alliance 204, 230; *see also* housing strike
Civic Progress 103, 203
Clark, Charles Dismas 137
Clay, William L. 9, 187–190; appearance 190; candidate for Congress 196–199; joins Steamfitters 196; *see also* Callanan, Larry; Jefferson Bank
Cohen, Mickey 243
Cold War 39–40, 41
Colson, Charles 208, 240
Communist Party 38, 71, 209
Community Stewards program 6, 80–81, 192; *see also* Calloway, Ernest
Congress of Industrial Organizations (CIO) 5, 18, 23; "CIO fever" in 1937 21; Flint, Michigan, sit-down strike 18
Congress of Racial Equality (CORE) 3–4; Clay leaves NAACP for CORE 187; CORE nine arrested 189; the CORE/warehouse union connection 63–64; formation of St. Louis CORE 59–61; Stix, Baer & Fuller campaign 61
Conn, Ernest 32
Cortor, Donald 131, 133
Costello, Joe 114–115, 129–135, 161; appearance 129
Council Plaza 142–144, 185, 245
Council Plaza Redevelopment Corp. 142

Crancer, Barbara Hoffa 145
Crancer, Robert 213
criminal types 91–93, 95–98; Apalachin meeting 157; "certain elements" 51; the "guys" 182, 184; Kansas City's North Side mob 126; mobs or The Mob? 127; the "Outfit" 126–128, 181–182, 184; *see also* Costello, Joe
Culter, Murah 19
Culter, William 19

Dagen, Irv 60, 67
Dagen, Maggie 60
Daley, Richard J. 128; *see also* criminal types
Daniel Hamm Drayage Co. 44
Davis, Sammy, Jr. 137, 182
Dean, John 208, 214, 221
Dean, Rolla "Blackie" 98
Defty, Sally Bixby 9
Delaware, Lackawanna & Western Railroad 12
Democratic Party (of St. Louis) 5, 78, "forces of progress" faction vs. "politicians" faction" 77–78; *see also* "forces of progress"; "politicians"
Department of Housing and Urban Development (HUD) 203, 230
Dilliard, Irving 94, 95; *see also* Post-Dispatch
Dioguardi, John ("Johnny Dio") 157–158, 161–162
Dismas House 137, 182
Dobbs, Farrell 42–43; prison term 43; St. Louis truck wildcat 44–45; *see also* Hoffa, James R.; Minneapolis strike; Trotsky, Leon; Trotskyists
"The Doctor's Son" (O'Hara) 21
Dodge, Joseph M. 117
Dorfman, Allen 145; *see also* criminal types
Douglas, Paul 109, 156–157
"dual unionism" 232
Dudman, Richard 62; *see also* "St. Louis' Silent Racial Revolution"
Duggan, Martin 9
Dulles, John Foster 162
Dunn, Michael 235–236
Dunne, Ray 44; St. Louis truck wildcat 44–45; talk with Gibbons 45–46; *see also* Trotskyists
Dwyer, Jack 88

Eagleton, Thomas F. 9, 168, 184n25, 213
East St. Louis, Illinois 91
Eisenhower, Dwight 111, 162

Emergency Education Program 16, 17; *see also* Herstein, Lillian
Emerson Electric Co. 23; *see also* sit-down strikes
Epsteen, Peter 181–182; *see also* criminal types
Erickson, Ralph 221
Ervin, Sam 161
"extension radicalism" 15, 58; *see also* Wisconsin Idea

Farmer, James 59
Farrow, Mia 182, 183
Federal Bureau of Investigation (FBI) 8, 13, 42, 141–142
Firmen-Desloge Hospital 35
First Congressional District: creation 195; mapping 195–196
Fisher, Bernice 3–4, 48, 58–60, 64–65; Stix, Baer & Fuller campaign 61
Fitzpatrick, Daniel 84, 94, 104; *see also* "forces of progress"; *St. Louis Post-Dispatch*
Fitzpatrick, John 16; *see also* Herstein, Lilliam
Fitzsimmons, Frank 173–175, 186, 206, 208, 236, 242, 244
Flynn, Thomas 97, 103*n*12, 106
"forces of progress" 77–78
Fortune magazine 115–116; *see also* Bell, Daniel

Gamache, Ron 8, 163, 202, 228, 229, 232–233, 237
Giancana, Sam 181; *see also* criminal types
Gibbons, Ann Maffette Culter (Harold's first wife) 20, 69, 70, 89, 140–142, 240–241; death 240; marriage 20
Gibbons, Annie (Harold's sister) 13
Gibbons, Antoinette "Toni" Stein (Harold's second wife) 242
Gibbons, Bridget Muldoon (Harold's mother) 11, 13
Gibbons, Harold 3, 4, 67–68, 138–140, 249; as AFT vice president 17; as anticommunist 38–42; in anti-war congress 217–219; appearance 4, 14, 41, 89; and Bernice Fisher 58; and Bill Clay 188; and Calloway, Ernest, 198, 200; in cement drivers' strike 102–107; the CORE/warehouse union connection 63–64; death 239; democracy in his union 52–54; explains guns to *Post-Dispatch* editor, cartoonist 94; fall 234–238; on FBI's "key figure" list 42, 46; and golf 180 ; and Hoffa 122–125, 150–151, 164–169, 172–175, 243; Hoffa's campaign for IBT presidency 123; indicted 112; the "intellectual Teamster" 137; in jail 110; joining Teamsters 74–76; and Kissinger 207–208, 210, 220; life threatened by mobsters 92; lifestyle 228; local home to black taxi drivers 54–55; local threatens warehouse general strike 100; marriage to Ann Culter 20; and the McClellan Committee 159–162; on mobs 167; Montgomery Ward strike 40–41; as night owl 70, 89; against Nixon 233; as orator 17, 29; as parent 70; "periods of ennui" 70; race relations in local 54–57; a racketeer? 113–114; raid on joint council 97–98; and Ray Tucker 103; RWDSU sends him to St. Louis 28; St. Louis leaves RWDSU 49; St. Louis truck wildcat 43–45; saved by carnival workers 144; second marriage 242; seeks permit for pistol 93; sense of humor 8; sexual affairs 140–141; Sinatra and show business friends 182–184; strike leader in South Bend, Indiana 18; and the taxi wildcat 129–133; textile workers' leader in Louisville, Kentucky 19; trade unionists as "citizen-members" 58; and Vietnam 206, 210–213; warehousemen become Teamsters 70–76; in Washington, DC, 148; winning St. Louis warehousemen's approval 28–30; in Yellow Cab strike 107–108; youth 11–14; *see also* Gibbons-Hoffa split; "Planning for an Integrated School System in St. Louis"; RWDSUGibbons-Hoffa split 163–164, 169, 170
Gibbons, Larry (son) 8, 89, 229
Gibbons, Patrick (Harold's father) 11, 13
Gibbons, Patrick (son) 8, 89, 249
globalization 246*n*638
Goebel, Mike 9, 245
Goldman, Emma 16
Goldschein, Max 110, 111
Goldstein, Ruby 137
Goldwater, Barry 158
Graham, Leroy 193, 200
Gravel, Mike 217
Greenlease, Bobby 130
Greenspun, Hank 145
Gruenberg, Gladys W. 9
Guilfoil, Thomas J. 9, 83–84, 179

Hackett, Buddy 185
Harriman, Averell 96
Harrington, Michael 208
Hearnes, Warren 195
Henry, Pat 210

Index

Herstein, Lillian 16, 17
Higginbotham, Leon 63
The Hill neighborhood 79
Hillman, Sidney 18, 26, 29, 30
Hoener, Gordon 9
Hoffa, James P. 244
Hoffa, James R. 6, 43, 72, 92, 95, 97, 106, 107, 167, 213–215; appearance 119; campaign for IBT president 123, 144–147; and commutation clause 214–215; and Dave Beck 122; Detroit background 92; disappearance 243; and Gibbons 122–125, 164–169, 172–175; and Israeli orphans 145; making AFL Teamsters more like CIO 151–152, 172; mob relations 120; personality 119–120; pessimism about capitalism 124; "that political and social stuff" 123; to prison 175, 186; and the Republican Party 116–118; sabotages Hanoi trip 222; on trial 170–171; and violence 121; in Washington, DC, 148; youth 119; *see also* Dobbs, Farrell; Gibbons-Hoffa split; James, Estelle: *Hoffa and the Teamsters*; James, Ralph: *Hoffa and the Teamsters*; RWDSU
Hoffman, Clare 117
Hogan, Edward J., "Jelly Roll" 14, 86; *see also* "politicians"
Holmes, Robert 237
Hoover, J. Edgar 20, 42
Horn, Harland 9, 225, 235
Houser, George 9, 59
housing strike 199–204; *see also* St. Louis Housing Authority; "social concern wing" of Local 688
Howard, Raymond 194; *see also* Congress of Racial Equality (CORE); Kinney, Mike
Humanity, Inc. 60, 61

Ibn Saud 162
Industrial Union Council of St. Louis 38
International Brotherhood of Teamsters (IBT) 5; IBT a GOP union? 154; mobsters seize St. Louis locals 92; St. Louis warehousemen become Teamsters 70–76; Teamsters become wards of U.S. government 244
International Longshore and Warehouse Union (ILWU) 25
"internationals" 25
Interstate 70 178
Ives, Irving 160

James, Estelle: *Hoffa and the Teamsters* 153, 165–166

James, Ralph: *Hoffa and the Teamsters* 153, 165–166
Jefferson Bank 188–190
Jessel, George 182, 183
J.H. Grady Co., strike 50, 88
Jim Crow in St. Louis 11–14, 60, 61, 62–64, 67
Joint Advisory Council 25

Kavner, Dick 48, 49–50, 92, 105, 126, 145, 150, 169, 178, 225–226, 236; as Gibbons' contract specialist 50; as Gibbons "hard drive" 49; as Wolchok's spy 48–49
Keathley, Ferguson 169, 180
Keathley, Yuki Kato 9, 34n19, 95, 148, 165, 169
Kefauver, Estes 82, 153
Kennedy, John F. 118; assassination 163; Hoffa and the Kennedy brothers 158–159; *see also* Gibbons-Hoffa split
Kennedy, Joseph P. 153–154, 159–160, 181
Kennedy, Robert F. 11, 118, 134, 153–159; Hoffa and the Kennedy brothers 158–159, 169
"key figure list" (FBI) 42
Kiel Opera House 99, 182, 236
King, Coretta Scott 217
King, Jean 203
King, Martin Luther, Jr. 3, 161
Kinney, Mike 86; *see also* "forces of progress"
Kissinger, Henry 6–7, 206–207, 223; double-crosses Hoffa, Gibbons 220; and Gibbons 207–208, 210, 220; *see also* Ngo Dinh Diem
Kleindienst, Richard 221
Konowe, Joe 151
Koppel, Ted 211
Kosciusko neighborhood 79, 80
Koss, Wanda 9, 240, 242
KSD-TV 104

Labor Health Institute (LHI) 34, formation of 34–36
La Follette, Robert M. 5
Lambert-St. Louis International Airport 102, 245
Latal, Bill 23, 30, 32, 225
Las Vegas casinos 126–127; *see also* Central States Pension Fund; Shenker, Morris; Williams, Roy
Lawler, John ("Doc") 196
Le Duc Tho 207, 212, 223
Lens, Sidney 40–41, 53, 71
Levy, Leonard 27
Lewis, John L. 18, 37–38, 148, 164

Index

Liston, Sonny 137
Livingston, David 209; *see also* Communist Party
Local/District 65 209; *see also* Livingston, David
Local 102 231; joins International Distributive Workers 232; *see also* Local/District 65; "miscellaneous" union; Kavner, Dick; Sanford, Levi
Local 688 179–180, 245; geographical dispersal of members 226; merger of AFL and CIO warehouse unions 73–76; *see also* J.H. Grady Co.; "miscellaneous" union 245
Lynd, Staughton 217

"Magic Chef" building 142
Martin, Dean 137, 182
Martin, John Bartlow 148
Mazey, Emil 209, 217, 219; *see also* United Auto Workers (UAW)
McCarthy, Jake 7, 95, 127, 136–138, 145, 146, 149–150, 202, 225–226, 229; as Gibbons' ghostwriter 137; as *Missouri Teamster* editor 170
McClellan, John 118
McClellan Committee 11, 107–108, 118, 133, 154, 155
McCoy, Kid 22; *see also* St. Louis warehouse unions
McGovern, George 212
McGuire, John M. 9
McMahon, Ed 210, 242
McNeal, Theodore 197; *see also* Hogan, Edward J. "Jelly Roll"
Meany, George 155
Metropolitan Sewer District (St. Louis) 6
Michaels, Sheila 9
Mill Creek Valley 78–79, 80
Miller, Mava 104, 105
Mills, C. Wright: *New Men of Power* 166
Minneapolis strike 43
"miscellaneous" union 52, 71
Missouri-Kansas Conference of Teamsters 125; *see also* Williams, Roy
Missouri Public Service Commission 5
Missouri Teamster 170, 226
Mitchell, Oldron A. 108; *see also* taxi strike tactics; Yellow Cab strike
Mohn, Einar 171
Mollenhoff, Clark 153–154
Montgomery Ward strike 40–41, and International Longshore and Warehouse Union 40; *see also* Retail, Wholesale and Department Store Union
Moran, Thomas L. 93*n*7, 94*n*9, 115

Mound City Macaroni Co. 32; *see also* Saffo, Pete
Murphy, Sean 9
Murray, Philip 47

National Labor Relations Board 22, 24; *see also NLRB v. Jones & Laughlin* (1937)
Ngo Dinh Diem 206; *see also* Kissinger, Henry A.
Niebuhr, Reinhold 58
Nineteen-sixty-nine focus groups 201, 226–228
Nixon, Richard M. 8, 207, 215, 230, 233–234
NLRB v. Jones & Laughlin (1937), 22, 166
"no strike pledge" 34, 37

O'Hara, John 12; *see also* "The Doctor's Son"
Oldham, Charles 60, 67, 197
Oldham, Marian 60
"organizing the bosses" 31, 88–89
Orr, Charles 19
Orr, Lois Culter 19

Pace, Jim 193, 226
Palm Springs, California 185
Payne, Keith 9, 180–182, 184, 235, 239–240, 241
Penney's (J.C. Penney Co. warehouse in St. Louis) 21, 25
Pentland, Robert 22
Perry, Ivory 193
Peurala, Alice 63
"Planning for an Integrated School System in St. Louis" 67
"politicians" 77–78, 133
Porter, William 212
Preisler, Doris 35
Presser, Jackie 244
Progressive movement 4, 15–16; Midwestern Progressivism's mix with socialism 15
Pruitt-Igoe housing complex 102

Rank-and-File Teamsters (RAFT) 230–231
Ratner, Payne 111, 117
Rauh, Joseph 168
Ravarino and Freschi Spaghetti Co. 35; *see also* Labor Health Institute
Reagan, Ronald 244
Reichardt, Phil 22, 23, 32, 130, 131, 225
Remphry, William "Bozo" 98
Retail, Wholesale and Department Store Union (RWDSU) 26, 71; factionalism in 47–49, 71; and Montgomery Ward strike 40–41; *see also* Wolchok, Samuel
Reuther, Victor 70, 167

Reuther, Walter 71, 167
Rice-Stix Co. 31
Rich, Evelyn 9
Rich, Marvin 9, 55, 60, 63, 67
Richman, Elmer 35
Riesel, Victor 162, 219–220
Robinson, James 9, 59
Rogers, William 208, 221, 222
Romney, George 203, 230n19
Roosevelt, Eleanor 16; *see also* Herstein, Lillian; Progressive movement
Roosevelt, Franklin D. 39, 43
Rosanova, Lou 181; *see also* criminal types
Rose, Arnold: *Union Solidarity: The Internal Cohesion of a Labor Union* 55
Rosenblum, Frank 18, 19
Rupinski, Bernard 212
Rustin, Bayard 59, 246–248
Ryan, Mike 9, 194, 195–195; *see also* 1969 focus groups 201, 226–228

Saffo, Pete 32, 51, 101, 112, 133, 225
St. Louis, Missouri: geographical shaping of politics 77–78; history 21; as "warehouse capital of the United States" 21
St. Louis Argus 135
St. Louis Globe-Democrat 104, 106, 176
St. Louis Housing Authority 199, 230; *see also* housing strike
St. Louis Joint Board of RWDSU 31, 38, 39; Joint Board renamed United Distribution Workers 49; and LHI 34; St. Louis leaves RWDSU 49
St. Louis Police Department 86–87; *see also* "forces of progress"
St. Louis Post-Dispatch 7, 23, 62
"St. Louis' Silent Racial Revolution" (Dudman) 62
St. Louis warehouse unions 21; AFL local 43; formation of CIO local 22–25; St. Louis truck wildcat 43–45
Salmon, David: *Recollections: Part 6: I Joined Teamsters Local 688* 28, 31, 60, 63
Sanders, William "Shotgun" 134
Sanford, Levi 9, 29, 97, 178, 193, 202, 236
Saturday Evening Post 148
Savannah Inn and Country Club 181
Schafers, Ted 10, 21, 95, 96, 129–130, 145
Schmeling, Max 96
Schoessling, Ray 237
School for Workers, University of Wisconsin 14–15
Seidman, Harold: *Labor Czars* 166
Seiler, George 25, 98
Sentner, Bill 38, 41, 42; *see also* Communist Party; Emerson Electric Co.

Sestric, Tony 88
Shaw, Ralph 22n6; *see also* Communist Party
Shenker, Morris 82–83, 137, 184n25
Shoulders, Louis, Jr. 134
Sinatra, Frank 137, 181, 182–185, 235, 242
sit-down strikes 18, 23
Smith, Gerald L.K. 62
Smith, Tucker 121
Smith, Wint 117–118
"social concern wing" of Local 688 200
"socialist kids" (School for Workers) 14–15
Socialist Party 4, 39
Southern Christian Leadership Conference 3
Steamfitters Local 562, 81, 179–180
Stein, Melburn F. 10, 87; *see also* St. Louis Police Department
Steinberg, Larry 121, 151, 169
Stevenson, Adlai 153–154
Stewards' Council 53–54, 100
Stix, Baer & Fuller campaign 61, 63
Student Nonviolent Coordinating Committee (SNCC) 3
Summer School for Women Workers 16; *see also* Herstein, Lillian
sweetheart contract 99–100

Tandy, Charlton Hunt 191
Tandy Area Council (TAC) 191, 200, 230; *see also* Calloway, Ernest; Chavez, Cesar; United Auto Workers (UAW)
Taub, William L. 215, 219, 221–223; con man? 215; and Le Duc Tho 216; his plan 216; telegram to Gibbons 217
taxi 18, 108
Taylor, Pennsylvania 11; *see also* "Archibald Patch"
Teamster charity shows 137
Teamsters Joint Council 13, 97; raid on Joint Council 97–98
Teamsters Local 405 (taxi drivers) 130; wildcat 130–133
Teamsters Local 682 (cement drivers) 101; strike 102–106
Teamsters Local 688 43, 89–90; local arms itself against mobsters 93n7, 97; local threatens general warehouse strike 100; the Pevely camp 142; police say local violent 93n9; St. Louis truck wildcat 43–45
Teamsters' "marble palace" 148
Thomas, Norman 121
Tobin, Dan 43, 148
Trotsky, Leon 39
Trotskyists 39

Tucker, Jerry 10, 70–71, 185–186, 193–194, 198, 217–219; *see also* United Auto Workers
Tucker, Raymond 78, 180; in cement strike 103–106; elected mayor 1953 85–86; *see also* "forces of progress"
Twist, Norman 25

Udall, Morris 244
United Auto Workers 70, 158–159
United Electrical Workers 23, 38, 41; *see also* Communist Party; Emerson Electric Co.; Industrial Union Council of St. Louis; Sentner, William; sit-down strikes in 1937
United Mine Workers 13, 37–38; *see also* Lewis, John L.
University of Chicago 3, 59
University of Missouri-St. Louis 6
University of Wisconsin 4; *see also* School for Workers
"urban renewal" in St. Louis 78–79, 79–80

Vasquez, Elizabeth Gibbons (daughter) 8, 89, 140, 242
Vietnam War 6, 233

"Ville" neighborhood 60
Vitale, John 129; *see also* criminal types
Voras, Max 22, 23, 24, 225

wages in St. Louis warehouses 21
War Labor Board 34, 37; and Montgomery Ward strike 40–41
Watergate burglary 213, 238
Wheeler, Sherman 30
Williams, Roy 125–127, 244; *see also* criminal types
Wilson, Harry B. 88–89
Wisconsin Idea 15, 58
Wolchok, Samuel 26, 47–49, 71
Woodcock, Leonard 218–219; *see also* United Auto Workers (UAW)
Woodner Hotel 148
Wortman, Buster 91, 98
Wyden, Peter 89

Yellow Cab strike 107–109

Zagri, Sidney 87; *see also* Calloway, Ernest; city charter referendums
Ziegler, Ron 220